THE ICSA MEETINGS AND MINUTES HANDBOOK

Andrew Hamer
with Andrew Robertson

ICSA Publishing Limited

Published by ICSA Publishing Ltd
16 Park Crescent
London W1B 1AH

Typeset in Stempel Schneidler by Fakenham Photosetting Ltd., Fakenham, Norfolk

Printed and bound in Great Britain by TJ International Ltd., Padstow, Cornwall

British Library Cataloguing in Publication Data

A catalogue record for this book is available from the British Library.

ISBN 1–86072–139–7

Contents

Table of Cases

Abbreviations

AC	*Appeal Cases (Law Reports)*
Ad. & El.	*Adolphus & Ellis*
All ER	*All England Law Reports*

App. Cas.	*Appeal Cases (Law Reports)*
BCC	*British Company Cases*
BCLC	*Butterworths Company Law Cases*
CA	*Court of Appeal*
Ch.	*Chancery (Law Reports)*
Ch. App.	*Chancery Appeals (Law Reports)*
Ch.D.	*Chancery Division (Law Reports)*
CPD	*Common Pleas Division (Law Reports)*
HLC	*English & Irish Appeals (House of Lords)*
KB	*Law Reports, King's Bench Division*
LJ	*Law Journal Reports*
LR	*Law Reports*
LT	*Law Times Reports*
LTJ	*Law Times Journal*
H & M	*Hemming & Miller Law Reports*
NSWLR	*New South Wales Law Reports*
PC	*Privy Council Appeals (Law Reports)*
QB	*Queen's Bench Reports*
QBD	*Queen's Bench Division*
SASR	*South Australian Law Reports*
SC	*Session Cases*
SJ	*Solicitors' Journal*
SLT	*Scottish Law Times*
TLR	*Times Law Reports*
WLR	*Weekly Law Reports*
WN	*Weekly Notes*

Table of Statutes

Note: Entries in bold are to Appendix A which sets out the main provisions of the Companies Act 1985 relating to company meetings.

Table of Statutory Instruments

Note: Entries in bold are to Appendix B (1985 Table A (as amended))

Companies (Table A to F) Regulations 1985 SI 1985/805 (as amended) 7–9, 14–17, 19, 23, 28, 44–46, 49, 53, 54, 58, 60, 61, 65, 67, 75, 76, 78, 85–88, 94, 111, 127, 128, 131–133, 143, 144, 157, 170, 171, 177, 179, 181, 182, 188, 207, 209, 240, 267, 268, 276, 289, 292, 295–298, 300, **411**

Table A—

reg. 1	16, **411**
regs. 2–6	**412**
reg. 2	106
regs. 7–12	**413**
reg. 8	41
reg. 9	41
regs. 12–22	37, 41
regs. 13–19	**414**
regs. 20–24	**415**
reg. 24	41
regs. 25–31	**416**
reg. 25	41
reg. 30	198
reg. 31	188, 198, 247, 444
regs. 23–37	**417**
reg. 34	8, 136, 196
reg. 36	97
reg. 37	41, 114, 117
regs. 38–42	**418**
reg. 38	125, 136, 137, 142, 143, 276, 444
reg. 39	145
reg. 40	163, 164, 166
reg. 41	165, 166, 267
reg. 42	54, 112, 240
regs. 43–47	**419**
reg. 43	241
reg. 44	248, 251, 444
reg. 45	245, 265, 268
reg. 46	201, 204, 205, 245, 268
reg. 47	202, 244, 302
regs. 48–55	**420**
reg. 48	205
reg. 49	206
reg. 50	54, 207, 210, 296
reg. 51	204, 206, 268

1

Introduction: Law and practice

This book deals with meetings of companies incorporated under the UK Companies Acts. It is intended as a guide for those involved with the management and administration of companies. Accordingly, it does not cover meetings in insolvency.

Unless otherwise indicated:

- all statutory references are to the relevant section number of the Companies Act 1985 as amended up to the end of May 2001 (e.g. 's. 379A' refers to a section of the Companies Act 1985 which was inserted by the Companies Act 1989 and which has subsequently been amended by statutory instrument);
- all references to regulations (e.g. reg. 72) are to the 1985 Table A which is contained in the Companies (Table A to F) Regulations 1985 as amended by the Companies Act 1985 (Electronic Communications) Order 2000 (see **1.5**).

Please note also that, throughout the book, the use of the word 'chairman', and the subsequent use of the masculine pronoun, applies equally to both men and women.

1.1 Are meetings necessary?

The overriding purpose of the law of meetings is to ensure that a company is actually able to make business decisions and that all those entitled to participate in making those decisions are given a reasonable and fair opportunity to do so.

A company is treated as a person in the eyes of the law and, as such, is able to do anything that a natural legal person can do for the purposes of running a business, e.g. own property, enter into contracts, and sue and be sued in its own name. Despite being accorded the status of a legal person, a company plainly does not have a mind of its own and cannot act without the intervention of human beings. Someone must act on behalf of the company.

Who may do so, and how, will depend largely on the company's memorandum and articles of association, the Companies Acts and the general law of meetings.

Logically, it is the members/shareholders, as 'owners' of the company, who represent the mind of the company and who should be able to direct what it does. This is fine in owner-managed companies where all the members are of the same mind. But what should be done if the members do not all agree? The obvious answer to this question is to allow decisions to be taken by a majority, with different majorities required for different types of decision. But how can one find out what the members think? Although their views could be ascertained by a postal ballot, this would not allow them to debate the issues before making decisions or give the minority an opportunity to put its case. The only way to ensure that this happens is to require decisions to be taken at formal meetings and, generally speaking, this is what the law requires. Members may sometimes act without holding a meeting, but only if they approve the transaction unanimously. For example, a private company may act by a written resolution signed by all its members (see **Chapter 24**).

It would be impossible to manage most companies if every decision had to be approved by the members in general meeting. Accordingly, it is usual for the members to delegate wide powers of management to the board of directors. This is done in the articles of association, the constitutional document that governs the relationship between the company, its members and its directors. The directors must act as a body (usually at a formal meeting) in order to exercise these powers. However, articles usually authorise the directors to delegate their powers to committees of directors, individual executive directors and other employees and agents. In addition, the articles of both public and private companies normally allow the directors to exercise their powers by written resolution, i.e. without holding a meeting (see **6.2**).

In practice, it is possible to manage a private company without holding formal meetings of either the members or the directors. As we have already seen, a private company may act by a written resolution signed by all its members and articles of association usually allow the directors to pass resolutions in a similar manner. Private companies may, if all the members agree, also dispense with the requirement to hold an annual general meeting and several of the formalities associated with it (see **Chapter 25**). This is particularly useful for small owner-managed companies and wholly owned subsidiaries.

1.2 Holding proper meetings

To ensure that those entitled to participate in a company's decision-making process are given a reasonable and fair opportunity to do so, certain procedures must be followed. In short, meetings must be properly convened, constituted and held. They must be called, held and conducted in accordance with the articles, the Companies Acts and the general law of meetings. Although the procedural requirements for general meetings are more onerous than those for meetings of directors, the essential components for both are as follows:

- the meeting must be called by someone with authority to do so and in the correct manner;
- notice of the meeting and the business to be transacted must be given in the correct manner to those entitled to receive it (generally those entitled to vote at the meeting);
- a quorum must be present (i.e. the minimum number of persons necessary to transact business);
- those entitled to attend and vote must be allowed to do so;
- a chairman must be elected or appointed;
- the business raised must be within the notice of the meeting;
- the meeting must be conducted properly, particularly in respect of voting; and
- the decisions of the meeting should be recorded in a minute book.

If these procedures are not followed, the validity of the meeting and any business transacted at it may be liable to challenge.

1.3 The law of meetings

One of the most difficult aspects of the law relating to company meetings is the complicated hierarchy of rules and procedures. Company meetings are governed by a combination of formal statutory rules, common law rules developed by the courts, and the company's own constitution (primarily its articles of association). Public companies that are listed on a stock exchange will also need to comply with additional rules. For example, companies listed on the London Stock Exchange must comply with the Listing Rules, now issued by the Financial Services Authority (FSA) in its capacity as the UK Listing Authority. Although failure to comply with these rules will not directly affect the validity of a meeting or a particular transaction, the FSA may impose sanctions and penalties for non-compliance. Listed companies may also need to have regard to codes of practice, such as the Combined Code on Corporate Governance and the ABI's Pre-emption Guidelines.

1.3.1 Statute

The main statutory rules relating to meetings are contained in the Companies Act 1985 ('the Act' or 'the 1985 Act'). This Act has been amended significantly since 1985 (most notably by the

Companies Act 1989, but also by numerous statutory instruments). The main provisions of the Act relevant to company meetings (as amended up to 31 May 2001) are set out at **Appendix A**. A number of legal publishers produce handbooks containing the latest version of applicable company legislation (including the 1985 Act), and anyone involved in running company meetings should ensure that they have an up-to-date edition of one of these books.

The term 'the Companies Acts' includes the Companies Act 1985, the Companies Consolidation Consequential Provisions Act 1985 and the insider dealing provisions of the Criminal Justice Act 1993 (s. 744). However, only the first of these is particularly relevant for the purposes of this book.

At the time of writing, the government is sponsoring a wide-ranging independent review of company law. The aim of the review is to modernise UK company law and thereby increase the competitiveness of the UK as a location for business. The review is expected to result in new legislation to replace the Companies Act 1985. This is unlikely to happen before 2003. For further details, see the Department of Trade and Industry website (www.dti.gov.uk/).

Types of company

Several different types of company can be formed under the Companies Act 1985 and each type can be subject to different statutory provisions. It is therefore essential to check whether the relevant statutory provisions or procedures are applicable to the type of company you are dealing with. The biggest differences in this regard arise between public and private companies. The rows in Table 1.1 show whether a company is public or private. The columns of the table also show other classifications used in the Act to limit or define the application of certain provisions.

Table 1.1

| | *Limited company* | | *Unlimited* |
	Limited by shares	*Limited by guarantee*	*company*
Public company	Public limited company (Plc)		
Private company	Private company limited by shares (Ltd)	Private company limited by guarantee (Ltd)	
	Private company limited by guarantee with a share capital (Ltd)		Unlimited company (–)

1.3.2 Common law and precedent

The common law is the body of rules and principles developed by the courts to decide the competing merits of litigants. Provisions contained in Acts of Parliament usually override the common law. A company may also exclude the operation of common law rules by making alternative provision in its memorandum or articles.

Despite this relatively lowly position in the legal hierarchy, the common law is still applicable in many areas relating to the law of company meetings. For example, no provision is made in the Act with regard to notice of board meetings. Accordingly, the common law rules regarding notice of meetings apply, subject to anything contained in a company's articles. Most articles specify that notice need not be given in writing but they do not specify the length of notice required. This must therefore be decided according to the common law rule, which provides that the notice given must be reasonable in the circumstances.

The courts are often called upon to rule on the interpretation and application of the Act and on the precise effect of provisions contained in a company's articles. Decisions in these cases provide precedents, which are useful in clarifying the law. Most cases concerning company law are heard initially in the Chancery Division of the High Court. Appeals can be made to the Court of Appeal and, ultimately, to the House of Lords whose decisions are more influential. Where the point at issue is the interpretation of an EU Directive, the case may be referred to EU courts and tribunals.

Decisions of the courts that have a bearing on the law of meeting are referred to in this book by their case names and reference. The case reference is to the law report in which the case was reported. For example, *Byng v. London Life Association Ltd* [1989] 1 All ER 560 refers to a case that was reported in the first volume of the *All England Law Reports* published in 1989 on page 560. A table of cases referred to in the text can be found at page xiii.

1.3.3 European law

A number of European Directives have had some influence on the law of meetings, e.g. the 12th Company Law Directive which requires Member States to allow private companies to be formed with only one member. However, because European Directives must be applied by national legislation in each Member State, it is rarely necessary to refer to the original Directive. For example, the 12th Directive was implemented in the UK by the Companies (Single Member Private Limited Companies) Regulations 1992 which amended the Companies Act 1985.

1.4 Memorandum of association

The memorandum and articles of association are the constitutional documents of the company. A memorandum of association must be submitted to the Registrar of Companies before a company can be incorporated. Most companies also submit articles of association for registration at the same time, although certain companies need not do so (see below).

During the incorporation process, the memorandum serves as the application form. It determines, among other things, what type of company the incorporators wish to be formed and therefore which provisions of the Act will apply to it. Once a company is registered, the memorandum becomes one of its core constitutional documents.

The memorandum of association must state the following:

- the name of the company;
- whether the registered office of the company is to be situated in England and Wales, or in Scotland;
- the objects of the company, i.e. the purpose for which it is formed – normally this clause will also set out the company's powers;
- whether it is a public or private company, limited by shares or guarantee or unlimited;
- in the case of a company limited by shares, the amount of share capital with which the company proposes to be registered and the division of the share capital into shares of a fixed amount, e.g. the share capital of the company is £100 divided into 100 shares of £1 each.

A provision that is required to be in the memorandum cannot be altered unless express provision is made by the Act allowing it to be altered and the formalities prescribed by the Act for that purpose have been complied with. No such provision is made with regard to the country in which the registered office is to be situated. However, specific provision is made for alteration of other clauses as follows:

- the company's name can be changed by special resolution (s. 28);
- the objects clause may be changed by special resolution, but minority shareholders may apply to the court to have the change declared invalid (ss. 4 and 5);
- a company may re-register as a different type of company provided that certain formalities have been followed (ss. 43 to 55);
- a company may alter its share capital by ordinary resolution, provided that its articles allow this (s. 121).

A company may include other provisions in its memorandum that are not required by the Act. These provisions may not be changed if the memorandum prohibits their alteration. If it provides a procedure for their alteration, that procedure must be followed, otherwise such provisions can be changed by special resolution, although the alteration may be challenged by minority shareholders in the same way as for a change to the objects clause (s. 17).

The memorandum must be signed by each subscriber. The subscribers to the memorandum are deemed to have agreed to become members of the company and on its registration should be entered as such in its register of members (s. 22(1)).

1.5 Articles of association

The articles of association ('articles') usually contain detailed provisions which govern the conduct of both general meetings and meetings of directors. Some of these provisions may be contained in the memorandum of association and this possibility should be borne in mind whenever reference is made to the articles. A company may alter any of its articles by special resolution unless its memorandum specifically provides otherwise (s. 9).

A company limited by shares need not submit articles of association with its application for registration. However, if it does not register its own articles, it will be deemed to have adopted a model set of articles prescribed by the Secretary of State, known as Table A (see below). Companies limited by guarantee and unlimited companies must submit articles of association with their application for registration.

Listed companies usually adopt articles that exclude Table A in its entirety. The Precedents section at the end of the book includes several examples taken from the articles of listed companies. Many private companies adopt 'short form' articles which state that the company has adopted Table A subject to a number of express exclusions, modifications or additions. In such circumstances, it is often helpful to produce a marked-up copy of Table A showing which regulations do not apply and any relevant modifications or additions. However, it should always be remembered that it is the 'short form' articles and not the new consolidated version that are registered at Companies House as the company's articles.

Articles must be printed, divided into paragraphs numbered consecutively and signed by each subscriber (s. 7(3)).

1.5.1 Table A

Table A is a model set of articles (suitable for public and private companies) which a company limited by shares will be deemed to adopt unless it registers its own articles. Even if a company registers its own articles, Table A will apply in so far as its own articles do not exclude or modify the provisions of Table A. The version of Table A that a company is deemed to adopt is the version that was in force at the date of its registration (s. 8(2)). If Table A is altered, the alteration does not affect a company registered before the alteration takes effect.

Several versions of Table A exist and the relevant version (if any) is therefore the one that was in force when the company was incorporated. The current version of Table A can be found in the Companies (Tables A to F) Regulations 1985. The version of Table A contained in those regulations was amended to facilitate the use of electronic communications by the Companies Act 1985 (Electronic Communications) Order 2000 on 22 December 2000. This amended version of the 1985 Table A is reproduced in full at **Appendix B**. The appendix also shows, by way of notes, the unamended text of the 1985 Table A. Any company subject to Table A that was incorporated between 1985 and 21 December 2000 will need to refer to this unamended version. The new version of Table A only applies directly to companies incorporated on or after 22 December 2000. All references to 'Table A' or to regulations (e.g. reg. 34) in this book are to the 1985 Table A (as amended by the 2000 Order) unless otherwise indicated. **Appendix C** contains an index to the 1985 Table A.

For companies incorporated under the Companies Act 1948, the relevant version of Table A is the one contained in that Act ('the 1948 Table A'), which is specifically preserved by the Companies Consolidation (Consequential Provisions) Act 1985, s. 31(8). Part I of the 1948 Table A applies (subject to the savings set out in the Companies Act 1980, s. 88(4)) in relation to private companies limited by shares as it applies in relation to public companies so limited (Companies Act 1980, Schedule 3, para. 36(1)). It is slightly different in many important respects to the 1985 Table A and these differences are highlighted throughout this book.

Some companies still exist that were formed while previous versions of Table A were in force. However, they are now so few in number that it is not considered necessary to refer to the position under these versions.

1.5.2   Relationship between Companies Acts and articles

Where articles refer to 'the Act', reference should be made to the article containing the definition of terms used (usually the first article) which will normally include the following or a similarly worded definition: 'the Act means the Companies Act 1985 including any statutory modification or re-enactment thereof for the time being in force'. For the present this means the Companies Act 1985 as amended.

In the case of the 1948 Table A, 'the Act' is defined as the Companies Act 1948. However, this and all references to section numbers in the 1948 Table A is deemed by virtue of s. 17(2) of the Interpretation Act 1978 to refer to the Companies Act 1985 and its equivalent provisions.

The Companies Act 1985 includes a good number of provisions relating to company meetings. Generally speaking these requirements override any provisions contained in the articles of association and must therefore be followed. Articles are usually drafted to ensure that no conflicts exist at the time of drafting. However, conflicts can arise subsequently as a result of amendments to the Act or, indeed, as a result of amendments made to the articles in ignorance of the statutory requirements. Changes were, for example, made to the Companies Act 1985 in 2000 to facilitate the use of electronic communications by companies and their members. These changes enable companies to take advantage of electronic communications, notwithstanding anything to the contrary contained in their articles. This was necessary because, at the time, most articles (including the unamended version of the 1985 Table A) contained provisions that would otherwise have prevented the use of electronic communications.

The position is further complicated by the fact that some of the provisions of the Act only apply if the articles do not make alternative provision (e.g. s. 370), while others invalidate the effect of articles not in accordance with certain minimum standards (e.g. s. 372(5) on the lodging of proxies). It is advisable to have amendments to the articles checked by a solicitor before they are made, to ensure that they are consistent with the requirements of the Act.

1.6 Contractual nature of the memorandum and articles

The memorandum and articles, when registered, bind the company and its members to the same extent as if they had been signed and sealed by each member and contained covenants on the part of each member to observe all the provisions of the memorandum and articles (s. 14). This is known as the 'section 14 contract'. The company can enforce the contract against its members (*Hickman's case* [1915] 1 Ch. 881) and the members can enforce it against each other (*Rayfield v. Hands* [1960] Ch. 1). The members can also enforce the contract against the company, but only in limited circumstances (see section 16.2). Section 14 is made subject to other provisions of the Act. So provisions in the memorandum or articles that conflict with the requirements of the Act will not be enforceable by the members or the company.

The section 14 contract differs in a number of ways from normal contracts. Provision is made in the Act for its terms to be altered by a special majority (see ss. 4 and 9 on the alteration of the memorandum and articles by special resolution). The consent of all the parties is required to vary normal contracts, and although the courts regard articles as commercial documents which should be construed so as to give them reasonable business efficacy (*Holmes v. Keyes* [1959] Ch. 199, 215, per Jenkins LJ), the Court of Appeal has held that terms cannot be implied into the articles in order to do so (*Bratton Seymour Service Co Ltd. v. Oxborough* [1992] BCLC 693).

1.7   Corporate governance

Corporate governance is concerned, among other things, with ensuring that decisions are taken in an appropriate manner by appropriate people after due consideration of the relevant facts. Should a matter be approved by the members? Or is it an area that can safely be left within the remit of the board of directors? If not, should the non-executive directors have some special role? Should the board be able to delegate responsibility to an executive director or a committee of directors? Should members be informed about the decisions taken on their behalf by the directors? And, if so, what action should they be able to take if they are not happy with those decisions?

The answers to these questions will have practical implications for the decision-making structure adopted by companies. Codes of practice have emerged largely to fill the gaps left by the Companies Acts. The existence of these gaps is, for the most part, deliberate. UK company law does not tend to interfere in the internal management of companies, mainly in recognition of the fact that it is difficult to find a single solution to suit the needs of all companies. Codes of practice on corporate governance have become highly influential on corporate behaviour generally. They are, however, directed mainly towards listed companies, i.e. companies where the vast majority of members are not involved in the day-to-day management, where highly paid professional managers fulfil that role, and where the members behave on the whole as investors rather than owners and are almost totally reliant when making investment decisions on information published by the directors.

1.7.1   Combined Code on Corporate Governance

The most important code for the purposes of this book is the Combined Code on Corporate Governance (see **Appendix F**). This code was issued in 1998 by a committee convened by the Financial Reporting Council and chaired by Sir Ronal Hampel (the Hampel Committee) following a review of existing corporate governance codes. As its name implies, the Combined Code consolidates (with some modifications) the recommendations made in other codes of practice. Its forerunners in this regard were the Cadbury Code and the Greenbury Code, both of which have now been superseded by the Combined Code.

The Combined Code includes recommendations on the following:

*   role of the company secretary (see **1.8**);
*   schedule of matters reserved to the board (see **3.12**);

- role of the chairman (see **4.7**);
- audit committees (see **5.11**);
- remuneration committees (see **5.12**);
- nomination committees (see **5.13**);
- retirement by rotation (see **23.10**).

The Combined Code is divided into two sections. The first section sets out a number of general principles, whereas the second sets out more detailed recommendations (in **Appendix F** the code provisions are shown under the relevant principles). Listed companies are required by the Listing Rules to include the following in their annual report and accounts:

- a statement explaining how they have applied the principles set out in the first section;
- a statement as to whether or not they have complied throughout the accounting period with the Code provisions and, if not, to give reasons for their non-compliance.

1.7.2 Cadbury Code and Report

Although the Cadbury Committee's Code of Best Practice has now been superseded by the Combined Code, the Cadbury Committee's report still contains useful guidance on many of the recommendations now contained in the Combined Code. References to 'the Cadbury Report' in this book are therefore to the *Report of the Committee on the Financial Aspects of Corporate Governance* (Gee Publishing).

1.7.3 Greenbury Code of Best Practice

The Cadbury Code required boards of directors to establish remuneration committees consisting of a majority of non-executive directors to make recommendations to the board on executive directors' salaries. However, the adoption of this recommendation did not put an end to public disquiet over the salaries paid to executive directors, particularly in the privatised utility companies. Accordingly, in February 1995, the CBI formed a study group chaired by Sir Richard Greenbury 'to identify good practice in determining directors' remuneration and to prepare a code of such practice for use by UK plcs'. The study group (the 'Greenbury Committee') published its final report and a code of practice on 17 July 1995 (*Directors' Remuneration: Report of a Study Group chaired by Sir Richard Greenbury*, Gee Publishing). The London Stock Exchange agreed to require UK listed companies to report on their compliance with the Greenbury Code and to include in their annual reports a report on directors' remuneration, disclosing, among other things, the following:

- the company's policy on executive directors' remuneration;
- full details of each director's remuneration package, share options, incentive schemes, service contracts.

Most of the recommendations made in the Greenbury Code have been retained in the Combined Code which, in any case, supersedes it. For the purposes of this book, these provisions are only relevant in relation to the role of the remuneration committee (see **5.12**).

1.8 Company secretary

Every company must appoint a company secretary (s. 283). The directors of a public company have a duty to appoint as secretary someone who is capable of carrying out the duties that the post entails (s. 286). This is normally satisfied by appointing a chartered secretary, lawyer or accountant, although the Act does not preclude the appointment of someone else who is appropriately qualified.

Although the Act does not specify the role of the company secretary, it makes the secretary liable to criminal prosecution as an officer of the company in circumstances where the company has failed to comply with its obligations under the Act. The list of offences for which the secretary may be held liable under the Act corresponds fairly closely with what might be considered the company secretary's core duties; and, although the directors can also be held liable for all these offences (and more besides), they tend to delegate responsibility to the secretary for ensuring compliance with obligations for which the secretary shares liability. This is particularly true with regard to compliance with the statutory provisions on company meetings and minutes.

Accordingly, the company secretary will normally be responsible for the administration of general meetings, board meetings and other meetings of directors. However, the secretary has no inherent power to ensure compliance with the applicable rules and regulations. He does not even have a right to attend any of these meetings (unless entitled in some other capacity). The secretary will therefore be totally reliant on the fact that the directors follow the secretary's advice or on powers delegated by the directors to the secretary.

The Combined Code on Corporate Governance states (at para. A.1.4): 'All directors should have access to the advice and services of the company secretary, who is responsible to the board for ensuring that board procedures are followed and that applicable rules and regulations are complied with. Any question of the removal of the company secretary should be a matter for the board as a whole.'

This recommendation was originally made by the Code of Best Practice published by the Cadbury Committee in 1992. In its report, the Cadbury Committee said:

> The company secretary has a key role to play in ensuring that board procedures are both followed and regularly reviewed. The chairman and the board will look to the company

secretary for guidance on what their responsibilities are under the rules and regulations to which they are subject and on how those responsibilities should be discharged. All directors should have access to the advice and services of the company secretary and should recognise that the chairman is entitled to the strong and positive support of the company secretary in ensuring the effective functioning of the board. It should be standard practice for the company secretary to administer, attend and prepare minutes of board meetings. (Cadbury Report, para. 4.25)

See also the ICSA's Code on Good Boardroom Practice at **Appendix I** for the ICSA's recommendations regarding the company secretary's right to attend meetings of the board and its committees.

The Cadbury Committee said 'the responsibility for ensuring that the secretary remains capable, and any question of the secretary's removal, should be a matter for the board as a whole' (Cadbury Report, para. 4.26). The Cadbury Committee also said that it 'expects that the company secretary will be a source of advice to the chairman and to the board on the implementation of the Code of Best Practice' (Cadbury Report, para. 4.27).

2

Electronic communications

2.1 Summary

- The Companies Act 1985 was amended on 22 December 2000 to facilitate the use of electronic communications for various purposes (see **2.2**).
- Table A was also amended on the same date and those amendments may be of significance to companies incorporated before 22 December 2000 (see **2.3**).
- Although companies need not amend their articles in order to take advantage of the statutory provisions on electronic communications, it is good practice to do so (see **2.4**).
- The term 'electronic communications' is defined in the Electronic Communications Act 2000 (see **2.5**).
- The Institute of Chartered Secretaries and Administrators has issued guidance for companies on the use of electronic communications in relation to general meetings (see **2.6**). This guidance is important, not least because Table A refers to it in relation to proof of service of electronic communications (see **11.3**).
- A company may only use electronic communications to send notices and copies of the accounts to members if they have elected to receive them in this manner (see **2.7**).
- Electronic signatures are now admissible as evidence in legal proceedings (see **2.8**).

2.2 Using electronic communications for statutory purposes

The Companies Act 1985 was amended on 22 December 2000 to facilitate the use of electronic communications for the following purposes by the Companies Act 1985 (Electronic Communications) Order 2000:

- issuing notices of general meetings and class meetings (see **11.3**);
- sending reports, accounts and summary financial statements to members (see **23.2**);
- appointment of proxies by members in relation to general meetings (see **14.11**);
- issuing a notice calling a meeting to pass an elective resolution under s. 379A of the 1985 Act (see **11.3**);
- where an elective resolution to dispense with AGMs is in force, to allow electronic transmission by a member of a notice requiring an AGM under s. 366A (see **25.3**);
- where an elective resolution to dispense with the laying of accounts at a general meeting is in force, to allow electronic transmission by a member or the auditors of a notice requiring the accounts to be laid under s. 253 (see **25.4**).

A company can take advantage of the above changes, notwithstanding anything to the contrary that may be contained in its articles.

2.3 Table A

The Companies Act 1985 (Electronic Communications) Order 2000 also amended Table A to facilitate the use of electronic communications by amending the regulations that contain Table A (i.e. the Companies (Tables A to F) Regulations 1985). The amended version of Table A contained in those regulations is now the current version of Table A for the purposes of the Act, and any company formed with Table A articles on or after 22 December 2000 will have adopted that amended version. However, the amendments made by the Order in this regard have no direct effect on the articles of companies that adopted Table A before the Order came into force. The relevant version of Table A for any company is the version that was in force on the date of its incorporation, and a company is not affected by any subsequent changes made to Table A. Accordingly, for companies incorporated before 22 December 2000, the relevant version of Table A remains the unamended version. The version of Table A at **Appendix B** shows the 1985 Table as amended by the Companies Act 1985 (Electronic Communications) Order 2000. However, it also shows, by way of notes, the relevant provisions prior to their amendment.

The articles of most companies incorporated before 22 December 2000 will, unless they have subsequently been amended, probably require notices of general meetings to be given in writing, appointments of proxies to made in writing, and may require physical copies of the accounts to be sent to members and others. The existence of such provisions in a company's articles will not preclude it from using electronic communications for statutory purposes. This is because the Act provides in each case that a company may take advantage of the statutory provisions on electronic communications, notwithstanding anything to the contrary in its articles. In addition, the Act provides in relation to notices and proxies that where a company's articles make no provision for the use of electronic communications, the provisions of Table A (as amended) shall apply. In other words, a company may take advantage of electronic communications despite the fact that its articles appear not to allow it to do so, and where this is the case, it may act as if the provisions of Table A in this regard had statutory force.

2.4   Amending articles for electronic communications

Although the Act allows a company to take advantage of electronic communications without first amending its articles, it is probably preferable to do so. Despite the government's best efforts to eliminate any problems in this regard, a company may find it difficult to decide whether its own articles or Table A should be applied in certain circumstances. It is, in any case, best to avoid having articles that conflict with the Act if at all possible. ICSA's guidance on electronic communications with shareholders (see **2.6**) recommends that companies should take steps to amend their articles to facilitate the use of electronic communications as soon as is practical. For companies with articles based on the original 1985 Table A, the best starting point may be to make the same amendments as were made by the Companies Act 1985 (Electronic Communications) Order 2000 to Table A itself. Schedule 1 of the Order sets out the necessary changes for this purpose which can be summarised as follows:

- to add in reg. 1 (interpretation) definitions for the word 'communication' and the phrase 'electronic communication' (both of which are deemed to have the same meaning as in the Electronic Communications Act 2000);
- to eliminate the requirements in regs 60, 61 and 62 for proxy appointments to be in writing;
- to make provision in regs 62 and 63 for delivery of proxy appointments by electronic communication;
- to provide in reg. 111 that any notice to be given to or by any person pursuant to the articles (other than a notice calling a meeting of directors) shall be in writing or given using electronic communications to an address for the time being notified for that purpose to the person giving the notice;
- to provide in reg. 112 for the giving of notices by electronic communication;
- to make provision in reg. 115 to the effect that proof that a notice contained in an electronic communication was sent in accordance with guidance issued by the ICSA shall be conclusive evidence that the notice was given;

- to provide that, for the purposes of regs 62, 111 and 112, an address in relation to an electronic communication includes any number or address used for the purposes of such communications.

A company may, of course, adopt provisions that have a different effect from Table A, and companies with articles that exclude Table A in its entirety will need to draft their own amendments. Questions that should be considered when amending articles in these circumstances might include the following:

- Are the provisions of Table A (as amended) suitable?
- What provision should the articles make with regard to deemed delivery of notices (and documents) sent electronically? Should they, for example, be treated the same as a notice sent by post? Or should documents sent using electronic communications be deemed to be served earlier? Should a notification of publication on a website be treated differently if sent by post or electronically?
- Should the articles require the company to send a paper copy of any notice or document where electronic transmission has failed or notify the member that a transmission has failed (if so, care would need to be taken not to prejudice any deemed service provisions)?
- Should the articles require the company to conduct a regular or periodic e-mail probe to check e-mail addresses held? The answer to this question will probably be negative, although this would not stop a company from conducting a probe.
- Should the articles specify how electronic communications may be authenticated or executed? It is probably best to give the directors discretion in this regard. This question may not only be relevant with regard to proxy appointments.
- Should specific provision be made regarding what constitutes proof that an electronic communication has been sent? Table A relies on guidance issued by the ICSA in this regard.
- In the case of a listed company, does any special provision need to be made for documents that the company must issue under the Listing Rules?

2.5 Definition of electronic communications

The term 'electronic communication' is defined in s. 15 of the Electronic Communications Act 2000 as:

> a communication transmitted (whether from one person to another, from one device to another or from a person to a device or vice versa) –
> (a) by means of a telecommunication system (within the meaning of the Telecommunications Act 1984); or
> (b) by other means but while in an electronic form.

A telecommunications system is defined in s. 4(1) of the Telecommunications Act 1984 as:

> a system for the conveyance, through the agency of electric, magnetic, electro-magnetic, electro-chemical or electro-mechanical energy of –
> (a) speech, music and other sounds;
> (b) visual images;
> (c) signals serving for the impartation (whether as between persons and persons, things and things or persons and things) of any matter otherwise than in the form of sounds or visual images; or
> (d) signals serving for the actuation or control of machinery or apparatus.

The term 'electronic communication' embraces the following methods of communication:

- e-mail;
- Internet delivery;
- telephone recordings and conversations;
- fax messages;
- text messages on mobile phones;
- radio and television signals.

Some lawyers have expressed doubts as to whether sending a document on a floppy disk or CD-ROM would fall within the definition of an electronic communication. At the time of writing, this issue has still not been resolved satisfactorily one way or the other. The Department of Trade and Industry, as the government department responsible for the Electronic Communications Act 2000, has indicated that the definition was intended to cover documents sent in this manner. However, companies should perhaps take advice before relying on these methods for statutory purposes.

It is questionable whether it would be appropriate to use some of the above methods for giving notices or sending copies of the accounts, particularly those that are of an ephemeral nature. Nevertheless, if a company and a member agreed to use one of these methods, there would seem to be nothing to prevent them from doing so. The methods most companies are likely to adopt are e-mail and other methods of Internet delivery. However, text messaging using mobile phones may become more popular in the future. Any method of electronic communication that allows the recipient to retain a copy for later use, and which is capable of giving the company assurance that proper service has been given, could be used.

2.6 ICSA guidance on electronic communications with shareholders

The Institute of Chartered Secretaries and Administrators has published a guide to best practice on electronic communications with shareholders (for a summary of recommendations, see **Appendix G**). Publication was timed to coincide with changes made to the Companies Act 1985 and Table A by the Companies Act 1985 (Electronic Communications) Order 2000. One of the modifications made to Table A by the Order was to amend reg. 115 to provide that proof that a notice contained in an electronic communication was sent in accordance with the ICSA guidance shall be conclusive evidence that the notice was given. The recommendations contained in Chapter 8 of the guide will be relevant for these purposes.

2.7 Election by members

A company must continue to send paper copies of the accounts and any notices of general meetings to any person who is entitled to receive them, unless that person has agreed to receive them via one of the available methods of electronic communications provided for by the Act. The Act provides two options in this regard:

- A company may use electronic communications to send a full electronic version of the accounts or notice to a person who has provided it with an address for that purpose (e.g. an e-mail address).
- Alternatively, a company may simply notify a person that the relevant documents have been published on a website together with details of how they may be accessed and, in the case of notices of general meetings, certain other prescribed particulars. A company cannot use this second method without the agreement of the person concerned. In addition, both the company and that person must agree on the manner in which the notification will be served. As long as both parties agree, the notification can be sent by post, by hand or by electronic communications. If it is to be sent by electronic communications, the person must have provided the company with an address to be used for that purpose.

Effectively, a company cannot use either of the above methods unless a person has made an active election to receive the relevant documents in that manner. A company cannot, for example, use e-mail to send notices to members if those e-mail addresses have been gathered for some other purpose. Before doing so it would have to get them to agree to accept notices by e-mail.

The Act does not require companies to obtain a member's

written consent before using electronic communications. Members could therefore be allowed to signify their consent in some other way, e.g. by registering on a website or sending an e-mail or even registering by telephone. Ideally, members should be required to authenticate their election in some way. If elections are made in writing, this can be done by signature or by any other accepted method of execution. If a company plans to allow members to make elections via e-mail, the Internet, telephone or fax, members could be required to authenticate their election by providing a personal identification number allocated to them for this purpose.

There is nothing in the Act to prevent a person from electing to receive certain types of document in one way and other types of document in a different manner. A company need not, however, allow a person to make such an election. Indeed, a company need not provide members with any choice at all as to the available methods. It could, for example, decide to publish the documents on a website and only offer members the opportunity to receive notifications regarding publication by e-mail.

Listed companies will not only need to obtain the consent of members for the various statutory purposes but also in respect of documents that they are required to send pursuant to the Listing Rules (Listing Rules, para. 1.27). The specimen form of election at **Precedent 2.7** has been adapted for this purpose. It provides an example of the sort of explanation that may need to be given to members. Companies will need to draft their own guidance for members depending on the options being made available and the provisions of their own articles.

Companies will need to comply with applicable data protection rules and practices when collecting, storing and using information provided by members for the purposes of electronic communications. Details of elections made by members and any electronic addresses provided by them should not be entered in any of the statutory registers in a manner that would require their disclosure to people inspecting the register. As the Act does not require these details to be entered in any statutory register, they are not covered by any of the applicable data protection exemptions for statutory registers. The form of election at **Precedent 2.7** includes a specimen data protection statement.

2.8 Electronic signatures

Section 7 of the Electronic Communications Act 2000 ('the ECA 2000') makes provision for the admissibility in legal proceedings of the following:

- an electronic signature incorporated into or logically associated with a particular electronic communication or particular electronic data;
- the certification by any person of such a signature.

An electronic signature (or any certification thereof) is admissible as evidence in relation to any of the following questions regarding the authenticity or integrity of a communication or data:

- whether the communication or data comes from a particular person or other source;
- whether it is accurately timed and dated;
- whether it is intended to have legal effect;
- whether there has been any tampering with or other modification of the communication or data.

The admissibility of electronic signatures may be of significance in the following areas covered by this book:

- the appointment of proxies using electronic communications (see **14.11**);
- the retention of signed minutes in computerised form (see **26.4**);
- for the purposes of other electronic communications between members and the company (ECA 2000, s. 15(2)).

An electronic signature is defined in s. 7(2) of the ECA 2000 as:

> so much of anything in electronic form as –
>
> (a) is incorporated into or otherwise logically associated with any electronic communication or electronic data; and
>
> (b) purports to be so incorporated or associated for the purpose of being used in establishing the authenticity of the communication or data, the integrity of the communication or data, or both.

This definition would allow a variety of methods to be used to apply an electronic signature. However, the security of the method used will have a bearing on the weight given to the evidence that is tendered in any legal proceedings. In order to ensure that an electronic signature is given at least the same (if not more) weight than a manual signature, it will be necessary to use the most modern cryptographic techniques. These involve the use of public and private keys to code and decode messages and algorithms which prevent the file that has been 'signed' from being tampered with.

Although it is possible to purchase commercially available software that will generate the public and private keys that must be used, most electronic signatures are purchased from commercial organisations which are able to certify for the benefit of third parties that the signature was purchased by the person that it purports to represent. The ECA 2000 provides that a person may certify an electronic signature by making a statement (whether before or after the making of the communication) confirming that the signature, a means of producing, communicating or verifying the signature, or a procedure applied to the signature, is (either alone or in combination with other factors) a valid means of establishing the authenticity of the communication or data, the integrity of the communication or data, or both (s. 7(3)).

A person could certify an electronic signature applied using an insecure method under this procedure. Difficulties may arise, however, where there is some dispute as to the validity of the electronic signature or as to whether the electronic signature was applied by or on behalf of the person it purports to represent. If the company is likely to need to rely on the validity of the electronic signature in legal proceedings, it is therefore preferable for it to insist that a secure method be used. This is certainly desirable with regard to the use of electronic signatures to sign the minutes.

Part I

Meetings of directors

Directors derive their powers from provisions that are usually contained in a company's articles of association. Generally speaking they must exercise those powers collectively at a board meeting. However, articles normally allow the directors to act by written resolution and to delegate their powers to some other body or person.

The procedures to be followed at meetings of directors are determined largely by a company's articles of association. The Companies Act 1985 interferes very little in this area. Where the articles are silent on any matter, the common law will apply. As most articles are modelled on Table A, it provides a convenient starting point for any study of this subject.

Articles usually provide that the proceedings of committees of directors are governed by the same rules as board meetings. The courts will not necessarily invalidate a transaction merely because the directors failed to follow proper procedures, particularly where the directors could rectify that failing by holding a proper meeting. The courts will not, however, tolerate such failures where a director is interested in the transaction.

3

Directors

3.1 Summary

- The Companies Act 1985 requires every private company to appoint at least one director and every public company to appoint at least two. The practical procedures for the appointment (and removal) of directors are dealt with in **Chapter 23**.
- Directors usually manage the business of the company on a day-to-day basis. However, the Act does not require this, nor does it confer on them any power to do so, either individually or as a body. Under the common law, a company's powers must be exercised by its members in general meeting unless its memorandum or articles of association provide otherwise (see **3.2**).
- Several factors must be taken into account when determining the extent of the directors' powers. For example, the directors cannot exercise a power that the company itself does not have (see **3.4**).
- A company's powers are set out in the objects clause in its memorandum of association (see **3.5**).
- Most articles include what is known as a general management clause. This clause usually gives the directors all the powers necessary to manage the company on a day-to-day basis. The powers are limited by the objects clause and other provisions in the memorandum or articles. In addition, the Act gives the members certain rights and powers that cannot be excluded by the articles (see **3.6**).
- The articles are deemed to be a contract between the members and the company which governs the way the company is run. It follows that the only way the shareholders can interfere in matters delegated to the directors is to change that contract (i.e. to amend the articles by special resolution so as to restrict the directors' discretion) or to issue directions in accordance with procedures contained in the articles. Even then, such resolutions or directions will have no effect on the validity of any transaction previously entered into by the directors on behalf of the company (see **3.7**).

- Other articles may give the directors special powers which they would not otherwise have, e.g. the power to delegate and the power to fix the remuneration of directors (see **3.8**).
- If the directors are unable to act for any reason, their powers may by default revert to the members in general meeting (see **3.9**).
- Articles usually allow the directors to delegate 'any of their powers' to committees of the board and/or to executive directors. However, it has been held that this does not necessarily include special powers given to them by the articles, e.g. the power to pay the directors special remuneration (see **3.10**).
- Articles usually give the board specific power to appoint agents by power of attorney or otherwise (see **3.11**).
- The Combined Code on Corporate Governance requires directors of listed companies to produce a schedule of matters reserved for the decision of the board (see **3.12**).

3.2 The board of directors

The Companies Act 1985 requires every public company formed after 1929 to have at least two directors and every other company to have at least one (s. 282). The directors usually undertake the day-to-day management of the company on behalf of the members. However, the Act does not require this and does not confer any powers on the directors to enable them to do so, either individually or as a body. Under common law, a company's powers must be exercised by its members in general meeting unless its memorandum or articles of association provide otherwise (*Mayor, Constables and Company of Merchants of the Staple of England v. Governor and Company of the Bank of England* (1887) 21 QBD 160). In other words, the directors will have no power to act on behalf of the company at all unless the memorandum or articles say so.

It is not normally practicable for the members to manage the business on a day-to-day basis. Every matter requiring a decision would have to be put to a general meeting called in accordance with the formal requirements of the Act. This would be impossible for a company with hundreds of shareholders. Even where there are relatively few members, it is easier for them to manage the company as directors rather than as members. This is mainly because the formalities associated with board meetings are less onerous, but also because that is the way most companies are run and doing it in any other way would complicate matters unnecessarily and probably involve significant legal expenses.

In practice, the articles of most companies delegate wide powers of management to the directors. Generally speaking, these powers must be exercised by the board of directors collectively (i.e. at a board meeting). However, the articles may allow the directors to act by written resolution. They may also allow the directors to delegate their powers to some other individual or body.

In the UK, all directors are members of the same board and usually have one vote each. Under this unitary system, each director has an equal say in matters put to the board (although the chairman may sometimes have a casting vote). Articles usually allow the board to appoint one or more of the directors to some sort of executive office within the company (e.g. managing director) and to delegate any of its powers to them. These executive directors are usually salaried and manage the business of the company on a full- or part-time basis. Directors who are not executives are known as non-executive directors.

The function of the board will be to take decisions that are outside the authority of the executive directors and to set the company's strategic objectives. Non-executive directors often play a key role in monitoring the performance of the executives and setting their pay.

On the continent, two-tier board systems are more common. The company is managed on a day-to-day basis by an executive board which is appointed by and accountable to a supervisory board. The supervisory board fulfils the monitoring role performed by non-executive directors in the UK and may include shareholder and employee representatives. The system is appealing to purists as it places the non-executives above the executives in the structural hierarchy. However, it is debatable whether these structural differences make it any easier for the part-time directors to supervise the executives.

The main advantage of the unitary system is said to be that it enables the non-executive directors to contribute more effectively to the formulation of the company's strategy and to monitor the performance of the executives; its major disadvantage is that it is more difficult for the non-executive directors to be impartial and independent. These criticisms were addressed in respect of listed companies in 1992 by the Committee on the Financial Aspects of Corporate Governance, chaired by Sir Adrian Cadbury. The committee produced a code of best practice for listed companies (the Cadbury Code) which made recommendations on the constitution of boards of directors and the role of non-executive directors. These recommendations were subsequently consolidated, together with the recommendations of the Greenbury Committee on directors' remuneration, into the Combined Code on Corporate Governance (see **Appendix F**). The Combined Code recommends that the board should include non-executive directors of sufficient calibre and number for their views to carry significant weight in the board's decisions, and that non-executive directors should comprise not less than one-third of the board (Combined Code, para. A.3.1). It also recommends that a majority of the non-executive directors should be independent of management and free from any business or other relationship that could materially interfere with the exercise of their independent judgement. Non-executive directors considered by the board to be independent in this sense should be identified in the annual report (Combined Code, para. A.2.2). The main purpose of this recommendation is to allow investors to make their own assessments as to the independence of the non-executive directors and therefore to make their own judgements as to whether the company is complying with these and other recommendations in the Code (e.g. regarding the constitution of the audit, remuneration and nomination committees).

3.3 Types of director

3.3.1 Executive directors

An executive director is a director who holds some executive or management position within the company. Under Table A, the directors may appoint one or more of their number as managing director or to any other executive office (e.g. finance director) and determine the terms and remuneration of any such appointment (reg. 84). These powers are special powers which cannot be delegated by the board under reg. 72 (see **3.10**). The appointment of executive directors and the terms of such appointments must therefore be approved by a resolution of the board (see **Precedent 3.3A**), unless the articles specifically allow another person or body to make appointments.

Regulation 72 allows the board to delegate its powers to individual executive directors. In delegating its powers, it may limit the executive's authority by imposing certain conditions. For example, the managing director may be given power to authorise capital expenditure up to a certain value with any expenditure above that amount requiring board approval. The terms of any delegation should be approved by a resolution of the board (see section 3.10).

Salaried executive directors should be appointed under a formal service agreement which should state the title of the job to be performed, the duties to be performed, the remuneration and other benefits associated with the appointment (including whether the remuneration payable is inclusive or exclusive of any director's fee that may be payable) and any restraints in the form of confidentiality undertakings and restrictive covenants in the event of leaving the service of the company. With regard to the duties to be performed it is normal for the service contract to include a more general provision stating that the director shall have such powers and duties as the board may determine from time to time (see **Precedent 3.3B**). This allows the board to modify authorisations generally without having to modify each executive director's contract. Limits on individual directors' authorities may also be reinforced by the adoption of a schedule of matters reserved to the board (see **3.12**).

The executive directors will be subject to any provisions in the articles on retirement by rotation, unless the articles specify otherwise. Under Table A, executive directors are exempt from retirement by rotation but not from the requirement to retire at the first annual general meeting following their appointment (reg. 84). The Combined Code recommends that all directors should retire and offer themselves for re-election at least once every three years (Combined Code, para. A.6.2).

3.3.2   Non-executive directors

Non-executive directors are directors who have not been appointed to any executive office within the company. The distinction between executive and non-executive directors will not always be clear-cut, particularly where the status of the chairman is concerned. The Combined Code recommends that the board should include non-executive directors of sufficient calibre and number for their views to carry significant weight in the board's decisions, and that non-executive directors should comprise not less than one-third of the board (Combined Code, para. A.3.1). It also recommends that a majority of the non-executive directors should be independent of management and free from any business or other relationship that could materially interfere with the exercise of their independent judgement. Non-executive directors considered by the board to be independent in this sense should be identified in the annual report (Combined Code, para. A.2.2). The main purpose of this disclosure obligation is to allow investors to make their own assessment as to the independence of the non-executive directors and therefore to make their own judgement as to whether the company is complying with other recommendations in the Code (e.g. regarding the constitution of the audit, remunerations and nomination committees). Various people have produced guidance on the criteria that should be used when assessing the independence or otherwise of non-executives. The most influential is probably issued by the National Association of Pension Funds (with the support of the Association of British Insurers), who together can claim to represent the vast majority of institutional investors. According to this guidance a non-executive director will be assumed by the ABI and NAPF to be independent unless, in relation to the company, the director:

- was formerly an executive;
- is, or has been, paid by the company in any capacity other than as a non-executive director;
- represents a trading partner or is connected to a company or partnership (or was prior to retirement) that does business with the company;
- has been a non-executive director for nine years, i.e. three three-year terms;
- is closely related to an executive director;
- has been awarded share options, performance-related pay or is a member of the company's pension fund;

- represents a controlling or significant shareholder;
- is a new appointee selected other than by a formal process;
- has cross-directorships with any executive director; and
- is deemed by the company, for whatever reasons, not to be independent.

Whether or not they are independent, non-executive directors participate in the management of the company by attending board meetings and any committees of the board of which they are a member. Reg. 72 of Table A does not allow the board to delegate any of its powers to an individual non-executive director. However, the same result can be achieved by delegating to a board committee consisting of only one non-executive director.

Under Table A, all directors are entitled to be repaid any expenses that they reasonably incur in connection with their duties (reg. 83). However, the fees paid to directors in their capacity as board members must be approved by an ordinary resolution of the members in general meeting (reg. 82). This applies to fees paid to executive and non-executive directors, although executive directors usually receive a salary instead of directors' fees and those salaries may be determined by the board without reference to the members (reg. 84). Regulation 82 is frequently modified to enable the board to fix the fees of non-executive directors without reference to the members or subject to a maximum amount approved by the members.

3.3.3   Alternate directors

An alternate director is someone appointed by a director to attend and vote at board meetings in their stead. The Act does not authorise a director to appoint an alternate or a proxy. Accordingly, an alternate director may only be appointed if the articles make specific provision, e.g. regs 65 to 69 of Table A (see further **4.11** and **Precedents 4.11A to D**).

3.3.4   *De facto* and shadow directors

De facto directors are people who act as directors and are held out to be directors by the company even though they have never actually been appointed as directors or have ceased to be directors. A shadow director is a person in accordance with whose instructions the directors of the company are accustomed to act. A person is not deemed to be a shadow director by reason only that the directors act on advice by that person in a professional capacity (s. 741). It is probably not possible for a person to be both a shadow director and a *de facto* director. Typically, the former tends to lurk in the shadows, sheltering behind others who, it is claimed, are the only directors of the company. The latter is a person who claims to act and purports to act as a director, though not validly appointed as such.

De facto directors and shadow directors can both be disqualified under the Company Directors Disqualification Act 1986 and may be liable for wrongful and fraudulent trading under the Insolvency Act 1986. Shadow directors are subject to some of the duties and penalties prescribed by the Companies Act 1985 (e.g. ss. 330 to 346 regarding restrictions on the making of loans to directors).

3.4 Extent of the directors' powers

In order to decide whether the directors are acting within their powers, the following questions should be asked:

- Is the proposed transaction within the powers of the company as set out in the objects clause? (See below.)
- If so, is there anything in the articles or the Act that specifically requires the transaction to be authorised by the members in general meeting? (See, for example, **Appendix D**.)
- If not, is the proposed transaction concerned with the management of the company?
- If so, the directors may act under the powers given by the general management clause unless:
  - some other provision in the articles restricts their powers under the general management clause in relation to the proposed transaction (see **3.6**)
  - the members have given the directors a valid instruction that restricts their freedom to enter into the transaction (see **3.7**).
- If not, is there a special power in the memorandum or articles that authorises the directors to act in this way? (See **3.8**.)

3.5 *Ultra vires* and the objects clause

The objects clause in the memorandum of association sets out the purpose for which the company was formed and may specify the powers of the company in that regard. By limiting the objects of the company, the clause limits its powers. For example, the objects clause may state that the company is to build and operate a railway. Such a company could not provide banking services and any transaction by the railway company with a third party in connection with banking would therefore be *ultra vires* (i.e. beyond the company's powers) and invalid.

Historically, a third party was deemed to have notice of any limitations on the company's powers by virtue of the fact that the memorandum containing the objects clause was filed at Companies House and available for public inspection. However, the *ultra vires* rule was modified in 1989 in order to comply with a European Directive, and s. 35(1) of the Companies Act 1985 now provides that the validity of an act done by a company shall not be called into question on the grounds of lack of capacity by reason of anything in the company's memorandum. Thus, if the directors enter into a contract with a third party for a purpose that is beyond the powers of the company, the third party can now rely on s. 35(1) to enforce it against the company (previously the contract would have been void and therefore unenforceable).

Nevertheless, s. 35(2) states that a member of the company may still bring proceedings to restrain an act that is beyond a company's capacity. In addition, s. 35(3) states that it remains the duty of the directors to observe any limitations on their powers flowing from the company's memorandum. Accordingly, the directors will be liable to compensate the company if it suffers a loss as a result of an *ultra vires* transaction approved by them. By participating in *ultra vires* acts, the directors are in breach of their fiduciary duty to the company, as preserved by s. 35(3).

The directors effectively bear most of the risks of an *ultra vires* transaction. However, the court can relieve the directors of their liability if it is satisfied that they have acted honestly and reasonably and ought fairly to be excused (s. 727). In addition, under s. 35(3) the members may by special resolution ratify the acts of the directors that were beyond the capacity of the company and by a separate special resolution relieve them of any liability incurred as a result of their actions.

It can be seen from the above summary that the *ultra vires* rule will not be a matter of great importance where the members are all directors and they all agree to a particular transaction. However, in other circumstances the directors would be well advised to act within the powers of the company as defined by the objects clause or risk heavy personal liabilities.

3.6 General management clause

Articles invariably contain a provision (known as the general management clause) that reverses the common law rule that the company's powers must be exercised by the members in general meeting. Regulation 70 of Table A is typical of this type of provision. It provides:

> **70.** Subject to the provisions of the Act, the memorandum and the articles and to any directions given by special resolution, the business of the company shall be managed by the directors who may exercise all the powers of the company. No alteration of the memorandum or articles and no such direction shall invalidate any prior act of the directors which would have been valid if that alteration had not been made or that direction had not been given. The powers given by this regulation shall not be limited by any special power given to the directors by the articles and a meeting of directors at which a quorum is present may exercise all powers exercisable by the directors.

It can be seen that reg. 70 gives the directors authority to exercise all the powers of the company that are not specifically excluded or reserved to the members by other provisions in the memorandum or articles or the Act. It also provides a special procedure under which the members in general meeting can give valid instructions to the directors (see **3.7**).

It has been held that a general management clause giving the directors all powers 'necessary in the management of the company' does not authorise them to present a winding up petition without the approval of the members because winding up is not connected with the management of the company (*Re Emmadart Ltd* [1979] Ch. 540). Although directors now have a statutory power to apply for a compulsory winding up under the Insolvency Act 1986, their powers may be subject to other limitations where this wording is adopted. Modern articles seek to avoid this problem by conferring powers on the directors without the condition that they be exercised in the management of the company. Regulation 70 of Table A uses the words 'the business of the company shall be managed by the directors who may exercise all the powers of the company'.

Under a general management clause it is usually safe to assume that the directors can do anything the company can do as long as they are not prevented from doing that thing by the Act or another provision in the memorandum or articles. Thus in *Re Patent File Co.* (1870) LR 6 Ch. 83, Mellish L.J. said: 'The articles give to the directors the whole powers of the company, subject to the provisions [of the articles and] of the Companies Act . . . and I cannot find anything either in the Act or in the articles to prohibit their making a mortgage by deposit.' There are, of course, exceptions to this rule.

The directors may not do anything that would be a breach of their fiduciary duty to the company unless the articles give them specific powers in that regard (e.g. pay themselves a salary). In addition, they may not delegate their powers unless the articles so provide (see **3.10**).

This might not appear very helpful to directors, who would no doubt prefer the articles to contain a list of things that they can do. However, such an approach would be unwieldy. The relevant article would need to be similar in nature, but perhaps longer, than the objects clause in the memorandum. As such, it is doubtful whether directors would actually find it any easier. Indeed, the objects clause is the closest the directors will get to a list of their powers, although this will not be of much assistance if the company adopts the short form object authorised by s. 3A of the 1985 Act (i.e. to be a general commercial company). In this case, s. 3A states that the company has power to do anything that is incidental or conducive to the carrying on of any trade or business by it.

3.6.1   Subject to the provisions of the Act

All powers conferred on the directors by the articles are subject to the provisions of the Companies Act 1985 (as amended), whether or not this is stated in the articles. Thus the directors cannot exercise any of the company's powers that are reserved to the members by the Act and must comply with the requirements of the Act when exercising their powers. For example, directors cannot allot new shares unless they have been authorised to do so in accordance with the requirements of s. 80. For further examples of transactions that require shareholder approval, see **Appendix D** which shows the type of resolution required for various types of business at general meetings.

The Act also requires the directors to have regard to the interests of employees (s. 309), imposes restrictions on the making of loans to themselves (Part X of the Act) and generally imposes duties on the directors to comply with certain procedural requirements when exercising their powers, e.g. to keep minutes of their meetings.

3.6.2   Subject to the memorandum and articles

The general management clause is always expressed as being subject to other provisions in the memorandum and articles of association. These may include provisions that:

- limit the capacity of the company and therefore the directors (i.e. the objects clause in the memorandum – see **3.5**);
- limit the powers of the directors (but not the members), e.g. a limit on directors' borrowing powers;
- reserve certain powers to the members, e.g. to approve the payment of dividend (although the articles may allow the directors to pay an interim dividend without reference to the members);
- determine the procedures that the directors must follow when exercising their powers, e.g. regulation of proceedings at meetings of directors;
- allow the directors to delegate their powers;
- relax the conditions that members must satisfy in order to exercise certain statutory rights, e.g. the articles could allow members holding less than one-tenth of the voting shares to demand a general meeting (the company cannot exclude the members' minimum statutory rights);
- provide additional procedures for removal of directors, e.g. by extraordinary resolution.

3.7   Directions given by the members

Unless the articles contain some special provision allowing the members to give directions, the only way they can interfere in the exercise by the directors of their powers is to alter the articles in such a way that those powers revert back to the company in general meeting. In *Automatic Self-Cleansing Filter Syndicate Co. Ltd v. Cunninghame* [1906] 2 Ch. 34, CA, the members in general meeting passed an ordinary resolution (i.e. by a simple majority of those voting) instructing the directors to sell part of the business to another company on certain terms. The directors refused to carry out the sale and the Court of Appeal held that they were not bound to do so because the power to sell any of the company's property had been vested in them by the articles.

Most articles provide an alternative method for the members to give instructions to the directors. In *Automatic Self-Cleansing Filter* the directors' powers were 'subject to such regulations as may from time to time be made by extraordinary resolution' (i.e. 75% majority of those voting). If the resolution to sell the business had been proposed and passed as an extraordinary resolution, the result would have been different. Whether or not such provision is made, the members may achieve the same result by proposing and passing a special resolution (which also requires a 75% majority but longer notice than an extraordinary resolution) to amend the articles so that, for example, the powers revert back to the company in general meeting. Having done that, they need only pass an ordinary resolution (50% majority of those voting) to approve the proposed course of action.

3.7.1   1985 Table A

In the case of reg. 70 of the 1985 Table A, the members may give the directors binding instructions by passing a special resolution. As the articles can be amended by special resolution, this does not place them in a significantly stronger position than if no such provision was made. The only real advantage is that it is not necessary for the resolution giving directions to be framed as an amendment of the articles. This allows the members to give directions in a specific instance without limiting the directors' powers generally. Although such a resolution would not, if passed, constitute an amendment to the articles, a copy of it would have to be filed at Companies House and attached to any copy of the articles issued after it had been passed.

3.7.2   1948 Table A

The wording of reg. 80 of the 1948 Table A is more obscure and has caused a number of difficulties. It provides:

> **80.** The business of the company shall be managed by the directors, who . . . may exercise all such powers of the company . . . subject, nevertheless, to any of these regulations, to the provisions of the Act and to such regulations being not inconsistent with the aforesaid regulations or provisions, as may be prescribed by the company in general meeting . . .

The difficulty with this type of article is in deciding what the word 'regulations' means. In *Quin & Axtens Ltd v. Salmon* [1909] AC 442, it was held that it meant 'articles' throughout. If this interpretation is correct, the members may only interfere by changing the articles and the condition that such regulations must not be inconsistent with the articles becomes superfluous. In *Scott v. Scott* [1943] 1 All ER 582, it was held that the members in general meeting could not give the directors instructions to pay an interim dividend by ordinary resolution under an article similar to reg. 80 of the 1948 Table A. Lord Clauson pointed out (at p. 444) that if an ordinary resolution could be considered to be a regulation within the meaning of those words it would still be ineffective because it would be inconsistent with the existing articles.

3.7.3 Other versions

Many companies adopt articles modelled on the 1948 Act Table A but with modifications. For example, some articles allow the members to give directions by extraordinary resolution. If they also provide that such directions must not be 'inconsistent with the aforesaid regulations or provisions', such provisions may be of limited use to the members if the word 'regulations' is taken to refer to the articles. It could be argued that any extraordinary resolution of the members that purports to fetter the discretion of the directors will be inconsistent with the articles. If so, the provision is almost superfluous because the only way the shareholders can avoid this is by amending the article that creates that inconsistency in the first place. This would seem to be a dangerous interpretation, particularly for companies whose lawyers have developed a slightly modified version of the 1948 Table A provision. In the following example taken from the articles of a UK listed company, an adverse ruling on this point could result in the members being able to give directions by ordinary resolution.

> 23.01 The business of the Company shall be managed by the Board which, in addition to all the powers and authorities by these Articles or otherwise expressly conferred on it, may exercise all such powers and do all acts and things as may be exercised or done by the Company as are not, by the Statutes or by these Articles, required to be exercised or done by the Company in general meeting, subject nevertheless to these Articles, to the provisions of the Statutes and to such directions (not inconsistent with these Articles and such provisions) as may be prescribed by the Company in general meeting.

3.7.4 Prior acts of directors not invalidated

Most articles follow reg. 70 of Table A in providing that no alteration of the memorandum or articles and no direction given in accordance with the articles shall invalidate any prior act of the directors that would have been valid if that alteration had not been made or that direction had not been given. This qualification ensures that the members cannot reverse a decision of the directors that has already been acted upon. Without it, third parties could never be sure that the company would be bound by the acts of its directors.

3.7.5 Practical points on general management clauses

If it is intended to restrict the ability of shareholders to give directions, reg. 70 of Table A should be followed. It is impossible to entrench the position of the directors any more than this as the members would be able to amend any such provision by passing a special resolution to that effect. Where the members want to retain the ability to give instructions to the directors on matters of management by ordinary resolution or extraordinary resolution, this should be stated explicitly in the articles. It is also best in such circumstances to avoid the condition that such directions must not be inconsistent with the articles or regulations. A simple modification of reg. 70 of the 1985 Table A would probably suffice for these purposes. Before making such changes, however, it is worth bearing in mind that the members may remove any of the directors by ordinary resolution (s. 303). Often the threat of removal will be sufficient to ensure that the directors act in accordance with the wishes of the majority. It is probably for this reason that the difficulties that have previously arisen with general management clauses have all but disappeared.

3.8 Special powers

Other articles may give the directors special powers, which they would not otherwise have under the general management clause because:

- they are not connected with the management of the company but with the relationship between the company and its members, e.g. the power to make calls (regs 12 to 22 of Table A); or
- the exercise of such a power would otherwise be a breach of their fiduciary duties, e.g. the power to fix the remuneration of executive directors (e.g. reg. 84 of Table A).

The articles may also include special provisions dealing with powers of management which the directors would ordinarily be assumed to have under the general management clause. It is normally presumed that the existence of a special power excludes the application of any power that the directors may have under a general management clause in that regard. For example, the articles may include a provision giving the directors specific power to borrow money up to a stated limit for certain defined purposes. The directors would normally be deemed to have the power to borrow under the general management clause. However, as the powers under the general management clause are expressed as being subject to other articles, it is clear that their power to borrow will be restricted, at least for the purposes stated. What may not be clear, however, is whether the directors are still authorised under the general management clause to borrow for other purposes. This will depend on the exact wording of the articles, but where there is any doubt, it should be assumed that the article containing the special power on borrowing represents the final word in this regard and excludes any powers that might normally exist under the general management clause.

Modern articles often reverse this presumption by stating in the general management clause that the powers given shall not be limited by any special power given to the directors by any other article (see for example reg. 70 of Table A). The purpose of these words is not to negate any restrictions contained in other articles but to preserve any powers the directors have under the general management clause that are not specifically excluded by other articles.

3.9   Default powers of the members

Where the board of directors is unable or unwilling to conduct the company's business, the members in general meeting may be entitled in default to exercise powers given to the directors. For example, in *Barron v. Potter* [1914] 1 Ch. 895, the company's articles provided that the power to appoint directors was vested in the board and fixed the quorum for board meetings as two. One of the two directors appointed refused to attend meetings so that no business could be done. It was held that the power to appoint additional directors in these circumstances reverted to the company in general meeting as this was the only way to break the deadlock.

In *Foster v. Foster* [1916] 1 Ch. 532, the company's articles provided that the directors could not vote on any contract in which they were interested and that the quorum for board meetings was two. Two of the three directors of the company each wanted to be appointed as its salaried managing director. Although unable to vote on their own appointment, both were able to block the appointment of the other. It was held that the power to appoint a managing director reverted by default to the general meeting.

In *Barron v. Potter* and to a lesser extent in *Foster v. Foster*, the board's failure to act paralysed the company and the general meeting merely acted in order to break the deadlock. The courts will not, however, allow the members to usurp the board's powers where the directors are unable to agree on a business decision but are otherwise capable of managing the business.

Thus in *Quin & Axtens Ltd v. Salmon* [1909] AC 442, the company's articles provided that no decision regarding the acquisition or letting of certain properties would be valid if either of two named directors dissented. One of the named directors (Salmon) dissented on such a proposal. An extraordinary general meeting was then held at which the shareholders, by a simple majority, passed similar resolutions. The House of Lords ruled that the shareholders' resolutions were inconsistent with the articles which conferred general powers of management on the directors to the exclusion of the members.

3.10   Delegation to committees and executive directors

Articles usually allow boards to delegate their powers to board committees and to individual executive directors. If no such provision is made in the articles, no committee or executive director may validly exercise the powers given to the directors.

The power to delegate to a committee cannot be used for an improper purpose, e.g. to exclude one or more of the directors from the forum where the board's decisions are taken (*Pullbrook v. Richmond Consolidated Mining Co.* (1878) 9 Ch.D. 610).

3.10.1   Table A

Regulation 72 of Table A is typical of the sort of provision one would expect to find on delegation in the articles. It provides:

> **72.** The directors may delegate any of their powers to any committee consisting of one or more directors. They may also delegate to any managing director or any director holding any other executive office such of their powers as they consider desirable to be exercised by him. Any such delegation may be made subject to any conditions the directors may impose, and either collaterally with or to the exclusion of their own powers and may be revoked or altered. Subject to any such conditions, the proceedings of a committee with two or more members shall be governed by the articles regulating the proceedings of directors so far as they are capable of applying.

3.10.2   Revocation and amendment of delegated authority

The board may at any time revoke a previous decision to delegate its powers (*Huth v. Clarke* (1890) 25 QBD 391). It follows that it must also be able to amend the extent of any delegation as it could achieve the same result by revoking the original powers and then delegating new powers. It is, of course, unnecessary to go through this convoluted procedure and a board resolution amending the delegated authority will suffice. Regulation 72 specifically states that any delegation by the board may be revoked or altered. However, this will be the case unless the articles specify otherwise.

3.10.3   Exclusive authority

In *Huth v. Clarke* it was also held that the body that delegates the powers retains the authority to exercise them itself. Thus, unless the articles provide otherwise, the board retains collateral power to act even though it has delegated those powers to a committee or executive director. Regulation 72 of Table A states that the directors may delegate their powers either collaterally or to the exclusion of their own powers. However, it also provides that the directors may revoke any delegated powers. Accordingly, even if it has delegated to a committee to the exclusion of its own powers, it could revoke that authority and act itself. It is doubtful whether the courts would intervene even if the board failed to revoke the delegated authority before acting itself if it was clear that the board would have done so if it had known that this was necessary. In practice, therefore, in order to grant exclusive authority the articles must allow the directors to delegate their powers irrevocably.

3.10.4   Sub-delegation

Committees and executive directors cannot sub-delegate their powers unless authorised to do so by the board (*Cook v. Ward* (1877) 2 CPD 255). This does not mean that a committee may not ask one or more of its members to make recommendations to a future meeting of the committee as long as the committee takes the final decision.

It is doubtful whether the articles need to make specific provision authorising sub-delegation. However, some listed companies have recently amended their articles to do so, presumably to clarify the position and to avoid any possibility of an adverse ruling following the *Guinness* case (see below). Companies have survived without making specific provision in this regard for hundreds of years. Although it is rare for board committees to sub-delegate, it is obvious that the managing director or chief executive of a large company must sub-delegate to other managers and employees of the company.

3.10.5   Restrictions on power to delegate

Although articles usually state that the directors may delegate 'any of their powers', this may not include special powers given to the directors by the articles (e.g. the power to fix the remuneration of directors). This is a difficult area and the answer will depend on the construction of the articles in each case. What is beyond doubt is that the general power to delegate will, unless otherwise stated, cover the powers given to the directors under the general management clause (e.g. reg. 70 of Table A).

In *Guinness plc v. Saunders* [1990] 1 All ER 652, the House of Lords held that an article giving 'the Board' of Guinness general power to delegate to committees did not authorise them to delegate a special power conferred by another article authorising 'the Board' to fix the special remuneration of a director serving on a committee. It reached this decision despite the fact 'the Board' was defined elsewhere in the articles as being 'The Directors for the time being (or a quorum of such Directors assembled at a meeting of Directors duly convened) or any Committee authorised by the Board to act on its behalf.' Lord Templeman, who gave the main judgement, said: 'It cannot have been intended that any committee should be able to grant special remuneration to *any* director who serves on *any* committee.'

This decision arose from a dispute between Guinness plc and one of its former non-executive directors, Mr Ward, who had been paid £5.2m for services rendered to Guinness during its bid for Distillers. The payment had not been authorised by the board but by two out of the three members of the committee established by the board (of which Mr Ward was a member) with full power and authority to settle the terms of the offer, to approve any revisions of the offer and to authorise and approve, execute and do all such documents, deeds, acts and things as they may consider necessary or desirable in connection with the making or implementation of the offer.

There can be no doubt that the House of Lords bent over backwards to ensure that Mr Ward accounted to Guinness for the money he had received and it may be that the effect of the judgment is only relevant to directors' remuneration. Directors are treated as fiduciaries under the common law and cannot claim remuneration unless the articles expressly provide for payment. The ability of the board to fix directors' remuneration is therefore dependent upon the existence of a special power contained in the articles. It seems from the *Guinness* case that this power cannot be delegated unless the articles make it absolutely clear that this is in fact intended.

However, it is possible that the *Guinness* case will have wider ramifications. Most articles include provisions giving the directors special powers in addition to the powers conferred by the general management clause, and these special powers are expressed as being given to the directors collectively. This is certainly the case under Table A which contains special powers authorising the directors:

- to declare a share to be wholly or in part free from a lien (reg. 8);
- to authorise a person to give effect to the sale of shares subject to a lien (reg. 9);
- to make calls (regs 12 to 22);
- to reject share transfers (regs 24 and 25);
- to call general meetings (reg. 37);
- to appoint and fix the remuneration of any managing or other executive director (reg. 84);
- to appoint the chairman of the board (reg. 91);

- to appoint and fix the remuneration of the secretary (reg. 99);
- to pay interim dividends (reg. 103).

It may well be that the board cannot delegate these powers under reg. 72 to a committee or an individual executive director. It is therefore advisable for the board to exercise these powers itself.

Following the decision in the *Guinness* case, some listed companies have adopted articles along the following lines to clarify that the general power to delegate is not intended to be limited by anything in the articles that requires powers to be exercised by the board.

> The power to delegate contained in this Article shall be effective in relation to the powers, duties and discretions of the Board generally whether or not express reference is made in these Articles to powers, duties or discretions being exercised by the Board or by a committee authorised by the Board.

3.11   Appointment of other agents

Articles usually give the directors specific power to appoint other agents. For example, reg. 71 of Table A provides:

> **71.** The directors may, by power of attorney or otherwise, appoint any person to be the agent of the company for such purposes and on such conditions as they determine, including authority for the agent to delegate all or any of his powers.

It is noteworthy that reg. 71 specifically states that the board may authorise an agent to delegate all or any of his powers. The power to appoint an agent would normally be deemed to include this power.

3.12   Schedule of matters reserved to the board

Where the board delegates any of its powers to committees and/or executive directors, it may no longer be entirely clear what matters must still be referred to the board for decision. In order to decide, it may be necessary to trawl through the terms of reference of every committee and executive director. However, even this may not suffice, because one may find that, in order to give committees or executives the powers necessary to fulfil their functions, they are also inadvertently given power to make decisions on which the board would have expected to have the final say.

To address this problem, and to provide 'a safeguard against misjudgments and possible illegal practices', the Cadbury Committee recommended that boards of listed companies should adopt a formal schedule of matters specifically reserved to them for their collective decision. This recommendation is repeated in the Combined Code on Corporate Governance (para. A.1.2) which has superseded the Cadbury Code. However, the Combined Code does not provide the same level of guidance as the Cadbury Report in this regard. For example, the Cadbury Report recommended that a copy of the schedule should be given to each director on appointment and kept up to date. It also recommended that the schedule should cover the following:

- the acquisition and disposal of assets of the company or its subsidiaries that are material to the company;
- investments;
- capital projects;
- authority levels;
- treasury policies; and
- risk management policies (Cadbury Report, para. 4.24).

The ICSA has published a model schedule of matters reserved for the board (see **Appendix H**). The model schedule is now slightly out of date as it still refers to stock exchange requirements rather than the Listing Rules, and makes no reference to the Combined Code which has now superseded the Cadbury Code. However, as the ICSA never intended the model schedule to be a definitive list or even an indication of best practice, it could still be useful as a starting point for boards of directors. The Cadbury Report also recommended that the schedule should make clear which transactions require multiple board signatures on the relative documentation and the procedures for dealing with urgent matters between board meetings (Cadbury Report, para. 4.24).

4

Board meetings

4.1 Summary

- Most matters concerning proceedings at meetings of directors are determined by the articles and, in default, by reference to the common law.
- Although companies have considerable freedom to establish their own internal board procedures, most adopt articles based on Table A. This is largely because its provisions have been tried and tested over many years and provide a solid foundation upon which new regulations and procedures can be added.
- This chapter focuses on the provisions of Table A and highlights areas where modifications to Table A are commonly made.

4.2 Collective exercise of powers

Under most articles, the directors must exercise their powers collectively, i.e. at a properly convened and constituted meeting of the board of directors, unless:

- the articles allow them to delegate their powers and they have delegated them (see **3.10**);
- the articles allow them to make decisions in some other way, e.g. by written resolution (see **6.2**);
- the directors all agree, in which case they may act informally (see **6.3**).

Where the directors are required to act collectively as a board, unanimity is not required. Under the common law, decisions may validly be made by a majority of the directors present at board meetings, provided that there are sufficient directors to form a quorum. Under the common law, a quorum exists where a majority of the directors are present at the meeting. Thus, if there are nine directors, five must be present to form a quorum. If five attend a meeting, only three of them (i.e. one-third of the directors in total) need vote in favour of a proposal to bind the company. If seven attend, four must vote in favour, and so on. The common law principle that a majority of the directors present may bind the company is usually adopted in the articles (e.g. reg. 88). However, articles usually specify a fixed quorum for meetings of directors and frequently allow the directors to alter that quorum (see **4.8**).

4.3 Who may call a meeting of directors

Articles usually provide that any director may call a meeting of directors and that the secretary at the request of a director shall do so (e.g. reg. 88 of Table A). It is usual for the board to fix the dates of its meetings in advance so that the directors can plan their diaries. However, there may be occasions when an additional meeting is needed to deal with urgent business.

In practice, meetings are usually called by the chairman and any director wishing to call a meeting would normally consult the chairman first. This ensures that the chairman is fully informed of the circumstances and may enable an alternative solution to be found. If approached by a director, the secretary should seek to persuade the director to follow this course. Although the secretary cannot refuse to call a meeting if instructed to do so by a director, it is advisable to inform the chairman at the earliest opportunity of the situation if the director refuses to follow this advice.

4.4 Date, time and place

Generally, the directors can hold their meetings wherever they wish, including overseas. However, if the court is satisfied that the reason that a particular venue has been chosen is to ensure that certain directors are unable to attend, it may prevent the meeting from taking place or declare the proceedings invalid (*Martin v. Walker* (1918) 145 LTJ 377).

The person calling the meeting should specify the date, time and place at which it is to be held as this information must be given in the notice of the meeting. If a director instructs the company secretary to call a meeting, he or she may specify these matters or leave them to be settled by the secretary, perhaps after contacting the other directors to find the most suitable time and place.

The articles may specify the time and place where regular meetings are to be held, e.g. on the second Thursday of each month at the company's registered office. Obviously, no such provision is made in Table A although the directors could specify a time and place in their internal procedures or standing orders.

4.5 Notice

The Act makes no provision with regard to notice of directors' meetings. Under the common law reasonable notice must be given to all the directors. If proper notice is not given, the meeting and any business transacted at it will be invalid. Most articles modify this basic principle, e.g. Table A provides that notice need not be given to a director who is absent from the United Kingdom. Most articles also specify the manner in which notice can be served, e.g. in writing, orally, by telephone, etc.

Where a dispute does arise as to the adequacy of the notice given, those complaining must initiate proceedings to have the meeting or its proceedings declared invalid as soon as possible otherwise they will be deemed to have acquiesced (assented to the notice given).

4.5.1 To whom notice must be given

As a general rule, notice must be given to all the directors. However, notice need not be given where:

- all the directors agree to waive it (see below);
- it can have no effect;
- the articles specifically provide.

With regard to the second heading, Lord Sterndale MR suggested in *Young v. Imperial Ladies Club Ltd* [1920] 2 KB 523 (at p. 528) that notice may not be necessary if, for example, a director is so seriously ill that he or she would be unable to attend. It was held in that case that notice must be given to any director who would be able to travel back in time for the meeting. In the days before air travel, this would have excluded any director in the United States. However, the rule is unlikely to be of assistance today except in the most extreme circumstances.

Articles normally contain a provision similar to reg. 88 of Table A which provides that a director who is absent from the United Kingdom is not entitled to receive notice of directors' meetings. The United Kingdom means England, Wales, Scotland or Northern Ireland. Reg. 88 is often modified so as not to exclude places outside the United Kingdom where the company's directors live.

Alternate directors are entitled under reg. 66 of Table A to receive notice of board meetings and of any meetings of board committees of which the director who appointed them is a member. Even if the articles make no provision in this regard, alternate directors are probably entitled to receive notice of such meetings under the common law principles.

Notice need not be given where the directors have agreed among themselves (or the articles prescribe) that meetings shall be held on a regular basis at a fixed time and place, e.g. on the first Thursday each month at 4.00pm at the company's registered office. In such circumstances, notice would, however, need to be given for any meeting held at a different time or place.

4.5.2 Waiver of notice

Unless the articles provide otherwise, directors cannot waive in advance their right to receive notice of a meeting (*Re Portuguese Consolidated Copper Mines Ltd* (1889) 42 Ch.D. 160). Table A makes no such provision and, subject to any other qualifications, notice must be given to all the directors even though some may have indicated that they are unable or unwilling to attend a future meeting. The following wording can be included in a company's articles on notice of directors' meetings to allow directors to waive notices: 'A Director may waive notice of any meeting either prospectively or retrospectively.'

Notice can, in any case, be waived if all the directors are present and agree to hold a board meeting without notice. In *Smith v. Paringa Mines Ltd* [1906] 2 Ch. 193, the two directors of a company met in the offices of one of them. The director who was the chairman proposed the appointment of a third director. Despite the objection of the other director to this appointment, the chairman declared the resolution carried by his casting vote. The appointment was held to be valid as they were both deemed to have agreed to treat their meeting as a board meeting. In *Barron v. Potter* [1914] 1 Ch. 895, a similar chance meeting between the directors of a company was held to be invalid as a board meeting as the director who proposed and purported to pass (by virtue of his casting vote) resolutions appointing new directors knew that the other director did not wish to attend any board meeting with him.

4.5.3 Length of notice

There is no strict rule as to the length of notice required for meetings of directors although there is an underlying assumption that it must be reasonable in the circumstances (*Browne v. La Trinidad* (1887) 37 Ch.D. 1). It is impossible to state conclusively the circumstances in which the notice given might be deemed unreasonable. It is fairly safe to assume that reasonable notice was given if none of the directors object or they all attend the meeting. On the other hand, it does not necessarily follow that the notice given was unreasonable merely because a director objects. If a director does object to the notice given, the other directors should consider their position very carefully, taking into account all the other relevant factors. These might include the following:

- the length of notice usually given for similar meetings in that company;
- the nature and urgency of the business to be transacted.

It goes without saying that the courts are more likely to intervene if it can be inferred that the purpose of calling the meeting at relatively short notice was to exclude a particular director from the decision-making process. A director should register his or her objection to the length of notice given immediately and should commence legal proceedings as soon as possible, otherwise the courts may refuse to intervene. In *Browne v. La Trinidad* the court accepted that the notice given to Mr Browne was unreasonable (less than ten minutes before the start of a board meeting at which it was decided to call an extraordinary general meeting to propose a resolution to remove him as a director). However, it refused to intervene, partly because he did not object at the time and only commenced proceedings shortly before the EGM was due to be held.

4.5.4   Form of notice

Articles usually specify the form in which notices required by the articles must be given. However, they usually state that these rules do not apply to meetings of directors. For example, reg. 111 of Table A (as amended) provides that notices may be given using electronic communications or, if that is not possible, in writing. However, it specifically states that these rules shall not apply to meetings of directors. In other words, it makes no provision whatsoever on the method of service that must be used for giving notice of directors' meetings. According to a case decided in 1887, in the absence of any specific provision in the articles, notice of directors' meetings may be given in writing or orally (*Browne v. La Trinidad* (1887) 37 Ch.D. 1). At the time, the only method that this excluded was giving notice by advertisement. However, it would now seem to preclude the use of electronic communications as well. This would seem odd when set against the fact that the Companies Act now allows electronic communications to be used to give notice of general meetings. It is, of course, possible that the courts would take a more modern approach if called upon to do so today. It is unlikely that they would prevent a company from using certain forms of electronic communication (such as fax or e-mail), particularly where a director had indicated his or her willingness to accept service of notices in this manner and had provided an electronic address for these purposes.

For companies subject to the unamended version of the 1985 Table A, reg. 111 states that notice of directors' meetings 'need not be given in writing'. This certainly means that notice may be given in writing or orally. It is also arguable that it allows companies to use electronic communications (as these are not given in writing). However, this form of words was used because Table A originally required other notices to be given in writing. In other words, by providing that notices of directors' meetings need not be given in writing, reg. 111 was making no provision at all on the methods that can be used. If so, the issues discussed above in relation to the amended version of Table A apply.

Because there is an element of doubt about the validity of using electronic communications to give notice of directors' meetings, it is preferable to make specific provision for its use in the articles.

If notice is given in writing, the provisions of the articles with regard to proof of posting and the deemed date of service will apply, e.g. reg. 115 of Table A. It may be served either personally or by delivering it to the address recorded as the director's usual address in the register of directors or to an alternative address supplied by the director for these purposes. Even though it is known that a director is not at his or her usual address, notice should still be sent to that address, unless the director has given an alternative address.

4.5.5 Content of notice

The notice must include the date, time and place of the meeting (see **Precedent 4.5**). It need not state the nature of the business to be transacted (*La Compagnie de Mayville v. Whitley* [1896] 1 Ch. 788). However, where notice of the business to be transacted is given, it must not be deliberately misleading. In *Re Homer District Consolidated Gold Mines, ex parte Smith* (1888) 39 Ch.D. 546, a board meeting was called at very short notice and a resolution was passed to rescind a decision made at a meeting held only two weeks previously. The notice of the meeting was held to be invalid for a number of reasons, one of which was that it was misleading in so far as it did not mention this item of business.

4.5.6 Practical issues

It is common practice to schedule regular board and board committee meetings for the forthcoming year. This allows the directors to organise their diaries so that they are able to attend meetings. The schedule is normally appended to or included in the minutes of a board meeting. This satisfies the legal requirements as to notice provided that a copy is sent to each director and it shows the date, time and place of each meeting. It is also normal for a copy of the agenda for the meeting to be given to each director prior to the meeting. As this normally includes the date, time and place of the meeting, it will also serve as notice of the meeting provided that it is sent out early enough to comply with the requirement that the notice given must be reasonable in the circumstances.

For small companies with relatively few directors, it may not be necessary or possible to plan so far ahead. Meetings may simply be called on an *ad hoc* basis at relatively short notice. Even in large public companies it is sometimes necessary to hold additional board meetings to deal with matters that cannot wait until the next scheduled meeting. In such circumstances, it is a good practice for the chairman or the secretary to contact each director in order to explain the circumstances and to offer a range of possible dates for the meeting, making it clear that the one on which the most are able to attend will be chosen. Once this has been done, each director should be notified in the usual manner.

4.6 The agenda

The agenda is a list of the business to be transacted at a meeting. Although it is not strictly necessary to give notice of the business to be transacted at meetings of directors, it is normal for an agenda to be prepared and sent to each director prior to the meeting, together with any supporting papers that may be necessary to facilitate discussion of that business. If an agenda is sent to the directors prior to the meeting, it will constitute notice of the business and, as such, the rule that it must not be deliberately misleading will apply.

If the notice of meeting includes notice of the business to be transacted, that part of the notice can be referred to as the agenda (see **Precedent 4.6A**).

Items of business on the agenda are usually placed in the order that the business is to be taken at the meeting, although the board is not bound to take them in that order (*Re Cawley & Co.* (1889) 42 Ch.D. 209).

4.6.1 Practical issues with respect to the agenda

It is normal for the agenda to refer only briefly to the nature of the business to be transacted and most items will contain some reference to supporting papers which contain the detailed proposals. If the business can be described accurately and briefly, the substance of the resolution to be put at the meeting may be included in the agenda. Even then, however, there may be some supporting papers and, if so, the agenda should include some reference to them. The overall objective when preparing the agenda should be to keep it as short as possible. This enables the directors to assess the business of the meeting at a glance.

Where supporting papers are required, they should be clearly identified, numbered and placed in the order in which they appear on the agenda. This task normally falls to the secretary, who should ensure that all reports and papers have been submitted and are listed in the proper form on the agenda.

The agenda and supporting papers should be sent so that they are in the hands of the directors about a week before the meeting. This gives them adequate opportunity to read the papers carefully. Many directors will not do so until the very last minute no matter when they receive the board papers. Nevertheless, they tend to forget this when they receive the board papers late and will not normally hesitate to complain.

4.6.2 'Any Other Business'

In view of the fact that it is not necessary to give notice of the business to be transacted at board meetings, it would seem to be perfectly in order for business not included in the notice or the agenda to be raised under the heading 'Any Other Business'. Two qualifications must be made to this principle. The first is that, in accordance with the ruling in *Homer*, the notice may be deemed to be invalid if the item is omitted so as to mislead members of the board that it will not be raised. The second is that it is unreasonable to expect the directors to make reasoned decisions if they are not given sufficient time to consider the merits of a proposal or the opportunity to consider any alternative proposals. Many chairmen refuse as a matter of principle to put matters raised under 'Any Other Business' to a vote until the following meeting. In practice, however, it may sometimes be necessary to do so, e.g. where there is likely to be a considerable delay before the next meeting.

4.7 Chairman

In theory, the duties of the chairman at a meeting of directors are largely the same as those of the chairman of a general meeting. However, meetings of directors are usually less formal than general meetings. Decisions are often reached on a consensual basis and the chairman is less likely to be called upon to exercise formal control over the proceedings. At general meetings, the chairman does not usually owe his position to the members but to his office as chairman of the board. In contrast, the chairman of the board is invariably elected by the board and can be removed by the board. Unless also the majority shareholder, the chairman's position may therefore be more tenuous. As a result, the chairman of the board tends to act more as facilitator or arbiter, as opposed to an autocrat or judge.

4.7.1 Role and duties

The common law duties of the chairman, as expressed by Chitty J in *National Dwelling Society Ltd v. Sykes* [1894] 3 Ch. 159, are also applicable to meetings of directors. It is therefore the duty of the chairman to ensure that:

- the meeting is properly conducted;
- all directors are given a fair opportunity to contribute to the deliberations;
- the sense of the meeting is properly ascertained and recorded; and
- order is preserved.

The chairman's authority is derived from the body that made the appointment. In other words, by electing a chairman, the directors are deemed to have conferred upon him or her all the powers necessary to fulfil the role. At general meetings, the chairman is deemed to have authority to rule on points of order and on other incidental questions that arise during the meeting (*Re Indian Zoedone Co.* (1884) 26 Ch.D. 70). This is probably the case at meetings of directors although, if challenged at the meeting, the chairman should bend to the will of the majority unless he or she is given specific authority by the articles to determine the matter. For example, reg. 98 of Table A provides that any question at a meeting of directors or of a committee of directors as to the right of a director to vote may, before the conclusion of the meeting, be referred to the chairman of the meeting and his ruling in relation to any director other than himself shall be final and conclusive.

In the unlikely event that a meeting is disorderly, the chairman will probably have inherent power to adjourn in order to restore order (*John v. Rees* [1969] 2 WLR 1294). Otherwise the power to adjourn will rest with the meeting and the chairman should not adjourn or close the meeting without the consent of the meeting until all the business is transacted.

4.7.2 Governance role

Most articles allow any director to call a meeting (e.g. reg. 88). In practice, it will be the chairman who usually decides whether meetings are necessary and who settles the agenda. In doing so, he will take account of the views of other directors (particularly the chief executive) and the advice of the company secretary (particularly on formal items of business, but also on matters of governance).

The Combined Code makes a number of recommendations about the status of the chairman and his role within the corporate governance structure (see **Appendix F**). Although these recommendations are similar to those made in the Cadbury Committee's Code of Best Practice which has now been superseded by the Combined Code, the Cadbury Committee's Report contained more detailed guidance on the role of the chairman. For example, the Cadbury Report suggested that the chairman should be primarily responsible for the following:

- the working of the board;
- its balance of membership (subject to board and shareholders' approval);
- ensuring that all relevant issues are on the agenda; and
- ensuring that all directors, executive and non-executive alike, are enabled and encouraged to play their full part in its activities (Cadbury Report, para. 4.7).

It also says that chairmen should be able to stand back sufficiently from the day-to-day running of the business to ensure that their boards are in full control of the company's affairs and alert to their obligations to their shareholders. It is for them to make certain that non-executive directors receive timely, relevant information tailored to their needs, that they are properly briefed on the issues arising at board meetings, and that they make an effective contribution as board members in practice. It is equally for the chairman to ensure that executive directors look beyond their executive duties and accept their full share of the responsibilities of governance (Cadbury Report, paras 4.7 and 4.8).

4.7.3   Appointment

Articles usually specify the method by which the chairman of the board of directors is to be appointed. For example, Table A provides:

> **91.** The directors may appoint one of their number to be chairman of the board of directors and may at any time remove him from that office. Unless he is unwilling to do so, the director so appointed shall preside at every meeting of directors at which he is present. But if there is no director holding that office, or if the director holding it is unwilling to preside or is not present within five minutes after the time appointed for the meeting, the directors present may appoint one of their number to be chairman of the meeting.

The main objective of this provision is to avoid the need to elect a chairman at each meeting of directors. A director appointed to the office of 'chairman of the board of directors' has a right to chair subsequent meetings until removed from office.

If, unusually, the articles make no provision with regard to the appointment of the chairman, the directors present at each meeting may elect one of their number to be the chairman of it.

If the office of chairman is unsalaried, a director is not deemed to have an interest in his or her appointment to that office and may therefore vote on a resolution to that effect (*Foster v. Foster* [1916] 1 Ch. 532). Where the office is salaried, a director will have a personal interest and may be prevented by the articles from voting on his or her own appointment. The same principles apply to any resolution to remove the chairman. A salaried chairman can therefore be removed more easily than an unsalaried chairman. Some articles specifically allow directors to be counted in the quorum at the meeting at which they are appointed to an office but not to vote, e.g. reg. 84(4) of the 1948 Act Table A.

4.7.4   Problems appointing a chairman

Under Table A, the person appointed as 'chairman of the board of directors' is automatically entitled (until removed from office) to:

- chair subsequent meetings of directors (reg. 91);
- exercise a casting vote at any meeting of directors which he chairs (reg. 88);
- chair meetings of the company (reg. 42); and
- exercise a casting vote at general meetings (reg. 50).

The ability to exercise a casting vote at board and general meetings could easily tip the balance of power and it is not unusual for the directors to be unable to reach agreement on the appointment of someone as 'chairman of the board of directors'. In these circumstances, the directors may prefer at each board meeting to elect one of their number as 'chairman of the meeting', leaving the office of 'chairman of the board of directors' vacant and the issue of who is to chair general meetings to be determined by the default provisions of reg. 42 (see further **18.2**). The person elected as chairman at each meeting would, however, still have a casting vote because reg. 88 confers that right on the 'chairman of the meeting' rather than on the 'chairman of the board of directors'.

Where reg. 88 or a similar article applies, it is not uncommon for the directors to be unable to agree on the appointment of a chairman at all, particularly where there are only two or some other even number of directors. To avoid this problem, it may be advisable at the outset to remove the chairman's right to a casting vote at meetings of directors and/or general meetings by amending the articles. This could be done by a written resolution of the members or the unanimous agreement of all the members (*Cane v. Jones* [1981] 1 All ER 533).

In the event of complete deadlock, the power to appoint the chairman may revert to the company in general meeting (*Foster v. Foster* [1916] 1 Ch. 532). However, if the two sides each control half the shares, this is unlikely to provide a solution. It may be possible for the directors to appoint someone as chairman of the meeting on the condition that they refrain from exercising the right to a casting vote, the assumption being that the person will automatically be removed if he or she attempts to exercise that right. It might, however, be safer to appoint no chairman at all.

4.7.5   No chairman

The board may act without a chairman. The chairman is said to derive authority from the meeting. If no chairman is appointed, the meeting retains those powers itself. Matters that the chairman would normally be called upon to decide could be resolved by the meeting. In addition, Table A merely provides that the directors 'may' appoint one of their number to be chairman of the board or chairman of the meeting. This would seem to imply that they need not do so. The directors could even invite someone who is not a director to chair or act as the facilitator at board meetings.

The board may also act without a chairman by way of written resolution in accordance with the provisions of the articles (if any) or by unanimous resolution of the directors (preferably evidenced in writing) if the articles do not specifically provide for written resolutions.

4.7.6 Chairman not present

Articles commonly provide that if the chairman of the board is not present within five minutes of the start of the meeting, the directors may elect one of their number to chair the meeting. If the chairman of the board arrives after the directors have elected a person to chair the meeting, the person elected is under no obligation to vacate the chair, although it is normal practice to do so.

4.8 Quorum

The quorum is the minimum number of directors who must be present and entitled to vote at a meeting of directors in order for it to transact business. A quorum must be present for each item of business considered and a director who is not entitled to vote (e.g. because he or she is interested in the transaction) cannot be counted in calculating whether a quorum exists for that item.

The quorum is normally fixed by the articles. If the articles are silent on the matter, the basic common law rule is that the quorum is a majority of the directors.

Articles normally give the directors limited powers to act where their number (i.e. the total number of directors in office and not merely the number present at the meeting) falls below the number fixed as the quorum.

A third party dealing with the company in good faith may, by virtue of s. 35A, be able to enforce a contract entered into by the directors in breach of the requirements of the articles. In such circumstances, the company could sue the directors for damages for breach of duty. It is therefore in the directors' interests to act in accordance with the articles and to ensure that a quorum is present when they make decisions.

4.8.1 Quorum fixed by or in accordance with the articles

Articles invariably specify the quorum for meetings of directors or a method of fixing one. For example, reg. 89 of Table A provides:

> **89.** The quorum for the transaction of business of the directors may be fixed by the directors and unless so fixed at any other

number shall be two. A person who holds office only as an alternate director shall, if his appointor is not present, be counted in the quorum.

The articles may fix a quorum of one, and there is nothing to prevent the directors from doing so under articles such as reg. 89 (*Re Fireproof Doors Ltd* [1916] 2 Ch. 142).

If the articles do not fix or provide for a method of fixing a quorum, the quorum for meetings of directors will be a majority of the directors currently holding office (*York Tramways Co. v. Willows* (1882) 8 QBD 685) or, where it can be shown that a standard practice has evolved over time, the number of directors who usually act in conducting the business of the company (*Re Tavistock Ironworks Co.* (1867) LR 4 Eq. 233). It goes without saying that where the articles make no provision as to the quorum, it is safer to assume that it is a majority of the directors. It is interesting to note that, while it is preferable for the articles to specify a quorum or a method of fixing one, the advantage of not doing so is that under the common law the number required to form a quorum (being a majority of the directors) automatically falls as the number of directors falls.

Where the articles do not specify a quorum but provide a method for fixing one, e.g. by a resolution of the directors, the quorum will be a majority of the directors until such time as alternative provision is made by that method (*York Tramways Co. v. Willows* (1882) 8 QBD 685). However, where the articles allow the directors to fix their own quorum and no resolution to that effect has ever been passed, the majority rule may be dispensed with if the court is satisfied that there was an understanding between all the directors which was followed (*Re Regent's Canal Iron Co.* [1867] WN 79). Again, it is safer to assume that the quorum is a majority of the directors unless the alternative quorum has been applied for a number of years.

4.8.2   Changing the quorum

Where the articles give the directors power to fix or alter the quorum, they may only exercise that power if they act in accordance with the existing rules and procedures governing their meetings, including the existing quorum requirements (*Re Portuguese Consolidated Copper Mines Ltd* (1889) 42 Ch.D. 160). In other words, they cannot change the quorum unless there are sufficient directors present at the meeting to form a quorum under the existing rules.

If the articles allow the directors to fix or alter the quorum, they may do so by a written resolution of all the directors as long as the articles allow them to act in this manner. It is doubtful whether such a resolution would be valid, however, if there were insufficient directors to form a quorum under the existing rules (*Hood Sailmakers Ltd v. Axford* [1996] 4 All ER 830).

If the quorum is fixed by the articles and they make no separate provision for alteration, the quorum can only be changed by passing a special resolution at a general meeting to amend the relevant article.

4.8.3 Disinterested quorum

Under the common law a quorum must be present for each item of business at a meeting and only those entitled to vote may be counted in calculating whether a quorum exists (*Re Greymouth Point Elizabeth Railway and Coal Co. Ltd* [1904] 1 Ch. 32). These principles apply to meetings of directors unless they are specifically excluded by the articles. Table A specifically provides that a director shall not be counted in the quorum present at a meeting in relation to a resolution on which he or she is not entitled to vote (reg. 95).

This rule can be of crucial importance because articles frequently restrict the right of directors to vote at meetings where a director has a personal interest in the matter under consideration, e.g. reg. 94 of Table A. Where such restrictions operate, a quorum may in fact be present for some but not all items of business. Care should be taken to check that a competent or disinterested quorum exists for each item of business.

The courts do not look favourably on techniques used by directors to avoid the operation of rules restricting their right to vote on matters in which they have an interest. Two such techniques were rejected in a case where a company's articles allowed directors to contract with the company but not to vote on any such contract. The quorum for board meetings had been fixed at three by the directors under powers given to them by the articles. At a meeting attended by four directors a contract in which two of them were interested was passed by two separate resolutions. Each interested director voted only on the resolution concerning the other director. These resolutions were held to be invalid because there was in reality only one item of business. Treating it as two separate resolutions was merely a device to avoid the operation of the articles (this rule would prevent directors from voting on a number of separate resolutions to take out directors' and officers' insurance cover for each director where only one policy to cover them all is to be taken out). At a subsequent meeting attended by three directors, those present voted to reduce the quorum to two so as to allow a resolution to be passed issuing a debenture to one of the directors present. The resolution to alter the quorum was also held to be invalid because its sole purpose was to enable something to be done indirectly that could not be done directly (*Re North Eastern Insurance Co. Ltd* [1919] 1 Ch. 198). In this case, the reason for altering the quorum was blatantly obvious. If it could be shown that the quorum was altered for other legitimate reasons, the resolutions at this second meeting would have been valid.

If the number of directors in office and the number required to form a quorum are equal and the articles include restrictions on the right to vote, the directors may be unable to deal with any item of business in which any of them has an interest. This sort of blanket prohibition may not be desirable as it could prevent the directors from acting in the best interests of the company merely because one of them has an interest in a particular transaction. It is usual therefore for the articles to specify a number of exceptions to the general prohibition on voting, e.g. reg. 94 of Table A. Modifications and additions can be made from time to time to these exceptions by amending the articles. In addition, articles often provide that the members in general meeting may by ordinary resolution suspend or relax the operation of any restrictions on directors' voting, e.g. reg. 96 of Table A. If so, it would normally be simpler to call a meeting to propose such a relaxation.

For small owner-managed companies, it is usually sensible to exclude or modify the relevant provisions of Table A (regs 94 to 96) so as to allow the directors to vote on any matter irrespective of any interest they may have in it (see **Precedent 4.8B**).

From a practical point of view, there is no need for a director to withdraw from the meeting when a matter in which he or she is interested is being considered, although it is usual to do so if the board so requests.

4.8.4   Alternate directors

Under the common law, directors must be present in person at the venue specified in the notice to be counted in the quorum. The articles may, however, provide otherwise, and commonly do so where provision is made for the appointment of alternate directors. They may also provide that directors who are in contact with the meeting by telephone or audiovisual links can be counted in the quorum (see **4.10**).

Where the articles provide for the appointment of alternate directors (a type of proxy), special provision will usually be made regarding the quorum. For example, reg. 89 of Table A provides that 'a person who holds office only as an alternate director shall, if his appointor is not present, be counted in the quorum'. It should be noted that this provision does not apply where the person appointed is already a director and it is highly questionable whether such a person can be counted in the quorum more than once. There is no other provision in Table A that specifically excludes the common law rule in these circumstances, even though the director appointed as the alternate would be entitled to more than one vote if a quorum was actually present by some other means (see reg. 88).

Table A also provides that an alternate director is deemed to be interested in any contract in which his or her appointor is interested (reg. 94). If a director is, by virtue of his or her interest in a contract, disqualified from voting and from being counted in the quorum, the alternate will be similarly disqualified. This may be the case even where the articles are silent on the matter as any other conclusion would enable the directors to circumvent restrictions on voting when they are interested in a contract. It should also be noted that an alternate director will also be disqualified from voting under reg. 94 where he or she is interested in the transaction.

4.8.5 Sole director

The default figure of two for the quorum at meetings of directors in reg. 89 is wholly inappropriate for a private company to be formed with only one director and suitably modified articles should be submitted with the application for registration (see **Precedent 4.8C**). If this is not done, the sole director will be incapable of acting and will need to apply to the court for an order under s. 371 calling a general meeting to appoint an additional director or to amend the article specifying the quorum. In practice, it would probably be cheaper and less time-consuming to form a new company.

4.8.6 Practical issues when fixing a quorum

Generally speaking, it is preferable to fix a low quorum. Doing so facilitates the conduct of the board's business. If the quorum is too high, one or more of the directors may be able to obstruct the board by deliberately absenting themselves from meetings. A director cannot be forced to attend board meetings against his or her will. In *Barron v. Potter* [1914] 1 Ch. 895, the quorum was two and Barron, one of only two directors, refused to attend board meetings. Had he done so, Potter, the other director who was entitled to a casting vote as chairman, would have been able to appoint his own nominee as an additional director. Potter tried to hold a board meeting at a railway station and again at the company's offices at which he purported to propose and carry with his casting vote a resolution to appoint his nominee as an additional director. Barron made it clear that he refused to attend board meetings and it was held that he could not be forced to do so against his will. The appointment by Potter was therefore invalid.

In *Re Opera Photographic Ltd* (1989) 5 BCC 601, a director tried to prevent the board convening a general meeting to remove him as a director by absenting himself from board meetings, thereby making it impossible to obtain a quorum at board meetings. The court ordered that a general meeting be called. In *Barron v. Potter,* it would have served no purpose for Potter to apply to the court for an order calling a general meeting. Barron had already requisitioned a general meeting to appoint new directors at which he would have been in the majority. Potter's only chance of success was therefore to entice Barron to attend a board meeting at which he had the casting vote.

Thus, although a director may be able to obstruct the business of the company by absenting himself from board meetings, the will of the majority will nearly always prevail as they will be in a position to remove him or to appoint additional directors unless the director has special class rights which enable him to veto appointments and removals.

It is, of course, sometimes desirable to establish a deadlocked company, e.g. where two members hold the same number of voting shares and are the only directors. In this case, it will be necessary to remove the chairman's casting vote at board and general meetings and fix a quorum of two at board meetings. If the directors fail to agree, it would serve no purpose applying to the court to call a general meeting as the balance of power would be the same.

The advantages of setting a relatively low figure as the quorum are plain. The other directors cannot call a meeting without giving reasonable notice. If the meeting is called to deal with routine or uncontroversial business, only sufficient directors to form a quorum need attend. However, whether all the directors attend or not, when an important or controversial item of business is considered, the will of the majority and not the minority will hold sway.

The final point that is worthy of consideration is that the quorum for board meetings may also affect the quorum for committees of the board where the articles provide that the regulations governing proceedings at board meetings shall also apply to committees of the board (see **5.6**).

4.8.7   Number below quorum

Articles that allow the directors to act notwithstanding any vacancy in their number do not allow them to act where their number falls below that required to constitute a quorum. This issue is, however, normally addressed in modern articles. For example, Table A, which specifies that the minimum number of directors shall be two unless otherwise determined by ordinary resolution (reg. 64) and that the quorum for meetings of directors shall be two unless otherwise fixed by the directors (reg. 88), provides:

> **90.** The continuing directors or a sole continuing director may act notwithstanding any vacancies in their number, but, if the number of directors is less than the number fixed as the quorum, the continuing directors or director may act only for the purpose of filling vacancies or of calling a general meeting.

Under this type of article the directors may act in the normal way where their number falls below the minimum prescribed by the articles but is still sufficient to form a quorum. However, if the number remaining is not sufficient to form a quorum the directors may only act to appoint new directors and to call a general meeting.

It should be noted that under s. 35A, a company will be bound by the acts of its board of directors in favour of a third party dealing with the company in good faith even though the board acted in breach of the company's memorandum or articles of association. Thus, whether the number of directors is less than the minimum prescribed by the articles or there are not sufficient directors to form a quorum, the directors may bind the company in a transaction with an innocent third party. By doing so, however, the directors will have acted in breach of duty and may therefore be liable to compensate the company.

4.9 Voting

The rules on voting at directors' meetings are based on the common law but are subject to modification by the articles. Board meetings and board committees are usually conducted with a great deal less formality than company meetings. Decisions are normally reached by consensus and matters are rarely put to a formal vote because it will normally be apparent which side would win without doing so.

When a resolution is put to a vote, each director will have one vote unless the articles provide otherwise. Questions are usually decided on a majority of votes cast for or against the resolution, although the articles may require a special majority for certain types of business. Most articles restrict the right to vote where a director has a personal interest in the matter under consideration. The chairman is commonly given a second or casting vote to be used in the event of a deadlock. Table A provides:

> **88.** . . . Questions arising at a meeting shall be decided by a majority of votes. In the case of an equality of votes, the chairman shall have a second or casting vote. A director who is also an alternate director shall be entitled in the absence of his appointor to a separate vote on behalf of his appointor in addition to his own vote.

4.9.1 Method of voting

Articles rarely specify the method of voting, e.g. reg. 88 of Table A simply states that questions shall be decided on a majority of votes. Voting is normally conducted by a show of hands with each director having one vote. This method may not be satisfactory if any of the directors is entitled to more than one vote, e.g. a personal vote and one as an alternate for another director. A director who is present at the meeting and who has more than one vote has a right to have each of those votes counted and may have a right to demand a poll if they are not counted (see *R. v. Wimbledon Local Board* (1882) 8 QBD 459). The method of voting used should take account of the fact that some directors may have more votes than others. It is not necessary to follow the formal procedures used at company meetings. Voting papers could be used where it is difficult for the chairman to calculate the true number of votes for and against the resolution on a show of hands.

4.9.2 Chairman's casting vote

Unless the articles so provide, the chairman has no right to a casting vote (*Nell v. Longbottom* [1894] 1 QB 767). Under reg. 88 of Table A the person who acts as the chairman of a meeting of directors is given a casting vote. A casting vote may only be used where there has already been a vote and the number of votes for and against the resolution are exactly equal. It cannot be used where there is a majority in favour or against in order to manufacture a tie.

There is no legal necessity for the chairman to use the casting vote in the event of a tie. Although failure to use the casting vote has the same effect as voting against the resolution, this may be preferable if the chairman wishes to remain impartial. The chairman need not use the casting vote in the same way as his or her original vote on the resolution.

In exercising a casting vote the chairman can follow one of two guiding principles (which are quite capable of producing the opposite result). The first, which is adopted by the Speaker of the House of Commons, is that the casting vote should be used to preserve the *status quo*. This may mean voting for or against the resolution depending on which way the resolution is worded. The second, which is perhaps more commonly applied, is that the chairman should use the casting vote in the best interests of the company. Clearly this second principle is more subjective than the first and depends on the chairman's view of what is in the interest of the company.

A casting vote may be exercised contingently. In *Bland v. Buchanan* [1901] 2 KB 75, the validity of a town councillor's vote was challenged during a meeting. The chairman realised that if the challenge proved to be well founded, there would be a tied vote on a particular resolution. As he was not certain of the true position, he stated that if there were an equality of votes, he would use his casting vote in a particular way. The court commended the chairman's actions, stating that he had taken 'a very practical and business like view'.

4.9.3 Weighted voting

Under the common law each director has only one vote unless the articles provide otherwise. It is unusual for any director to have more than one vote except where the chairman is given a casting vote or a director is also an alternate for another director. However, weighted voting is sometimes used in owner-managed companies to ensure that the founder or major shareholder can outvote the other directors at board meetings. It is not strictly necessary for a director who is the majority shareholder because he or she would be able to remove any other director by passing an ordinary resolution at a general meeting. Neither will it offer a director who is a minority shareholder protection against removal as a director, unless he or she is also entitled to additional votes on a resolution to remove him or her at a general meeting.

4.9.4   Record of votes

Directors have a right to have their opposition to a resolution recorded in the minutes, whether a formal vote was put to the meeting or not. This is mainly because a director who was not present when a decision was taken or who voted against it at the meeting will not be liable for the consequences of that transaction, unless it can be proved that he or she subsequently acquiesced in the decision.

4.9.5   Restrictions on voting

Articles frequently impose restrictions on the right to vote where a director has a personal interest in the subject of the resolution. As has already been seen, these restrictions can cause the board to become inquorate as a director who is unable to vote on a resolution cannot normally be included in calculating whether a quorum exists for that item of business (see reg. 95 of Table A). However, provided that a quorum exists there is nothing to prevent the other directors from entering into a contract in which a director is interested.

In practice the restrictions on voting are themselves normally subject to a number of qualifications and articles usually provide a mechanism that allows the members to suspend or relax the restrictions contained in the articles (e.g. reg. 96 of Table A).

Reg. 94 of Table A provides that a director shall not vote at a meeting of directors or a committee of directors on any resolution concerning a matter in which he or she has, directly or indirectly, an interest or duty that is material and which conflicts or may conflict with the interests of the company. However, it goes on to list a number of exceptions to this general rule. These exceptions cover the giving of guarantees, security or indemnities, subscribing for shares or other securities, underwriting an issue of securities, and pension scheme arrangements.

Reg. 94 also states that an interest of a person who is, for any purpose of the Companies Act 1985 (as amended at the time the company was formed), connected with a director shall be treated as an interest of the director. It also provides in relation to an alternate director that an interest of his appointor shall be treated as an interest of the alternate director without prejudice to any interest that the alternate director has otherwise. Thus alternate directors may not vote if either they or their appointors have a relevant interest.

The Listing Rules used to require the articles of listed companies to prohibit directors from voting on matters in which they have an interest subject to certain limited exceptions. However, this requirement was deleted in January 2000.

4.9.6 Practical issues on voting

It is difficult to frame many of the issues discussed at board meetings as formal resolutions and it can sometimes be counter-productive to do so. When the chairman feels that a consensus has been reached, he or she should attempt to summarise it. This gives the other directors an opportunity to object to that interpretation and is obviously helpful for the secretary in preparing the minutes. What often happens, however, is that the chairman will often end the discussion by saying: 'I think we are all agreed on that subject and suggest we move on to the next item of business.' In such circumstances, if one were to go round the table asking each director what they thought had been agreed, each one would probably give a different answer. The other directors should not allow the chairman to get away with this, although it is often left to the secretary to ask the chairman to summarise what has been decided so that it can be properly recorded in the minutes.

4.10 Meetings by telephone

Recent cases have confirmed that the board may act without holding a formal meeting if all the directors give their consent informally (see **6.3**). There is no reason that such informal consent should not be given over the telephone. A more difficult question is whether directors can participate in board meetings over the telephone (or by audiovisual link). In other words, can they be counted in the quorum and can they vote even though they are not personally present so that the board can act without unanimity in the usual manner?

To avoid the need for argument as to the common law position, some companies have amended their articles to provide expressly for the holding of board meetings by telephone. For an example of an article that allows meetings to be conducted using conference-type telephone systems, see **Precedent 4.10**. Such articles need to clarify that directors who are in contact with the meeting by conference telephone connection may be counted in the quorum. Without such an article the board could be deemed by the courts to be incapable of transacting any business where the number of directors physically present at the meeting is not sufficient to meet the quorum fixed by or established in accordance with the articles.

If sufficient directors are physically present at a meeting to form a quorum (proper notice having been given to all directors entitled to receive it), there is no doubt that those directors are able to transact business in the usual manner. This will be the case even where some directors vote by telephone, provided that the votes of those directors would not have altered the outcome of any vote on a resolution. The matter is only open to argument when the result of a vote would have been different if those participating by telephone had not voted.

Reg. 88 of Table A provides that questions arising at a meeting shall be decided by a majority of votes, but also that, subject to the provisions of the articles, the directors may regulate their proceedings as they think fit. As Table A makes no specific provision as to the method by which directors must vote at meetings of directors, it can be argued that the directors may make their own regulations which allow them to vote by telephone.

The courts have already demonstrated a willingness to accept the fact that participants in a general meeting need not all be in the same room (in other words, that a meeting may take place at several different locations at once). In *Byng v. London Life Association Ltd* [1989] 1 All ER 560, the company provided overflow facilities at an extraordinary general meeting to accommodate members who were unable to find a place at the venue given in the notice of that meeting. The overflow facilities were in the same complex and were meant to be connected to the main body of the meeting by audiovisual links. However, during the meeting those audiovisual links did not work as intended and the chairman purported to adjourn it to another place on the same day. The plaintiff sought to have the extraordinary resolution passed at the adjourned meeting declared invalid on a number of grounds. The first of these was that the original meeting was not a valid meeting because it was held in more than one place and as such could not be adjourned. The Court of Appeal dismissed this argument. In the leading judgment Browne-Wilkinson V-C stated (at p. 565):

> The rationale behind the requirement for meetings in the 1985 Act is that the members shall be able to attend in person so as to debate and vote on matters affecting the company. Until recently this could only be achieved by everyone being physically present in the same room face to face. Given modern technological advances, the same result can now be achieved without all the members coming face to face; without being physically in the same room they can be electronically in each other's presence so as to hear and be heard and to see and be seen. The fact that such a meeting could not have been foreseen at the time the first statutory requirements for

meetings were laid down, does not require us to hold that such a meeting is not within the meaning of the word 'meeting' in the 1985 Act.

Although in this case the Court of Appeal accepted that a general meeting need not be held in one room, it indicated that, for general meetings at least, the participants must be in visual as well as audio contact. In addition, it should be noted that while the overflow facilities were obviously in different rooms, they were both in the place given in the notice of the meeting. In his judgment in the *Byng* case, Mustill LJ said (at p. 572):

> I also accept that it possible to have a meeting, not all of whose members are present in the same room. It is unnecessary to consider the extreme case where none of the participants are face to face, but are linked by simultaneous audiovisual transmissions. This would require consideration of whether it is possible to convene a meeting which does not take place in any single location, and which consists only of the exchange of electronic impulses. No such problem arises here. If the arrangements had gone according to plan, and if the participants had first occupied Cinema 1 until it was full, and had then all found a place in the adjacent rooms by the time the business had commenced, and if they had been able to see hear and communicate with the other participants I would have seen no intellectual or practical objection to regarding this as a 'meeting'. Moreover, it would have been a meeting held at the place of which notice had been given, namely Cinema 1, since this was where the centre of gravity of the meeting was to be found.

In this respect *Byng* does not seem to advance the cause for telephone board meetings much further. However, it at least demonstrates the courts' willingness to adapt long-established legal principles in order to allow technology to be used to facilitate meetings. It should also be borne in mind that the courts normally impose less stringent rules for meetings of directors.

4.10.1   Series of telephone calls

Except where the directors approve a proposal unanimously, it seems unlikely that the courts would accept as valid a resolution of the board reached as a result of a series of one-to-one telephone calls conducted by the chairman, unless the articles made specific provision to this effect. This would stretch the common law concept of a meeting too far. It would not allow the simultaneous transfer of views. It is not a meeting of minds at a particular point in time. Those who were contacted first may have changed their minds by the time the chairman has spoken to the last director. They might also have reached a different conclusion if they had heard the views of other directors. The same might be true of those who are contacted later in the series of calls if the chairman fails to explain adequately the views of the minority.

Some companies have articles that specifically allow decisions of the board to be reached in this manner. On the whole such a method of decision making is only suitable for issues that are simple or mere formalities.

4.11 Alternate directors

At common law there is no automatic right to vote by proxy. The Act confers a statutory right on the members to vote by proxy but does not make similar provision with regard to the directors. Thus a director who is unable to attend a meeting of directors will be unable to vote at that meeting unless the articles provide otherwise.

Table A provides a mechanism that allows directors to appoint another person to attend and vote in their stead at board and committee meetings. A person so appointed is known as an alternate director.

Reg. 68 provides that alternate directors may be appointed or removed by notice to the company signed by the director making or revoking the appointment or in any other manner approved by the directors (see **Precedents 4.11A–D**). However, reg. 65 states that the approval of the board is required regarding the appointment as an alternate of a person who is not a director. Such approval is not required where another director is appointed and reg. 88 provides that a director who is also an alternate director shall be entitled in the absence of his or her appointor to a separate vote on behalf of his or her appointor in addition to his own vote.

Reg. 89 provides that a person who holds office only as an alternate director shall, if his or her appointor is not present, be counted in the quorum. This provision does not deal with the position of a director who is also appointed as an alternate for one or more of the other directors (see **4.8**).

Reg. 69 provides that an alternate director shall be deemed to be a director and shall alone be responsible for his or her own acts and defaults and shall not be deemed to be the agent of the director appointing him or her. Thus the chairman need not be concerned as to whether the alternate is voting in accordance with the instructions of his or her appointor. If the appointee is not already a director of the company, his or her appointment as alternate director will cause him or her to be regarded as a director and the usual formalities (such as notification of appointment on form 288a) should be followed.

Reg. 94 provides in relation to alternate directors that an interest of his or her appointor shall be treated as an interest of the alternate director without prejudice to any interest that the alternate director has otherwise. Thus an alternate director may not vote if either he or his appointor is interested in a transaction put to the vote at either a board or committee meeting.

An alternate director may sign a written resolution instead of his appointor under reg. 93.

4.12   Interests in contracts

Under s. 317, directors have a duty to declare at a meeting of directors the nature of any direct or indirect interest they may have in any contract or proposed contract with the company. This provision is intended to assist in avoiding conflicts of interest on the part of directors and to ensure that the requirements of the articles (e.g. reg. 94 of Table A) restricting a director's right to vote on such matters are observed. The type of interest that is relevant for these purposes is extremely wide and would include being a director of another company that is to be a party to a proposed transaction.

Section 317(3) allows general notice of a director's interests as a shareholder of other companies to be given to the company. This notice has no effect unless it is given at a meeting of directors or the director takes reasonable steps to ensure that it is brought up and read at the next meeting of directors after it is given. This procedure cannot be used where a director's interest is only as a director of another company and in such circumstances separate disclosure is required in relation to each relevant transaction.

In the case of a proposed contract, the declaration must be made at the meeting of the directors at which the question of entering into the contract was first considered or, if the director was not at the date of that meeting interested in the proposed contract, at the next meeting of directors held after he or she became so interested. If a director becomes interested in an existing contract, the declaration must be made at the first meeting of directors after he or she becomes so interested.

The requirements of s. 317 are not satisfied by giving notice of an interest at a meeting of a committee of the board and it makes no difference that all the board members knew of the interest in question (*Guinness plc v. Saunders* [1988] 2 All ER 940). It has also been held that a sole director must comply with the formalities of s. 317 by holding a meeting and making a declaration at that meeting (*Re Neptune (Vehicle Washing Equipment) Ltd* [1995] 1 BCLC 352).

Articles frequently provide that directors may be a party to or otherwise interested in certain transactions or arrangements with the company provided that they have disclosed the nature and extent of that interest in accordance with s. 317. Any failure on the part of a director to comply with such an article renders any contract between the company and the director concerned voidable at the instance of the company (*Hely-Hutchinson v. Brayhead Ltd* [1967] 3 All ER 98).

4.13   Adjournment

Articles rarely make specific provision with respect to
adjournment of directors' meetings other than to state that the
directors may adjourn. As a result, the common law rules on
adjournment will normally apply and the power to adjourn will
rest with the meeting (*National Dwelling Society Ltd v. Sykes* [1894]
3 Ch. 159). It follows that, in order to exercise that power, a
quorum must be present. Thus it is impossible to adjourn a board
meeting at which a quorum is not present, unless the articles
make specific provision to that effect, and a further meeting will
need to be called.

If a quorum is present, the directors may adjourn. In practice, it
is unusual for directors' meetings to be adjourned for any longer
than a few hours, perhaps to allow lunch to be taken or further
negotiations to take place before a final decision is made.
Although there is strictly no need to give notice of an adjourned
meeting (*Scadding v. Lorrant* (1851) 3 HLC 418), it is normal
practice to notify directors who were unable to attend the original
meeting, if only to ensure that there is a quorum at the adjourned
meeting. The quorum required at an adjourned meeting will be
the same as for the original meeting.

4.14   Standing orders and internal regulations

Articles frequently provide that, subject to the articles, the
directors may regulate their proceedings as they think fit (e.g. reg.
88 of Table A). As a result, boards may adopt standing orders or
internal regulations that govern their own conduct and
procedures. The areas in which the board may establish such
regulations might include the following:

- length of notice of board meetings;
- location and frequency of meetings;
- requirements to give notice of business to be transacted in the
  agenda;
- procedures for the approval and circulation of the minutes of
  meetings;
- schedule of matters reserved to the board.

Assuming that such regulations are consistent with the articles,
the question arises as to their status and enforceability. Much will
depend on the way they are drafted. If they are framed as a code
of best practice (in other words they are aspirational rather than
mandatory), they are unlikely to be enforceable. If, however, they
are drafted as regulations and are intended to be mandatory, it is
arguable that they should be complied with as if they were
contained in the articles.

Articles often confer a similar power on the directors to fix the
quorum at board meetings. It has been held that they may only

exercise that power if they act in accordance with the existing rules and procedures governing their meetings, including the existing quorum requirements (*Re Portuguese Consolidated Copper Mines Ltd* (1889) 42 Ch.D. 160). In other words, they cannot change the quorum unless there are sufficient directors present at the meeting to form a quorum under the existing rules.

It could be argued that the same principle applies to internal regulations made by the board under reg. 88 or a similar article. For example, an internal regulation requiring at least seven days' notice of board meetings could not be amended at a meeting held with notice of less than seven days. In theory, the board meeting would not have been validly called and any business transacted at it would therefore be invalid. In practice, the validity of the meeting would only be liable to challenge by a director or, in the event of insolvency, an administrator. No one else would be likely to have notice of the breach. Third parties would be protected from any breach by the indoor management rule (see **7.2**). A director wishing to challenge the validity of the proceedings would need to act quickly otherwise he or she may be deemed by the courts to have acquiesced in the breach. The board could, of course, subsequently ratify the decisions taken at the meeting and the court could refuse to declare the proceedings invalid where it is satisfied that the irregularities could be cured by the board going through the proper process (*Bentley-Stevens v. Jones* [1974] 1 WLR 638).

4.15   ICSA code on good boardroom practice

The Institute of Chartered Secretaries and Administrators (ICSA) issued a code on good boardroom practice in 1991 (see **Appendix I**). The ICSA code recommends that boardroom procedures should be periodically reviewed to ensure both the satisfactory operation of its code and the identification of matters that individual companies could advantageously bring within its scope. Some of the recommendations in the ICSA code were subsequently repeated in the Cadbury Code and, ultimately, in the Combined Code on Corporate Governance. However, it still provides useful guidance on board procedures.

5

Committees of directors

5.1 Summary

- Committees of directors should be appointed by a resolution of the board which should specify its membership and duties (see **5.2**).
- Only directors may be appointed as members unless the articles provide otherwise (see **5.2**).
- Articles usually provide that the proceedings at committees of directors shall be governed by the regulations governing board meetings (see **5.4** to **5.9**) except where a committee of one director is appointed (see **5.10**).
- The Combined Code recommends that all listed companies should establish an audit committee (see **5.11**), a remuneration committee (see **5.12**) and a nomination committee (see **5.13**).

5.2 Appointment of committees

The power to delegate to committees of directors is a special power which must be exercised by the board at a properly convened and constituted meeting of the board. In other words, the establishment of a committee with delegated powers must be the subject of a valid board resolution.

The resolution establishing a committee must deal with the following:

- its membership;
- its duties and powers; and
- any conditions imposed by the board on the exercise of those powers.

This can sometimes be done in one simple resolution (see **Precedent 5.2A**). However, it is normal to pass a resolution establishing the committee's terms of reference (including its delegated powers) and to deal with appointments separately when establishing a standing committee.

5.2.1 Membership

Most articles state that the directors may appoint a committee of one or more directors. However, the power to delegate to a committee is deemed to include the power to delegate to a committee consisting of only one director, unless the articles specifically provide otherwise (*Re Fireproof Doors Ltd* [1916] 2 Ch. 142).

In most cases, it will be preferable to appoint named individuals to a committee. This will be so for standing committees such as the audit and remuneration committees which are usually comprised wholly or mainly of non-executive directors. It is, however, perfectly acceptable to appoint post-holders rather than named individuals. This might be a more suitable method for an executive committee where the membership is drawn from particular office holders.

5.2.2 Committees of 'any two directors'

It is also quite common for boards of directors to establish a committee of 'any two directors' or 'any three directors', etc. (see **Precedent 5.2B**). This method is most commonly used to allow one or more directors to complete a transaction that the board has already authorised or to sign a document on behalf of the board. In such cases, it is arguable whether it is necessary to establish a committee. It would be sufficient for the board to resolve, for example, that any two directors be authorised to sign the documents on behalf of the board.

The 'any two director' method is slightly less satisfactory where the committee is to be given discretionary powers. The technique was used by the board of Guinness during its takeover of Distillers in the 1980s to appoint a committee of any three directors:

> with full power and authority to settle the terms of the offer, to approve any revision of the offer which the committee might consider it desirable to make and [among other things] (vi) to authorise and approve, execute and do, or procure to be executed and done all documents, deeds, acts and things as they may consider necessary or desirable in connection with the making or implementation of the offer and/or the proposals referred to above and any revision thereof ... (see *Guinness plc v. Saunders* [1990] 1 All ER 654)

Appointing such a committee could be viewed as appointing the whole board as a committee and fixing the quorum at the number of directors specified. In theory, all the directors are potential members of such a committee and are therefore entitled to receive notice of its meetings. It is, however, debatable whether this method could be used to avoid any restrictions in the articles as to the quorum at committee meetings. If it is possible to appoint a committee of any two directors, it must also be acceptable to appoint a committee of 'any two' of a number of named directors. The end result is, of course, the same as if the board had appointed a committee of, say, four named directors and specified the quorum as two. If the articles prevent the board doing this by the normal method, it must be doubtful whether it can achieve the same result by using the 'any two director' method of appointment. It is worthy of note on this score that the articles of Guinness gave the board specific power to fix the quorum of committees of the board.

It is also questionable what the position would be if, say, four directors attended a meeting of a committee of 'any two directors'. Could they all vote? And what would happen if two were in favour and two opposed to a proposal? Which (if any) of the directors would constitute the committee? In *Guinness plc v. Saunders*, Lord Templeman said, somewhat pointedly perhaps, that the three directors in that case 'constituted themselves as a committee'. Could three other directors have constituted themselves as a committee with the same powers?

In order to avoid these problems, there ought, perhaps, to be some sort of control exercised on the calling of meetings of such a committee. Usually this will be the task of the person who prepares the documentation for the meeting. Indeed, it may be preferable to specify in the board resolution establishing the committee that it may not meet unless the company secretary or some other specified person is present. These sort of safeguards may not be necessary where the committee is established to execute a document or perform some other mechanical process.

5.2.3 Coopted members

Only directors may be appointed as members of board committees unless the articles provide otherwise. Reg. 72 of Table A makes no such provision. Non-directors cannot therefore be appointed as voting members, although they can be given rights of attendance.

Until recently, the Listing Rules required directors to form the majority on board committees of listed companies whose articles allow coopted members, and insisted that such committees act only where the majority of members present were directors. Although this rule was abolished in 1995, the articles of many listed companies still include such restrictions.

5.3 Powers and duties of committees

The extent of the powers delegated to a committee should be specified in the board resolution or the terms of reference approved by the board. Generally speaking, this will be apparent from the committee's duties or functions. However, it is safer to set out these powers explicitly. For example, if a committee is to be established to negotiate, agree and execute a contract for the purchase of a specified freeehold property, it might be preferable to state explicitly that the committee has the power to appoint surveyors and solicitors and incur other costs which are necessary in the performance of its duties.

It is not necessary to delegate any powers to a committee established solely to make recommendations to the board. Any director may make recommendations to the board. However, committees established for this purpose may also benefit from having certain incidental powers (e.g. to retain external professional advisers) and it is preferable to specify these powers at the outset.

It is normal to draft more formal rules for standing committees. A standing committee is one that is established permanently to perform certain duties on a regular basis. Terms of reference for such committees are usually adopted by a specific board resolution. Named individuals are then appointed as members of such committees by a separate resolution(s). See **Precedent 5.11** for specimen terms of reference of an audit committee and **Precedent 5.13** for a nomination committee.

5.4 Proceedings at committee meetings

The proceedings at committees of the board will be governed by the articles and in default by the common law of meetings. Articles usually provide that the proceedings at committee meetings shall be governed by the articles regulating the proceedings at board meetings so far as they are capable of applying. Regulation 72 of Table A adopts this style but only with respect to committees of two or more directors. The issues raised in connection with meetings of only one director are covered at **5.10**.

5.4.1 Conditions imposed by the board

Regulation 72 provides that the board may impose conditions on the exercise by a committee of its delegated powers. The application to committees of the articles governing the proceedings at board meetings is made subject to any such conditions imposed by the directors. The word 'conditions' would seem to imply that the board may impose additional restrictions but may not relax the application of the articles. For example, the board could appoint the chairman of the committee and thereby limit the application of reg. 91 which would otherwise allow the committee to choose its own chairman. However, the board could not relax the application of reg. 95 which states that a director shall not be counted in the quorum present at a meeting in relation to a resolution on which he or she is not entitled to vote. To do so would be to remove an obstacle rather than impose an additional obstacle. It is acknowledged, however, that this theory can cause problems with regard to the quorum at committee meetings (see **5.6**).

Some articles use the word 'regulations' instead of 'conditions'. This might give the directors more latitude in disapplying the articles. It should be noted, however, that even this form of wording would not allow the directors to disapply an article that specifically states that it shall apply to committees of directors as well as the board, e.g. reg. 94 of Table A which sets out the circumstances in which a director cannot vote on a resolution.

5.5 Appointment of committee chairman

Under Table A, the committee members may appoint (and remove) one of their number as chairman of the committee (applying reg. 91 and reg. 72), unless the board appoints a chairman itself. The board may nominate the chairman as a condition on the exercise of the committee's powers. A chairman appointed in this manner cannot be removed by the committee and will have a casting vote if the articles confer a casting vote on the chairman of the board of directors, unless, of course, the board removes the casting vote as a condition on the exercise of the committee's powers.

The board may also appoint one or more deputy or vice-chairmen to act in the chairman's absence. If it fails to do so and the committee's quorum is such that meetings can be held without the nominated chairman, the committee members present will have the power (in accordance with reg. 91) to appoint one of their number to chair meetings in the absence of the chairman.

5.6 Quorum

The common law rule is that a committee can only act if all its members are present. This rule can, of course, be modified by the articles. For example, the articles may give the board specific power to fix the quorum for board committees. Where this is the case, the common law rule will apply in default if the board fails to specify a quorum (*Re Liverpool Household Stores Association Limited* (1890) 59 LJ Ch. 616). Even though this may be what the board intended, it is preferable to state the quorum in the resolution appointing the committee or the terms of reference approved by the board.

Unfortunately, most articles do not give the board specific power to fix the quorum for committees but rely on provisions like reg. 72 of Table A which states that the proceedings of committees shall be governed by the articles regulating the proceedings of the board so far as they are capable of applying. In these circumstances, the article that deals with the quorum at board meetings will also govern the quorum at board committees so far as it is capable of applying. The Table A provision dealing with the quorum at board meetings (reg. 89) is capable of applying (see below). However, if the number of members appointed to a committee (say, three) is less than the number specified by the articles as the quorum at board meetings (say, four), that article will not be capable of applying and the common law rule will apply in default. In other words the quorum will be all three members of the committee.

Under Table A, the quorum for the transaction of the business of the directors may be fixed by the directors and unless so fixed at any other number shall be two (reg. 89). This article also governs the quorum at committee meetings by virtue of reg. 72. However, it is capable of more than one interpretation when applied to a committee. It could mean that the quorum for the transaction of the business of a committee of directors may be fixed by the *board of directors* and, unless so fixed at any other number, shall be two; or it could mean that the quorum for the transaction of the business of a committee of directors may be fixed by the *committee* and, unless so fixed at any other number, shall be two. Both interpretations cannot be correct, otherwise the committee would be able to change the quorum fixed by the board. It is suggested that the first of these interpretations is correct and that if the board fails to fix the quorum at some other number, it will be two.

5.6.1   Quorum of one

The basic common law rule established in *Sharp v. Dawes* is that in order to hold a valid meeting there must be a meeting of minds; in other words, that there must be at least two people present who are entitled to attend and vote. However, even the common law recognises that a valid meeting can be held with only one person present where he or she is the only person entitled to attend and vote at meetings of that body, e.g. the sole holder of a class of shares (*East v. Bennett Bro. Ltd* [1911] 1 Ch. 163).

In any case, the principle laid down in *Sharp v. Dawes* is a common law rule and, as such, is liable to modification by the articles. If the articles allow the directors to fix a quorum of one at board meetings and provide that the regulations governing board meetings shall also apply to committee meetings, it would seem that they may also fix a quorum of one for a committee of more than one director (*Re Fireproof Doors Ltd* [1916] 2 Ch. 142). Regulation 89 of Table A allows the directors to fix a quorum of one for board meetings and therefore to do likewise for any committee.

5.6.2   Disinterested quorum

Reg. 95 of Table A provides that a director shall not be counted in the quorum present at a meeting in relation to a resolution on which he or she is not entitled to vote. This is merely a restatement of the common law rule and will always be the case unless the articles make specific provision to the contrary. Any article on this matter will also apply to meetings of a committee of directors by virtue of reg. 72 and it is doubtful whether the directors can exclude the application of any such article by imposing a condition in accordance with reg. 72. It is also arguable that reg. 95 should be read in conjunction with reg. 94 which specifically states that it is applicable to committees of directors.

5.6.3   Minimum number

Articles specifying the minimum number of directors are clearly not intended to apply to committees of the board and can be considered to be excluded by the words 'so far as they are capable of applying' in reg. 72 and similarly worded articles. The board may, however, specify as a condition in the board resolution establishing the committee the minimum number of members of that committee. If so, the committee will not be authorised to act if the number of members falls below that figure, say as a result of the death or resignation of committee members (*Re Liverpool Household Stores Association Limited* (1890) 59 LJ Ch. 616). If the board resolution states that the committee shall consist of three members and then proceeds to name them, that would be equivalent to fixing a minimum number.

Regulation 90 of Table A provides that the continuing directors or sole continuing director may act notwithstanding any vacancies in their number. If reg. 90 applies to committees by virtue of reg. 72, it would appear that a committee may act notwithstanding any vacancies provided that there are sufficient members present to form a quorum. This would seem to defeat the object of setting a minimum in the first place. However, one might also say the same about the situation with regard to the board of directors.

5.7   Voting

At common law, directors are excluded from voting where they are interested in the contract under discussion. This rule can be modified wholly or partially by the articles and any such provisions will apply to board committee meetings. Regulation 94 of Table A allows the directors to vote in certain limited circumstances where they are interested but otherwise imposes a general prohibition. It specifically states that it applies to committees of directors as well as the board.

Where non-directors are appointed as members of a board committee, it is a good idea to clarify in the terms of reference their duties with regard to disclosure of interests and their right to vote on contracts in which they have an interest. Non-directors do not have a statutory duty to disclose such interests and articles on voting usually refer only to directors.

Articles sometimes provide that the majority of members present at a meeting must be directors where they allow non-directors to be appointed. This could also be included as a condition in the committee's terms of reference.

Under the common law, each member of the committee will have one vote. The articles may, however, make alternative provision with regard to board meetings and any such provisions may be adopted by default for committees by virtue of clauses like reg. 72. The most obvious example is where the articles provide for the appointment of alternate directors. If a director appoints another director as his or her alternate, the director so appointed will have two votes. Great care should, however, be taken where one or more directors have weighted voting rights in respect of the exercise by the board of certain powers and it is proposed to delegate those powers to a committee.

5.7.1 Disclosure of interests

In order to comply with s. 317, it is not sufficient for a director to declare an interest in a contract at a committee meeting. This must be done at a board meeting (*Guinness plc v. Saunders* [1988] 2 All ER 940). The same will be true with regard to any article that requires disclosure in accordance with the requirements of the Act, e.g. regs 85 and 86.

5.7.2 Alternate directors

There is no automatic right to appoint a proxy or an alternate at meetings of committees. The right to appoint an alternate depends entirely on the articles. Table A deals explicitly with the position of alternates with regard to committees (see regs 65 to 71). To summarise, it provides that an alternate is entitled to receive notice of all meetings of committees of which his or her appointor is a member and to attend and vote at any such meeting in the absence of his or her appointor. It is doubtful whether a non-director who is a member of a committee can appoint an alternate unless the articles specifically provide.

5.8 Defects in appointment

Section 285 and articles based on it (e.g. reg. 92 of Table A) serve to validate the acts of committees where it is subsequently discovered that there is a defect in the appointment or qualification of directors who were members of it (see **7.3**).

5.9 Written resolutions

Most articles on directors' written resolutions specifically extend
this form of decision-making to committees of the board
(see **6.2**). This is certainly the case with regard to reg. 93 of Table
A, although not reg. 106 of the 1948 Table A.

5.10 Committee of one director

As a general rule, there must be at least two people present in
order to hold a meeting (*Sharp v. Dawes* (1876) 2 QBD 26). The
power to delegate to a committee is, however, deemed to
include the power to delegate to a committee of only one
director unless the articles provide otherwise (*Re Fireproof Doors
Ltd* [1916] 2 Ch. 142). Although it is not necessary, most articles
specify that the board may delegate its powers to a committee of
one director.

Most articles follow reg. 72 of Table A by providing that the
articles governing proceedings at board meetings shall apply to
committees consisting of two or more directors. In other words,
they make no provision for proceedings at meetings of
committees of one director. Even if the articles do not follow this
precise form, the words 'so far as they are capable of applying'
will exclude the application of many of the articles. However, any
article that specifically states that it is applicable to committees of
directors will still be relevant, e.g. reg. 93 (written resolutions)
and reg. 94 (restrictions on voting). In theory, it is still necessary
for a director who is the sole member of a committee to hold
meetings. In practice, it will not be necessary to give notice of
any such meeting and whenever such a director exercises his or
her delegated powers, it can be said that he or she is holding a
meeting. What is important is that the director maintains a formal
record of his or her decisions. Regulation 100 requires the
directors to keep minutes of all proceedings at meetings of
committees of directors. Probably the best way of doing this is for
the director to act by written resolution (see **Precedent 6.2A**) and
for each resolution to be entered into a minute book kept for that
purpose.

5.11 Audit committee

The Combined Code on Corporate Governance recommends that
boards of directors should establish an audit committee with
written terms of reference. It also makes recommendations
regarding the constitution and duties of the audit committee. The
vast majority of listed companies now follow these
recommendations, and those that do not are required by the
Listing Rules to give reasons for any non-compliance (Listing
Rules, para. 12.43A).

The Combined Code recommends that the committee should

consist of at least three non-executive directors, a majority of whom should be 'independent', and that their names should be disclosed in the report and accounts (Combined Code, para. D.3.1). This disclosure obligation is intended to allow investors to make their own assessment regarding the independence of the non-executives (see **3.3**).

5.11.1   Duties of the audit committee

The establishment of an audit committee is not intended to undermine the ultimate responsibility of the board for reviewing and approving the annual report and accounts and the half-year report. Rather, it is intended to ensure that the non-executive directors become actively involved in that process and have access to the resources necessary to enable them to make independent judgements. It also offers the auditors a direct link with the non-executive directors. To summarise, it provides an important assurance that a key area of the board's duties will be rigorously discharged. Para. D.3.2 of the Combined Code states that the duties of the audit committee should include keeping the following under review:

- the scope and results of the audit;
- its cost effectiveness;
- the independence and objectivity of the auditors; and
- where the auditors also supply a substantial volume of non-audit services to the company, the nature and extent of such services, seeking to balance the maintenance of objectivity and value for money.

More detailed guidance on the role of the committee can be found in the Cadbury Report which also includes specimen terms of reference (see **Precedent 5.11**). It said that the duties of the audit committee should include reviewing and making recommendations to the board on the following:

- the appointment of the external auditor, the audit fee, and any question of resignation or dismissal;
- the nature and scope of the audit and coordination where more than one audit firm is involved;
- the half-year and annual financial statements before submission to the board;
- problems and reservations arising from the interim and final audits, and any matters that the auditor may wish to discuss (in the absence of management where necessary);
- the auditor's management letter and management's response;
- the company's statement on internal control prior to endorsement by the board;
- the internal audit programme;
- the major findings of internal investigations and management's response.

5.11.2   Powers

The primary purpose of the audit committee is not to exercise powers delegated by the board but to monitor and review matters connected with the financial statements and to make recommendations to the board arising from these activities. Strictly speaking, there is no need to delegate any powers to the committee for these purposes. However, the audit committee may need to be given certain incidental powers to enable it to function effectively. It could, for example, be given explicit powers of internal investigation and rights of access to any company information it requires. In theory, this would enable the audit committee to cut through the usual chain of authority when conducting investigations, although it is questionable whether the committee could enforce such powers without recourse to the board in the face of concerted opposition by the executive directors. The committee will almost certainly need to be given power to retain independent professional advisers. This is a far more concrete power and undoubtedly involves the delegation of powers by the board.

5.11.3   Secretary

The specimen terms of reference for an audit committee contained in the Cadbury Report (see **Precedent 5.11**) envisage that the company secretary will act as the secretary to the audit committee. This is consistent with the Combined Code which states that all directors should have access to the advice and services of the company secretary. However, it may not be desirable for a company secretary who is also a director to fulfil this role.

5.12   Remuneration committee

Although articles often require directors' fees to be approved by the members in general meeting (e.g. reg. 82 of Table A), they usually give the board of directors power to fix the salaries of the executive directors (e.g. reg. 84 of Table A). Executive directors may be paid directors' fees in addition to any salary they may receive. If so, those fees must be approved in the manner prescribed by the articles. Articles invariably give the board of directors power to determine executive salaries and the members will normally have no direct say in the amount that executives are paid. These arrangements are necessary because executive directors are usually employed under a service contract, the terms of which need to be settled before the executive joins the board. Members could be given a role in determining these salaries if the executive directors' contractual entitlements were made subject to the approval of the members in general meeting. However, any company that tried to impose such arrangements would probably find it impossible to recruit executives of desired calibre.

The usual procedure is therefore for the board to enter into a contract with the executive director on behalf of the company when it appoints him or her. If the director is subsequently dismissed (e.g. by the members at the next annual general meeting), he or she will be entitled to damages for breach of contract (see for example reg. 84 of Table A). The amount of damages will depend on the directors' remuneration but also on the period of notice that the company is required to give under the contract.

The members are therefore reliant on the board to exercise restraint in the matter of executive salaries. Not surprisingly, shareholders often feel that the salaries of executive directors approved by the board are too generous. Where the majority of directors are executive directors, it is generally believed that the board cannot be sufficiently impartial. Although each director is unable to vote on his or her own salary and benefits, the suspicion is that they tend to approve larger increases for their colleagues than perhaps they ought on the basis that their colleagues will approve a similar increase for them.

In 1992, the Cadbury Committee recommended that boards of directors should establish remuneration committees consisting of a majority of non-executive directors to be responsible for making recommendations to the board on executive directors' salaries. Although the vast majority of listed companies complied fully with the Committee's recommendations, there continued to be considerable public disquiet over the salaries paid to executive directors, particularly in the privatised utility companies, and in February 1995 the CBI formed a study group chaired by Sir Richard Greenbury 'to identify good practice in determining directors' remuneration and to prepare a code of such practice for use by UK plcs'. The study group (the 'Greenbury Committee') published its final report and code of practice on 17 July 1995 (*Directors' Remuneration: Report of a Study Group chaired by Sir Richard Greenbury*, Gee Publishing). The London Stock Exchange agreed to adopt the new Code with certain minor modifications and introduced a requirement for listed companies incorporated in the United Kingdom to report on their compliance with its recommendations on remuneration committees and include a detailed report on directors' remuneration in their annual reports.

In 1998, the Hampel Committee, which was convened by the Financial Reporting Council to review the operation of the Cadbury and Greenbury Codes, published what is now referred to as the Combined Code on Corporate Governance. This code supersedes both the Cadbury and Greenbury Codes, and listed companies are now required to report on their compliance with the Combined Code (Listing Rules, para. 12.43A).

5.12.1 Combined Code provisions on remuneration committees

The Combined Code recommends that boards of directors should establish remuneration committees of independent non-executive directors. The committee should have written terms of reference and its duties should include the following:

- making recommendations to the board, within agreed terms of reference, on the company's framework of executive remuneration and its cost; and
- determining on their behalf specific remuneration packages for each of the executive directors, including pension rights and any compensation payments (Combined Code, para. B.2.1).

The Code recommends that the remuneration committees should consist exclusively of non-executive directors who are independent of management and free from any business or other relationship that could materially interfere with the exercise of their independent judgement (Combined Code, para. B.2.2). It also recommends that the membership of the committee should be listed each year in the board's remuneration report to shareholders (Combined Code, para. B.2.3). This disclosure obligation is intended to allow investors to make their own assessment regarding the independence of the non-executives (see **3.3**). The Combined Code recommends that the remuneration committee should consult the chairman and/or chief executive officer about their proposals relating to the remuneration of other executive directors and have access to professional advice inside and outside the company (Combined Code, para. B.2.5). This recommendation should be borne in mind when establishing terms of reference for the committee. If it is to be truly independent, it is arguable that the committee should be given power to appoint its own external advisers.

The Combined Code includes detailed recommendations on directors' remuneration (see **Appendix F**), and the Listing Rules still require listed companies to include a detailed report on directors' remuneration in the annual report and accounts (Listing Rules, para. 12.43A).

5.13 Nomination committee

The Combined Code recommends that, unless the board is small, a nomination committee should be established to make recommendations to the board on all new board appointments (Combined Code, para. A.5.1). It also recommends that a majority of the members of the committee should be non-executive directors and that the committee chairman should either be the chairman of the board or a non-executive director. See **Precedent 5.13** for specimen terms of reference for a nomination committee drawn up by the ICSA's Company Secretaries Panel.

A practical issue that will arise in operating a nomination committee is that the minutes/reports to the board of the committee will, for reasons of discretion, usually not include details of internal candidates considered in principle but rejected. The names of outside candidates under serious consideration by the committee (e.g. for non-executive directorship) would, again for reasons of discretion, no doubt be 'sounded out' with the full board prior to the committee commencing discussions with the person concerned with a view to possibly making a recommendation for his or her appointment.

6

Directors' written resolutions and informal consent

6.1 Summary

- The Act allows members of a private company to act by written resolution but makes no equivalent provision with regard to directors. However, articles commonly allow the board of directors and any committee of directors to act without holding a meeting by passing a written resolution. Articles normally require all the directors to sign the resolution in order to act in this way. However, they may make different provision (see **6.2**).
- A decision of the directors will not necessarily be invalid simply because they failed to approve the transaction at a meeting or in accordance with some other procedure provided for in the articles. The courts often apply the common law principle of unanimous consent where it is clear that all the directors approved the transaction or can be deemed to have acquiesced to the decision (see **6.3**).

6.2 Written resolutions

There is no equivalent for directors to the statutory procedure for written resolutions of the members (see **24.2**). The ability of the directors to act without holding formal meetings is therefore entirely dependent on the common law and the articles.

Most articles (including Table A) make specific provision for written resolutions of the directors even though it is now firmly established that the directors may act outside formal board meetings if they all agree. This is partly because of the uncertainties in the common law but also because articles usually provide a slightly more relaxed regime. For example, reg. 93 of Table A provides:

93. A resolution signed in writing by all the directors entitled to receive notice of a meeting of directors or of a committee of directors shall be as valid and effectual as if it had been passed at a meeting of directors or (as the case may be) a committee of directors duly convened and held and may consist of several documents in the like form each signed by one or more directors; but a resolution signed by an alternate director need not also be signed by his appointor and, if it is signed by a director who has appointed an alternate director, it need not be signed by the alternate in that capacity.

Under the common law, the unanimous agreement of the directors is required. Under reg. 93 the resolution need only be signed by the directors entitled to receive notice of a meeting of directors or of a committee of directors as the case may be (see **Precedent 6.2A** for an example of the form of a directors' written resolution).

6.2.1   Director not entitled to receive notice

Under Table A, the only occasion on which a director is not entitled to receive notice is when he or she is absent from the UK (reg. 88). Thus, in normal circumstances, the resolution must be signed by all the directors. If, however, one or more directors are outside the UK, then the requirement for unanimity no longer applies. This could give rise to some peculiar results. Say, for example, four out of seven directors travel abroad on a business trip, it would appear that the three directors who remain in the UK could pass a written resolution even though they are in the minority in terms of numbers. This is not particularly unusual because the same directors could convene a board meeting and pass the resolution in the usual manner. However, a more difficult question is whether the written resolution would still be valid where the quorum for board meetings was four.

The High Court was recently called upon to rule on a similar question under reg. 106 of the 1948 Table A, which is broadly the same as reg. 93 of the 1985 Table A. Carnwath J held that a directors' written resolution, passed in accordance with reg. 106 of the 1948 Table A, signed by only one director where the quorum for the transaction of business by the directors was two, was invalid, notwithstanding that the only other director was outside the UK and thus not entitled to notice of a meeting of directors (*Hood Sailmakers Ltd v. Axford* [1996] 4 All ER 830). In reaching this decision, he relied on the fact that reg. 99 of the 1948 Table A refers to 'the quorum necessary for the transaction of the business' (as does reg. 88 of the 1985 Table A), and said that even though reg. 106 of the 1948 Table A indicates that a written resolution of the directors will be as valid and effectual as if it had been passed at a meeting of directors, the requirement for a quorum must be treated as a separate matter.

The absence of a director from the UK can also cause difficulties because neither version of Table A specifies the point at which the test of whether a director is entitled to receive notice should be applied. There would be no problem if the director was away on the day that all the directors in the UK signed the resolution. However, if the directors sign on different days, it is not clear whether a person who was absent for only part of the period between the first and last signatures should also sign. Say, for example, a company has four directors (A, B, C and D) who are each given a copy of a written resolution. A and B do not agree with the proposal and do not sign it. They leave the UK on business before C and D sign the resolution. If the critical point for the test is when the last director signs, then the resolution would be valid because A and B are absent from the UK and not therefore entitled to receive notice when C and D sign it.

Alternatively it could be argued that there is no single critical point, i.e. that a director who is present in the UK at some stage during the process must sign the resolution. The process could be deemed to start from the point when the first director signed and finish at the point when the last director signed. This would not make any difference in the above example but would if either C or D had signed a copy of the resolution before A and B left the UK. Finally, as the test is whether a director is entitled to receive notice, it could be argued that if a director actually receives a copy of a written resolution while in the UK and does not sign it, the resolution will not be valid without his or her signature.

6.2.2   Alternate directors

Where the articles make provision for the appointment of alternate directors and one or more of the directors have appointed an alternate, it would seem that their signature will also be necessary unless some sort of saving provision is included in the articles. This is because the word 'director' will be deemed to include alternates and because alternate directors are usually entitled to receive notice of all meetings of directors and committees of which their appointor is a member. Reg. 93 provides that a written resolution signed by an alternate director need not also be signed by his appointor and, if it is signed by a director who has appointed an alternate director, it need not be signed by the alternate in that capacity.

A director who is signing in his or her own capacity and as an alternate for another director should make this clear. If a director has appointed an alternate, the alternate's signature will be required where his or her appointor is not entitled to receive notice. However, reg. 93 would seem to suggest that the signature of the alternate might also be acceptable in other circumstances.

6.2.3   Director interested in contract

It is questionable whether a written resolution will be valid where one or more of the directors has an interest in the contract which would prevent them from voting on the resolution if it were proposed at a board meeting. In *Re Charles Arkins and Co. Ltd* [1929] SASR 129, an Australian case based on an article that allowed decision by way of written resolution signed by all the directors currently in office, a written resolution was challenged on the basis that it had been signed by a director who was interested in the contract. Napier J rejected this argument and said: 'The signature to the resolution is not a vote ... I can see no reason why I should qualify that article by implying something which is not expressed, namely, that the subject of the resolution must be one upon which all the directors are able to vote.' However, the decision in *Hood Sailmakers Ltd v. Axford* (see above) would seem to suggest that a written resolution will not be valid unless, among the directors signing it, there are sufficient to form a disinterested quorum.

6.2.4   Practical points on written resolutions

Most company secretaries prefer to obtain the signatures of all the directors on the same day. If that is not possible, it is normally preferable to send out copies and obtain all the relevant signatures as quickly as possible. It is quite common for copies of the written resolution to be faxed to the directors and for the directors to be asked to sign it and fax a copy of it back to the company the same day.

It should be noted that the signature of all the directors will be required if the articles require directors who are absent from the UK to be given notice of meetings. Although this is not the case under Table A, the articles may provide for other circumstances in which a director is not entitled to receive notice. It should also be noted that there may still be some residual common law exceptions to the requirement to give notice which can be summarised as applying where the notice would not have any effect, e.g. where a director is so seriously ill that he or she would be unable to attend a meeting.

There is nothing to prevent the inclusion in articles of procedures to enable the directors to pass resolutions in writing if, for example, only three out of four directors or a certain percentage of them sign it. Provision can also be made to allow directors to approve the resolution by fax or electronic communications (see example at **Precedent 6.2B**).

6.2.5   Effective date and minutes

It must be presumed that a written resolution will not be effective until the last director signs. Original signed copies of the resolution should be included in the minute book (s. 382).

6.3   Informal consent

If the directors unanimously agree on a particular course of action, there is no need for that decision to be taken at a formal meeting of directors. It is unwise to rely on this common law rule, particularly where the articles provide an alternative method of acting without holding a meeting, e.g. written resolutions. In each of the following cases, none of the directors disputed the fact that they had concurred in the decision that was challenged in the courts. If they had, it is possible that the court's rulings would have been different. It is advisable therefore to have written evidence of the fact that all the directors agreed to act in a certain way.

In *Re Bonnelli's Telegraph Co.* (1871) LR 12 Eq. 246, the quorum for board meetings was three. Two out of the four directors signed a letter to C stating that they would secure the agreement of the other directors to C's appointment as agent in the sale of company's business on terms set out in the letter. The remaining two directors subsequently signed and sent a copy of that letter to C signifying their agreement to the appointment. Bacon V-C held that the directors had acted in a manner that was capable of binding the company. Unfortunately, in stating his reasons, he seemed to suggest that it was only necessary for three out of the four (i.e. a quorum) to agree, even though all the directors had agreed in the case before him. This reasoning runs counter to the generally accepted principle with regard to informal decisions of the members (see *Re Express Engineering Works Ltd* [1920] 1 Ch. 466; *Re Duomatic Ltd* [1969] 1 All ER 161). Indeed, for many years this flaw caused some commentators to question the application of the principle of unanimous informal consent to meetings of directors.

The issue has now been clarified by two recent cases. In *Charterhouse Investments Trust Ltd v. Tempest Diesels Ltd* [1986] BCLC 1, the board of Tempest Diesels Ltd had not formally considered the disputed term in a contract for the sale of its business signed on behalf of the board by one of the directors. Hoffman J held that the term was binding because the other directors, by their actions and subsequent testimony, were clearly content to acquiesce in whatever lawful terms were agreed by that director.

In *Runciman v. Walter Runciman plc* [1992] BCLC 1084, variations in a director's service contract were not put to the board for formal approval. Following a takeover, the new owners of the company challenged the validity of those variations and, in particular, an increase in the period of notice from three to five years. In holding that they were valid, Simon Brown J said: 'The articles say nothing as to how or when the directors are to arrive at their determination. In my judgment, therefore, provided only and always that by the time the term relied upon is sought to be enforced all the other directors can be shown to have concurred in the agreement of that term, it can fairly and properly be said that they have indeed determined it as the article requires.'

The *Runciman* case also highlights one of the factors that could easily defeat this type of informal decision making, namely the requirement to be found in most articles for directors to disclose their interest in any contract approved by the board. Failure to do so will normally make the contract voidable at the instance of the company (in other words the company can decide whether to avoid the contract or to enforce it) (*Hely-Hutchinson v. Brayhead Ltd* [1967] 3 All ER 98). In *Runciman*, Simon Brown J refused to apply this principle to the detriment of the director on the basis that it was a mere technical breach. In other cases, however, the courts might take a more stringent view (see **4.12**).

Although it is not clear from the reports of the two recent cases, it is highly likely that the articles of both companies allowed the directors to act by written resolution. If so, it appears that the board may act by the unanimous consent of its directors without holding a formal meeting irrespective of the existence of specific provisions in the articles on written resolutions.

7

Failure by directors to comply with proper procedures

7.1 Summary

Although the directors have a duty to act in accordance with the provisions of the company's memorandum and articles of association in order to avoid personal liability, their failure to do so will not always invalidate the transaction, at least as far as innocent third parties are concerned. Protection against defects in the decision-making process is provided by statute, articles and the common law where, for example:

- the directors fail to follow proper procedures (see **7.2**);
- under the principle of unanimous consent, the directors fail to follow the proper formal procedures but can be shown to have all agreed informally to the proposed transaction (see **6.3**);
- there is a defect in the appointment or qualification of a director (see **7.2**);
- the number of directors is less than the minimum prescribed by or in accordance with the articles (see **7.4**);
- the directors act beyond their powers (see **7.5**);
- the directors act beyond the company's powers (see **7.6**).

7.2 Indoor management rule

The 'indoor management rule' protects third parties dealing with the company from irregularities in the decision-making process, including acts of the board, board committees and individual directors. It can be applied in three different situations:

- Where a director has no authority to act (*Re County Life Assurance Co. Ltd* (1870) LR 5 Ch. App. 288).

- Where the director would have had authority had certain conditions been satisfied (*Royal British Bank v. Turquand* (1856) 119 ER 886).
- Where the director has authority to act but fails to follow the correct procedure (*Duck v. Tower Galvanising Co. Ltd* [1901] 2 KB 314).

7.3 Defects in appointment or qualification of directors

7.3.1 CA 1985, section 285

Section 285 serves to validate the acts of a director or manager notwithstanding any defect that may afterwards be discovered in his or her appointment or qualification. This allows third parties to deal with the company through its directors without having to investigate whether they have been properly appointed. Articles usually contain similarly worded provisions, e.g. reg. 92 of Table A (see below). Section 285 and such articles operate between the company and outsiders and between the company and its members (*Dawson v. African Consolidated Land & Trading Co.* [1898] 1 Ch. 6).

Anyone seeking to rely on such provisions must have acted in good faith. A person who merely has notice of the facts that give rise to the defect will not be prevented from relying on s. 285 unless they are also aware of the consequences of those facts (*Channel Collieries Trust Ltd v. Dover, St Margaret's and Martin Hill Light Railway Co.* [1914] 2 Ch. 506). The requirements of good faith will normally prevent a director from benefiting under s. 285. However, it has also been held that a director who allotted himself shares in the knowledge that his appointment was invalid (i.e. in bad faith) could not subsequently avoid the allotment on the ground that it could not therefore be validated by a clause similar in terms to reg. 92 of Table A (*York Tramways v. Willows* (1882) 8 QBD 685).

Section 285 applies only where there has been an appointment and not where there has been no appointment or reappointment at all. Thus, a provision similar to s. 285 in a company's articles did not validate the acts of a director who had vacated office at the end of the year in which he was due to retire by rotation owing to the fact that no annual general meeting had been held in that year at which he could be reappointed (*Morris v. Kanssen* [1946] AC 459). See, however, below on reg. 92 of Table A.

Section 285 operates to validate the acts of a director appointed without the necessary share qualification required by the articles (*Channel Collieries Trust Ltd v. Dover, St Margaret's and Martin Hill Light Railway Co.*). It also operates where a director becomes disqualified because 'he ceases to hold the requisite number of shares or does some act or suffers something to happen which causes him to vacate his office' (Farwell J in *British Asbestos Co. v. Boyd* [1903] 2 Ch. 439). In *British Asbestos*, the director was appointed secretary and became disqualified by virtue of the articles which prohibited the person appointed as secretary from being a director.

7.3.2 Reg. 92 of Table A

Reg. 92 of Table A goes further than s. 285 and the relevant article in the *Morris v. Kanssen* case by validating acts of a director who has vacated office. It provides:

> **92.** All acts done by a meeting of directors, or of a committee of directors, or by a person acting as a director shall, notwithstanding that it be afterwards discovered that there was a defect in the appointment of any director or that any of them were disqualified from holding office, or had vacated office, or were not entitled to vote, be as valid as if every such person had been duly appointed and was qualified and had continued to be a director and had been entitled to vote.

It should also be noted that reg. 92 also seeks to validate the acts of a director who is not entitled to vote at any meeting of directors or any committee thereof.

7.4 Number of directors less than the prescribed minimum and quorum

Under the common law, where articles prescribe a minimum number of directors and the actual number of directors falls below that minimum, the continuing directors cannot exercise any of their powers even though there are sufficient of them to form a quorum (*Re Alma Spinning Co.* (1880) 16 Ch.D. 681). This rule can give rise to serious problems because the continuing directors will be unable to exercise either their power to appoint new directors or their power to call a general meeting to allow the members to do so. Indeed, the only way to resolve the problem may be for a member or a director to make an application to the court under s. 371 for an order calling a general meeting to allow the members to appoint new directors.

In order to avoid such difficulties, it is normal for the articles to include a clause allowing the continuing directors to act notwithstanding any such vacancy in their number, e.g. reg. 90 of Table A. This type of article allows the directors to continue to act if their number falls below the minimum specified in the articles. For example, where a company's articles provided that the number of directors shall be not less than four, that two directors shall constitute a quorum and that the continuing directors may act notwithstanding any vacancy in the board, an allotment of shares by only two directors following the resignation of two out of the original four was held to be valid (*Re Scottish Petroleum Co.* (1883) 23 Ch.D. 413).

However, a similar article giving the continuing directors power to act notwithstanding any vacancy in their body was held not to operate where the minimum number of directors prescribed by the articles had never been reached (*Re Sly, Spink and Co.* [1911] 2 Ch. 430).

A question that begs to be asked is whether there is any point prescribing a minimum number of directors if the articles say that such a minimum can be ignored. The best answer that can be given is that the remaining directors may have a general duty to take steps to fill the vacancies so as to bring their number back to the prescribed minimum. In other words, they could not continue indefinitely to operate below the prescribed minimum. It may also be that if they fail to fill the vacancies, the members in general meeting may do so in default regardless of anything in the articles to the contrary (see **3.9**).

The articles of a company with four equal shareholders might require a minimum of four directors, the implication being that each of the members will be appointed as a director. The promoters or incorporators of a company may set a high figure to give the impression that the company is more respectable and that the executive directors will be monitored by an independent element on the board.

In reality, prescribing a minimum number of directors in the articles that is higher than the statutory minimum is likely to cause more problems than it is worth and company formation agents frequently modify Table A accordingly, not least to allow private companies to be established with only one director.

7.4.1   Number of directors falls below quorum

Articles that allow the directors to act notwithstanding any vacancy in their number do not operate where the number of directors is less than that required to constitute a quorum unless specific provision is made. Modern articles usually give the continuing directors limited powers to act in these circumstances. For example, reg. 90 of Table A provides:

> **90.** The continuing directors or sole continuing director may act notwithstanding any vacancy in their number, but, if the number of directors is less than the number fixed as the quorum, the continuing directors or director may act only for the purpose of filling vacancies or of calling a general meeting.

Under this type of article the continuing directors may only act for the purposes stated where their number is less than the number fixed as the quorum if the minimum number of directors prescribed by the articles has at some time been reached. Some articles go further than reg. 90 by giving the continuing directors power to act where there is a matter that must be dealt with urgently.

7.5 Acts beyond the powers of the directors

In favour of a person dealing with a company in good faith, the power of the board of directors to bind the company, or authorise others to do so, is deemed by virtue of s. 35A to be free of any limitation under the company's constitution. Limitations under the company's constitution are deemed to include limitations deriving from a resolution of the company in general meeting or a meeting of any class of shareholders or from any shareholders' agreement (s. 35A(3)). This section does not apply where a director is a party to the transaction (s. 322A) (see below).

A person will not be regarded as acting in bad faith by reason only of his or her knowing that an act is beyond the powers of the directors under the company's constitution and will be presumed to have acted in good faith unless the contrary is proved (s. 35A(2)).

A member may still bring proceedings to restrain the doing of an act that is beyond the powers of the directors provided that the act is not required to be done in fulfilment of a legal obligation arising from a previous act of the company (s. 35A(4)).

The liability incurred by the directors, or any other person, by reason of the directors' exceeding their powers is also not affected (s. 35A(5)). The company could therefore sue the directors itself. A shareholder would not normally be allowed to sue the directors on behalf of the company where the act complained of was outside the authority of the directors but within the powers of the company, unless it could be shown that the directors control the company and have profited from their actions (see **16.3**).

Although it is possible for an act by the board of directors that is not *ultra vires* the company but which is beyond the board's powers to be ratified by an ordinary resolution of the company in general meeting after the event, it is not possible to authorise such acts in advance (*Irvine v. Union Bank of Australia* (1877) 2 App. Cas. 366 and *Grant v. UK Switchback Railways Co.* (1888) 40 Ch.D. 135).

Section 35B provides that a third party is not bound to make any enquiries as to the limitations on the powers of the board, whether these limitations derive from the objects of the company as stated in its memorandum or some other source.

7.6 Acts beyond the company's capacity

The validity of an act done by a company cannot be called into question on the ground of lack of capacity by reason of anything contained in the company's memorandum (e.g. the objects clause). A member may still bring proceedings to restrain the doing of an act that is beyond the company's capacity; but no such proceedings shall lie in respect of an act to be done in fulfilment of a legal obligation arising from a previous act of the company (s. 35(2)).

It remains the duty of the directors to observe any limitations on their powers flowing from the memorandum, and action by the directors that, but for s. 35(1), would be beyond the company's capacity may only be ratified by the company by special resolution. A resolution ratifying such action shall not, however, affect any liability incurred by the directors or any other person. Relief from such liability must be agreed to separately by special resolution (s. 35(3)).

7.6.1   Where a director is party to a transaction

Both s. 35 and s. 35A are qualified with respect to transactions to which directors or their associates are a party by s. 322A. It provides that where the board of directors exceeds its powers under the company's constitution and one of the parties to the transaction with the company is a director of the company or its holding company or an associate of such a director, the transaction will be voidable at the instance of the company. This means that the company may decide whether to treat the contract as void or to enforce its contractual rights. Whether or not the transaction is avoided, the director or his or her associate will be liable to account to the company for any gain that he or she has made directly or indirectly by the transaction and to indemnify the company for any loss or damage resulting from the transaction (s. 322A(3)).

The transaction ceases to be voidable if:

- restitution of any money or other asset that was the subject of the transaction is no longer possible; or
- the company is indemnified for any loss or damage resulting from the transaction; or
- rights acquired in good faith for value and without actual notice of the directors' exceeding their powers by a person who is not a party to the transaction would be affected by the avoidance; or
- the transaction is ratified by the company in general meeting, by ordinary or special resolution or otherwise as the case may require (s. 322A(5)).

Part II

General meetings

A general meeting is a meeting of the members of the company. The term embraces both annual general meetings and extraordinary general meetings. General meetings are sometimes referred to as company meetings or shareholders' meetings.

Articles usually provide that all general meetings other than the annual general meeting shall be called extraordinary general meetings (e.g. reg. 36 of Table A). The same convention is used throughout this book, and the phrase 'general meetings' is used to refer to both annual general meetings and extraordinary general meetings.

Many of the rules and procedures applicable to general meetings also apply to class meetings, meetings of debenture holders and meetings in insolvency. Class meetings are covered separately in **Chapter 9**. However, meetings in insolvency are outside the scope of this book.

8

Types of general meeting

8.1 Summary

- The expression 'general meeting' embraces both annual general meetings and extraordinary general meetings (see **8.2**).
- All public companies and all private companies that have not passed an elective resolution to dispense with annual general meetings must hold an annual general meeting once every calendar year and not more than 15 months after the date of the last annual general meeting. Special rules apply to the first annual general meeting (see **8.3**).
- Companies usually use the annual general meeting to deal with business that must be put to a general meeting some time during the year, e.g. laying the accounts and reports before the members, reappointing auditors or any other business that requires shareholder approval (see **8.4**).
- Certain documents must be made available for inspection at the annual general meeting (see **8.5**).
- See also **Chapter 17** – Organising General Meetings.
- Extraordinary general meetings are called to deal with urgent business between annual general meetings or, in the case of a private company that has elected to dispense with annual general meetings, to deal with all items of business that cannot be disposed of in some other manner (see **8.6**).
- The rules regarding notice of extraordinary general meetings and annual general meetings are different (see **8.7**).
- The members may requisition an extraordinary general meeting (see **10.6**) and require the directors to circulate a statement in connection with any business to be proposed at any extraordinary general meeting (see **11.13**).

8.2 General meetings

The expression 'general meeting' embraces both annual general meetings and extraordinary general meetings. Accordingly, a matter that requires the approval of the members in general meeting can be dealt with either at an annual general meeting (AGM) or an extraordinary general meeting (EGM). Articles usually specify that all general meetings other than the AGM shall be called EGMs. Some older articles refer to the AGM as the ordinary meeting and may use different terminology for EGMs.

EGMs must be distinguished from class meetings which are meetings of a specific class of members, usually held to approve a variation of those members' rights (see **Chapter 9**).

8.3   Annual general meetings

For many years all companies were required to hold an AGM each year. However, the Act was amended in 1989 to allow private companies to dispense with holding AGMs and some of the associated formalities, such as the laying of the report and accounts and the annual appointment of auditors. In order to take advantage of these dispensations, a private company must pass a unanimous resolution of all its members (see further **Chapter 25**).

Every public limited company must hold an AGM in each calendar year. Every private company must also do so unless it has elected to dispense with AGMs by passing an elective resolution to that effect. A calendar year starts on 1 January and ends on 31 December and is not calculated by reference either to the date of formation or to the accounting reference date.

Not more than 15 months should elapse between the date of one AGM and the next (s. 366(3)). A month means a calendar month, i.e. the period expiring on the corresponding day in the following month. If there is no corresponding day in that month, the period expires at the end of that month, e.g. 15 months after 31 March is 30 June in the following year.

If a company fails to comply with any of the above requirements, its officers (i.e. its directors and secretary) and the company itself are liable to a fine of up to £5,000. If a company fails to hold a meeting in a particular calendar year and more than 15 months has elapsed since the last AGM, two separate offences are committed, each of which may result in a separate fine.

A newly registered company must hold its first AGM within 18 months of incorporation. As long as it complies with this requirement, it need not hold an AGM in its year of incorporation or the following year, e.g. a company formed on 20 July 2001 would not need to hold its first AGM until 19 January 2003 (i.e. it need not hold one in 2001 or 2002).

The above requirements are not satisfied by holding an EGM during the period in question, even if the business at that EGM is the same as that which would normally be dealt with at the AGM. This is because s. 366 requires the notice that must be sent to members before the AGM to specify that the meeting will be held as the AGM.

8.3.1 Choosing a date for the AGM

Before choosing a date for the AGM, it is necessary to calculate the last date on which the meeting must be held. Having done this, it is possible to select the preferred date within the remaining period.

It is normal to aim for a date that allows the report and accounts to be laid before the meeting and it may be advisable to delay the meeting in order to do so (if that is possible in view of the above requirements). Private companies must lay their accounts before the members in general meeting at least ten months after the year end and public companies must do so within seven months (s. 244). Although it is sensible to hold the AGM on a date within that period, it should be borne in mind that the date chosen may also affect the timing of future meetings.

For example, a private company with a 31 March year end has until 31 January in the following year (i.e. ten months) to lay and deliver its report and accounts. If the last AGM was held in December the previous year, the last available date would be 31 December in the current year because of the requirement that a meeting must be held at least once every calendar year. If it is not possible to finalise the accounts in time to lay them at this meeting, an EGM will also need to be held in January. However, if the last AGM was held on, say, 20 January in the current year, the next meeting could be held as late as 20 June in the following year (in accordance with the 15-month rule). It might be preferable in these circumstances to opt for a date on or before 31 January to enable the report and accounts to be laid at the meeting.

The existence of other companies within the group with the same or similar accounting reference periods may influence the choice of date. It may be desirable to hold the AGMs of all subsidiary companies on the same day, particularly if the membership of each company is similar. The AGM cycle for such subsidiaries could be brought forward to coincide with that of the parent, although consideration should be given to dispensing with the requirement to lay the accounts and hold AGMs for wholly owned subsidiaries (see **Chapter 25**).

Listed companies will often seek to avoid holding their AGM on the same date as other companies in the same sector. Other factors that may determine the date chosen might include the availability of the chairman and other directors, the availability of a suitable venue, and the availability of the auditors, registrars and other advisers. In order to ensure that all these factors can be coordinated, it may be necessary to begin planning the AGM a long way in advance. Many listed companies book the venue of the AGM up to two years in advance.

Finally, it should not be forgotten that 21 clear days' notice of the meeting must be given unless the consent of all the members

Table 8.1 Dates by which accounts must be laid and filed with the Registrar

Year end	31 March		31 July		30 September		31 December	
	Plc	Ltd	Plc	Ltd	Plc	Ltd	Plc	Ltd
Accounts laid by	31 Oct	31 Jan	28/29 Feb	31 May	30 Apr	30 July	31 July	31 Oct

to shorter notice can be obtained (see further **11.11**). If the accounts that are to be laid at the meeting are sent out less than 21 days before the meeting, separate consent will also be required (s. 238(4)) (see **23.2**).

8.3.2 Coordinating AGM date following a change of accounting reference date (ARD)

Problems can arise with respect to the date of the AGM when a company changes its ARD. For example, following a change in its ARD (year end), a company that routinely holds its AGM in January might wish to move it to a date in August so that it can continue to lay its report and accounts at the AGM. It would not be possible to postpone the AGM until August without breaching the 15-month rule. The simple solution might seem to be to hold an AGM in both January and August in the relevant year. However, most commentators agree that s. 366 does not allow more than one AGM to be held in any one year. If this interpretation is correct (and it has never been tested in the courts), then the second AGM would not be valid as an AGM. It would therefore follow that the AGM held in August of the following year would be in breach of the 15-month rule. If the second AGM in the year was not an AGM, there could be problems with any retirement by rotation provisions.

Although it might seem to be unfair to be penalised for over-compliance, the safest course of action in these circumstances is probably to stagger the change, e.g. in the first year to hold the AGM in April and in the second to hold it in July, only moving to August in the third year. This should not pose insuperable problems in any of those years as long as the accounts can be finalised earlier than normal during the transition period. Alternatively, the accounts could be laid at an EGM until such time as the AGM and accounts timings coincide.

8.4 Purpose and business of the AGM

The purpose of the AGM is as follows:

- to enable members to question the directors face to face and thereby hold them accountable for their management of the company;
- to enable members to put forward resolutions for consideration by the company without having to requisition a meeting – the conditions that a member must satisfy to propose a resolution at the AGM (see **11.13**) are less onerous than those for requisitioning an EGM to propose such a resolution (see **10.6**);
- to enable members to vote on resolutions that the directors are obliged under the articles or the Act to put to the members in general meeting.

The Companies Act does not specify the business of the AGM. However, unless an elective resolution is in force, all companies must at some stage do the following:

- lay the report and accounts before the members at a general meeting (s. 241) (see **23.2**);
- appoint or reappoint auditors at that meeting (s. 385(2)) (see **23.3**); and
- fix the auditors' remuneration (s. 390A) (see **23.6**).

Although these matters need not be dealt with at the AGM, it is plainly sensible to do so in order to avoid having to hold an EGM and an AGM.

It is also common to deal with the following matters at the AGM:

- appointment of directors (see **23.8**);
- reappointment of directors retiring by rotation (see **23.10**);
- approval of dividend recommended by the board (see **23.7**);
- renewal of directors' authority to allot shares in accordance with s. 80 (if required);
- special resolution to disapply pre-emption rights in accordance with s. 95 (if required);
- special resolutions to amend memorandum or articles of association (if required);
- other business required by the articles to be conducted at the AGM;
- any other business that needs shareholder approval and which it is convenient to deal with at the time; and
- resolutions validly proposed by the members (see **11.13**).

8.4.1   No business to be transacted

If the accounts are not ready to be laid at the AGM, the only business to be conducted could be the reappointment of directors retiring by rotation in accordance with the articles of association. If the articles make no such provision or none of the directors is subject to retirement by rotation, there may be no business to be transacted at the AGM. Nevertheless, a meeting must still be held and notice of the meeting must be sent to members (indicating that no business is to be proposed). It may be difficult to obtain a quorum for such a meeting in which case it will be necessary to comply with the articles governing adjournment in these circumstances (see **21.4**). Some members may, however, still attend the meeting to seek an explanation as to why the accounts are not ready.

8.5   Documents to be displayed at the AGM

Companies are required to maintain a register of directors' interests in shares or debentures of the company (s. 325). The register must be made available at the AGM for inspection by any person attending the meeting (para. 29 of Schedule 13 of the Companies Act 1985).

Listed companies must make copies of directors' service contracts available for inspection by any person at the place of the AGM for at least 15 minutes prior to and during the meeting (Listing Rules, para. 16.9). The Listing Rules also make detailed provision as to the information that must be included or attached to the service contracts made available for inspection at the meeting (Listing Rules, paras 16.10 and 16.11). The definition of 'directors' service contracts' used in the Listing Rules is wider than the one in the Act (see the Definitions section of the Listing Rules).

The Listing Rules used to require the notice convening the AGM to contain a note informing members as to when and where directors' service contracts would be made available for inspection. This requirement was deleted in June 1996.

8.6   Extraordinary general meetings

For the purposes of this book and most articles, the phrase 'extraordinary general meeting' is used to describe any meeting of the shareholders other than an annual general meeting.

It may be necessary throughout the year to call an EGM of the company to deal with business that cannot be left until the next AGM or, in the case of a private company, be dealt with by written resolution. For example, a private company that has elected to dispense with holding AGMs under the elective regime (see **Chapter 25**) may need to call an EGM to deal with business that needs shareholder approval if it is not able to dispose of it by written resolution.

It is not necessary to lay the accounts, reappoint auditors or fix their remuneration at the AGM. The Act simply requires accounts to be laid at a general meeting and for the auditors to be reappointed at that meeting. In other words, this can be done at an EGM.

The members may requisition an EGM (see **10.6**) and require the directors to circulate a statement in connection with any business to be proposed at any EGM (see **11.13**).

8.7 Procedures for EGMs

Subject to the following, the rules governing proceedings at AGMs and EGMs are exactly the same.

8.7.1 Notice

The Act requires 14 days' notice to be given to the members of any EGM other than one called for the passing of a special resolution, in which case 21 days' notice is required (s. 369). It would also be necessary to give 21 days' notice of the intention to propose an ordinary resolution requiring special notice and any elective resolution (see **11.12** and **Precedent 11.5B**).

It is usual for the notice to specify the meeting as an EGM, although it is sufficient for it to refer to it as a 'meeting' or a 'general meeting' of the company.

8.7.2 Consent to short notice

An EGM may be held with shorter notice than the statutory minimum, provided that the company obtains the consent of a majority in number of the members entitled to vote at the meeting holding between them not less than 95% in nominal value of the shares giving the right to vote (see **11.11**). Consent would also have to be obtained from the same proportion of members to propose a special resolution at such a meeting.

8.7.3 Members' resolutions

The members cannot force the directors to include resolutions on the agenda of an EGM called by the directors. They may only do this in respect of AGMs (see **11.13**). In order to propose resolutions at an EGM, the members must requisition the meeting themselves (see **10.6**).

8.7.4 Resolutions

Not all resolutions passed at EGMs must be passed as extraordinary resolutions. The type of resolution required to approve an item of business put to an EGM depends in the usual manner on the Act and the company's articles of association (see **Chapter 12**).

9

Class meetings

9.1 Summary

- Not all members of a company will necessarily have the same rights. Where this is the case, the company has different classes of members. The rights of each class of members will be specified in the memorandum or articles of association. This may occur in a company with a share capital (see **9.2**) and a company limited by guarantee (see **9.3**).
- Class meetings are meetings of the holders of a specific class of shares or of a specific class of members. A class meeting may be required where a company has more than one class of shares and proposes to vary the rights attached to a particular class or where the articles provide that a transaction requires the separate consent of a meeting of the holders of a certain class of shares.
- Special procedures must be followed to vary the rights attached to different classes of shares. These procedures differ according to the manner in which those rights are conferred and whether the memorandum or articles make specific provision for variation of those rights (see **9.4**).

9.2 Classes of shares

The memorandum or, more usually, the articles, of a company with a share capital will normally provide that it may divide its share capital into shares of more than one class (e.g. reg. 2 of Table A). This means that the company can issue shares that give their holders different rights from the holders of other shares. Shares that give their holders the same rights are deemed to be shares of the same class. Holders of a different class of shares will usually have different rights regarding dividends, voting at general meetings, participation in capital and surplus assets on winding up, or some other matter.

Different classes of shares are usually given different designations (e.g. 'A' shares, 'B' shares, preference shares, etc.) in order to distinguish them from other shares with different rights.

However, this will not always be the case and shareholders holding shares of the same name may have different rights and constitute a separate class. This may arise as a result of a separate shareholder agreement under which the shareholders agree to modify the rights of the respective shareholders.

The rights attached to shares are usually specified in the memorandum or articles. If they are contained in the memorandum, it is more difficult to vary them. It is therefore more common for them to be set out in the articles. Articles sometimes allow the directors to determine the rights attached to shares, in which case the rights will be set out in the terms of issue approved by the board.

The holders of all classes of shares are members of the company. They are therefore entitled to receive notice of general meetings of the company and to attend and vote at such meetings unless those rights are withdrawn or restricted.

The most commonly found classes of shares are as follows:

- *Ordinary shares* The ordinary shares are the basic shares of the company which carry the right to vote at general meetings, to receive dividends and to participate in any surplus when the company is wound up. Where a company has only one class of shares, these will be the ordinary shares.
- *Preference shares* Preference shares are shares that carry preferential dividend rights, usually a fixed percentage of their nominal value, which must be paid out of profits available for distribution before dividends are paid to the ordinary shareholders. These rights are often cumulative, which means that any dividends payable to the preference shareholders that are in arrears must be paid before the ordinary shareholders are paid a dividend. The articles usually give preference shareholders the right to vote at general meetings if their dividends are more than six months in arrears, but not otherwise. If the company is wound up, preference shareholders will usually have the right to have their capital returned before the ordinary shareholders but are not usually entitled to share in any surplus.
- *'A' and 'B' shares* A company may have more than one class of ordinary shares. This is common in joint venture companies where each partner will hold a separate class of shares which give them the right to appoint one or more directors but which otherwise have the same rights. Having two categories of ordinary shares may also be used to give a minority shareholder (often the founder) certain entrenched rights, e.g. by giving him or her enhanced voting rights on any resolution to remove him or her as a director (see *Bushell v. Faith* [1970] AC 1099 which is discussed at **23.11.1**).
- *Non-voting shares* These are usually issued to ensure that the founder shareholders retain control. They usually have the same rights as the ordinary shareholders to receive dividends, etc. However, they do not have the right to vote at general meetings.

Holders of non-voting shares will, however, be entitled to vote at any meeting of the non-voting shareholders held to approve a variation of their rights, e.g. to authorise the terms of their conversion into voting shares.

9.3 Classes of members in guarantee companies

A company limited by guarantee may have different classes of members. Typically, the company's articles will allow the board of directors to establish different classes with different rights. An example might be a sports club that has full members, weekend members and junior members. Section 125 does not apply to the variation of these rights. In practice, such matters are normally left to the board or the members as a whole. If separate approval of a class of members is required for any matter, the articles should specify how those meetings should be conducted. In the absence of any such provision, it is arguable that common law principles will apply.

9.4 Variation of class rights of shareholders

The rights of different classes of shares may only be varied in accordance with the relevant provisions of the memorandum or articles and s. 125 of the Act which provides safeguards to ensure that the interests of one class of shareholders are not prejudiced by another. The section applies to any variation of the rights attached to any class of shares in a company. It does not apply to the variation of the rights of different classes of members of a company limited by guarantee.

The procedures that must be followed to vary class rights under s. 125 differ according to the manner in which those rights are conferred and the existence in the memorandum or articles of provision for variation. Any alteration of a provision contained in a company's articles for the variation of the rights attached to a class of shares, or the insertion of any such provision into the articles, is itself to be treated as a variation of those rights (s. 125(7)). For the purposes of s. 125 and any provision for the variation of class rights contained in a company's memorandum or articles, references to the variation of those rights are to be read as including references to their abrogation (i.e. cancellation) (s. 125(8)).

9.4.1 Rights not set out in memorandum and no provision in articles regarding variation

Where the rights are attached to a class of shares otherwise than by the company's memorandum, and the company's articles do not contain provision with respect to the variation of the rights, s. 125(2) provides that those rights may be varied if, but only if:

(a)   the holders of three-quarters in nominal value of the issued shares
      of that class consent in writing to the variation; or

(b)   an extraordinary resolution passed at a separate general meeting
      of the holders of that class sanctions the variation;

and any requirement (howsoever expressed) in relation to the
variation of those rights is complied with to the extent that it is
not comprised in paragraphs (a) and (b) above.

The holders of not less in aggregate than 15% of the issued
shares of the class in question (being persons who did not vote in
favour of the variation) may apply to the court to have a variation
passed under s. 125(2) cancelled, and if such application is made,
the variation has no effect unless or until it is confirmed by the
court (s. 127).

9.4.2   Provision for variation made in the memorandum or articles but variation concerns s. 80 authority or reduction in capital

Where the memorandum or articles contain provision for the
variation of rights attached to a class of shares and the variation
of those rights is connected with the giving, variation, revocation
or renewal of an authority for allotment under s. 80 or with a
reduction of the company's share capital under s. 135, s. 125(3)
provides that those rights shall not be varied unless:

(a)   the holders of three-quarters in nominal value of the issued shares
      of that class consent in writing to the variation; or

(b)   an extraordinary resolution passed at a separate general meeting
      of the holders of that class sanctions the variation;

and any requirement of the memorandum or articles in relation to
the variation of rights of that class is complied with to the extent
that it is not comprised in that condition.

9.4.3   Provision for variation made in the memorandum or articles and variation concerns other matters

Where the variation is not connected with the authority of the
directors to allot shares under s. 80 or a reduction in capital in
accordance with s. 135 and:

(a)   the rights are attached to a class of shares in the company by the
      memorandum and the articles contain provision with respect to
      their variation which had been included in the articles at the time
      of the company's original incorporation; or

(b)   the rights are attached to a class of shares by some other means and
      the articles provide for their variation (whenever first so included),

s. 125(4) provides that those rights may only be varied in
accordance with that provision of the articles.

The holders of not less in aggregate than 15% of the issued shares of the class in question (being persons who did not consent to or vote in favour of the variation) may apply to the court to have the variation cancelled where the memorandum or articles authorise variation of class rights subject to the consent of a specified proportion of the holders or by a resolution at a meeting of that class, and if such application is made, the variation has no effect unless or until it is confirmed by the court (s. 127).

9.4.4 Rights attached by memorandum and no provision for variation in memorandum or articles

Where the rights are attached to a class of shares by the memorandum, and the memorandum and articles do not contain provision with respect to the variation of those rights, s. 125(5) provides that those rights may only be varied if all the members of the company agree to the variation.

9.4.5 Application of provisions on general meetings

Section 125(6) provides that the following provisions shall apply, so far as they are applicable and with certain specified modifications, in relation to any class meeting held to consider a variation of the rights attached to that class of shares:

- s. 369 (length of notice for calling company meetings);
- s. 370 (general provisions as to meetings and votes);
- ss. 376 and 377 (circulation of members' resolutions); and
- the provisions of the company's articles relating to general meetings.

The modifications specified in s. 125(6) are that:

- the quorum at a class meeting held to consider a variation of rights shall be two persons holding or representing by proxy at least one-third in nominal value of the issued shares of the class in question;
- at an adjournment of such a meeting the quorum shall be one person holding shares of the class in question or his or her proxy; and
- any holder of shares of the class in question present in person or by proxy may demand a poll.

The provisions of s. 125(6) with regard to the quorum can give rise to problems where the articles contain some other provision, e.g. where the articles provide for a quorum of ten at class meetings but make no provision as to the percentage of nominal value those members must hold. Read in isolation, the requirements of s. 125(6) on the quorum appear very stark. They are not expressed as being subject to the articles or as a minimum standard. This would seem to indicate that the Act takes precedence over anything in the articles where a variation of rights is concerned, and most modern articles follow precisely the same formula as the Act. However, some modern articles of listed companies provide that the quorum for a variation of rights shall be one or more persons, instead of two, representing at least one-third by nominal value. In order to justify this, one has to assume that the words in s. 125(6) on the quorum modify the numerical requirements in s. 370 but not the fact that s. 370 only applies in the absence of some other provision in the articles – in other words that the provisions of s. 125(6) on the quorum only apply in the absence of some other provision in the articles. This is a fairly risky assumption to make. There can, however, be a degree of risk in making the opposite assumption where the articles make more onerous provision than the Act. The safest course in all circumstances is to attempt to comply with the more onerous requirement in respect of the number of members and the most onerous requirement in respect of percentage of nominal value. If this proves to be impossible, the default provisions for adjourned meetings in s. 125(6) may apply, although yet again there can be conflicts between the articles and the statutory provisions.

It has been held in relation to class meetings that a single person may constitute a meeting where that person holds all the issued shares of a particular class (*East v. Bennett Bro. Ltd* [1911] 1 Ch. 163).

9.4.6 Notice

Section 369 (which is applied by s. 125(6) in relation to meetings for the variation of class rights) requires a company to give at least 14 days' notice of any meeting to the holders of that class of shares (see **Precedent 11.5B**) or, in the case of an unlimited company, at least seven days' notice.

By virtue of s. 369(3) a majority in number of the holders of a class of shares together holding not less than 95% in nominal value of the shares giving a right to attend and vote at the meeting may consent to shorter notice.

As a resolution authorising a variation of rights must be passed as an extraordinary resolution, there are no additional notice requirements in connection with the passing of such a resolution.

Section 370 (also applied by s. 125) provides by implication that notice of a class meeting shall be served on every holder of shares of that class in the manner in which notices are required to be served under Table A unless the articles make some other provision. Most articles do make other provision regarding the service of notices and will often restrict the right to receive notice (e.g. to the first named joint holder only). However, it is arguable that, unless the articles specify that these provisions also apply to class meetings, the provisions of Table A will apply in this regard. The counter-argument to this is that s. 125(6) also provides that the provisions of the articles on general meetings shall also apply with the necessary modifications to class meetings held to consider a variation of rights. In the absence of specific provision in the articles, however, it is difficult to say which of these statutory provisions takes precedence.

9.4.7   Right to call a meeting

Section 370(3) provides that two or more members holding not less than one-tenth of the issued share capital may call a meeting. With the necessary modification, this means that, unless the articles provide otherwise, two or more holders of a class of shares holding not less than one-tenth of the issued share capital of that class may call a meeting of that class of shares to consider a proposal for the variation of rights.

9.4.8   Appointment of chairman

Section 370(5) provides that any member elected by the members present at a meeting may be chairman. Making the necessary modifications this means that, unless the articles provide otherwise, the holders of a class of shares present at a meeting of that class of shares may elect the chairman of that meeting. In fact articles often provide that the chairman of the board of directors or a director nominated by the board shall act as the chairman of any meeting (e.g. reg. 42 of Table A); and the class members will normally only be able to elect the chairman in default of these provisions.

9.4.9   Voting

Section 370(6) provides that in the case of a company having a share capital, every member has one vote in respect of each share or each £10 of stock held by him or her. This provision will apply to class meetings, subject to any provisions in the articles. For example, articles usually contain provisions restricting the right to vote in certain circumstances (see **15.4**).

9.4.10   Attendance

In *Carruth v. Imperial Chemical Industries Ltd* [1937] AC 707, the directors convened an extraordinary general meeting of the company and two class meetings to approve a reduction of capital. The meetings were held on the same day and at the same venue. As one meeting finished, the next meeting was started and each meeting was attended by the holders of the other classes of shares. The resolution passed at one class meeting was challenged by a member of that class on the basis that people who were not members of that class were present at the meeting. The resolution was held to be valid and Lord Russell said:

> There are many matters relating to the conduct of a meeting which lie entirely in the hands of those persons who are present and constitute the meeting. Thus it rests with the meeting to decide whether notices, resolutions, minutes, accounts, and such like shall be read to the meeting or be taken as read; whether representatives of the Press, or any other persons not qualified to be summoned to the meeting, shall be permitted to be present, or if present, shall be permitted to remain; whether and when discussion shall be terminated and a vote taken; whether the meeting shall be adjourned. In all these matters, and they are only instances, the meeting decides, and if necessary a vote must be taken to ascertain the wishes of the majority. If no objection is taken by any constituent of the meeting, the meeting must be taken to be assenting to the course adopted.

9.5 Proceedings at other class meetings

It is possible, though unusual, for articles to require meetings of a class of members to be held to consider matters that do not constitute a variation of rights. In such circumstances, and provided that the meeting will not be called upon to consider a proposal for the variation of rights, s. 125 does not apply. Although articles sometimes refer to class meetings as a 'general meeting of that class', it is doubtful whether a meeting of a class of members is a 'general meeting'. Accordingly, unless the articles make specific provision as to the proceedings at these 'class meetings', issues such as the quorum may need to be determined according to the common law. It is therefore preferable to make specific provision in the articles where such meetings may be required.

10

Calling general meetings

10.1 Summary

- Unless the time and place at which meetings are to be held each year is fixed, someone must be given the power to call meetings, i.e. to direct that a meeting will be held at a certain time and place to consider certain business.
- A general meeting must be convened (i.e. called) by a person or body with appropriate authority otherwise the meeting and any business transacted at it will be invalid. The articles usually give the board power to convene general meetings (see **10.2**).
- However, they usually provide alternative procedures for situations where the board of directors is unable or unwilling to exercise its powers (see **10.3**).
- The Secretary of State (see **10.4**) and the court (see **10.5**) also have powers under the Act to direct that general meetings be held.
- Members who are able to satisfy certain requirements may require the directors to convene an extraordinary general meeting to consider business proposed by them (see **10.6**).
- Any member of a private company that has dispensed with the holding of AGMs may require the directors to convene an AGM (see **25.3**).

10.2 Meetings convened by the board of directors

Articles usually give the board of directors power to convene general meetings (e.g. reg. 37 of Table A). The directors may exercise such powers whenever they think it appropriate in the interests of the company to do so (*Pergamon Press v. Maxwell* [1970] 1 WLR 1167).

Where the articles state that the directors may call general meetings, they must exercise that power collectively at a duly convened and constituted meeting of the board (*Browne v. La Trinidad* (1887) 37 Ch.D. 1), although a written resolution of the directors (e.g. under reg. 93 of Table A) will have equivalent effect. This is probably the case, even though the articles provide that the directors may delegate 'any of their powers' to a committee of directors or to individual executive directors. This is because the power to convene general meetings is a special power and not subject to the standard article on delegation. Modern articles attempt to get round this by stating that the power to delegate shall be effective in relation to the powers, duties and discretions of the directors generally whether or not express reference is made in the articles to powers, duties or discretions being exercised by the directors. Care should therefore be taken to ensure that the power to delegate is applicable and where there is any uncertainty, it is probably safest to assume that it is not.

The directors' resolution should state the date, time and place of the meeting and its purpose (see **Precedent 10.2A** and **Precedent 10.2B**). A draft copy of the notice together with any additional documents that will accompany it should also be approved. The board should authorise someone (usually the secretary) to sign and issue the notice to all those entitled to receive it.

A further board meeting would be needed to approve the addition of any further item of business or to amend the substance of the notice.

10.2.1   Ratification of invalid notice

Notice of a general meeting given by any person without the sanction of the directors or other proper authority will be invalid (*Re Haycroft Gold Reduction Co.* [1900] 2 Ch. 230). This is the case even though it was issued by the secretary in response to a valid requisition by the members under s. 368 (*Re State of Wyoming Syndicate* [1901] 2 Ch. 431). However, a meeting called without proper authority will be valid if it is ratified before the meeting by the body with authority to call the meeting. Thus, a notice issued by a director or the company secretary without the authority of the board will be valid if it is subsequently ratified prior to the general meeting by the directors at a properly convened and constituted meeting of the board (*Hooper v. Kerr Stuart & Co.* (1900) 83 LT 729).

A general meeting convened by an irregularly constituted board (e.g. at an inquorate meeting) will be invalid. However, a defect in the appointment of any of the directors may be cured by an article in the form of reg. 92 of Table A which provides that all acts done by any meeting of directors, a committee of directors or by any person acting as a director, notwithstanding that it be afterwards discovered that there was some defect in the appointment of any such director or that they or any of them were disqualified, had vacated office, or were otherwise not entitled to vote, be valid as if every person had been duly appointed, was qualified to be a director and entitled to vote (*Transport Ltd v. Schomberg* (1905) 21 TLR 305) (see further **7.3**).

10.2.2 Practical procedures for convening AGMs

In practice, a proof of the AGM notice is usually tabled at the board meeting held to approve the report and accounts and its contents are used to frame the appropriate board resolution convening the meeting. The board resolution should specify the date, time and place and the business to be transacted. The directors should also authorise the secretary to sign the notice and send copies to all persons entitled to receive it (i.e. the members and the auditors and anyone else specified in the articles) (see **Precedent 10.2B**).

As soon as the proof print of the report and accounts has been approved by the directors, the balance sheet, directors' report and auditors' report should be signed and dated by the appropriate people. A further copy should be prepared with the names of the signatories and the dates on which they signed inserted at the appropriate points. This copy can then be printed together with final copies of the notice and, if necessary, any circular or proxy cards.

The notice usually goes out under the name of the secretary who signs 'by order of the board'. It is usually dated for the day on which it is sent out and this date can be included in the proofs sent to the printers even though the notice may not yet have been physically signed. It is, however, also common for the notice to be signed and dated on the day it is approved by the board. Strictly speaking, of course, the date on the notice should be the date on which it was actually signed. Accordingly, if it is to show the date on which the notice is to be sent out, it should also be signed on that date.

If accounts are to be laid at the AGM, copies of the report and accounts must be sent to members not less than 21 days before the meeting. As members must be given 21 clear days' notice of the AGM it is sensible to send both together. The notice of the meeting can be incorporated in the document containing the annual report and accounts.

10.3 Problems convening meetings

10.3.1 Number of directors below quorum

Articles usually provide that where the number of directors falls below the number fixed as the quorum, the continuing directors may act for the purposes of calling a general meeting (e.g. reg. 90 of Table A). Reg. 90 also allows the continuing directors to exercise their powers under reg. 79 to appoint a director either to fill a casual vacancy or as an additional director. This type of article can only be invoked where the remaining directors would be unable to fulfil the quorum requirements even if they all attended a board meeting.

10.3.2   Insufficient directors in UK

Most articles include a provision similar to reg. 37 of Table A which provides that any director or any member(s) may call a general meeting if there are insufficient directors in the UK to do so. Reg. 37 is of no assistance if there are sufficient directors in the UK even though they are not capable of acting to form a quorum for these purposes, e.g. because of illness. The wording of Table A can be modified as follows to cover such circumstances:

> If at any time there are not within the United Kingdom sufficient Directors *capable of acting to form a quorum,* any Director or any two members of the Company may convene an Extraordinary General Meeting in the same manner as nearly as possible as that in which meetings may be convened by the Board.

Without this type of modification, an application may need to be made to the court under s. 371 or to the Secretary of State under s. 367 (see below).

10.3.3   Director refuses to attend board meetings

In small companies, it is quite common for a director who is in the minority to attempt to frustrate the will of the majority by refusing to attend board meetings. If that director's presence is necessary in order to form a quorum, this tactic will make it impossible for the other directors to pass resolutions. Although it may not be the intention of the dissident director(s) to prevent the calling of a general meeting, this is often one of the side effects of such tactics. If they are not opposed to calling a meeting, and assuming the articles allow this, it might be possible to call the meeting by written resolution (see further **6.2**). A more dubious method might be to call a board meeting while the director(s) who refuse to attend are outside the UK and to call the general meeting under reg. 37 of Table A or its equivalent. Reasonable notice of such a board meeting would still need to be given and notice would need to be sent to the directors' usual address. The members could requisition a general meeting under s. 368 and, if the directors do not convene a meeting within 21 days, convene a meeting themselves in accordance with s. 368(4) (see **10.6**). If all else fails, an application may need to be made to the court under s. 371 or, in respect of an AGM in default, to the Secretary of State under s. 367 (see below).

10.3.4 Directors refuse to call meeting

Where the directors refuse to call a general meeting, the members can requisition one under s. 368 and convene it themselves if the directors fail to do so within 21 days. Any member of the company may request the Secretary of State to call or direct the calling of an AGM in default. In addition any director or member may apply to the court for an order in respect of a general meeting (see below).

10.4 Power of Secretary of State to call AGM in default

Where a company is in default of the requirements of s. 366 for holding an AGM, any member may apply to the Secretary of State for an order calling or directing the calling of a general meeting (s. 367).

In making such an order, the Secretary of State may give such ancillary or consequential directions as he or she thinks fit. These directions may modify or supplement the company's articles in relation to the calling, holding and conduct of meetings and may include a direction that one member present in person or by proxy be a quorum for that meeting.

A meeting called under s. 367 will, subject to any direction to the contrary by the Secretary of State, be deemed to be an AGM of the company. If, as will often be the case, an AGM called on the direction of the Secretary of State is not held in the year in which it became due, it will not be treated as the AGM of the year in which it is held unless at that meeting the company resolves by ordinary resolution that it be so treated (s. 367(4)). Although the wording of this section is obscure, it is usually taken to mean that the company may resolve that it be treated as the AGM of the year in which it was held as well as the AGM for the year in which it is overdue. As prior notice of any such resolution would be required, this is unlikely to be a common occurrence bearing in mind the circumstances. A copy of any such resolution must be submitted to the Registrar of Companies within 15 days (s. 367(5)).

10.5 Powers of the court to call a general meeting

If for any reason it is impracticable to call a general meeting, or to conduct the meeting in the manner prescribed by the company's articles or the Act, the court may order a meeting of the company to be called, held and conducted in any manner it thinks fit (s. 371(1)). The court may make such an order on the application of any member who would be entitled to vote at the meeting or any director. In doing so, the court may give such ancillary or consequential directions as it thinks fit, which may include a direction that one member present in person or by proxy be deemed to constitute a meeting (s. 371(2)). Any meeting called, held and conducted in accordance with an order of the court made under s. 371 is deemed for all purposes to be a meeting of the company duly called, held and conducted (s. 371(3)).

These powers have been exercised where it was impracticable to hold a meeting with a quorum in accordance with the articles (*Re Edinburgh Workmen's Houses Improvement Co. Ltd* 1934 SLT 513) and where the directors, being minority shareholders, failed to call a general meeting (including an AGM) thus preventing the majority shareholder from exercising his right to remove them (*Re El Sombrero Ltd* [1958] Ch. 900 and *Re H.R. Paul & Son Ltd* (1973) 118 SJ 166). The court has also used these powers to direct that a vote be taken by postal ballot because previous general meetings had been disrupted by protesters in such a violent manner that it was likely that most ordinary members would not attend any future meetings (*Re British Union for the Abolition of Vivisection* [1995] 2 BCLC 1).

The court may also convene a meeting under s. 425 where a compromise or arrangement is proposed between the company and its creditors.

10.6 Members' requisition

A member or members holding one-tenth of the company's paid-up capital carrying the right to vote may require (requisition) the directors to convene an extraordinary general meeting at the company's expense. If the directors fail to call a meeting, the requisitionists may do so themselves and recover their expenses from the company (s. 368). Members holding a much smaller proportion of the voting rights can also force the directors to include a resolution on the agenda of the AGM (s. 376). However, the company can require the requisitionists to pay its expenses in giving effect to a requisition made under s. 376. It may therefore be preferable from the requisitionists' point of view to requisition an EGM under s. 368 if they can muster the necessary support.

10.6.1 Conditions for demand

The directors are required by s. 368 to convene an EGM of the company on receipt of a demand made:

- in the case of a company limited by shares, by members holding at the date of deposit of the requisition not less than one-tenth of the paid-up capital of the company which at that date carries the right to vote at general meetings of the company; or
- in the case of a company not having a share capital (e.g. a company limited by guarantee), the demand must be made by members representing not less than one-tenth of the total voting rights of all members who have at the date of deposit of the requisition a right to vote at general meetings.

In calculating whether a valid demand has been made by members of a company limited by shares, the critical factor is the amount of paid-up capital held by the members rather than the number of votes attached to those shares. Where all the shares are of equal value and carry the same number of votes, this calculation will be simple. However, care should be taken to ensure that shares that confer the right to vote in limited circumstances are included in the calculation if those circumstances operate at the time of the deposit. For example, ABC Ltd has a share capital of 5,000 £1 ordinary shares and 2,000 £1 preference shares. The preference shareholders only have a right to vote if their dividends are in arrears. As long as the preference dividends are not in arrears, any ordinary shareholder(s) holding 500 or more shares can requisition a meeting. If the dividends are in arrears, a member(s) holding 700 or more shares (either ordinary shares, preference shares or a combination of the two) would be needed.

It should be noted that articles commonly remove the right to vote when any calls on a share are unpaid (e.g. reg. 57 of Table A). It has also been held that the right to requisition a meeting requires paid-up share capital (*Re Bradford Investments plc* [1990] BCC 740).

Articles cannot impose more stringent conditions than those established under s. 368. They may, however, provide for a less stringent regime.

10.6.2   Form of requisition

The requisition must be signed by the requisitionists and deposited at the registered office of the company (see **Precedent 10.6A**). In the case of joint holders, the requisition must be signed by each of them (*Patent Wood Keg Syndicate v. Pearse* [1906] WN 164). The requisition may consist of several documents in like form each signed by one or more requisitionists (s. 368(3)). This allows a master document to be prepared and for copies to be circulated to members for signature.

The requisition must state the objects of the meeting and the board cannot refuse to act on the requisition unless the objects cannot legally be carried into effect (*Isle of Wight Railway Co. v. Tahourdin* (1883) 25 Ch.D. 320). The object is very similar to the general nature of the business (see **13.5**). It does not need to be stated as a specific resolution although the requisitionists may also need to submit resolutions in order to do the things stated as their object in the requisition.

In *Rose v. McGivern* [1998] 2 BCLC 593, the board of directors of the Royal Automobile Club refused to give effect to a requisition supported by more than one-tenth of the members on three grounds:

1.   The requisitionists had induced members to add their names to the requisition by giving misleading information in a letter.

2. The proposals in the requisition were invalid and would, if passed as resolutions, be invalid.

3. Even if other resolutions could be put to any meeting called pursuant to the requisition, they would be ineffective.

As the judge ruled that the requisitionists' letter was not misleading to any material degree he was not called upon to decide whether this could be a valid ground for refusing to call a requisitioned meeting. The company had argued that cases relating to misleading notices should also be applied in these circumstances. However, the judge noted that the circumstances of this case were different from those cited by the RAC and that different rules could therefore apply.

With regard to the second ground, the members' requisition stated that the meeting was being called to consider 'the Resolutions' set out in a letter circulated to shareholders seeking their support for the requisition. That letter stated:

> At the EGM, resolutions will be put:
>
> (a) to elect a new Board (Committee) of not more than ten members and which will not include the Executive Officers who will be concentrating on running the business of RACMS, and
>
> (b) to authorise and instruct the new board (Committee) to proceed with the Scheme and report back to a further General Meeting at an early date.

Even if these 'resolutions' had been passed at a general meeting of the RAC, neither would, for obvious reasons, have had any legal effect. The company argued therefore that they were not obliged to call a meeting. The requisitionists argued that, though expressed as resolutions, the requisition was merely intended to set out the purpose of the meeting and that the directors should have called the meeting and included in the notice a series of resolutions that they had subsequently submitted to the company to give effect to the requisition.

The judge accepted that the requisitionists could have submitted resolutions to give effect to their requisition if they had made it clear that what were stated as resolutions were merely their object or purpose in calling the meeting. However, he ruled that they were precluded from doing so because they had used the word 'resolutions' in the body of the requisition.

He also held that, even if the additional resolutions submitted by the requisitionists had been valid on this count, the company would not have been bound to put them all to the meeting because the requisitionists had failed to get their timings right. The RAC's articles contained the standard provisions requiring members wishing to propose a person as a director to give the company at least two months' notice. Although the requisitionists had submitted the required notices, in order for them to be effective the directors would have had to have delayed calling the meeting. However, s. 368 requires the directors to call a meeting forthwith on receipt of a valid requisition, i.e. immediately. If the directors had done so, the appointment resolutions would have been defective under the articles. Accordingly, the judge ruled that the directors would not have been obliged to include them in the notice.

10.6.3   Directors must duly convene meeting

On receipt of a valid requisition, the directors must convene an EGM of the company in the proper manner (s. 368(1)). In the case of a requisitioned meeting at which a resolution is to be proposed as a special resolution, the directors are deemed not to have properly convened the meeting if they do not give the minimum statutory notice required for special resolutions (s. 368(7)). The meeting will also not be duly convened if it is called for a date more than 28 days after the date of the notice convening the meeting (s. 368(8)). This provision is intended to prevent the directors defeating the objects of the requisitionists by delaying the holding of the meeting.

When it convenes the meeting, the board may add other items to the agenda for the requisitioned meeting by giving notice in the normal manner. However, a member cannot raise any other matter at the meeting that was not specified in the requisition. For example, a member may not propose a resolution to remove a director at a requisitioned meeting where that was not one of the objects of the requisitionists (*Ball v. Metal Industries Ltd* 1957 SLT 124).

10.6.4   In default requisitionists may convene meeting

If the directors do not properly convene a meeting within 21 days from the date of deposit of the requisition, the requisitionists (or any of them representing more than one half of their total voting rights) may convene a meeting, which must be held within three months of the date of deposit (s. 368(4)).

The meeting must be convened by the requisitionists in as near to the same manner as possible as it would if the directors had convened it (s. 368(5)) (see **Precedent 10.6B**). Thus, if the articles do not provide for notice to be given by advertisement, the requisitionists are not entitled to give notice in that manner.

The requisitionists are entitled to be repaid any reasonable expenses they incur as a result of the failure of the directors to convene a meeting. These expenses will be payable by the company which must retain an equivalent sum from any fees or other remuneration payable by the company to the defaulting directors in respect of their services (s. 368(6)).

10.7 Requisition by auditor

An auditor may resign his or her office by giving the company notice in writing to that effect together with a statement of circumstances (s. 392 & 394). If the statement is of circumstances that the auditor believes should be brought to the attention of members, he or she may deposit at the same time a signed requisition calling on the directors of the company to convene an EGM for the purpose of receiving and considering his or her explanation of the circumstances of his or her resignation (s. 392A). The auditor also has a right to have a statement in writing of the circumstances connected with his or her resignation circulated to the members before any meeting convened on his or her requisition.

The directors (but not the secretary) are liable to a fine if they do not take reasonable steps within 21 days from the date of the deposit of the requisition to convene a meeting for a day not less than 28 days after the notice convening the meeting is given (s. 392A(5)). However, the auditor has no right to convene a meeting in default.

11

Notice of general meetings

11.1 Summary

- The Act makes detailed provision as to the length of notice that must be given to members and the methods of giving notice. Most other aspects are dealt with by the articles or, failing them, by the common law.
- The Act requires a minimum of 21 days' notice to be given of AGMs and any meeting to pass a special or elective resolution or one that requires special notice to be given. Other meetings may be called with only 14 days' notice. Clear days' notice is required unless the articles provide otherwise (see **11.2**).
- Notice may be given in writing or electronically (see **11.3** and **11.4**).
- In order to calculate when notices must be sent, it is necessary to make allowance for the statutory notice period and the date on which the notice will be deemed to have been served (see **11.5**).
- In addition to the date, time and place, the notice must state the business of the meeting. The exact text or the entire substance of the resolution should be stated for certain types of resolution. However, it is normally sufficient to state the general nature of the business. Circulars and other documents sent with the notice can be used for this purpose and will be read in conjunction with it for the purposes of determining the validity of the notice (see **11.6**).
- All the members are entitled to receive notice of general meetings unless the articles provide otherwise (see **11.9**).
- Articles usually provide that the accidental omission to give notice to a member will not invalidate the proceedings (see **11.10**).
- The members may consent to receive shorter notice than the statutory minimum. However, the conditions imposed by the Act are so rigorous that this is only likely to be possible for closely held private companies and subsidiaries (see **11.11**).
- Special notice requirements exist for resolutions to remove a director, appoint a director aged 70 or more, or remove or replace the auditors (see **11.12**).

- Members who satisfy certain qualifications have a statutory right to require the directors to give notice of resolutions that they wish to propose at an AGM. They may also require the directors to circulate a statement in connection with the business of any general meeting (see **11.13**).

11.2 Length of notice

The Act requires at least 21 days' notice to be given of AGMs (s. 369). The minimum notice required for an EGM will depend largely on the type of resolutions that are to be proposed at the meeting. Table 11.1 provides a simple guide for these purposes. Generally speaking, if it is intended to propose at an EGM a resolution for which 21 days' notice must be given, it will be necessary to give 21 days' notice of the meeting. If no such resolutions are to be proposed, then only 14 days' notice of the meeting will be required.

A company's articles may specify a longer period of notice than the statutory minimum for AGMs, EGMs or both (s. 369(1) and (2)). Unless the members consent to receive short notice in accordance with the statutory requirements (see **11.11**), meetings called with less than the notice required by the Act or the articles (if they specify a longer period of notice) will be invalid.

11.2.1 Clear days

Articles usually provide that the period of notice required in respect of general meetings shall be clear days (e.g. reg. 38 of Table A). It has been decided in the English courts that unless the articles provide otherwise, the number of days' notice required under the Companies Act shall be interpreted as being clear days (*Re Hector Whaling Ltd* [1936] Ch. 208). This is usually taken to mean that the day the notice is deemed to be served and the day of the meeting should not be counted. However, a more recent Scottish case has thrown this interpretation into doubt by ruling

Table 11.1 Length of notice

Type of resolution	Type of meeting to be proposed at	Minimum notice, CA 1985
Any resolution	AGM	21 days, s. 369(1)
Extraordinary resolution	EGM	14 days, s. 369(1)
Ordinary resolution	EGM	14 days, s. 369(1)
Elective resolution	EGM	21 days, s. 379A(2)
Special resolution	EGM	21 days, s. 378(2)
Ordinary resolution for which special notice is required to be given	EGM	21 days, s. 379(2)

that when calculating the period of notice required under the Companies Act the day of service must be excluded, but the day of the meeting may be counted (*Neil McLeod & Sons Ltd, Petitioners* [1967] SC 16). Articles sometimes define the meaning of clear days in order to avoid any uncertainty in this regard. If the articles do not contain any definition, it is safer for companies registered in England or Wales to apply the standard interpretation rather than the Scottish case.

11.2.2   AGM best practice

In its *Guide to Best Practice for AGMs*, the Institute of Chartered Secretaries and Administrators recommends that notice of AGMs should be circulated at least 20 working days before the meeting, i.e. excluding weekends and bank holidays. This recommendation is also repeated in the Combined Code on Corporate Governance (at para. C.2.4). Neither document specifies whether the expression 'working days' is intended to mean clear working days. However, unless this intention is assumed, the 'best practice recommendations' will often be very little better than the current legal requirements.

11.2.3   Detailed provisions on EGMs

The provisions of the Act relating to notice of EGMs are rather more complex than indicated above. However, the detailed provisions will only be relevant if a company fails to comply with the basic principles summarised in Table 11.1. Section 369 actually requires at least 14 days' notice to be given of any EGM other than one held for the passing of a special resolution, and provides that any provision in a company's articles will be void in so far as it specifies a shorter time. Although it does not specify the period of notice required for an EGM called for the passing of a special resolution, it is clear from s. 378(2) that at least 21 days' notice is required (see **12.4**), unless the members consent to receive shorter notice (see **11.11**). Because the Act also requires 21 days' notice to be given of the intention to propose an elective resolution (s. 379A(2)) or an ordinary resolution subject to the special notice requirements of s. 379, it will also be necessary in practice to give 21 days' notice of an extraordinary resolution called for the passing of such a resolution unless, in the case of an elective resolution, the members unanimously consent to receive shorter notice.

Failure to give at least 21 days' notice of an EGM called for the passing of an elective resolution (without the members' unanimous consent) or of an ordinary resolution requiring special notice will invalidate those resolutions but not the meeting itself, provided at least 14 days' notice has been given in accordance with s. 369. In other words, it would still be possible to pass any ordinary or extraordinary resolutions included in the notice.

The same is probably true for an EGM called for the passing of a special resolution. However, the situation is complicated by the fact that s. 369 deliberately makes an exception to the normal 14 days' notice requirement for 'a meeting for the passing of a special resolution' without specifying a minimum notice period for such a meeting. Section 378 states that a special resolution must be passed at a meeting of which not less than 21 days' notice specifying the intention to propose the resolution as a special resolution has been given, although the members may consent to receive shorter notice in accordance with s. 378(3). It is therefore arguable that unless the members consent to receive short notice, a meeting called at less than 21 days' notice is not 'a meeting for the passing of a special resolution' in the context of s. 369. In other words, the ordinary 14 days' notice rule would apply in default. However, if this is the case, there would seem to be little point in having the exception in s. 369 for meetings for the passing of special resolutions.

11.3 Electronic service of notices

The Companies Act and Table A both used to require notice of general meetings to be given in writing. Although never conclusively decided, it was generally assumed that this meant in paper form and precluded the use of electronic communications. In order to facilitate the use of electronic communications for these purposes, both the Act and Table A were amended by the Companies Act 1985 (Electronic Communications) Order 2000. The amendments came into force on 22 December 2000. As a result, all companies may now use electronic communications to give notice of general meetings, provided they satisfy certain statutory conditions (s. 369). This is the case notwithstanding anything to the contrary that may be contained in a company's articles (s. 369(4E)). If, however, a company is not able to comply with the applicable statutory conditions for using electronic communications (the most important of which is to obtain the prior consent of the person entitled to receive notice), it must continue to send notices in writing (i.e. in paper form) to that person. See **2.5** regarding the meaning of electronic communications and **2.6** for guidance on matters that will need to be considered before using electronic communications for these purposes.

Most articles make detailed provision on the service of notices. Any company incorporated on or after 22 December 2000 that adopts Table A will have articles that make specific provision for the service of notices using electronic communications. However, the articles of companies incorporated before that date will not make any such provision, unless they have been amended specifically for that purpose. The original (unamended) version of the 1985 Table A requires notice to be given in writing and to be served either personally or by post. Accordingly, that is what the articles of any company that adopted Table A before 22 December 2000 will still provide (unless those articles have subsequently been amended). The modifications made to Table A and the Act do not have the effect of amending the articles of these companies. A company that adopts Table A, whether in full or in part, adopts the version of Table A that was in force on the date of its incorporation, and its articles are not affected by subsequent amendments to Table A (s. 8). This does not mean, however, that these companies cannot use electronic communications to give notice of general meetings. The amendments made to the Act on 22 December 2000 enable all companies to use electronic communications, notwithstanding anything to the contrary that may be contained in their articles. The Act also provides that in so far as a company's articles make no specific provision for the service of electronic notices, notices must be served in the manner required by the version of Table A in force at that time (s. 369(4F)). This means that the provisions of Table A (as amended by the Order) will apply to all companies as if they were contained in the Companies Act 1985 until such time as a company makes different provision in its articles.

Because of the way the Act is drafted, it is practically impossible to draft articles that prevent a company and its members from taking advantage of the new electronic regime, should they wish to do so. A company cannot, however, force a person to accept service of notices electronically, and a person entitled to receive notice cannot force the company to serve it electronically if it does not wish to do so.

The Act makes provision for two different methods of serving notices electronically:

1. A company may use electronic communications to send a copy of the notice in full to any person who has agreed to accept service in this manner and has provided an 'address' for that purpose (s. 369(4A)).

2. Alternatively, if the person entitled to receive notice agrees, the company may simply notify them in an agreed manner that a copy of the notice has been made available on a website and leave it up to them whether or not to view it or download it (s. 369(4B)).

Both options require the agreement of both parties, i.e. the company and the person entitled to receive notice. It should be noted that the members will not necessarily be the only people entitled to receive notice and that electronic communications can be used to give notice to any other person entitled to receive it (e.g. the auditors) provided that they have agreed to accept service in this manner.

11.3.1 Sending notices in full

If a company and its members wish to use the method provided by s. 369(4A), the company must send the whole of the notice electronically. Bearing in mind that other documents sent with the notice can be deemed to be part of the notice, the company may also need to send those other documents in electronic form at the same time. If, as will often be the case in relation to the proposed dividend, this includes the annual report, the electronic files could become very large. This would not matter a great deal if the files were sent on a CD-ROM or other electronic storage media. It might, however, cause consternation among members who had elected to receive these documents by e-mail. Attention will also need to be paid to the format in which the documents were sent and whether members will be able to read or view them.

These factors are likely to make this method of electronic communication impractical and unpopular for all but the most simple documents. It would, for example, be suitable for a notice that could be incorporated in a plain text e-mail. A company could also send the documents as attachments to an e-mail, although this could easily give rise to problems of software compatibility unless the documents are sent in commonly used file formats.

11.3.2 Placing the notice on a website

If a person entitled to receive notice agrees, the company may satisfy the requirements of the Act by notifying that person (in an agreed manner) that the notice of meeting has been made available on a website (s. 369(4B)). The notification given by the company in these circumstances must be given in a manner agreed between the company and the person concerned. This could be in writing or by electronic communications. Irrespective of the manner in which it is given, the notification must:

- specify the address of the website, the place on that website where the notice may be accessed, and how it may be accessed;
- state that it concerns a notice of a company meeting served in accordance with the Act;
- specify the place, date and time of the meeting; and
- state whether the meeting is to be an AGM or EGM.

Where this method of giving notice is used, notice of the meeting will be deemed to have been given when the notification itself has been given (see below). Whether the requisite period of notice has been given will then be determined under the normal rules (see **11.2**). If not, and the members have not consented to receive short notice, the meeting would be invalid. In addition, where this method is used, the meeting may be invalid if the notice is not published on the website throughout the period beginning with the giving of the notification and ending with the conclusion of the meeting. The Act provides that failure to publish the notice throughout this period will not invalidate the proceedings of the meeting if it was wholly attributable to circumstances that it would not be reasonable to have expected the company to prevent or avoid (s. 369(4D)). Although the Act does not specifically state that other failures will invalidate the proceedings, this is clearly a distinct possibility, particularly if the failure occurred during the statutory period of notice and the members have not consented to receive shorter notice. The conditions that must be satisfied to come within the ambit of the exception for failures are fairly onerous, and should any failure occur during the period it may be difficult to state conclusively whether the meeting can be validly held. The saving grace as far as a company is concerned is that this will not really be a problem unless someone actually challenges the validity of the proceedings. However, companies with active dissident shareholders should perhaps bear these requirements in mind and take extra precautions to avoid failures (for example, by making the notice available on two or more websites on different servers and notifying members of the address of each of these sites).

11.3.3   Disapplication of pre-emption rights

Electronic communications cannot be used if a special resolution to disapply statutory pre-emption rights in relation to a specified allotment is to be proposed under s. 95(2). This is because the Act still requires a written statement by the directors to be circulated with the notice in these circumstances (s. 95(5)). However, no such statement is required where a special resolution to disapply statutory pre-emption rights is to be proposed under s. 95(1). As this is the type of resolution that most listed companies routinely put to the AGM, they should not be precluded from using electronic communications.

11.3.4   Circulars and other documents

If it is necessary to circulate other documents with the notice of a general meeting, care should be taken to ensure that they can also be served electronically. The Act makes specific provision with regard to the annual report and accounts and summary financial statements (see **23.2**), both of which will commonly be circulated with the AGM notice.

Under para. 1.27 of the Listing Rules, any document that the company is required by the Listing Rules to send to holders of listed securities may be sent using electronic communications, provided that the person entitled to receive the document has agreed to accept service of such documents in that manner. It is important to note that it is not sufficient that the person has agreed to accept service of notices and other Companies Act documents electronically. They must also specifically agree to accept electronic service of documents required to be circulated under the Listing Rules. Listed companies will need to reflect this in any documentation sent to shareholders on electronic communications (see **Precedent 2.7**).

Although the Act does not require companies to issue proxy forms, it can be an offence under s. 372(6) to issue proxy forms to some, but not all, of the members. Section 372(6) does not specifically allow, nor prevent, a company from issuing proxy forms electronically. It merely makes it an offence to issue selective invitations. To ensure that proxy forms sent using electronic communications have been 'issued' for these purposes, it may be preferable to ensure that provisions in the articles relating to deemed service of notices also apply to proxy forms.

Provision is made in the Listing Rules to allow listed companies to send proxy forms using electronic communications (see **14.13**).

Requisitioned resolutions and statements required to be circulated under s. 376 may be served in any manner permitted for giving notice of the meeting (s. 376(3) and (4)).

11.3.5   Table A provisions on electronic service

The provisions of Table A (as amended) on electronic service of notices and notifications are deemed to apply to all companies unless their articles make separate provision in this regard (s. 369(4F)). Regulations 111 and 112 of Table A (as amended) both provide that a company may give any notice to a member using electronic communications by sending it to an address for the time being notified for that purpose to the company. They also provide that an 'address', in relation to electronic communications, includes any number or address used for the purposes of such communications.

Regulation 112 also provides that a member whose registered address is not within the UK and who gives to the company an address within the UK at which notices may be given to him or her, or an address to which notices may be sent by electronic communications, shall be entitled to have notices given to him or her at that address, but otherwise no such member shall be entitled to receive any notice from the company.

Regulation 115 of Table A (as amended) provides that a notice sent by electronic communications shall be deemed to have been given at the expiration of 48 hours after the time it was sent. Some companies have already adopted articles that provide for a shorter period in this regard. This is sensible, particularly where the articles already provide for a shorter period for notices sent through the post, but also because for certain types of electronic communications (but not all) service will in reality be effected, if not instantaneously, then within a much shorter time frame.

Regulation 115 also provides that proof that notice contained in an electronic communication was sent in accordance with guidance issued by the Institute of Chartered Secretaries and Administrators shall be conclusive evidence that the notice was given. The guidance referred to in this regulation is an ICSA booklet entitled *Electronic Communications with Shareholders*. Chapter 8 of the guide includes several best practice recommendations which companies will need to follow in order to satisfy the requirements of reg. 115 (see **Appendix G**).

11.4　Written notice

If any of the conditions for giving notice of general meetings electronically are not complied with, notice must be given in writing (s. 369 and reg. 111 of Table A). Under Table A, notices given in writing must be served either personally or by post in a prepaid envelope to the member at his or her registered address (reg. 112). Written notice may be served personally by handing it to the member. Service by post includes ordinary and registered post and recorded delivery (*Re Thundercrest Ltd* [1995] 1 BCLC 117 and *TO Supplies (London) Ltd v. Jerry Creighton Ltd* [1951] 2 All ER 992).

Under Table A, members whose registered address is not within the UK are not entitled to receive notices unless they supply the company with an address (postal or electronic) in the UK for that purpose (reg. 112). The Listing Rules used to require listed companies to make such facilities available to overseas members. However, this requirement was deleted in January 2000. Under articles similar to reg. 112, the company must maintain a separate record of the addresses supplied by overseas members for these purposes and their registered address should not be changed unless they specifically request that it be changed. It is open to question whether the company can send other documents to the address supplied by an overseas member for the purposes of receiving notices. For example, s. 238 requires a copy of the report and accounts to be sent to every member but does not specify where it should be sent. The obvious place would be the registered address. However, it may be that the company may send it to the address supplied by an overseas member for the purposes of receiving notices.

Listed companies must use air mail or an equivalent service when sending notices and other documents to members resident in countries outside the European Union (Listing Rules, para. 9.29).

Table A is commonly modified to allow notices to be served by advertisement. This is clearly necessary for companies that allow members to hold shares in bearer form. However, the ability to give notice by advertisement can also be useful in the event of a postal strike. It has been held that a provision in a company's articles (similar to reg. 115 of Table A), which stated that notices shall be deemed to have been served a certain period after posting, did not apply where disruption to the postal service was such that placing the letters in a letter-box could not reasonably be expected to result in delivery to members within that time (*Bradman v. Trinity Estates plc* [1989] BCLC 757). Public companies are increasingly taking power in their articles to give notice by advertisement in such circumstances. Such articles need to be carefully worded to ensure that they apply where there is only a partial disruption of the postal service. The Listing Rules used to require notices given by advertisement to be inserted in at least one national newspaper. However, this requirement was deleted in January 2000.

11.4.1 Date of service

A written notice that is handed or given to a member personally is deemed to have been served on the day it was given. Table A provides that written notice sent by post shall be deemed to have been given 48 hours after the envelope containing it was posted (reg. 115). As Table A makes no distinction between first- and second-class post, there is nothing to be gained from using first-class post. However, articles sometimes clarify whether first- or second-class post should be used or make separate provision depending on which is used. For example, the articles could provide that notices sent by first-class post shall be deemed to have been served 24 hours after posting and those sent by second class, 48 hours after posting.

If a company's articles are silent on the deemed date of service, s. 7 of the Interpretation Act 1978 will apply, and a notice that has been properly addressed and posted will be deemed to have been given at the time when the letter would be expected to be delivered 'in the ordinary course of post'. In the case of a letter sent by first-class post, this is the 'day next after posting', and in the case of second-class post, the 'day next but one after posting', although in both cases any day on which there is no delivery of post must be excluded. Unless otherwise proved, it will be assumed that second-class post has been used (*Practice Direction* [1968] 3 All ER 320).

Notices given by advertisement are deemed to have been served the day after the newspaper is published (*Sneath v. Valley Gold Ltd* [1893] 1 Ch. 477) unless the articles provide otherwise.

11.4.2 Proof of service

The common law provides that a meeting will be invalid unless notice of it is given to all those entitled to receive it. When notices are sent by post, there is, of course, a danger that some may be lost and not delivered. To avoid the possibility of a meeting being invalidated for this reason, articles usually provide that proof that an envelope containing a notice was properly

addressed, stamped and posted shall be conclusive evidence that
the notice was given (e.g. reg. 115). When sending out written
notices of meetings, it is advisable to obtain and retain a receipt
(proof of posting) from the Post Office for this purpose. For
companies with large shareholder registers, this may be
impractical and an undertaking by the registrars that the proper
procedures were followed will probably be sufficient.

Although it might be possible in theory to calculate the number
of notices that should be sent out and to compare this with the
number that were actually sent, it may be impossible in practice
to discover the reason that the two figures do not reconcile. In *Re
West Canadian Collieries Ltd* [1962] Ch. 370, it was held that a
failure to send notices to nine shareholders was accidental where
the reason for the omission was that it had been forgotten that
the plates for printing their addresses had been separated from
the rest because earlier communications had been returned
undelivered.

It has been held that articles similar to reg. 115 are effective
only where there is uncertainty as to whether a document has
been delivered and not where it is clear that it has not been
delivered (*Re Thundercrest Ltd* [1995] 1 BCLC 117). The notice in
this case was given in connection with an offer of shares in
accordance with ss. 89 and 90. It was sent by recorded delivery (a
method that requires the recipient to sign as acknowledgement of
receipt). When it was returned to the company by the Post Office,
it was therefore obvious that it had not been delivered. Judge Paul
Baker said:

> The purpose of deeming provisions (such as reg. 115) in the
> case of management of companies is clear. In the case of
> uncertainty as to whether a document has been delivered, with
> large numbers of shareholders and so forth, there has to be
> some rule under which those in charge of the management can
> carry on the business without having to investigate every case
> where some shareholder comes along and says he has not got
> the document. The directors have to proceed and transact the
> company's business on the basis of the deeming provisions.
> But in my judgment, all that falls away when you find it is
> established without any possibility of challenge that the
> document has not been delivered.

Despite the best efforts of the judge to limit the application of
this ruling, it is clear that it could cause problems if applied to
notices of general meetings that are returned undelivered. This
would not be a problem if the notice was actually delivered to the
proper address but returned by the present occupiers. However, it
could cause a problem where, say, the building has been
demolished and it was not possible for the Post Office to deliver
the letter at all. In practice, companies and registrars tend to
ignore this problem, presumably on the basis that the case was

either wrongly decided or that the same principles would not be
applied to notices of meetings.

11.5   Practical issues on timing of notices

The date by which notices should be sent out needs to be
calculated carefully in accordance with the above rules to ensure
that proper notice is given. If the date of the meeting is already
known it is necessary to work backwards from that date to
establish the latest date by which the notices should be posted or
served. For companies registered in England or Wales, the basic
rules are as follows:

- the statutory period of notice commences the day after the notice
  has been served or is deemed to have been served on the
  member; and
- the meeting must be held after the last day of the period of notice
  required by statute or, if longer, by the articles.

In Scotland the meeting may be held on the last day of the period
of notice required by statute or, if longer, the articles (see **11.2**
above).

To take an example, an English company that has adopted
Table A in full must post the notice of its AGM at least 24 days
before the date of the meeting. If the notices were posted on 1
April they would be deemed to have been served 48 hours later,
i.e. on 3 April. The period of 21 days' notice would not
commence until 4 April, the first clear day, and would expire on
24 April. The earliest date that the meeting could be held would
therefore be on 25 April, the first clear day after the notice period
has expired. A meeting of a Scottish company could be held on
24 April.

The same principles would apply to an EGM, and notices
would have to be posted a minimum of 17 days before the date
of the meeting.

Both the ICSA's *Guide to Best Practice for AGMs* and the
Combined Code recommend that listed companies should
circulate the notice of their AGMs at least 20 working days before
the meeting, excluding weekends and bank holidays. This
recommendation is intended to give nominees more time to
obtain and submit proxy votes on behalf of underlying investors.
Neither the ICSA guide nor the Combined Code specifies whether
this is intended to mean 20 clear working days. However, unless
that interpretation is adopted, compliance with recommendation
makes only a slight difference to the date on which the notices
must be sent out, unless there is a bank holiday within the period
of notice.

11.6 Contents of notice

Notice of general meetings should:

- include the name of the company (s. 349(1)(b));
- include the time and place of the meeting;
- include the type of meeting (e.g. whether the meeting is the AGM in accordance with s. 366(1) and reg. 38 of Table A) (see below);
- include the business to be transacted at the meeting (see **11.7**);
- include the full text of any resolution to be proposed as special or extraordinary resolution (s. 378), an elective resolution (s. 379A), or as an ordinary resolution for which special notice is required (s. 379);
- state on whose authority it is issued (e.g. the board, requisitioning members, court, etc.) and the name of the person who signed it on their behalf (e.g. the name of the secretary) (but see *Re Brick and Stone Company* [1878] WN 140);
- be dated;
- in the case of a company having a share capital, include with reasonable prominence a statement of a member's right to appoint a proxy or, if a public company, one or more proxies and a statement that a proxy need not be a member of the company (s. 372(3)) – the articles of a company not having a share capital may entitle members to appoint a proxy and may require a similar statement to be included;
- in the case of a company whose shares have been admitted to CREST, specify in the notice a time, not more than 48 hours before the time fixed for the meeting, by which a person must be entered on the relevant register of securities in order to have the right to attend and vote at the meeting (Uncertificated Securities Regulations, reg. 34).

Although the Act and most articles only require the notice to specify AGMs as such, it is plainly sensible to specify EGMs as such, although the words 'a meeting of XYZ Limited' would be sufficient for this purpose, the assumption being that it must be an EGM if it is not specified as an AGM. However, it would not be sufficient to use the words 'a meeting of XYZ Limited' for a meeting of the holders of any class of shares of XYZ Limited.

Listed companies used to be required by the Listing Rules to include a statement in the notice regarding inspection of directors' service contracts. However, this requirement was deleted in June 1996.

A notice may be required by the Act, the articles or the Listing Rules to be accompanied by statements (see **11.13**), circulars (see **11.8**) and proxy forms (see **14.9**).

A notice will be invalid if it states that the meeting will only be held in certain predetermined circumstances (e.g. on the passing of a resolution by members of a different class), unless the articles specifically allow such notices to be given (*Alexander v. Simpson* (1889) 43 Ch.D. 139 and *Re North of England Steamship Co.* [1905] 2 Ch. 15). However, resolutions may be included in the business of a meeting that are contingent upon other events.

11.6.1 Signing the notice

At least one copy of the notice should be signed by or on behalf of the person or body under whose authority it is issued. In practice, it is normally signed and dated by the secretary or one of the directors above the words 'By order of the board'. The original signed copy should be retained by the company for evidential purposes. Copies of the notice sent to shareholders do not need to be signed but should include the name and position of the person who signed it on behalf of the board (see **Precedent 11.5A**). It is helpful if the notice can be dated for the day on which it is to be posted or the advertisement is to be placed. However, this is not strictly necessary and will not always be possible in view of the fact that it should be dated for the day on which it is actually signed.

11.7 Notice of the business

The notice need not give the exact text of the resolutions to be proposed, unless required by the Act, i.e. in relation to special, extraordinary and elective resolutions and ordinary resolutions requiring special notice (see **Chapter 12**). Doing so does not guarantee, in any case, that sufficient notice of the business has been given. Under the common law, the notice must give a 'fair and candid and reasonable explanation' of the purposes for which the meeting is called (*Kaye v. Croydon Tramways Co.* [1898] 1 Ch. 358).

Whether a notice is adequate will depend on the particular facts in each case. In *Normandy v. Ind, Coope & Co.* [1908] 1 Ch. 84, notice was given of a resolution to consider and, if thought fit, to approve a new set of articles to replace the existing articles. No indication of the content or effect of the new articles was given in the notice although it stated that copies were available for inspection at the company's office. It was held that the notice was defective because it did not properly inform the shareholders of the nature of the business.

The articles may modify this rule, e.g. by specifying certain business as 'ordinary business' (see below). Where the articles require the notice to specify the 'general nature of the business', the common law rules will apply (e.g. reg. 38 of Table A).

Notices are not construed with excessive strictness. The test that the courts apply is what the notice would fairly convey to an ordinary person (*Henderson v. Bank of Australasia* (1890) 45 Ch.D. 330). In determining the validity of the notice the courts often apply the absent shareholder test. In *Tiessen v. Henderson* [1899] 1 Ch. 861, Kekewich J said (at p. 886):

The question is merely whether each shareholder as and when he received notice of the meeting, in which I include the circular of the same date, had fair warning of what was to be submitted to the meeting. A shareholder may properly and prudently leave matters in which he takes no interest to the decision of the majority. But in that case he is content to be bound by the vote of the majority; because he knows the matter about which the majority are to vote at the meeting. If he does not know that, he has not a fair chance of determining in his own interest whether he ought to attend the meeting, make further inquiries, or leave others to determine the matter for him.

He added (at p. 870):

The man I am protecting is not the dissentient, but the absent shareholder – the man who is absent because having reviewed and with more or less care looked at this circular, he comes to the conclusion that on the whole he will not oppose the scheme, but leave it to the majority. I cannot tell whether he would have left it to the meeting to decide if he had known the real facts. He did not know the real facts; and, therefore, I think the resolution is not binding upon him.

There must be adequate disclosure of all material facts relevant to the question on which members will be asked to vote. In *Kaye v. Croydon Tramways Co.* [1898] 1 Ch. 358, a notice that failed to disclose the financial interest of the directors in a proposed reconstruction was held to be invalid. In *Baillie v. Oriental Telephone & Electric Co. Ltd* [1915] 1 Ch. 503, notice of a resolution to sanction the remuneration of the directors in connection with services rendered to certain subsidiaries was held to be inadequate because it did not specify the amount of that remuneration.

Business that has not been sufficiently notified or which is substantially different from that notified cannot be validly transacted (*Re Bridport Old Brewery Co.* (1867) 2 Ch. App. 19). However, amendments that are relevant to, and arise fairly out of, an item of business of which notice has been given may be proposed at the meeting (*Re Trench Tubeless Tyre Co.* [1900] 1 Ch. 408). For example, it has been held that a notice 'to elect directors' was sufficient for the meeting to elect directors up to the number permitted by the articles even though the notice only named one director (*Choppington Collieries Ltd v. Johnson* [1944] 1 All ER 762). Amendments may not be made to the substance of resolutions proposed as special, extraordinary or elective resolutions or resolutions requiring special notice (see further **22.3**).

The business actually carried out must substantially correspond to what was included in the notice. If notice is given of a single resolution that contains more than one proposal, it is not possible to adopt only part of it, because it is impossible for the court to know how many shareholders were satisfied with the arrangement as proposed and therefore abstained from attending the meeting (*Clinch v. Financial Corporation* (1898) LR 5 Eq. 450). Where notice was given of a meeting to consider resolutions for reconstruction and for winding up as incidental thereto, and only a resolution to wind up was passed, it was held to be invalid as it resulted in a position fundamentally different from that contemplated by the notice (*Re Teede and Bishop* (1901) 70 LJ Ch. 409). However, where the notice specified several separate resolutions and one of those was to wind up the company, that resolution was effective even though the other resolutions, which were concerned with the sale of the undertaking and consequent reorganisation, were found to be *ultra vires* and therefore void (*Thomson v. Henderson's Transvaal Estates Co.* [1908] 1 Ch. 765). The difference between these two cases is that in the first the notice implied that a resolution to wind up would only be passed as part of a reconstruction. In the second, the notice of the resolution to wind up was capable of standing in its own right. It follows that if it is intended to make a resolution contingent on the passing of another resolution, this should be done either by combining the two proposals in one resolution or clearly stating in the notice that the resolution(s) is (are) contingent upon the passing of another resolution(s).

11.7.1 Ordinary and special business

Many companies still have articles that distinguish between ordinary and special business. These are usually based on reg. 52 of the 1948 Table A which defines special business as any business

> that is transacted at an EGM, and also all that is transacted at an AGM, with the exception of declaring a dividend, the consideration of the accounts, balance sheets, and the reports of the directors and auditors, and the election of directors in the place of those retiring and the appointment of, and the fixing of the remuneration, of the auditors.

Any resolution that is not special business will be ordinary business.

Reg. 50 of the 1948 Table A (see **Precedent 11.7**) provides that in the case of special business the notice shall specify 'the general nature of that business'. Thus it must give a 'fair and candid and reasonable explanation' of the business to be transacted and give all material information to enable it to be understood.

No such requirement exists with regard to ordinary business and the effect of such provisions is to enable notice of AGMs to be given without setting out the general nature of the ordinary business. The members will be assumed to know what the ordinary business includes by virtue of the articles.

In practice, most listed companies also specify the general nature of ordinary business in notices. Indeed, although articles may distinguish between ordinary and special business, they may still require the general nature of ordinary business to be specified in the notice. Whether or not this is the case, it would be impracticable for a listed company to do otherwise. This is because the form of proxy sent to members must allow them to instruct their proxy how to vote on all resolutions intended to be proposed at the meeting (Listing Rules, para. 13.28), and it would be confusing for members if resolutions were included on the proxy form but not in the notice.

The Listing Rules also include a definition of ordinary business which is used to determine the details a listed company must include in its notification of the results of the meeting (see Listing Rules, para. 9.31 and the definition of 'ordinary business' in the Listing Rules Definitions section). Although this definition can differ from the one found in a company's articles, it has no bearing on the question of notice.

11.8   Circulars

Where the business is complex or important it is desirable to supplement the notice with an explanatory circular (*Young v. South African & Australian Exploration & Development Syndicate* [1896] 2 Ch. 268). Where a circular is sent with the notice, it will normally be read in conjunction with the notice in order to determine whether adequate notice has been given (*Tiessen v. Henderson* [1899] 1 Ch. 861). The same is true of the directors' report (*Boschoek Proprietary Co. Ltd v. Fuke* [1906] 1 Ch. 148) and presumably of any other document referred to in, or sent with, the notice.

Whenever a listed company gives notice of a meeting that includes business other than ordinary business at an AGM, that notice must be accompanied by an explanatory circular. If such other business is to be considered on the same day as the AGM, the explanation may be incorporated in the directors' report (Listing Rules, para. 14.17). A circular in connection with a resolution proposing to approve the adoption or amendment of the memorandum or articles of association; trust deeds; or employee share schemes must satisfy the requirements of Chapter 13 of the Listing Rules.

Paragraph 13.9 of the Listing Rules provides that a circular to shareholders in connection with proposed amendments to the memorandum and articles of association must:

- include an explanation of the effect of the proposed amendments;
- include either the full terms of the proposed amendments, or a statement that the full terms will be available for inspection:

- from the date of dispatch of the circular until the close of the relevant general meeting at a place in or near the City of London or such other place as the Exchange may determine; and
- at the place of the general meeting for at least 15 minutes prior to and during the meeting; and
- comply with the requirements of para. 14.1 (contents of all circulars).

Paragraph 14.1 of the Listing Rules provides that any circular sent by a company to a holder of its listed securities must:

(a) provide a clear and adequate explanation of its subject matter;

(b) if voting or other action is required, contain all information necessary to allow the holders of the securities to make a properly informed decision;

(c) if voting or other action is required, contain a heading drawing attention to the importance of the document and advising holders of the securities who are in any doubt as to what action to take to consult appropriate independent advisers; (Note 1)

(d) where voting is required, contain a recommendation from the directors as to the voting action shareholders should take, indicating whether or not the proposal described in the circular is, in the opinion of the directors, in the best interests of the shareholders as a whole; (Note 1)

(e) state that where all the securities have been sold or transferred by the addressee the circular and any other relevant documents should be passed to the person through whom the sale or transfer was effected for transmission to the purchaser or transferee; (Note 1)

(f) where new securities are being issued in substitution for existing securities, explain what will happen to existing documents of title;

(g) not include any reference to a specific date which has not been agreed in advance with the Exchange on which listed securities will be marked 'ex' any benefit or entitlement;

(h) where it relates to a transaction in connection with which securities are proposed to be listed, include a statement that application has been or will be made for the securities to be admitted to the Official List and, if known, a statement of the following matters:
  (i) the date dealings are expected to commence;
  (ii) how the new securities will rank for dividend or interest;
  (iii) whether the new securities rank *pari passu* with any existing listed securities;

(iv) the nature of the document of title;

(v) the proposed date of issue; and

(vi) the treatment of any fractions; and

(i) where a person is named in the circular as having advised the issuer or its directors, a statement that such adviser has given and has not withdrawn its written consent to the inclusion of the reference to the adviser's name in the form and context in which it is included.

Note 1: These items do not apply in the case of a circular or other document convening an AGM.

Circulars that do not fall within the definition in para. 14.5 of the Listing Rules (circulars of a routine nature) must be submitted to the UKLA for prior approval. Two copies of every circular in its final form (whether or not it is required to be submitted for approval) must be lodged with the UKLA at the same time as it is dispatched to shareholders (Listing Rules, para. 14.4).

Specific guidance on the content of circulars relating to the following business is also provided in Chapter 14 of the Listing Rules:

- authority to allot shares [para. 14.7];
- disapplication of pre-emption rights [para. 14.8];
- increase in authorised share capital [para. 14.9];
- reduction of capital [para. 14.10];
- capitalisation issue [para. 14.11];
- scrip dividend alternative [paras 14.12 to 14.14];
- scrip dividend mandate schemes [paras 14.15 and 14.15A];
- purchase of own securities [para. 14.16];
- early redemption [paras 14.22 to 14.24]; and
- reminders of conversion rights [paras 14.25 and 14.26).

11.9   Persons entitled to receive notice

Notice of meetings must be given to all persons entitled to receive it by virtue of the articles of association. Where the articles are silent on the matter, notice must be given to every member of the company (s. 370(1)). This would include joint shareholders, members whose calls are in arrears or who are resident abroad, and the holders of all classes of shares whether or not they have a right to attend and vote. Articles usually modify or exclude the rights of these members to receive notice (see below). Articles usually specify that notice shall be given to the directors (e.g. reg. 38), although the Act makes no such provision.

Auditors have a statutory right to receive notices of meetings and any other communications relating to any general meeting that a member is entitled to receive (s. 390(1)). An auditor who has been removed under s. 391(4) or who has resigned from office under s. 392A(8) retains the rights conferred by s. 390 in relation to any general meeting at which his or her term of office would otherwise have expired, or at which it is proposed to fill the vacancy caused by his or her removal. An auditor who has resigned also retains the rights conferred by s. 390 in relation to any general meeting requisitioned by him or her (s. 392A(8)).

The right to receive notice is suspended for members who are enemies or who are situated in enemy territories. A meeting will be properly convened if no notice is served on such persons (*Re Anglo-International Bank* [1943] Ch. 233).

A listed company must ensure that at least in each member state of the EU in which its securities are listed all the necessary facilities and information are available to enable holders of such securities to exercise their rights. In particular it must inform holders of securities of the holding of meetings that they are entitled to attend and enable them to exercise their right to vote, where applicable (Listing Rules, para. 9.24).

11.9.1 Restrictions on right to receive notice

Articles usually specify who is entitled to receive notice of meetings. For example, reg. 38 of Table A provides that, subject to any restrictions imposed on shares, notice shall be given to all the members, all persons entitled to a share in consequence of the death or bankruptcy of a member, the directors and the auditors.

Other regulations in Table A specify the circumstances in which members are not entitled to receive notice. It should be noted that a person may have a right to receive notice but not a right to attend or vote at the meeting. A person may also have a right to attend and vote at a meeting but not to receive notice of it, e.g. a member whose registered address is outside the UK. The following restrictions on the right to receive notice of meetings are commonly found in articles:

- *Joint shareholders* A notice sent to the joint holder whose name stands first in the register of members in respect of the joint holding shall be sufficient notice to all the joint holders, e.g. reg. 112 of Table A. Companies often allow joint shareholders to split their holding, if it is capable of being split, so that two or more accounts are entered in the register of members each with a different name as the first named holder. By doing so, each joint holder whose name stands first in one of the accounts in the register is assured of receiving notice of any meeting.
- *Address not within the UK* A member whose registered address is not within the UK may not be entitled to receive notices unless he or she has given the company an address within the UK at which notices may be served, e.g. reg. 112 of Table A. This type of article requires the company to keep a separate record of UK addresses notified by such persons as their address in the register of members will still be outside the UK. (See *Parkstone Ltd v. Gulf Guarantee Bank plc* [1990] BCLC 850 for a case on reg. 113 of the

1948 Table A.) For listed companies, see also para. 9.24 of the Listing Rules.

- *Subsequent purchaser* A person who becomes entitled to have his or her name entered in the register of members as a member shall be bound by any notices given to the person from whom he or she derives his or her title, e.g. reg. 114 of Table A.
- *Calls unpaid* Articles commonly restrict the rights of members whose calls are in arrears to vote at a general meeting, e.g. reg. 57 of Table A. Such members must still be given notice of that meeting unless the articles specify otherwise. Table A makes no provision in this regard.
- *Preference shareholders* It is common for companies with preference share capital to restrict the rights of preference shareholders to receive notice of, or to attend and vote at, general meetings. However, Table A makes no such provision and any company that intends to issue preference shares and wishes to restrict these rights should amend its articles accordingly. Typically, the preference shareholders might be entitled under the articles to receive notice of any general meeting at which it is proposed to wind up the company or where a resolution is to be proposed that will affect the rights and privileges of the preference shareholders. Where the right to receive dividends is cumulative, the preference shareholders will normally be entitled to receive notice of (and to attend and vote at) general meetings if those dividends are in arrears for a specified period (normally six months). Where preference dividends were payable each year out of profits earned in that year only, it was held that dividends were not in arrears for a particular year where there were no profits in that year. Accordingly the preference shareholders had no right to receive notice (*Coulson v. Austin Motor Co.* (1927) 43 TLR 493).
- *Non-voting shares* Again, Table A makes no provision for non-voting shares and such members must be given notice unless the articles specify otherwise.

11.9.2   Record date

Companies whose securities have been admitted to CREST may set a record date for determining entitlement to receive notice of meetings. The date must not be more than 21 days before the date on which the notices are sent out (i.e. the actual date of posting and not necessarily the date of signing shown on the notice). If a company sets such a record date, only those members whose names have been entered on the relevant register of securities at the close of business on that date will be entitled to receive notice (Uncertificated Securities Regulations 1995, reg. 34 (see **Appendix K**)). Boards may set a record date by including in their resolution to approve the notice something on the following lines (although no reference needs to be made in the notice itself to this resolution):

For the purposes of regulation 34 of the Uncertificated
Securities Regulations 1995 the members entitled to receive
notice of [description of meeting] shall be those entered on the
company's register of [members/other securities] at the close of
business on [date].

11.10   Failure to give proper notice

Unless all the members actually attend the meeting, failure to
give proper notice to any person entitled to receive it invalidates
the meeting (*Smyth v. Darley* (1849) 2 HLC 789). However, articles
often provide that the accidental omission to give notice of a
meeting or the non-receipt by a member of notice of a meeting
shall not invalidate the proceedings at that meeting (e.g. reg. 39
of Table A). Such an article was held to validate a meeting for
which notice had not been given to several members because the
address plates for those members had inadvertently been
separated from the rest because their dividends had been returned
uncashed (*Re West Canadian Collieries Ltd* [1962] Ch. 370).
However, a deliberate failure to send a notice to a member will
not be validated even if the company had reason to believe that
the notice would not reach the member at his or her registered
address (*Musselwite v. C H Musselwite* [1962] Ch. 964). Once it is
shown that some members were not given notice, the onus lies
with those claiming that the meeting was valid to show that the
omission was accidental (*POW Services Ltd v. Clare* [1995] 2 BCLC
435).

Some companies have adopted articles that provide that a
member shall not be entitled to receive notice if on the three
most recent occasions on which they were sent documents by the
company, they were returned undelivered, unless they have
subsequently confirmed their address or notified a new address.

Articles commonly provide that a member present, either in
person or by proxy, at any meeting of the company or of the
holders of any class of shares shall be deemed to have received
notice of the meeting and of the purposes for which it was called
(e.g. reg. 113 of Table A). Even without such a provision a
member who was present and voted at a meeting of which
irregular notice had been given may be deemed to have
acquiesced in the irregularity (*Re British Sugar Refinery Co.* [1857]
26 LJ Ch. 369).

11.11   Consent to short notice

11.11.1   AGMs

An AGM may be called with less than 21 days' notice if all the
members entitled to attend and vote give their consent. If
accounts are to be laid at the AGM, consent will probably need to
be given to accept the report and accounts less than 21 days

before the meeting (see **Precedent 11.11A**). The consent of all the members is required to do this whether the accounts are to be laid at the AGM or an EGM (s. 238(4)).

11.11.2 EGMs

In the case of any other meeting, consent to short notice need only be given by a majority in number having a right to attend and vote at the meeting holding together not less than 95% in nominal value of the shares conferring that right (ss. 369(3) and (4)) (see **Precedent 11.11B**).

It should be noted that the majority required is calculated by reference to the rights of all the members and not simply by reference to the rights of those who actually attend the meeting. Where a majority of 95% is required, one member cannot form a majority in number and overrule the minority in this regard. However, a sole member would clearly be able to satisfy the requirements for both AGMs and EGMs.

11.11.3 Separate consent required for special and extraordinary resolutions

If it is intended to propose a special resolution at a meeting held at short notice, consent will also need to be obtained to dispense with the notice requirements of s. 378 in respect of special resolutions (see **Precedent 11.11C**). In this case consent must be given by a majority in number of the members having the right to attend and vote holding together not less than 95% in nominal value of the shares conferring that right (s. 378(3)).

By using this procedure it is also possible to pass a special resolution that was not included in the notice of the meeting. However, it does not override the need for the consent of all the members to be given in relation to short notice of an AGM. Equally, consent to short notice of the intention to propose a special resolution must be given at a meeting for which consent to short notice has itself been given.

11.11.4 Elective resolutions

Consent to short notice may be given in respect of elective resolutions. Previously no such provision was made. However, the Deregulation (Resolutions of Private Companies) Order 1996 inserted a new subsection (2A) in s. 379A which provides that an elective resolution shall be effective notwithstanding the fact that less than 21 days' notice in writing of the meeting is given if all the members entitled to attend and vote at the meeting so agree. Although this is a more onerous requirement than for special and extraordinary resolutions, it should not present any difficulties in practice because elective resolutions

must also be approved unanimously by all the members entitled
to vote.

11.11.5 Some notice still required

By consenting to short notice in accordance with the statutory
provisions, the members do not consent to receive no notice at
all. Some notice (however short) must be given prior to the
meeting and that notice must be served in a manner allowed by
the articles, unless all the members attend the meeting and, in the
case of a special or extraordinary resolution, vote in favour of the
resolution.

11.11.6 When consent cannot be given

The Act makes no provision for consent to short notice of
resolutions requiring special notice (e.g. a resolution to remove
the auditors or a director). This is logical because the special
notice requirements are intended to allow the auditors or the
director concerned to prepare a statement for circulation to the
members.

11.11.7 Practical points

In practice, consent to short notice will only be useful for
companies with relatively few members, e.g. small private
companies and subsidiaries. It is not strictly necessary for the
members to consent in writing. A resolution passed by the
appropriate majority at the start of the meeting will suffice. It is,
however, advisable to obtain the written consent of members
prior to the meeting. It may prove to be impossible to obtain the
necessary majority at the meeting perhaps because some
members do not attend or have not submitted proxies. Consent
in writing is also preferable as a method of proving compliance
with the requirements of the Act. The form(s) of consent signed
by the members should be entered in the minute book for this
purpose.

As a final point of detail, notice still needs to be given to any
person entitled to receive it who is not entitled to vote at the
meeting. This would include the auditors who have a statutory
right to receive notice but, having received it, cannot object to the
meeting being held at short notice. The articles might also require
notice to be given to other classes of member or the directors.

11.11.8 Elective resolution to reduce percentage required to consent

A private company may by elective resolution reduce to 90%
the majority required to consent to the holding of an EGM and
for the passing of special resolutions at short notice (see
further **25.7**).

11.12 Special notice

Certain resolutions cannot validly be proposed at a general meeting unless special notice has been given in accordance with the requirements of s. 379. Special notice is required by the Act in relation to the following resolutions:

- to remove a director by ordinary resolution before the expiration of his or her period of office under s. 303(1) or to appoint somebody instead of a director so removed at a meeting at which he or she is removed (s. 303(2));
- to appoint or approve the appointment of a director who has attained the age of 70 (s. 293(5));
- to fill a casual vacancy in the office of auditor (s. 388(3)(a));
- to re-appoint as auditor a retiring auditor who was appointed by the directors to fill a casual vacancy (s. 388(3)(b));
- to remove an auditor before the expiration of his or her term of office (s. 391A(1)(a)); and
- to appoint as auditor a person other than a retiring auditor (s. 391A(1)(b)).

Any such resolution will be invalid unless notice of the intention to propose it has been given to the company at least 28 days before the meeting at which it is to be proposed (see **Precedent 11.12A**). Subject to one exception, this is the case whether the resolution is to be proposed by a dissident member or to be included in the notice of a general meeting at the instigation of the board of directors. The exception to the rule is that if, after notice of the intention to propose the resolutions has been given to the company, a meeting is called for a date 28 days or less after the notice has been given, the notice will be deemed to have been properly given, though not given within the time required (s. 379(3)). It should also be noted that, provided it is served at least 28 days before the meeting, special notice may be validly served on the company after the notice of meeting has been circulated.

It can be implied from the words used in the Act that special notice must be given to the company by someone who would be entitled to propose the resolution at a general meeting. Plainly, this includes any member, but might also, at a stretch, include the person who will chair the general meeting (usually the chairman of the board of directors). However, if the resolution is to be proposed at the instigation of the board, it is infinitely preferable for a member (e.g. a director who is a member) to give the necessary notice to the company.

11.12.1 Company's obligations on receipt of special notice

On receipt of notice of the intention to propose one of the above resolutions, the company must comply with the additional requirements relating to that type of resolution (see below). In addition, s. 379(2) provides that a company shall give its members notice of any such resolution at the same time and in the same manner as it gives notice of the meeting or, if that is 'not practicable' (e.g. where the notice of meeting has already been circulated), shall give them notice by advertisement in a newspaper having an appropriate circulation or in any other mode allowed by the company's articles, at least 21 days before the meeting (see **Precedent 11.12B**).

The Act makes no provision for a penalty in the event of a failure by the company to give notice of the resolution in accordance with s. 379(2). In fact, it has been held that a company is not obliged to include a resolution submitted by a member in the notice of the meeting, or to give members notice of it in any other manner, unless the member who submitted it has also satisfied the conditions of either s. 368 (EGM on members' request) or s. 376 (circulation of members' resolutions) (*Pedley v. Inland Waterways Association Ltd* [1977] 1 All ER 209). Hoffman J ruled that the wording in s. 379(2) was merely intended to confer on the members of a company the right to receive notice of any resolution of which special notice is required and has been duly given that is to form part of the agenda to be dealt with at the relevant meeting. Thus, a member who cannot comply with the conditions of s. 368 or s. 376 cannot force the company to include the resolution in the notice of the meeting or to give notice of it in any other manner. A company may, of course, choose to include the resolution on the agenda even though the member has not satisfied these conditions and, if it does, it must allow the member to propose the resolution at the meeting.

Although the Act does not specifically state that a resolution subject to the special notice rules cannot be proposed if the company has not given notice of it to the members in accordance with s. 379(2), this must be assumed to be the case. It is notable, for example, that s. 379(3) makes no specific provision in this regard. All it does is to rectify any failure on the part of a member to give notice of the intention to propose the resolution at least 28 days before the meeting where, after receiving the notice from the member, the company calls a meeting for a date 28 days or less after it received the notice. In other words, it prevents a company from manipulating the requirements of s. 379 to avoid any obligation it may otherwise have to give notice of the resolution. It should also be borne in mind that if such a resolution were to be requisitioned under s. 376 in relation to the AGM, it would be an offence under that section for the company to fail to give notice of it in accordance with the requirements of that section. An AGM can, of course, be called at less than 21 days' notice if all the members agree. If all the members did consent and the meeting was held at less than 21 days' notice, it would not be possible to propose any resolution for which special notice must be given. Accordingly, one would not normally expect a member who wished to propose such a resolution to agree to the meeting being held at short notice.

There is nothing in s. 379 that requires a company to convene a meeting to consider a resolution for which special notice has been given. Indeed, a company that has elected to dispense with AGMs might never hold a meeting at which such a resolution could be proposed unless the member also gave notice under s. 366A requiring it to hold an AGM or requisitioned an EGM under s. 368.

11.12.2   Additional requirements

In addition to the requirement to notify the members on receipt of special notice of the intention to move a resolution, the company must also comply with special requirements for each resolution which are set out in the relevant section of the Act (see further **Chapter 23**). For example, s. 293 requires the company to include in the notice sent to members the age of the director whom it is proposed to appoint. On receipt of notice from a member of his or her intention to propose a resolution to remove a director or auditor, the company must immediately send a copy of the notice to the person named in the resolution. In the latter case, the director or auditor concerned then has a right to have a statement circulated with the notice of the meeting.

11.12.3   No consent to short notice

No provision is made in the Act for consent to short notice with respect to a resolution requiring special notice. Therefore such a resolution cannot be passed at a meeting held at short notice. It should also be noted that 21 days' notice must still be given of a resolution requiring special notice if the resolution is to be validly proposed at an EGM.

11.13   Circulation of members' resolutions and statements

In addition to the right to requisition an EGM under s. 368, the members of a company have a statutory right under s. 376 to require the company to give notice of resolutions that they intend to propose at AGMs. They also have a right to have statements circulated by the company in connection with any business that is to be dealt with at any general meeting. This includes a statement on any matter pending before an EGM of the company and any business that is to be dealt with at an AGM, including a requisitioned resolution.

11.13.1   Conditions for valid requisition under s. 376

The conditions that must be satisfied for a members' requisition under s. 376 are less onerous than those for requisitioning an EGM under s. 368 (see **10.6**). This is logical because the company is not required to call an additional meeting but merely to do something in relation to a meeting that must be held. Section 376(2) provides that a valid requisition may be made by the following:

(a) any number of members (which includes one) holding not less than one-twentieth of the total voting rights of all the members having at the date of the requisition the right to vote at the meeting to which the requisition relates; or

(b) not less than 100 members holding shares in the company on which there has been paid up an average sum, per member, of not less than £100.

It should be noted that under (a) above the validity of the requisition must be determined by reference to the number of members who would have been entitled to vote if the meeting had been held on the date of the requisition. Thus, if preference dividends are in arrears on the date of the requisition and the company's articles give preference shareholders the right to vote in such circumstances, the requirements for a valid requisition will be more onerous (see Table 11.2 below).

Table 11.2 Examples of the minimum requirements for members' requisitions

Number of voting shares in issue	Notice of AGM resolution/circulation of statement under s. 376(2)(a)	under s. 376(2)(b)	Convene EGM under s. 368
100 fully paid £1 ordinary (voting) shares	One or more members holding together 5 shares	N/A	One or more members holding together 10 shares
200,000 fully paid £1 ordinary (voting) shares	One or more members holding together 10,000 shares	100 members holding together 10,000 shares	One or more members holding together 20,000 shares
1 million fully paid £1 ordinary voting shares	One or more members holding together 50,000 shares	100 members holding together at least 10,000 shares	One or more members holding together 100,000 shares
1 million fully paid £1 ordinary voting shares and 500,000 £2 preference shares carrying the right to vote	One or more members holding together 75,000 shares (ordinary or preference)	100 members holding shares (ordinary or preference) on which an average of not less than £100 per member has been paid up	One or more members holding together shares (ordinary or preference) representing £200,000 of the paid-up capital

In relation to (b) above, the number of shares that members must hold is calculated in relation to the nominal value of the shares. For example, if the nominal value is £1, each member must hold on average 100 fully paid shares. If the nominal value is 25p, each member must hold on average 400 shares.

A copy of the requisition under s. 376 signed by the requisitionists (or two or more copies which between them bear the signatures of all the requisitionists) must be deposited at the company's registered office (see **Precedents 11.13A and B**). The requisition must be deposited as follows:

- in the case of a requisition requiring the company to give notice of a resolution, not less than six weeks before the meeting (s. 377(1)(a)(i)); or
- in the case of a requisition requiring the company to circulate a statement, not less than one week before the meeting (s. 377(1)(a)(ii)).

A company is not bound to comply with a demand made after the above dates. However, after the requisition has been deposited at its registered office, it cannot avoid its obligations by calling an AGM to be held within six weeks. In these circumstances, the requisition will be deemed to have been properly deposited (s. 377(2)). This provision can cause immense problems, particularly for companies with a large membership. If one assumes that a meeting is not called until all the notices have been sent out (or, worse, until they have been served on the members), this means that a member may validly requisition a meeting after the notice has been printed. It is possible to take a more robust view if one assumes that a meeting is called when the directors convene it. This appears to be more in keeping with the spirit of the Act which presumably seeks to prevent the directors from avoiding their obligations by calling a snap meeting after they receive a valid requisition. However, there is sufficient doubt as to the meaning of the word 'called' for many companies to apply the more rigorous test to their own detriment.

11.13.2   Company's duty

On receipt of a valid requisition, a company has a duty to:

- in the case of a requisition requiring the company to give notice of a resolution, give to the members of the company entitled to receive notice of the next AGM notice of any resolution that may be properly moved and is intended to be moved (by the requisitionists) at that meeting (s. 376(1)(a)); or
- in the case of a requisition requiring the company to circulate a statement, circulate to members entitled to have notice of any general meeting sent to them any statement of not more than 1,000 words with respect to the matter referred to in any

proposed resolution or the business to be dealt with at that meeting (s. 376(1)(b)).

Although the Act imposes these duties on the company, it will fall to the directors to ensure compliance, and it is noteworthy that under s. 376(7) the directors, but not the company, are liable to a fine in default.

Under s. 376(1)(a) the members may require the company to give notice of a proposed resolution only in respect of an AGM. A company is not required to include such a resolution in the notice of an EGM to be held before the next AGM. If the members are not prepared to wait until the next AGM, they should requisition an EGM under s. 368, assuming that they are able to satisfy the more onerous conditions.

The company must give notice of the requisitioned resolution and circulate any requisitioned statement to members of the company who are entitled to have notice of the meeting sent to them by serving a copy of the resolution or statement in any manner permitted for service of notice of the meeting (s. 376(3)) (see **Precedents 11.13C and 11.13D**). Notice of the resolution must also be sent to the company's auditors who are entitled to receive all notices of, and other communications relating to, any general meeting that a member of the company is entitled to receive (s. 390(1)) and to any other persons entitled to receive notices under the articles.

Members who are not entitled to have the notice sent to them but who are entitled to receive notice by some other means (e.g. holders of bearer shares who are entitled to be given notice by advertisement) must be given notice of the general effect of the resolution in any manner permitted for giving such members notice of meetings (s. 376(4)). It should be noted that this provision does not apply to a requisitioned statement which need only be circulated to members who are entitled to have notice of the meeting sent to them (s. 376(1)(b)). The copy or notice of the general effect of the resolution must be served or given in the same manner and (where practicable) at the same time as the notice of the meeting or as soon as practicable thereafter (s. 376(5)).

Notwithstanding anything in a company's articles, any business of which notice is given in accordance with the requirements of s. 376 may be dealt with at an AGM and an accidental omission to give notice of a requisitioned resolution to one or more members shall not invalidate the proceedings (s. 376(6)).

11.13.3 Cost of circulating a resolution

A company need not comply with a requisition unless the requisitionists deposit or tender with it a sum that is reasonably sufficient to meet its expenses in giving effect to the requisition (s. 377(1)(b)). However, the members may vote by ordinary resolution to release the requisitionists from any obligations they may have to pay the company's costs (s. 376(1)).

It is difficult for the requisitionists to make an accurate assessment of the company's costs and they will normally seek guidance from the company before depositing the requisition. If there is a dispute between the company and the requisitionists as to the sum required, the directors would be well advised to give effect to the requisition as they could be liable to a fine for failing to comply with the requirements of s. 376 if the court takes the view that the sum deposited or tendered by the requisitionists was reasonably sufficient.

The cost of giving effect to a members' resolution should not be prohibitive if it is deposited in time for inclusion in the notice calling the AGM, although this deadline will often be more than six weeks before the meeting in the case of listed companies. If the company has already printed the notice at the time of the deposit, it should attempt to minimise the cost of giving effect to the requisition by issuing a separate notice of the resolution rather than, for example, having the original notice reprinted, particularly if that notice is embodied in the annual report and accounts.

In practice, the company (i.e. the directors) may sometimes agree to give effect to a requisition without charge to the requisitionists. Section 377(1)(b) does not prevent the company (i.e. the directors) from doing this. It merely provides that the company 'need not' (rather than 'shall not') give effect to a requisition unless the requisitionists have deposited or tendered with it a sum reasonably sufficient to meet the company's costs in giving effect to it. And, in giving effect to the requisition without charge, the directors can be assumed to have waived any liability the requisitionists may have under s. 376(1) to pay the company's costs.

If the directors do not agree to give effect to the requisition without charge, the requisitionists may wish to include in their requisition a proposal that the company bears its own costs in giving effect to the requisition. Requisitionists sometimes achieve this by embodying a proposal regarding costs in the requisitioned resolution. This has the advantage of ensuring that they will not be required to pay if the resolution is passed. However, it may be preferable from their point of view for the proposal to be drafted as a separate requisitioned resolution, particularly where their main proposal is one that requires a special majority. This is because the resolution regarding costs need only be passed as an ordinary resolution.

The ICSA's *Guide to Best Practice for AGMs* recommends that unless the company agrees at the outset to absorb all the costs of circulation, shareholder resolutions requisitioned under s. 376 of the CA 1985 should automatically be accompanied (in any notice) by another resolution giving shareholders the opportunity to decide whether the company or the requisitionists should bear the relevant costs. If the directors feel that any particular case does not justify the adoption of such a resolution, they should, however, be free to recommend a vote against it. The guide also suggests that companies should consider including shareholder resolutions in the notice without charge unless they are vexatious, frivolous, substantially repetitive or seeking a purpose that will clearly have no legal effect.

11.13.4 Cost of circulating a statement

Although a requisition requiring a statement to be circulated can be deposited after the notice has been sent out, the cost of circulating it at this late stage will obviously be greater. Unless the directors agree to waive the costs of circulating a statement, the requisitionists will have no choice but to pay them. If the requisitioned statement is deposited at least six weeks before the meeting, the requisitionists could, however, also requisition a resolution proposing that the company bears its own costs in giving effect to the requisitioned statement.

It should be noted that as an alternative to requisitioning a statement under s. 376, any member may (on payment of the prescribed fee) demand a copy of the company's register of members (s. 356) and use the names and addresses of the members to circulate a statement to all or part of the membership. This may be cheaper if it is only necessary to target, say, shareholders holding more than 5% of the company's equity.

11.13.5 Abuse of rights under s. 376

If the court is satisfied that the rights conferred by s. 376 are being abused to secure needless publicity for defamatory matter, it may on the application of the company or any other aggrieved person order that the company is not bound to circulate any such statement and that the requisitionists pay the company's costs in making such an application (s. 377(3)). In an Australian case on a similarly worded provision, it has been held that the applicant must demonstrate that the statement is defamatory *and* that the section is being abused to secure needless publicity (*Re Harbour Lighterage Ltd* (1968) 1 NSWLR 438). In the same case, it was held that the court had no power to order the deletion of the defamatory parts of a member's statement. It could only order that the whole statement should not be sent.

12

Resolutions

12.1 Summary

- The type of resolution required to deal with an item of business is determined primarily by the Companies Act but can also depend on other factors. For each type of resolution, there are different requirements with regard to the notice that must be given and the majority required to pass the resolution.
- An ordinary resolution can be passed by a simple majority of the members voting at a meeting for which proper notice has been given (see **12.2**).
- Extraordinary resolutions require a majority of 75% of the members voting and are generally required in connection with the winding up of companies (see **12.3**).
- Special resolutions are far more common and are generally required where it is proposed to alter the rights of members or the constitution of the company. The majority required is the same as for extraordinary resolutions. However, the requirements as to notice are more stringent (see **12.4**).
- Elective resolutions can only be passed by private companies and are used to dispense with various requirements connected with the holding of AGMs. All the members of the company must vote in favour of the resolution otherwise it will be invalid (see **12.5**).
- A copy of all special, extraordinary, elective and some ordinary resolutions must be filed at Companies House 15 days after they have been passed and be embodied in or annexed to every copy of the articles issued after the passing of the resolution (see **12.6**).
- A resolution will normally be passed on the date of the meeting (see **12.7**).

12.2 Ordinary resolutions

As a general rule, unless the Companies Acts or a company's articles specify otherwise, all business at general meetings may be dealt with by ordinary resolution, although listed companies also need to have regard to the requirements of the Listing Rules and various codes of practice. Where a provision in the Companies Acts requires a matter to be authorised 'by the company in general meeting', this means by ordinary resolution.

There is no definition of ordinary resolution in the Act. However, it is well established that a resolution will be passed as an ordinary resolution when it is passed by a simple majority of the votes cast (whether in person or by proxy) at a meeting of which proper notice has been given. An abstention is not considered to be a vote for these purposes. Put quite simply therefore, an ordinary resolution will be passed if the number of votes cast in favour of the motion exceeds the number against.

Articles often give the chairman of the meeting a casting vote where an equal number of votes are cast for and against a resolution proposed as an ordinary resolution, e.g. reg. 50 of Table A. If they do not make any such provision, the chairman will not have a casting vote and the resolution will have been defeated.

Table 12.1 Matters that may be passed by ordinary resolution under the Act

Nature of resolution	Companies Act 1985
Giving directors authority to allot shares (Note 1)	s. 80
Transfer to public company of non-cash asset in initial period	s. 104
Alteration of share capital	s. 121
Increase of share capital (Note 2)	s. 123
Authority for market purchase of own shares (Notes 1 and 3)	s. 166
Removal of a director (Notes 4 and 5)	s. 303
Approval of payment for loss of office to director	s. 312 & 313
Director's contract of more than five years	s. 319
Approval of substantial property transaction involving directors	s. 320
Resolution to revoke elective resolution (Note 1)	s. 379A
Appointment of auditors by company in general meeting	s. 385 & 385A
Resolution to fix remuneration of auditors	s. 390A
Removal of auditors (Note 4)	s. 391
Making provision for employees on cessation or transfer of business	s. 719

Notes
1. Resolution must be filed at Companies House under s. 380.
2. Resolution must be notified to Companies House on Form 123.
3. The ABI's Pre-emption Guidelines actually require listed companies to pass a special resolution.
4. This resolution requires special notice to be given in accordance with s. 379.
5. Articles cannot exclude the members' right to remove a director by ordinary resolution.

Listed companies must forward 'without delay' to the UK Listing Authority two copies of any ordinary resolution passed at a general meeting other than resolutions concerning ordinary business at an AGM (Listing Rules, para. 9.31). Ordinary business for these purposes includes receiving the accounts and reports, re-appointing the auditors and fixing their remuneration, and the re-election of directors retiring by rotation (Listing Rules, Definitions).

Table 12.1 shows the matters that may be passed by ordinary resolution under the Act. Unless otherwise indicated, the articles may specify a higher majority.

12.3   Extraordinary resolutions

An extraordinary resolution must be passed by a majority of not less than 75% of the members who are entitled to vote and who actually vote (whether in person or by proxy) at a general meeting of which notice specifying the intention to propose the resolution as an extraordinary resolution has been duly given (s. 378(1)).

On a show of hands the majority required is 75% of the members actually voting (including corporate representatives but not proxies unless, unusually, the articles confer on them the right to vote on a show of hands). An abstention is not a valid vote for these purposes. Thus, if 100 members are present at a meeting and 79 actually vote on a show of hands, 60 must vote in favour in order to pass a resolution as an extraordinary resolution (i.e. 75.59% – 59 would be a majority of only 74.68%). An extraordinary resolution will, however, be passed where the majority in favour is exactly 75%, e.g. 75 in favour, 25 against. On a poll, where each member is entitled to votes in proportion to their holdings, the number of votes required is calculated by reference to the total number of votes cast for and against the resolution.

An extraordinary resolution will be invalid if the notice does not specify the intention to propose it as an extraordinary resolution (*MacConnell v. E. Prill & Co. Ltd* [1916] 2 Ch. 57) and if it does not state the text or entire substance of the proposals to be submitted (*Re Moorgate Mercantile Holdings Ltd* [1980] 1 All ER 40).

There are no specific requirements as to the period of notice that must be given for extraordinary resolutions. Accordingly, the period of notice required will be determined by the requirements for the type of meeting at which the resolution is to be proposed. It also follows that, unlike special resolutions, if consent to short notice is being sought for a meeting, separate consent is not required for an extraordinary resolution that is to be proposed at that meeting.

A copy of every extraordinary resolution passed by a company must be filed with the Registrar of Companies within 15 days of

Table 12.2 Matters that must be passed by extraordinary resolution

Nature of resolution	Source
Voluntary winding up of a company that cannot continue its business by reason of its liabilities	Insolvency Act 1986, s. 84(1)
Members' voluntary winding up, to sanction liquidator's proposals for a compromise with the company's creditors	Insolvency Act 1986, s. 165(2)
Variation of class rights (not attached by memorandum) for which the articles make no alternative provision with respect to variation	Companies Act 1985, s. 125(2)
Distribution by a liquidator of surplus assets in kind instead of realising them in cash	Table A, reg. 117

it being passed (s. 380(1)) and a copy must be annexed or embodied in every copy of the articles issued after the passing of the resolution (s. 380(2)) (see **12.6**).

Listed companies must send the UK Listing Authority two copies of any extraordinary resolution passed at a general meeting (Listing Rules, para. 9.31). See Table 12.2.

12.4 Special resolutions

A resolution will be a special resolution when it has been passed by a majority of not less than 75% of members who are entitled to vote and who actually vote (whether in person or by proxy) at a general meeting of which not less than 21 days' notice has been given of the intention to propose it as a special resolution (s. 378(2)). The majority required is calculated in accordance with the principles set out for extraordinary resolutions above.

At least 21 days' notice must be given of the intention to propose a special resolution at a general meeting. However, consent to short notice may be given in accordance with s. 378(3) which requires the agreement of a *majority in number* of the members having the right to attend and vote at such a meeting, holding not less than 95% in nominal value of the shares giving that right. In the case of a company not having a share capital, the majority required is a majority in number together representing not less than 95% of the voting rights.

The intention to propose a resolution as a special resolution should be clearly stated in the notice calling the meeting. The notice should also specify either the text or the entire substance of the resolution (*Re Moorgate Mercantile Holdings Ltd* [1980] 1 All ER 40) (see **22.3**).

A copy of every special resolution passed by a company must be filed at Companies House within 15 days of it being passed (s. 380(1)) and must be annexed or embodied in every copy of the articles issued after the passing of the resolution (s. 380(2)) (see **12.6**).

Table 12.3 Matters that must be passed by special resolution under the Companies Act 1985 and the Insolvency Act 1986

Nature of resolution	Companies Act 1985
Change of situation of registered office to Wales in memorandum of association	s. 2(2)
Alteration of objects in memorandum of association	s. 4(1)
Alteration of articles of association	s. 9(1)
Alteration of conditions in memorandum that could lawfully be contained in the articles	s. 17(1)
Change of company name	s. 28(1)
Ratification of (and relief for) action by directors that is outside the capacity of the company	s. 35(3)
Re-registration of private company as public	s. 43(1)
Re-registration of unlimited company as public	s. 48(2)
Re-registration of unlimited company as limited	s. 51
Re-registration of public company as private	s. 53(1)
Disapplication of pre-emption rights	s. 95(1) & s. 95(2)
Resolution that uncalled share capital shall not be called up except in a winding up	s. 120
Reduction of share capital	s. 135
Financial assistance by private company for acquisition of own shares	s. 155
Resolution authorising terms of off-market purchase of own shares	s. 164
Purchase of own shares under contingent purchase contract	s. 165(2)
Assignment or release of company's right to purchase own shares	s. 167
Purchase of own shares (payment out of capital of private company)	s. 173
Resolution of dormant company not to appoint auditors	s. 250
Resolution making liability of directors unlimited	s. 307
Approval of assignment of office by a director	s. 308
	Insolvency Act 1986
Resolution to wind up voluntarily	s. 84(1)
Authorise liquidator to transfer assets of company to new company in exchange for securities in the new company	s. 110(3)
Resolution to be wound up by court	s. 122(1)

Listed companies must also forward to the UK Listing Authority two copies of any special resolution passed at a general meeting (Listing Rules, para. 9.31). See Table 12.3.

12.5 Elective resolutions

A private company may elect to dispense with certain formalities by passing an elective resolution (see Chapter 25). An elective resolution will not be effective unless:

- at least 21 days' notice in writing is given of the meeting, stating that an elective resolution is to be proposed and stating the terms of the resolution; and
- the resolution is agreed to at the meeting, in person or by proxy, by all the members entitled to attend and vote at the meeting (s. 379A(2)).

However, less than 21 days' notice in writing of the meeting may be given if all the members entitled to attend and vote at the meeting agree (s. 379A(2A)). A private company can also avoid the statutory notice requirements by passing an elective resolution as a written resolution (see **Chapter 26**).

A copy of every elective resolution passed by a private company must be filed at Companies House within 15 days of it being passed (s. 380(1)) and must be annexed or embodied in every copy of the articles issued after the passing of the resolution (s. 380(2)).

12.6 Filing of resolutions

The Act requires copies of certain resolutions to be filed with the registrar of companies at Companies House within 15 days of being passed (s. 380) (see **Precedent 12.6**). The resolutions that must be filed include the following:

- any special resolution;
- any extraordinary resolution;
- any elective resolution; and
- a number of ordinary resolutions specified in s. 380(4) (see Table 12.1).

If any of the above are done by written resolution, they must still be filed. In addition any agreement that has the same effect as a resolution (e.g. a shareholders' agreement which has the effect of modifying the articles) must also be filed under s. 380.

12.7 Date a resolution is passed

The date on which a resolution is passed is the date of the meeting or, if the resolution was passed at an adjourned meeting, the date of the adjourned meeting (s. 381). However, where the business of a meeting is suspended for the purposes of conducting a poll at a later date, the date of the resolution will be the date on which the result of the poll is ascertained, unless the articles provide otherwise. If a resolution is passed by written resolution, it is passed on the date the last member signed it.

13

Quorum

13.1 Summary

- The quorum is the minimum number of persons entitled to vote who must be present or represented at a meeting in order for it to transact any business. Articles usually specify the quorum for general meetings. In default, the Act provides that the quorum shall be two members who must be personally present (s. 370).
- Corporate representatives are counted in calculating whether a quorum exists. Proxies should not be counted unless the articles provide otherwise. An individual may be counted more than once for the purposes of calculating whether a quorum exists where he or she represents more than one member (see **13.2**).
- However, a meeting cannot normally take place with only one person present even if that person represents sufficient members to form a quorum or, indeed, represents all the members (see **13.3**).
- Articles usually provide that a general meeting will be automatically adjourned if a quorum is not present within a specified period after the time appointed for the start of the meeting (see **13.4**).
- A quorum must be present throughout the meeting unless the articles provide otherwise (see **13.5**).
- The court may intervene where a member is abusing the quorum requirements to frustrate the will of the majority (see **13.6**).
- Articles may make provision for special quorum requirements in certain circumstances (see **13.7**).
- The Act provides that the quorum at meetings of single-member companies shall be one member present in person or by proxy (see **13.8**).
- Special quorum requirements exist for class meetings held to consider a variation of the rights of class members (see **9.4**).

13.2 Who may be counted in the quorum

To be counted in the quorum, a person must first and foremost be eligible to vote (*Young v. South African & Australian Exploration & Development Syndicate* [1896] 2 Ch. 268; cf. *Re Greymouth Point Elizabeth Railway and Coal Co. Ltd* [1904] 1 Ch. 32). A member may be ineligible to vote for a variety of reasons (see **15.4**); for example, because a call is outstanding on his or her shares (reg. 57 of Table A).

Members must also be personally present, unless the articles provide otherwise. Corporate representatives are deemed to be members for these purposes and should always be counted unless they are not eligible to vote (*Re Kelantan Coco Nut Estates Ltd* [1920] WN 274). However, members represented by a proxy should not be counted unless the articles allow. Proxies may not be counted under articles like reg. 53 of 1948 Table A which states:

> **53.** No business shall be transacted at any general meeting unless a quorum of members is present at the time when the meeting proceeds to business; save as herein otherwise provided *three members present in person shall be a quorum*. [The words in italics were substituted by the words 'two members present in person or by proxy shall be a quorum' by the Companies Act 1980, Sch. 3 and these words apply to any company registered on or after 22 December 1980.]

In contrast, reg. 40 of the 1985 Table A explicitly allows members represented by proxy to be counted in the quorum. It provides:

> **40.** No business shall be transacted at any meeting unless a quorum is present. Two persons entitled to vote upon the business to be transacted, each being a member or a proxy for a member or a duly authorised representative of a corporation, shall be a quorum.

Where the articles allow members represented by proxy to be counted in calculating whether a quorum exists, care should be taken to ensure that:

- proxies are not counted when the member who appointed them is also present;
- a member represented by more than one proxy is only counted once.

Table 13.1 shows what combinations would qualify for the purposes of reg. 40 of 1985 Table A.

Table 13.1 Possible combinations for a quorum under reg. 40 of 1985 Table A

First person	Second person
Member	Member
Member	Proxy
Member	Corporate representative
Proxy	Proxy
Proxy	Corporate representative
Corporate representative	Corporate representative

13.3 More than one person

A quorum may exist even though the actual number of persons present is less than the number specified as the quorum by the articles. This is because a person may represent more than one member. For example, in *McLeod (Neil) & Sons, Petitioners*, 1967 SC 16, the quorum specified in the articles was three members personally present. It was held that a quorum was present at a meeting even though there were only two people present at a meeting where one of those members attended in his own capacity and as a trustee.

This rule is subject to the basic common law principle that for a meeting to take place there must be a coming together of at least two people. In *Sharp v. Dawes* [1876] 2 QBD 26, Mellish LJ said: 'It is clear that, according to the ordinary use of the English language, a meeting could no more be constituted by one person than a meeting could have been constituted if no shareholder at all had attended.' Thus, a meeting attended by only one member who held proxies for all the other members was held to be invalidly constituted (*Re Sanitary Carbon Co.* [1877] WN 233). Similarly, where a company's articles provided that two or more members present in person or by proxy shall be a quorum, one member present in his own capacity and in his capacity as the first named trustee for two trusts and as proxy for another member did not constitute a valid meeting (*Prain & Sons Ltd, Petitioners*, 1947 SC 325).

There are a number of important exceptions to the general rule that a meeting cannot take place without at least two persons.

If default is made in holding an AGM, the Secretary of State may call or direct the calling of a general meeting and direct that one member present in person or by proxy be deemed to be a quorum (s. 367(1) and (2)). The court may make a similar direction where it has ordered a general meeting to be called under s. 371.

It has been held in relation to class meetings that a single person may constitute a meeting where that person holds all the issued shares of a particular class (*East v. Bennett Bro. Ltd* [1911] 1 Ch. 163). This principle does not apply where all the shares in a public company fall into the hands of a single member. In these circumstances the correct procedure would be for the member to transfer at least one share into the name of another person (normally a nominee) so that a meeting may be held. If this is not possible, an application should be made to the Secretary of State (s. 367) or the court (s. 371) for an order that a meeting may be held with a quorum of one.

A private company that has only one member may, notwithstanding any provision to the contrary in the articles, hold meetings with a quorum of one by virtue of s. 370A (inserted by the Companies (Single Member Private Limited Companies) Regulations 1992, reg. 2, Schedule, para. 5).

13.4 Failure to obtain a quorum

Reg. 41 of the 1985 Table A provides that if a quorum is not present within half an hour from the time appointed for the meeting, the meeting shall stand adjourned to the same day in the next week at the same time and place or such time and place as the directors may determine. Where this article applies, the quorum required for the transaction of business at the adjourned meeting will be the same as for the original meeting. However, it is common for this article to be modified so that if at the adjourned meeting a quorum is not present within a certain time 'the members present shall be a quorum' (see example at **Precedent 13.4**). Thus the normal requirement of, say, eight members present in person or by proxy would be reduced to at least two. If the articles allow proxies to be included, it would seem that the words 'members present' would allow them to be included for this purpose. However, the principle in *Sharp v. Dawes* would probably prevent a meeting of one person being allowed in such circumstances even if that person held proxies for other members (see *Daimler Co. Ltd v. Continental Tyre & Rubber Co. (Great Britain) Ltd* [1916] 2 AC 307).

It is also common for articles to provide that a meeting convened on the requisition of members shall be dissolved if a quorum is not present within the allotted time (see example at **Precedent 13.4**). Where such provision is made, the company would be well advised to ensure that a quorum is present if it has taken the opportunity to propose resolutions at the meeting.

If it is impracticable or impossible to hold a meeting with a quorum in accordance with the articles, application can be made to the court under s. 371 for an order calling a meeting to be held with some other quorum (*Re Edinburgh Workmen's Houses Improvement Co. Ltd* 1934 SLT 513) (see **10.5**). The Secretary of State has similar powers in relation to AGMs (see **10.4**).

13.5 Failure to maintain a quorum

For companies with articles similar to reg. 40 of the 1985 Act Table A, which provides that no business shall be transacted unless a quorum is present, the quorum must be maintained throughout the meeting. Reg. 41 of the 1985 Table A provides that if during a meeting such a quorum ceases to be present, the meeting shall stand adjourned to the same day in the next week at the same time and place or such time and place as the directors may determine. Strictly speaking, under reg. 41, a meeting will be adjourned automatically if sufficient members leave the meeting and the number remaining is not sufficient to form a quorum, even if those who have left actually return shortly thereafter. Where the number of members present is only just sufficient to form a quorum, the chairman should ask members not to leave the meeting without informing him that they are about to leave. This would allow him to propose a formal motion to adjourn the meeting to a time and place that is agreeable to the members before the member leaves and forces the meeting to be adjourned automatically.

In order to avoid this problem altogether, articles commonly provide that a quorum need only be present 'at the time when the meeting proceeds to business' (e.g. reg. 53 of 1948 Act Table A). If so, the meeting may continue to transact business even though the quorum is not subsequently maintained (*Re Hartley Baird* [1955] Ch. 143) provided that the number of persons present does not fall below two, in which case the *Sharp v. Dawes* principle applies (*Re London Flats Ltd* [1969] 1 WLR 711). This type of article also prevents a dissenting minority obstructing the transaction of business by absenting themselves from the meeting once they realise that things are not going their way.

13.6 Abuse of quorum requirements

If a minority shareholder attempts to frustrate the will of the majority by refusing to attend a meeting and thereby preventing the formation of a quorum, the court may order the holding of a meeting under s. 371 (see further **10.5**) and direct that the quorum for that meeting shall be less than the number normally required (*Re El Sombrero Ltd* [1958] Ch. 900 and *Re H. R. Paul & Son Ltd* (1973) 118 SJ 166). The court will only do so where the quorum is a fixed number of shareholders and the minority shareholder's ability to prevent the holding of meetings is merely a consequence of the number of shareholders there are at that time. It will not do so where the articles specifically provide that a meeting shall not be quorate without the presence of that shareholder (see below).

13.7 Special quorum requirements

The quorum requirements can be used to protect the interests of certain shareholders. The articles or a shareholders' agreement may provide that a quorum shall not exist unless a particular member or the holder of a particular class of shares is present. These special requirements can be restricted to certain types of business, e.g. the appointment and removal of directors. Such provisions will usually be framed so that they attach special rights to a certain class of shares. The courts have held that where they apply to a named shareholder, that shareholder will be treated as having class rights which may not be modified unless the proper procedures for variation are followed. The Court of Appeal has also held that, where the articles or a shareholders' agreement create class rights by requiring the presence of the holder of a certain class of share for meetings to be quorate, it would not be right for the court, on an application under s. 371 (see section 10.5), to order that a meeting be held with some other quorum requirement (*Harman v. BML Group Ltd* [1994] 1WLR 893). Dillon LJ said: 'it is not right, in my view, to invoke s. 371 to override class rights attached to a class of shares which have been deliberately – in this case by the shareholders' agreement – imposed for the protection of the holders of those shares'.

An article that requires all the members entitled to vote to be present in person or by proxy in order to form a quorum (irrespective of the number of members there is at any particular time) may offer similar protection. However, such an article would not normally be advisable except for companies with very few members.

13.8 Single-member companies

The Act provides that, notwithstanding anything to the contrary in the articles of a private company limited by shares or guarantee having only one member, one member present in person or by proxy shall be a quorum at general meetings of the company (s. 370A).

14

Proxies and corporate representatives

14.1 Summary

- A company that is a shareholder in another company can appoint a proxy to attend and vote on its behalf. However, the rights of proxies are limited in comparison to the rights of members present in person at a meeting. As a company clearly cannot attend and vote in person, it would be at a disadvantage if it were not given special rights of representation. In order to place a corporation on the same footing as individual members, the Act allows a corporation to appoint a person to act as its representative at company meetings (see **14.2**).

- A corporate representative is entitled to exercise the same powers on behalf of the corporation as the corporation could exercise if it was an individual member, creditor or debenture-holder of the company (see **14.3**).

- The Act prescribes the method of appointment, although articles may allow appointments to be made in other ways (see **14.4**).

- There is some debate as to whether a company may appoint more than one representative. The DTI has recently proposed that the Act should be clarified to allow companies to appoint more than one representative (see **14.5**).

- The right to vote at general meetings enables members to influence or control the company. In order to maintain the balance of power, it is essential that members have the right to exercise their votes even though they are not able to attend the meeting in person. The Act achieves this by giving members a statutory right to appoint another person (a proxy) to attend the meeting and vote on their behalf (see **14.6**).

- The Act confers certain rights on proxies which cannot be excluded by a company's articles. The articles may, however, extend those rights (see **14.7**).

- The notice of every general meeting must include a statement explaining to members their right to appoint a proxy (see **14.8**).
- The directors may issue proxy forms at the company's expense. However, they may not invite selected members to appoint a specific person as their proxy (see **14.9**).
- Articles usually require proxies to be appointed in writing and may prescribe the form that must be used to make the appointment. Irrespective of anything contained in its articles, a company may, however, allow members to notify their appointment using some form of electronic communications.
- Listed companies are required to send shareholders a proxy form which allows them to instruct their proxy how to vote. These may be sent electronically if the shareholder has agreed to receive documents required by the Listing Rules to be sent to him or her in this manner (see **14.10**).
- Articles usually require proxy forms to be deposited with the company at least 48 hours before the time appointed for the meeting (see **14.14**).
- A proxy deposited in time for the original meeting will also be valid for any adjournment of that meeting (see **14.16**).
- Articles usually make special provision for the deposit of proxies in connection with a poll not taken at the meeting (see **14.17**).
- A member may revoke the appointment of a proxy. Articles normally require notice of revocation to be given to the company. However, a member may revoke the appointment of a proxy without giving notice by attending and voting in person at the meeting (see **14.18**).
- A member may change his or her voting instructions at any time before the vote is taken (see **14.20**).
- Articles usually make special provision with regard to the validity of proxies appointed by joint shareholders (see **14.21**) and proxies appointed by members who subsequently die or suffer from some mental disorder (see **14.19**).
- A proxy cannot be forced to attend or vote on behalf of his or her appointor unless there is a contractual relationship between the parties or the proxy has a fiduciary duty to do so. The chairman may have a fiduciary duty to vote in accordance with the instructions of members who have appointed him (see **14.22**).
- The chairman is usually given authority by the articles to rule on the validity of proxy votes (see **14.23**).

14.2 Right to appoint representatives

In order to place corporations on the same footing as individual members, s. 375(1)(a) allows a corporation that is a member of another company to appoint a person to act as its representative at any meeting of the company or any meeting of any class of members of the company. This right is also extended to meetings of creditors and debenture-holders where the corporation is a creditor or debenture-holder as the case may be (s. 375(2)). A person so appointed by a company is usually known as a corporate representative.

For the purposes of s. 375, a corporation includes any body that has separate legal personality (including companies incorporated outside Great Britain), but does not include a corporation sole or a Scottish firm (s. 740).

14.3 Rights of corporate representatives

A corporate representative is entitled to exercise the same powers on behalf of the corporation as the corporation could exercise if it was an individual member, creditor or debenture-holder of the company (s. 375(2)). Thus a corporate representative will, for example, be counted as a member for the purposes of calculating whether there is a quorum (*Re Kelantan Coco Nut Estates Ltd* [1920] WN 274). Unlike a proxy, a representative will always be entitled to vote on a show of hands and have a right to speak at any meeting. Unless prevented from doing so under the terms of appointment, a corporate representative may also appoint a proxy. Table 14.1 shows a comparison of the rights of proxies and corporate representatives.

14.4 Appointment of corporate representatives

A corporation may appoint a person as its representative by a resolution of its board of directors or other governing body (s. 375(1)). For these purposes a 'corporation' includes any UK or foreign company and the words 'other governing body' can include a liquidator (*Hillman v. Crystal Bowl Amusements and Others* [1973] 1 WLR 162, CA).

As far as the Act and Table A are concerned, there is no requirement for a corporation to deposit a form of appointment prior to the meeting. The articles of listed companies normally specify that a representative may be required by the company to

Table 14.1 Comparison of the rights of proxies and corporate representatives

Rights	Proxy	Corporate representative
Counted in quorum	Only if articles specify	Yes
Attend	Yes	Yes
Vote on show of hands	Only if articles specify	Yes
Speak at meetings: Private company	Yes	Yes
Public company	Depends on articles	Yes
Appoint a proxy	No	Yes

produce evidence of his or her authority on admission or at any time during the meeting or in connection with the exercise of any right to vote on a poll (see **Precedent 14.4A**). Although Table A does not make specific provision in this regard, a company can and should take steps to ensure that those who attend and vote are eligible to do so. For individual shareholders and creditors, proof of identity will be sufficient for these purposes. Clearly this will not be the case with regard to a corporate representative and it will be necessary in addition to obtain evidence of their appointment.

As a resolution of the directors is required, the evidence should be provided in the form of a certified copy of a board minute. The board resolution can be authenticated (certified) by any director, secretary or other authorised officer of the company by virtue of s. 41. However, it is not uncommon for appointments to be made under seal. In these circumstances, it can be assumed that the appointment was properly authorised even though no evidence of a resolution of the directors has been provided.

The appointment of a representative may relate to a specific meeting or, as is commonly the case, may be of more general application (see **Precedent 14.4B**).

14.5   One or more representatives

It is open to debate whether a corporate member can appoint more than one person to act as its representative. Section 375 uses the word 'person' in the singular. However, s. 6 of the Interpretation Act 1978 states that in any Act, unless the contrary intention appears, words in the singular include the plural. The intention of s. 375 is clearly to place a corporation in the same position as an individual shareholder and not in a more advantageous position. If a corporation is allowed to appoint more than one representative, each joint representative would, by virtue of s. 375(2), be 'entitled to exercise the same powers on behalf of the corporation which he represents as the corporation could exercise if it was an individual shareholder, creditor or debenture holder'. There is therefore a school of thought that a corporation is only entitled to appoint one representative to attend, speak and vote on the same occasion. Any other interpretation, it is argued, would enable a corporation that owned only one share to appoint as many people as it could muster as its representatives, each having the right to speak at the meeting, join in a demand for a poll and vote on a show of hands. An individual shareholder could not achieve the same result even if entitled to appoint more than one proxy. His or her proxies would not have the right to vote on a show of hands or, with regard to meetings of public companies, speak at a meeting. If the word 'person' in s. 375 is not intended to include the plural all these problems are eliminated at a stroke, and it is hardly surprising that this is the view that most companies adopt.

It may be that in order to rebut the basic principle contained in s. 6 of the Interpretation Act the courts would require stronger evidence of a contrary intention. The restrictive interpretation would prevent a corporation appointing different representatives for different blocks of shares that form part of the same holding as well as preventing the appointment of two or more persons as representatives for the same block of shares. It is clear from s. 372(2)(b) (a member of a private company may only appoint one proxy unless the articles otherwise provide) that the parliamentary draftsmen were aware that the word 'person' in s. 372(1) (and presumably in s. 375) was capable of meaning more than one person.

If, contrary to the generally accepted view, a corporation can appoint more than one person to act as its representative for the same holding, it is submitted that it is far from certain whether the consequences are as dire as some might suggest. If the word 'persons' is substituted for the words 'a person' in s. 375(2) and appropriate grammatical changes are made, it would read 'persons so authorised are entitled to exercise the same powers on behalf of the corporation which they represent as the corporation could exercise if it was an individual shareholder, creditor or debenture holder'. This could be interpreted as meaning that the representatives must act jointly in the exercise of the corporation's rights. The corporation, as a member, would still be entitled to only one vote on a show of hands. Which of the representatives should cast that vote in practical terms would be a matter for them to decide between themselves. It is only if s. 375(2) is interpreted as conferring on *each* representative the same rights as an individual member that the problem of more than one vote on a show of hands arises. Articles usually provide that each member shall be entitled to one vote on a show of hands but, in the case of joint holders, that the company shall only accept the vote of the senior joint holder who tenders a vote. No precedent exists on the voting rights of joint holders where the articles are silent on this matter. However, it has been held that in the absence of any provision to the contrary in the articles, joint holders should be counted as a single member for the purposes of demanding a poll (*Cory v. Reindeer Steamship Co.* (1915) 31 TLR 530). There is no reason to believe that the courts would not adopt a similar approach with regard to corporate representatives by treating them as one member for the purposes of voting.

14.5.1   DTI consultation

In 1996, the Department of Trade and Industry issued a consultative document (*Shareholder Communications at the Annual General Meeting*) which proposed that s. 375 should be amended to allow corporate shareholders to appoint more than one representative to attend general meetings. The proposal was made for the benefit of nominee companies that would like to be able to appoint their underlying investors as corporate representatives rather than as proxies. Another alternative considered in the consultation document was to amend s. 372 so as to give proxies of members of public companies the same right to speak as the member who appointed them.

14.6 Statutory right to appoint a proxy

Every member of a company with a share capital who is entitled to attend and vote at a meeting of the company has a statutory right to appoint another person (who need not be a member of the company) to attend and vote on his or her behalf at that meeting (s. 372(1)). A person so appointed by a member is known as a proxy.

The ability to appoint someone who is not a member is important as it ensures that a member can find someone who is willing to act. This would not necessarily be the case if only members could be appointed.

For members of public companies the right to appoint another 'person' in s. 372(1) is deemed by virtue of s. 6 of the Interpretation Act 1978 to mean one or more persons. A member of a private company is not entitled to appoint more than one proxy to attend the same meeting unless the articles confer that right (s. 372(2)(b)). This does not prevent a member of a private company appointing an alternate proxy. However, they may not both attend. It should be noted that reg. 59 of Table A allows a member to appoint more than one proxy to attend on the same occasion.

The right to appoint a proxy in the case of companies limited by guarantee that do not have a share capital will depend on the articles. There is no common law right to vote by proxy (*Harben v. Phillips* (1883) 23 Ch. D. 14). The statutory right to appoint a proxy does not apply in the case of a company not having a share capital, e.g. a company limited by guarantee (s. 372(2)(a)).

The word 'proxy' is commonly used to describe the person appointed by a member, the form of appointment sent to members and the votes held by a proxy (e.g. the chairman of the meeting). Only the first of these is strictly correct. A proxy is a person appointed by a member to attend and vote on his or her behalf. To avoid confusion, the instrument of appointment can be referred to as the 'proxy form' and votes cast by a proxy as 'proxy votes'.

14.7 Rights of proxies

Proxies have a statutory right to attend and vote on behalf of the members who appointed them. The right to attend will, however, be subject to the usual rules on ejection in cases of severe disorder.

A proxy appointed by a member of a private company has the

same right as that member to speak at the meeting (s. 372(1)). The Act makes no such provision with regard to proxies appointed by members of a public company. The articles of public companies sometimes confirm or deny proxies' right to speak. Where they are silent, the question may be determined by the chairman with the consent of the meeting in accordance with the principles laid down in *Carruth v. Imperial Chemical Industries Ltd* (see **18.5**). In its *Guide to Best Practice for Annual General Meetings*, the ICSA recommends that chairmen of listed companies should seek the consent of the meeting to proxies speaking and participating in the debate. However, some listed companies still prefer not to do so because they believe protest groups might abuse that right.

All proxies may demand or join in a demand for a poll (s. 373(2)). This will be the case even where the articles provide that proxies may not speak. All proxies are entitled to vote on a poll but not on a show of hands unless the articles so provide (s. 372(2)(c)). Table A does not allow proxies to vote on a show of hands. However, some listed companies now allow proxies to vote on a show of hands.

Proxies must attend the meeting in person in order to vote. Proxies appointed to attend and vote at the original meeting have a right to attend and vote at any adjournment of that meeting unless the articles provide otherwise (*Scadding v. Lorrant* (1851) 3 HLC 418), e.g. they require members to submit a new instrument of proxy for any adjourned meeting. It makes no difference in this regard whether the articles allow members to appoint proxies between the date of the original meeting and the adjourned meeting. In this case, instruments of proxy deposited for the original meeting and those deposited in accordance with the articles for the adjourned meeting will both be valid (see further **14.16**).

On a poll, a member who is entitled to more than one vote need not use all his or her votes or cast all the votes he or she uses (whether in person or by proxy) in the same way (s. 374). There is nothing to prevent a person acting as proxy for more than one member.

A proxy may in certain circumstances act as the chairman of a meeting (*Re Bradford Investments plc* [1990] BCC 740).

14.8   Statement in the notice of the meeting

A statement must be included with reasonable prominence in the notice of every general meeting of a company that has a share capital to the effect that a member entitled to attend and vote is entitled to appoint a proxy or, where that is allowed, one or more proxies to attend instead of him or her and that a proxy need not be a member (s. 372(3)). If the articles of a private company allow members to appoint more than one proxy, the statement should make this clear. The statement is usually positioned at the end of the notice (see **Precedent 11.5A**). If the articles of a company without a share capital allow members to appoint a proxy, they usually require a similar statement to be included in the notice.

14.9 Invitations to appoint a proxy

The Act does not require companies to send proxy forms to members, although listed companies are required to do so by para. 9.26 of the Listing Rules (see para. 14.13). Any company may, however, issue proxy forms to members at the company's expense. Generally, any expenses incurred in good faith in the best interests of the company to secure votes in support of the directors' policy are payable out of the funds of the company. Thus, the directors may send proxy forms made out in their own names to shareholders accompanied by a stamped addressed envelope to encourage a greater response (*Peel v. London & North West Ry. Co.* [1907] 1 Ch. 5).

Invitations to appoint a person (e.g. the chairman) or one of a number of persons may only be issued at the company's expense if they are sent to all the members entitled to receive notice of the meeting. An officer of the company who knowingly or wilfully permits the issue of invitations to selected members is liable to a fine unless the invitation was issued in response to a written request by a member for a form of appointment naming the proxy or a list of persons willing to act as proxy and that form or list was freely available to all other members entitled to vote by proxy at the meeting (s. 372(6)). For the purposes of s. 372(6), an invitation will include any proxy form with the name of a person already inserted as the proxy or any document, circular or letter inviting members to appoint a particular person or persons as their proxy.

It should be noted that s. 372(6) does not prevent anyone (including the directors) from soliciting proxies at their own expense.

14.10 Appointment of a proxy

The relationship between a member and his or her proxy is one of principal and agent. In the normal course of events, an agent can be appointed either in writing or orally or by any other legal method, including the use of electronic communications. Although a person may validly appoint an agent without notifying anyone of the appointment, third parties usually demand to see evidence of an agent's authority so that they can satisfy themselves that the principal will be bound by the acts of his purported agent. Companies usually require members to notify proxy appointments well in advance of the meeting so that they can check the validity of the appointment, but also so that they know in advance who must be admitted to the meeting and who may be excluded. If prior notification were not required, the company would have to try to check the validity of appointments at the meeting.

Articles usually require appointments to be made in writing and to be signed by the relevant member or joint members, although a company may now allow members to make appointments electronically (see **14.11**). In the normal course of events, the signed proxy forms provide evidence that any poll called at the meeting was properly conducted and that the votes cast by proxies on behalf of members were valid. They could, however, be used by someone seeking to challenge the result to show that some fraud had been committed (e.g. that their signature had been forged). Whether this would have any effect on the outcome of the meeting will depend partly on whether the company's articles give the chairman power to rule on the validity of votes cast at the meeting (see **14.23**). However, the courts would be unlikely to allow a company to rely on such an article where the company (or the chairman) was a party to the fraud.

The Act does not dictate how proxies must be appointed. It does, however, impose certain restrictions on provisions that may be contained in a company's articles.

14.11   Electronic appointments

Section 372 used to require appointments of proxies to be made in writing; or, at least, this was assumed to be the case by virtue of the fact that s. 372(5) referred to an 'instrument appointing a proxy', which was generally assumed to mean an instrument in writing. Whether this was the case was never tested. However, the question is now academic because the offending words have now been deleted and specific provision is now made in the Act to facilitate the use of electronic communications. These changes were made by the Companies Act 1985 (Electronic Communications) Order 2000 which came into force on 22 December 2000.

As there is nothing in the Act that dictates how proxies must be appointed, it is open to companies to make their own provision in their articles. As it was assumed that the Act required appointments to be made in writing, that is what the articles of any company incorporated before 22 December 2000 will probably require, unless its articles have subsequently been amended. To ensure that such companies are not precluded from using electronic communications for these purposes, s. 372(2A) provides that the appointment of a proxy may, notwithstanding any provision to the contrary in a company's articles, be contained in an electronic communication sent to such address as may be notified by or on behalf of the company for that purpose (see **2.5** regarding the meaning of electronic communications).

In addition, s. 372(2B) provides that, in so far as the articles of a company make no other provision in that behalf, the appointment of a proxy may be contained in an electronic communication in accordance with the provisions of Table A.

Table A was also amended by the Companies Act 1985 (Electronic Communications) Order 2000 to allow the use of electronic communications with effect from 22 December 2000 (see **Appendix B**). Although the amendments have no direct effect on the articles of any company incorporated before that date, they must be applied as if they were incorporated in a company's articles, if a company decides to allow members to use electronic communications to appoint proxies and its articles make no direct provision to allow this.

A company need not allow members to make appointments using electronic communications. If it chooses not to do so, appointments must be made in accordance with its articles, which will normally require the appointment to be made in writing.

Although it is not necessary for a company to amend its articles before allowing members to make proxy appointments by e-mail or via a website (or any other electronic method), it is desirable to do so (see **2.4**).

If a company wishes to allow members to make proxy appointments using some form of electronic communications, it must notify them of the fact that this facility is being made available and specifically notify them of the address to be used for this purpose. In practice, this address will normally be an e-mail address or the address of the company's website. However, the definition of electronic communications is so wide that members could also be allowed to use other methods of communication, including the telephone, mobile phone text messaging service or a fax message. An address in these cases would mean a telephone number.

The Act makes no specific provision to allow a company to send proxy forms to members electronically. This is because the Act does not require companies to send proxy forms to members. Listed companies are required to do so by the Listing Rules which have been modified to allow them to be sent electronically (see **14.13**).

In practice, most companies will probably only allow members to use methods of electronic communication that enable the company to ensure that the member uses its standard form of appointment and provides all the information necessary to ensure that the appointment is valid. Methods that satisfy these criteria include web-based forms and appointments made by fax or over the telephone.

14.11.1   Authentication/execution

If a company intends to allow members to make electronic proxy appointments, it will need to devise a method of authentication. Where appointments are made in writing, they are authenticated by being executed, i.e. by the signature of an individual or the seal of a company. Although a company will often have no way of knowing whether the signatures on proxy forms are genuine, the existence of signed proxy forms enables this to be established after the event, should the need arise. They also provide the basis on which the chairman would make any ruling on the validity of votes tendered by proxy.

A company could, subject to its articles, allow members to notify proxy appointments electronically without providing any authentication at all. In other words, it could simply trust to luck that there will be no challenge as to the validity of any votes. Should there be a challenge, the chairman might find it difficult to rule on the validity of votes tendered by proxy in this manner, and his decision could conceivably be challenged in legal proceedings even where the articles provide that his ruling shall be conclusive in this regard. It is submitted therefore that members ought to be required to provide some sort of authentication when making electronic proxy appointments. It is notable in this regard that regs 60 and 62 of Table A still require appointments to be 'executed', which would seem to indicate that a substitute for manual signatures will be required where individuals make electronic appointments (see **Precedent 14.11** for an alternative form of words which may be used in this regard).

The closest equivalent to a manual signature for these purposes is the so-called electronic signature. Under the Electronic Communications Act 2000, electronic signatures are now admissible as evidence in legal proceedings (see **2.8**). An electronic signature may be applied to an electronic transmission using complex cryptographic techniques. These ensure that the document may only be unlocked by applying the public key of the person who encrypted it. If the document can be opened using the public key of the person who sent it, it must also have been encrypted using that person's private key. Using this type of electronic signature also ensures that the message cannot be tampered with before being opened by the recipient. Electronic signatures are in many ways more secure than manual signatures, unless the owner has allowed his or her private key to fall into the hands of some unauthorised person. However, they are, at present, only suitable for authenticating messages transmitted in computerised form, whether as an e-mail or via the Internet or otherwise. In addition, most people still do not have one. Accordingly, it is unlikely that many companies will be able to insist on this level of authentication if they wish to encourage members to use electronic communications.

Instead, most companies will probably require members to authenticate their appointment by confirming a unique identification number which the company or its registrars has allocated to them for that purpose, or which it may have already allocated for some other purpose. For example, most service registrars allocate a unique reference number to each shareholder which is often printed on share certificates and proxy forms. For reasons of security and practicality, it may be preferable to allocate a separate identification number for the purposes of electronic communications. Shareholders may, for example, want to change their number if they suspect that it has been compromised. However, unless shareholders are reminded what their number is each year, they are likely to forget it, and therefore be unable to use electronic communications. One way round this would be to enable shareholders to access their unique number via a website if they were able to provide answers to certain questions that were deemed sufficient to establish their identity.

Members could, of course, be allowed from the outset to allocate their own password or identification number. This would enable them to use the same code for their holdings in other companies. It is clear that the solution to these problems will always involve a trade off between security and usability. In practice most listed companies will probably rely on systems devised by their service registrars for these purposes. And, at the moment, it appears that service registrars are planning to use specially allocated personal identification numbers for the purposes of authentication.

Although this method of authentication would come within the Electronic Communications Act 2000 definition of an electronic signature, it is clear that it would not be given the same weight as an electronic signature applied using modern cryptographic techniques in any legal proceedings. Generally speaking, this will not cause a problem in view of the provisions that are found in most articles regarding the validity of votes (see **14.23**).

14.11.2   Procedures for electronic appointments

The Act provides that in so far as the articles of a company make no other provision in that behalf, the appointment of a proxy may be contained in an electronic communication in accordance with the provisions of Table A (s. 372(2B)). It is notable that the word 'may' is used here rather than the word 'shall'. This would seem to imply that a company need not insist that members comply with the procedures in Table A.

Regulation 62 of Table A (as amended) provides that the appointment of a proxy may be made by electronic communications, where an address has been specified for that purpose:

- in the notice convening the meeting, or
- in any instrument of proxy sent out by the company in relation to the meeting, or
- in any invitation contained in an electronic communication to appoint a proxy issued by the company in relation to the meeting.

Under reg. 62 an appointment sent using electronic communications to any other address would not be valid, and an appointment sent to the proper address would not be valid unless it was received at least 48 hours before the time for holding the meeting or adjourned meeting at which the person named in the appointment proposes to vote.

In theory, reg. 62 also allows electronic communications to be used to send any authority under which the appointment is executed or a copy of such authority certified notarially or in some other way approved by the directors. Where the authority has been executed in writing, this would normally be impossible. Practices will, however, undoubtedly emerge to allow authenticated copies of such authorities to be delivered electronically. An authority executed by electronic signature could also be delivered electronically.

14.12 Appointments in writing

Where a company decides not to allow appointments of proxies to be made electronically, all appointments will need to be made in accordance with the procedures set out in its articles. The articles of any company incorporated before 22 December 2000 will probably still require proxy appointments to be made in writing. This will therefore continue to be the default method of appointment for these companies. Theoretically, it is now possible for a company's articles to require all appointments to be made using some form of electronic communications; the Act does not require companies to allow appointments to be made in writing. In practice, few companies will want to do this, and where specific provision is made to allow appointments to be made electronically, articles should continue to make provision allowing appointments to be made in writing. This is the model adopted in reg. 62 of Table A.

Prior to 22 December 2000, reg. 60 provided that an instrument appointing a proxy shall be in writing executed by or on behalf of the appointor. It also specified the form of words that could be used to make the appointment. Although the amended version of reg. 60 still requires appointments to be executed by or on behalf of the appointor and specifies the form of words that may be used, it no longer requires appointments to be made in writing. Similar amendments have been made to reg. 61, which specifies the form of words that may be used by members to instruct their proxy how to vote.

In addition, reg. 62 of Table A now provides separate procedures for notifying the company of appointments made in writing and those made electronically. Where the appointment is made in writing, the instrument (proxy form) must be deposited at the office or such other place within the UK as is specified in the notice convening the meeting or in any instrument of proxy sent out by the company in relation to the meeting not less than

48 hours before the time for holding the meeting or adjourned meeting at which the person named in the instrument proposes to vote.

The amendments made to Table A by the Companies Act (Electronic Communications) Order 2000 have not changed the procedures to be followed where appointments are made in writing. Instead, they merely allow appointments to be made by an alternative method if the company chooses to allow members to use it.

The provisions of Table A regarding the procedure for making appointments in writing are widely followed in most articles. Thus most articles require the proxy form to be executed by or on behalf of the appointor. In the case of an individual, this means signed. A corporation that is a member of a company may execute a proxy under its common seal or by signature in accordance with s. 36A (in England) and s. 36B (in Scotland). It is open to debate whether a company can refuse to accept a proxy executed under the hand of a duly authorised officer. Listed companies used to be required by the Listing Rules to allow companies to execute proxies in this manner. Although the requirement was deleted in January 2000, the articles of most listed companies still make specific provision allowing this. Where this method of execution is allowed, the articles will normally allow the directors to require the company to provide evidence of that person's authority (e.g. in the form of a certified board minute).

Older articles sometimes require the instrument appointing a proxy to be attested (i.e. signed in the presence of a witness). An instrument of proxy that does not comply with such a requirement contained in the articles will be invalid (*Harben v. Phillips* (1883) 23 Ch. D. 14) and a proxy cannot attest his or her own appointment in such circumstances (*ex parte Cullen* [1891] 2 QB 151).

It is not necessary for a named person to be nominated as proxy as long as the person appointed is capable of being identified (*Bombay-Burmah Trading Corporation Ltd v. Dorabji Cursetji Shroff* [1905] AC 213). Shareholders may, for example, nominate 'the chairman of the meeting' as their proxy.

Articles usually allow the appointment of a proxy to be executed on behalf of a member. In these circumstances, they normally require the authority under which the person executed the instrument of appointment (e.g. a power of attorney) or a copy of it to be deposited by the deadline for deposit of the instrument of proxy, e.g. reg. 62 of Table A. Articles sometimes give the directors power to dispense with this requirement.

A member may authorise (either in writing or orally) another person to complete the proxy form by filling in the name of the person entitled to vote (*Re Lancaster* (1877) 5 Ch. D. 911). A blank proxy form signed by a member given to a person in connection with a requisitioned meeting together with authority to fill it up was held to be valid for a later requisitioned meeting called for the same purpose after the original requisition had been withdrawn (*Sadgrove v. Bryden* [1907] 1 Ch. 318). The secretary has no authority to enter the date of the meeting in proxy forms returned without a date unless authorised by the member to do so, although that authority may be implied in some circumstances (*Ernest v. Loma Gold Mines* [1897] 1 Ch. 1).

Proxy forms are commonly required to be deposited at the offices of the company's registrar and the reverse of the proxy form will normally be in the form of a pre-addressed and pre-paid postcard.

14.12.1   Form of proxy under Table A

Reg. 60 of Table A provides that appointments shall either be:

- in the same form as the specimen provided in that regulation (see below) or as close to it as circumstances allow;
- in any other form that is usual; or
- in any other form that the directors approve.

Under Table A, it can be assumed that proxy forms sent to members by the company have been approved by the directors for these purposes. Where proxy forms are not sent to members with the notice of the meeting, as will often be the case in private companies, members should use the specimen in the articles (if any) or, failing that, the form of words used in reg. 60 (which it would be difficult for the directors to assert is unusual). Whether any other form of words would be considered a usual form may depend on the type of company and its previous practice in this regard.

The following form of proxy is prescribed by reg. 60:

> XYZ Limited
> Form of proxy
> I/We, [name of member/names of joint holders], of [address/addresses], being a member/members of the above-named company, hereby appoint [name of proxy] of [address of proxy], or failing him, [name of alternate proxy, if any] of [address], as my/our proxy to vote in my/our name(s) and on my/our behalf at the annual/EGM of the company to be held on [date], and at any adjournment thereof.
> Signature(s)   [Date]

Although this form of proxy appears to give the person appointed as proxy complete discretion as to how to vote, a member can issue separate voting instructions (see **14.22** for a discussion of a proxy's obligation to vote in accordance with instructions).

Reg. 61 of Table A prescribes the following form of proxy for use 'where it is desired to afford members an opportunity of instructing the proxy how he should vote':

> PLC/Limited
> I/We, [name of member/names of joint holders], of [address], being a member/members of the above-named company, hereby appoint [name of proxy] of [address of proxy], or failing him, [name of alternate proxy, if any] of [address], as my/our proxy to vote in my/our name(s) and on my/our behalf at the annual/EGM of the company to be held on [date], and at any adjournment thereof.
> This form is to be used in respect of the resolutions mentioned below as follows:
> Resolution No 1 *for *against
> Resolution No 2 *for *against.
> *Strike out whichever is not desired.
> Unless otherwise instructed, the proxy may vote as he thinks fit or abstain from voting.
> Signed this   day of   20....

The words 'where it is desired to afford members an opportunity of instructing the proxy how he should vote' in reg. 61 seem to imply that the directors may, where it is not so desired, reject an appointment made in the form prescribed by that regulation (i.e. on a two-way proxy form). In fact, it is submitted that this form of appointment is now so common that it should be accepted under the heading 'or in any other form that is usual' in reg. 60.

14.13 Listing Rules

Listed companies must send shareholders two-way proxy forms. Para. 9.26 of the Listing Rules requires a proxy form to be sent with the notice convening any meeting of the holders of listed securities to each person entitled to vote at the meeting. The proxy form must comply with the requirements of paras 13.28 and 13.29 of the Listing Rules which state:

- it must provide for two-way voting on all resolutions intended to be proposed (except that it is not necessary to provide proxy forms with two-way voting on procedural resolutions) (para. 13.28(b));
- it must state that a shareholder is entitled to appoint a proxy of his or her own choice and provide a space for insertion of the name of such proxy (para. 13.28(c));
- it must state that if it is returned without an indication as to how the proxy shall vote on any particular matter, the proxy will exercise his or her discretion as to whether, and if so how, he or she votes (para. 13.28(d)); and
- if the resolutions to be proposed include the re-election of retiring directors and the number of retiring directors standing for re-

election exceeds five, the proxy form may give shareholders the opportunity to vote for or against the re-election of the retiring directors as a whole but must also allow votes to be cast for or against the re-election of the retiring directors individually (para. 13.29).

Proxy forms that comply with the requirements of Chapter 13 of the Listing Rules and which have no unusual features (see, for example, **Precedent 14.13**) do not need to be approved by the UK Listing Authority before they are dispatched. However, two copies must be lodged with the UK Listing Authority no later than the date on which they are dispatched to the holders of the relevant securities (Listing Rules, para. 13.2). It is difficult to say what might be considered an unusual feature on a proxy form.

The Listing Rules specifically allow companies to use electronic communications to send proxy forms to holders of listed securities provided that the member/holder has agreed to accept service in this manner (Listing Rules, para. 1.27). It is not sufficient for these purposes that the holder has agreed to accept service of notices and other statutory documents in this manner. Instead, they must specifically agree to accept electronic service of documents that the company is required under the Listing Rules to send them. The Listing Rules allow such documents to be served in full using any form of electronic communications provided that the person has agreed to accept service in this manner and provided an address for this purpose. They also allow a company to send the person a notification that the documents have been made available on a website, provided that the person has agreed to accept service in this manner and the company and the holder have agreed as to the manner in which that notification is to be served. Provided that the company and the holder both agree on the method to be used, the notification can be given in writing through the post or by any of the available methods of electronic communication.

14.14   Time limit for deposit of proxies

A company may require proxy appointments (and any document relating to or necessary to show the validity of any such appointment) to be lodged or delivered by a specified time before the meeting. This is normally done to allow the validity of the instruments to be checked and the votes for and against the resolution to be counted before the meeting. If no such provision is made in the articles, the company must accept a vote tendered by proxy at the meeting even though the proxy is unable at the meeting to establish his or her authority (*Re English, Scottish & Australian Bank* [1893] 3 Ch. 385).

Any provision in a company's articles will be void in so far as it requires the appointment of a proxy (or any document relating to or necessary to show the validity of any appointment) to be received by the company or its agent more than 48 hours before the meeting or adjourned meeting (s. 372(5)). In such circumstances, proxies received any time before the commencement of the meeting would be valid.

Most articles require proxies to be deposited not less than 48 hours before the time for holding the meeting or adjourned meeting. Proxy forms received after the time specified in the articles will not be valid for that meeting and should not be accepted under any circumstances. If a meeting is held on a Monday or a Tuesday, it will normally be necessary for someone to be present at the nominated office at the deadline to ensure that proxies delivered after that time are not accepted.

14.15   Faxed proxies

Although a company may, if it wishes, allow members to make appointments by fax under the provisions of s. 372, questions of validity may still arise where it did not notify members of its willingness to accept appointments in this manner or provide a fax number for this purpose. It has been held that a proxy form delivered by fax is valid for the purposes of a creditors' meeting in relation to an individual voluntary arrangement to be entered into pursuant to the Insolvency Act 1986 (*Re a debtor* (No. 2021 of 1995) [1996] 1 BCLC 538). Although Laddie J stressed that his ruling in this case did not apply to meetings held under the Companies Act 1985 or, indeed, to other creditors' meetings held in accordance with the Insolvency Act 1986, the case may be of wider significance because it hinged on the question of whether the signature on a faxed proxy satisfied the requirements of rule 8.2(3) of the Insolvency Rules 1986 that 'a form of proxy shall be signed by the principal, or by some person authorised by him'. Laddie J held that it did and, after examining the authorities, said:

> I have come to the conclusion that a proxy form is signed for the purposes of r 8.2(3) if it bears upon it some distinctive or personal marking which has been placed there by, or with the authority of, the creditor. When a creditor faxes a proxy form to the chairman of the creditors' meeting he transmits two things at the same time, the contents of the form and the signature applied to it. The receiving fax is in effect instructed by the transmitting creditor to reproduce his signature on the proxy form which is itself being created at the receiving station. It follows that, in my view, the received fax is a proxy form signed by the principal or by someone authorised by him.
> ... From the chairman's point of view, there is nothing about a received fax which puts him in a worse position to detect forgeries than when he received through the post or by hand delivery a document signed by hand by a person whose signature he has never seen before or one signed by stamping. The reality is that fax transmission is likely to be a more

reliable and certainly is a more speedy method of communication than post.

The validity of a faxed proxy received in similar circumstances in relation to a general meeting may depend upon the construction of the articles. There is certainly nothing in the Act to prevent appointments being made in this manner. Most articles require proxies to be 'executed by or on behalf of the appointor'. Where execution can be effected by signature, it seems that the ruling in *Re a debtor* will be relevant. The only other question would seem to be whether faxing the proxy form would satisfy the requirement in most articles that it be 'deposited at the office'.

14.16 Proxies at adjourned meetings

An instrument of proxy deposited prior to the original meeting will also be valid for any adjournment of that meeting, unless the articles provide otherwise (*Scadding v. Lorrant* (1851) 3 HLC 418) (see **21.8**).

14.17 Proxies on a poll

A proxy delivered after the time specified in the articles will not be valid on the suspension of business for the purposes of taking a poll (*Shaw v. Tati Concessions* [1913] 1 Ch. 292) unless the articles expressly allow proxies to be deposited at a specified time before the poll is taken, e.g. reg. 62 of Table A. Reg. 62 provides that in the case of a poll taken more than 48 hours after it is demanded, proxies must be deposited after the poll has been demanded and not less than 24 hours before the time for the taking of the poll. Therefore a proxy deposited after the time allowed for the original meeting but before the poll was actually demanded would still not be valid for these purposes.

Reg. 62 also provides that in the case of a poll taken less than 48 hours after the meeting at which it was demanded, proxies may be delivered at the meeting at which the poll was demanded to the chairman or to the secretary or to any director. In this case, it would seem that all proxies delivered late for the original meeting would be invalid unless they were delivered at the meeting. This provision can cause problems in the case of a member who is represented at the original meeting by a proxy other than the chairman who is unable to attend the poll. The member would not be able to appoint a further proxy and would therefore have to attend the poll in person in order to vote. This problem can best be avoided by nominating the chairman of the meeting as an alternate by using the words 'or failing him, the chairman of the meeting'.

14.18   Revocation of proxies

The appointment of a proxy in relation to a share will automatically be revoked (terminated) on the registration of a transfer of that share. The death or insanity of a member automatically revokes any appointment by that person of a proxy unless the articles provide otherwise. Articles commonly provide that a proxy appointed by a member who subsequently dies will be valid unless the company receives notice in writing of the death of that member.

Revocation can also be effected by notifying the company that the appointment has been revoked or that the authority under which the instrument of proxy was signed has been revoked, e.g. the revocation of a power of attorney (*R. v. Wait* (1823) 11 Price 518). A proxy that is expressed as being irrevocable cannot be revoked.

Articles usually require notice of revocation to be given before the meeting or the time appointed for the taking of a poll. For example, reg. 63 of Table A states:

> **63.** A vote given or poll demanded by proxy or by the duly authorised representative of a corporation shall be valid notwithstanding the previous determination of the authority of the person voting or demanding a poll unless notice of the determination was received by the company at the office or at such other place at which the instrument of proxy was duly deposited before the commencement of the meeting or adjourned meeting at which the vote is given or the poll demanded or (in the case of a poll taken otherwise than on the same day as the meeting or adjourned meeting) the time appointed for taking the poll.

Notice usually means notice in writing (e.g. reg. 111 of Table A). If, unusually, the articles make no provision as to the manner in which notices must be served, a member may revoke his or her proxy by giving notice at the meeting itself. If the articles do not make specific provision in respect of a poll not taken at the meeting, the revocation must be notified before the meeting at which the poll was demanded. The articles could make provision to allow members to use electronic communications for these purposes.

A proxy may vote on behalf of the member who appointed him or her even though that member attends the meeting. However, the proxy is impliedly revoked if the member votes in person (*Knight v. Bulkley* (1859) 5 Jur. (NS) 817). This will be the case even where the articles require notice of revocation to be given to the company a specified period before the meeting (*Cousins v. International Brick Co. Ltd* [1931] 2 Ch. 90, CA).

The execution and deposit of a second or later instrument of proxy in respect of the same holding within the time allowed under the articles will act as a revocation of any previous appointment where members are entitled to appoint only one proxy. This may also be the case where the deadline for appointments has expired, which could result in the member not being represented at the meeting. Where more than one appointment is made within the period specified by the articles, the company should accept whichever was the last appointment to the exclusion of the first. Where it is not possible to determine the date on which one or both appointments were made, the company may need to resolve the matter in some other way, e.g. by assuming that the appointment last received was the last to be executed.

Where members are entitled to appoint more than one proxy, the deposit of a second instrument appointing a different person will not always be conclusive evidence of the intention to revoke the original appointment, except perhaps where the second appointment is accompanied by new voting instructions.

The ability to appoint more than one proxy allows nominee companies to appoint separate proxies to attend and vote on behalf of the various underlying holders. Several instruments of appointment, each representing different shares within the same registered holding, can be deposited. However, if the sum of the parts exceeds the whole, the company will obviously need to find some way of limiting the number of votes cast. It might inform the various proxy holders in the hope that they are able to come to an arrangement between themselves. If all the proxies attempt to vote, the company must scale down the votes of one or more of the proxies. One way of doing so might be to assume that the last proxy submitted had the effect of revoking (either in whole or in part) one or more of the previously submitted proxies on a first in, first out basis.

14.19   Personal representatives

Normally the death or insanity of a member automatically revokes the appointment by that person of a proxy. Articles sometimes provide that any proxy appointed by a member who subsequently dies will be valid unless the company receives notice in writing of the death of that member (see **Precedent 14.19**). A person who becomes entitled to a share in consequence of the death or bankruptcy of a member will not normally be entitled to attend or vote at any meeting of the company until he or she is registered as the holder of the share, see for example reg. 31 of Table A. It follows that such a person will not be entitled to appoint a proxy.

Reg. 56 of Table A deals with the position of a member in respect of whom an order has been made by the court on the ground of mental disorder. A receiver, *curator bonis* or other person authorised by the court in that regard may appoint a proxy provided that evidence of the authority of the person claiming the right to do so is deposited not less than 48 hours before the meeting at the same place as instruments of proxies must be deposited.

14.20 Change of voting instructions

Members may change the instructions given to their proxy at any time before a vote is taken. This may cause particular problems for companies that issue two-way proxy forms inviting members to appoint the chairman of the meeting as their proxy. The chairman should act on any change of instructions received in respect of those shares up to the time that the poll is taken.

It is common practice for chairmen to seek to deter members from demanding a poll by indicating at the meeting the number of proxies that they hold for and against the resolution, the implication being that the result is a foregone conclusion. In fact, the chairman can never be certain of the result of a poll until it is actually taken because his authority as a proxy may be revoked by a member voting in person at the meeting and members may alter their instructions at any time prior to the taking of the poll.

14.21 Joint shareholders

Most companies' articles include a provision similar to reg. 55 of Table A which sets out the voting rights of joint shareholders. This is necessary to prevent each joint shareholder having a vote on a show of hands and to allow the company to determine which of the members' votes it should accept if more than one of them votes on a poll. Regulation 55 of Table A states:

> In the case of joint holders the vote of the senior who tenders a vote, whether in person or by proxy, shall be accepted to the exclusion of the votes of the other joint holders; and the seniority shall be determined by the order in which the names of the holders stand in the register of members.

If the joint holders of a share attend a meeting and vote in different ways on a resolution, only the vote of the most senior should be counted. If the senior does not vote, the vote (if any) of the next most senior should be counted. The same principle applies to votes tendered by proxy.

Companies often insist that proxy forms are signed by or on behalf of all the joint holders. It is, however, doubtful whether this practice is correct. Section 372(1) provides that any member of a company entitled to attend and vote at a meeting is entitled to appoint a proxy to attend and vote instead of him or her. Each of the joint holders is a member (see s. 22(2)) and each has a right to attend and (if none of the more senior joint shareholders votes) to vote. It is arguable therefore that they should each be entitled to appoint a proxy. Under reg. 55, the vote of a proxy appointed by the senior joint holder (or by the senior and any of the other joint holders) should be counted to the exclusion of any votes tendered by proxies appointed by any of the other joint holders. The vote of the senior tendered by proxy should also be counted to the exclusion of any vote tendered in person by any of the junior joint holders. The vote of a junior holder in these circumstances is not a revocation of the proxy of the senior. This will probably be so even where the proxy was appointed by all the joint holders.

14.22   Proxies' obligations and discretions

A person who agrees to act as a proxy is considered to be the legally constituted agent of the member who makes the appointment (*Re English, Scottish & Australian Bank* [1893] 3 Ch. 385). However, the relationship of principal and agent 'can only be established by the consent of the principal and the agent' (per Lord Pearson in *Garnac Grain Co. Inc. v. HMF Faure & Fairclough Ltd* [1967] 2 All ER 353). Thus, a person appointed by a member as his or her proxy need not act in that capacity unless there is a binding contract between the parties or the proxy has a legal or equitable obligation to do so.

Where there is a contractual agreement to vote in a certain way, the court may enforce that contract by mandatory injunction (*Puddephatt v. Leith* [1916] Ch. 200). The member may also be entitled to damages for any loss he or she incurs as a result of his or her proxy failing to vote in accordance with instructions in breach of a contractual or fiduciary duty.

Where a proxy is appointed without consideration, a gratuitous agency will exist which gives rise to negative obligations on the part of the agent (e.g. not to vote contrary to the member's instructions, if any) but not positive obligations (e.g. to attend and vote). In *Oliver v. Dalgleish* [1963] 1 WLR 1274, several members nominated the same person as their proxy but gave him different instructions as to how to vote on a series of resolutions. The proxy voted in favour of the resolutions without specifying how many votes he was casting. It was held that the chairman had acted improperly in rejecting all the proxy's votes. He should have accepted those for which the proxy had instructions to vote in favour of the resolutions. As the votes of those who had instructed the proxy to vote against the resolution would not have affected the outcome, the court did not rule on the proxy's obligation to vote. However, it was impliedly accepted that the proxy did not have an obligation to use them (see, however, below on the position of the chairman).

Not surprisingly the courts have sought ways to ensure that proxy votes are given effect without tampering with the law of agency. The problem was first identified by Maugham J in *Re Dorman Long & Co. Ltd* [1934] Ch. 635 which arose after the court had made an order under a scheme of arrangement calling a meeting and requiring the directors of the company to issue two-way proxies to those entitled to attend and vote. Maugham J held that, as a result of the court's order, the directors had a duty to use the proxy votes and the people who gave them were entitled to assume that they would be used. However, he doubted whether directors had a general duty to attend and vote in respect of proxies and he noted that it would be difficult to allow the proxies to have force if none of the directors named as proxy holders attended the meeting. He said:

> In a sense, in all these cases, the dice are loaded in favour of the views of the directors: ... proxy forms are made out in favour of certain named directors and, although it is true that the word 'for' or 'against' may be inserted in the modern proxy form, the recipients of the circulars very often are in doubt as to whether the persons named as proxies are bound to put in votes by proxy with which they are not in agreement.

14.22.1   Chairman's obligations

The position of the chairman in relation to proxies is particularly important. Most two-way proxies name 'the chairman of the meeting' as the default proxy. Accordingly, the vast majority of shareholders appoint the chairman as their proxy. By doing so they at least ensure that their nominated proxy attends the meeting. They also secure the added benefit of appointing a person who has a duty to ascertain the sense of the meeting. In *Second Consolidated Trust Ltd v. Ceylon Amalgamated Tea & Rubber Estates Ltd* [1943] 2 All ER 567, the chairman of a public company failed to call a poll even though he had the power to do so under the company's articles and held sufficient two-way proxies to reverse a decision taken at a meeting on a show of hands. It was held that he had acted in breach of his duty to ascertain the sense of the meeting. Uthwatt J said:

> It appears to me that the power to demand a poll is a power possessed by the chairman which is to be exercised or not to be exercised according to his decision whether it is necessary to exercise his power in order to ascertain the sense of the meeting upon the matter before them; in other words it is a power directed towards enabling him to carry on the meeting for the purpose for which it was convened. In addition to this duty to demand a poll or to exercise his power to demand a poll ... he would be under a duty in law to exercise all the proxies which he held as chairman in accordance with the instructions they contained.

It would seem to be irrelevant for these purposes whether or not the chairman of the meeting is a director of the company. And, according to the judgment of Uthwatt J, the duty to vote arises independently of the duty to demand a poll. It will therefore also apply where a poll is demanded by the members.

14.22.2   Proxies' discretion

Where a member uses a form of proxy similar to that contained in reg. 60 of Table A, the proxy has complete discretion as to how to vote on any resolution before the meeting.

Where a member issues voting instructions, the extent of the proxy's discretion will depend on the wording of those instructions and the form of appointment. The form of proxy in reg. 61 allows members to instruct their proxy how to vote, and states that in the absence of any instructions the proxy may vote as he or she thinks fit or abstain from voting. This obviously means that the proxy may exercise his or her discretion on those resolutions of which the member has had notice but has not issued voting instructions. A more difficult question is whether the proxy can also vote on resolutions that come before the meeting of which the member has had no notice, such as amendments, proposals to adjourn, etc. In *Re Waxed Papers Ltd* [1937] 2 All ER 481, a meeting was held to approve, with or without modifications, a proposed scheme of arrangement. Various members appointed the chairman of the meeting as their proxy with instructions to vote in favour of the proposed scheme 'either with or without modification as my proxy may approve'. The chairman cast those votes against an amendment that would have deferred consideration of the scheme until the accounts for the current year had been finalised. It was held that he had acted properly. On the wording of the instrument of appointment, the power conferred on the proxy was not limited to voting for or against the proposed scheme and was sufficiently wide to enable him to vote on any incidental matter that might arise before the main question.

In *Re Waxed Papers Ltd* the chairman exercised his discretion in a manner that was consistent with the voting instructions he had been given. He would not have been able to carry out his instructions properly if he had allowed the amendment to be passed. In addition, it was not clear whether the members would have been in any better position had consideration of the proposed scheme been deferred. It is, however, relatively easy to envisage situations where it would be more advantageous for members if their proxy had not exercised his or her discretion in this way. Modern forms of proxy attempt to cater for this by using words such as the following:

> I/We hereby authorise and instruct the proxy to vote on the resolutions to be proposed at such meeting as indicated in the boxes below. Unless otherwise directed, the proxy will vote or abstain from voting as he or she thinks fit. Should any

resolutions, other than those specified, be proposed at the meeting, the proxy may vote thereon as he or she thinks fit.

Where this form of words is used, there can be no doubt that the proxy has complete discretion when voting on amendments, adjournments, etc. Whether the proxy should follow any guiding principles in determining how to vote on such matters is a difficult question. The answer is probably no where there is no contractual or fiduciary relationship between the proxy and his or her appointor. However, where such a relationship exists the proxy presumably has a duty to act in the best interests of his or her appointor. It is arguable that the chairman of the meeting is in such a position, particularly where the company has issued proxy forms inviting members to appoint him as their proxy. The difficulties this can cause can be demonstrated by the chairman's options on a proposal to adjourn.

The approach taken by most chairmen on a proposal from the floor to adjourn is to assume that those members who have given instructions to vote in favour of the remaining resolutions proposed in the notice of meeting approve of the conduct of the business before the meeting at this time, and, accordingly, would wish to vote against the proposal to adjourn. The chairman might also cast against the proposal those votes where he has been given discretion how to vote and abstain in relation to those members who have instructed him to vote against any of the remaining resolutions proposed in the notice of meeting. However, the chairman can hardly be expected to follow these guiding principles where he has proposed an adjournment to facilitate the conduct of the meeting. In such circumstances, he will normally assume that those who have instructed him to vote in favour of the resolutions would vote in favour of the adjournment. If the resolution is passed on a show of hands and would, in view of his discretionary votes, be passed on a poll, it would appear that he would not be under any obligation to demand a poll.

Likewise, chairmen nearly always assume that those who have issued instructions to vote in favour of a resolution would wish to vote against any amendment to that resolution. This will normally be sufficient to defeat any amendment. Listed companies commonly require proposals to amend resolutions to be notified in advance of the meeting. This enables the chairman to take legal advice before the meeting on any proposed amendments and, almost certainly, serves to minimise the number of amendments proposed. In view of the fact that the vast majority of votes at meetings of listed companies are cast by proxy and the fact that a proxy has no real way of knowing how his appointor would have voted, this is perhaps a sensible precaution.

14.23 Validity of proxies

All decisions on the validity of proxies fall to the chairman to decide (*Re Indian Zoedone Co.* (1884) 26 Ch. D. 70). The chairman should not reject a properly executed proxy merely because he believes it has been obtained by misrepresentation (*Holmes v. Jackson* (1957) *The Times* April 3) or because it contains a minor error, e.g. it describes the meeting as an AGM instead of an EGM (*Oliver v. Dalgleish* [1963] 1 WLR 1274).

However, in ruling on the validity of proxies, the chairman is effectively ruling on the validity of votes and is therefore protected by any article that provides that the chairman's ruling on any question of the validity of votes shall be final and conclusive (e.g. reg. 58). In *Wall v. London and Northern Assets Corporation (No. 2)* [1899] 1 Ch. 550, one of the two scrutineers raised objections to the validity of certain proxy votes on a poll. Despite the fact that his objections appeared to be well founded and that the disputed votes would have affected the outcome of the meeting, the chairman ruled that they were valid and declared the resolution carried. The company's articles stated that every vote, whether given in person or by proxy, not disallowed at the meeting would be deemed valid for all purposes. North J held that the scrutineer (who was also a shareholder) could not object after the event unless it could be shown that there had been fraud.

15

Voting

15.1 Summary

- Every member of a company has a statutory right to vote unless the articles provide otherwise (see **15.2**).
- Membership is determined by the register of members (see **15.3**).
- Articles usually specify the voting rights of members and the circumstances in which those rights are restricted or removed (see **15.4**).
- The articles may give some members enhanced voting rights in certain circumstances (see **15.5**).
- Members entitled to attend and vote at general meetings have a statutory right to appoint a proxy to attend and vote in their stead (see **14.6**). Corporate members have a statutory right to appoint a person as their representative to attend and vote at meetings (see **14.2**).
- Voting is usually conducted by a show of hands, at least initially. On a show of hands, each member and corporate representative is entitled to one vote (see **15.6**). This method of voting does not reflect the fact that some members may be entitled to more votes than others by virtue of the number of shares they hold. In addition, proxies are not normally entitled to vote on a show of hands.
- The declaration by the chairman of the result of a vote on a show of hands is usually conclusive (see **15.7**).
- Accordingly, members and proxies are given a statutory right to demand a poll (see **15.8**). The number of votes each member may cast on a poll depends on the number and type of shares they hold and the provisions of the articles.
- The articles may give the chairman a casting vote (see **15.9**).
- The chairman may be called upon to rule on the validity of votes tendered at the meeting. At common law, the validity of a resolution passed at a general meeting may be challenged if the result would have been different had certain votes not been wrongly counted or excluded. To avoid any uncertainty in this

regard, articles usually provide that the chairman's ruling will be final or conclusive (see **15.10**).

- Generally speaking, members are free to exercise their votes as they wish (see **15.11**).
- A working party has made detailed recommendation for streamlining and improving the quality of the voting process in respect of UK listed companies (see **15.12**).

15.2   Right to vote

The Act provides that every member of a company having a share capital shall have one vote for each share (or each £10 of stock) held and, in the case of a company limited by guarantee, that every member shall have one vote (s. 370(6)). However, this provision only applies if the articles do not make some other provision. Almost without exception, articles override s. 370(6) by setting out the voting rights of members. This is usually done by an article which sets out members' basic voting rights (e.g. reg. 54 of Table A), which is usually expressed as being subject to other restrictions or enhancements set out in the articles (see below).

15.2.1   Record date for securities admitted to CREST

A company whose shares (or other securities) have been admitted to CREST may specify in the notice a time, not more than 48 hours before the time fixed for the meeting, by which a person must be entered on the relevant register of securities in order to have the right to attend and vote at that meeting (or meeting of the holders of those securities) (Uncertificated Securities Regulations, reg. 34 – see **Appendix K**).

Such a provision is necessary because CREST operates on a real-time basis and the dematerialised part of the register could be changing right up to (and even during) the meeting.

As reg. 34 uses the expression 'a time', it is probably safer to give a specific time in the notice rather than to use an expression like 'the close of business' (which could cause some uncertainty if the CREST system is operating unusual hours on that date). Where the meeting is to be held on a Monday or a Tuesday, the notice could specify, say, 11.00 pm on the Sunday preceding the meeting or a time early on Monday morning before any entries will have been made on the register.

It may be preferable to specify a time in the notice that is considerably less than the 48-hour maximum allowed under reg. 34 in order to avoid any problems that could arise if the meeting has to be adjourned for a short time. Provision might also need to be made in the notice for any adjournment that results in the meeting being reconvened more than 48 hours after the time specified in the notice for the original meeting. For a suggested form of wording, see **Precedent 11.5A**.

15.2.2   Statutory restrictions on the right to vote

Where a special resolution is required under s. 174 to make a
payment out of capital to redeem shares, the votes attaching to
the shares to be redeemed must be ignored. Similarly, when a
special resolution is required under s. 164 to confer authority on a
company to purchase its own shares in an off-market transaction,
the votes attaching to the shares that are to be purchased must be
ignored.

The Secretary of State, in carrying out an investigation under s.
442 or s. 444 into the ownership of a company's shares, may
impose voting restrictions on those shares. He or she may also do
so where a person has been convicted of an offence under s. 210
(disclosure of interests in shares). The court may make a similar
order where a person has failed to give the information required
following service of a s. 212 notice.

15.3   Membership

The register of members is evidence of membership for the
purpose of voting (*Pender v. Lushington* (1877) 6 Ch. D. 70). The
subscribers to the memorandum of association become members
on incorporation and no entry on the register of members is
required (*Nichol's Case* (1885) 29 Ch. D. 421; see also s. 22(1) of
the Companies Act 1985). Every other person who agrees to
become a member, and whose name is entered in the register of
members, is a member of the company (s. 22(2)). The holders of
preference shares or any other class of shares are members of the
company for the purposes of s. 22(2). They will therefore have
the same right to vote as the ordinary shareholders unless the
articles provide otherwise.

15.3.1   Bearer shares

A bearer share is a share that is evidenced by a certificate that
does not show the name of the holder and which can be
transferred by the holder to another person by giving up
possession. For obvious reasons, the names of the holders of
bearer shares are not entered in the register of members.
Accordingly, they are not members for the purposes of s. 22 and
are not entitled to receive notices of meetings or to vote unless
they surrender their certificates and become registered holders
before the meeting. The articles of companies that may issue
bearer shares usually require notices to be published in national
newspapers and provide a simpler procedure to allow the holders
of bearer shares to vote at general meetings. This normally
involves depositing their certificates at a nominated bank before
the meeting.

15.4   Restrictions on voting in the articles

Companies have considerable discretion in determining who may vote and under what circumstances. The statutory rights of members as stated in s. 370(6) are usually modified by the company's articles. Restrictions on the right to vote can usually be found in articles that deal with the transmission of shares, calls and the votes of members. The following paragraphs summarise some of the more common examples that may be found in the articles. Other restrictions may be imposed and it is important to examine the articles carefully in order to ascertain the true position.

15.4.1   Joint holders

Where members are allowed to hold shares jointly, the articles will determine (as between the company and the joint holders) which of the holders shall be entitled to vote in respect of any shares jointly held. Most companies adopt an article similar to reg. 55 of Table A which provides that the vote of the senior who tenders a vote (whether in person or by proxy) shall be accepted to the exclusion of the votes of the other joint holders, seniority being determined by the order in which the names appear in the register of members (see **14.21**).

Joint holders can circumvent these restrictions by having their holdings split into two or more joint holdings, each having a different person registered as the senior joint holder (*Burns v. Siemens Brothers Dynamo Works Ltd* [1919] 1 Ch. 225). By doing so, the joint holders gain an advantage with respect to voting on a show of hands and, in most cases, satisfying the requirements for demanding a poll.

15.4.2   Death and bankruptcy

Most articles restrict the right of a person who becomes entitled to a share in consequence of the death or bankruptcy of a member to attend and vote at any meeting of the company. Under the general law a personal representative is entitled to be registered as the holder of shares in the absence of any provisions to the contrary (*Scott v. Frank F Scott (London) Ltd* [1940] Ch. 794). Reg. 30 of Table A provides that a personal representative or a trustee in bankruptcy may, upon providing satisfactory evidence of appointment, elect to become the holder of the share (by giving notice to that effect) or to have some other person registered as the holder (by executing an instrument of transfer). Reg. 31 further provides that personal representatives or trustees in bankruptcy shall not be entitled to attend or vote until they have been registered as the holders of the share. If they do not elect to become the holder of the shares or to have them registered in the name of someone else, it is advisable to stop sending them notices of meetings and proxy forms (although it will still be necessary to send copies of the annual report and accounts). If a company continues over a period of time to send notices of meetings and proxy forms to the representatives or trustees, it is possible that it may be estopped from denying their right to attend and vote because it has created a reasonable expectation on their part that they may do so.

Normally the death of a member automatically revokes the appointment by that person of a proxy. However, articles sometimes provide that any proxy appointed by a member who subsequently dies will be valid unless the company receives notice in writing of the death of that member (see example at **Precedent 14.18**).

Personal representatives are entitled to determine the order in which their names appear on the register of members (*Re Saunders & Co Ltd* [1908] 1 Ch. 415).

A bankrupt who remains registered as a member of the company is entitled to vote at general meetings but must vote in accordance with the directions of his or her trustee (*Morgan v. Gray* [1953] Ch. 83). It should be noted, however, that the company is not bound to ensure that those instructions have been followed.

15.4.3 Mental disorder

Articles usually make provision on the voting rights of members who are suffering from some sort of mental illness. For example, reg. 56 of Table A provides that a member in respect of whom a mental health order has been made by any court having the jurisdiction (whether in the UK or elsewhere) may vote by his or her receiver, *curator bonis* or other person appointed by a court to act in a similar capacity. Evidence of authority must be deposited at the registered office, or at such other place as is specified by the company for the deposit of proxies, not less than 48 hours before the meeting at which the right to vote is to be exercised.

15.4.4 Calls unpaid

Most articles restrict the voting rights of members in respect of shares on which calls or other sums presently payable have not been paid. The scope of the restrictions that can be imposed vary and care should be taken to ensure that the power to disenfranchise is properly exercised. Reg. 65 of the 1948 Table A provides that no *member* shall be entitled to vote at any general meeting unless *all* calls or other sums presently payable by him or her in respect of shares have been paid. In other words, a member will be disqualified from voting even if a call on only one of his or her shares remains unpaid. Modern articles often impose similar restrictions but give the directors the option not to enforce them (see example at **Precedent 15.4A**). Reg. 57 of the 1985

Table A is far less restrictive in that it merely restricts the right to vote in respect of those shares on which money is still due.

It has been held that where shares in a public company are allotted for consideration other than cash without an independent valuation, the effect of s. 103(6) is to create an immediate liability which, together with an article similar to reg. 65 of the 1948 Table A, has the effect of disenfranchising the allottees (*Re Bradford Investments plc* [1990] BCC 740).

15.4.5 Failure to respond to s. 212 inquiry

Public companies often take power in their articles to disenfranchise shares held by a member who has not replied to a notice served under s. 212 of the Companies Act (see example at **Precedent 15.4B**). The Listing Rules used to state that where such power is taken in the articles the sanction may not take effect earlier than 14 days after the service of the notice. This requirement was deleted in January 2000.

15.4.6 Non-voting or restricted voting shares

Articles usually provide that the company may issue more than one class of shares. Shares will be of a different class if they give their holders different rights from other shares. The rights of the holders are usually set out in the articles. A company may issue shares with restricted or no voting rights.

15.4.7 Preference shares

Preference shares are perhaps the most common class of shares issued in addition to the ordinary shares. They usually have priority over the ordinary shares with respect to the payment of dividends and repayment of capital on winding up. Articles usually remove the right to vote except where dividends are in arrears.

15.5 Enhanced voting rights

The articles may give members enhanced voting rights in certain circumstances. The most common example is as a protection for a founder member against removal as a director of a private limited company (see **Precedent 15.5**). The method employed in **Precedent 15.5** does not create a different class of shares – any member who is a director will be entitled to more votes per share on a resolution to remove him or her as a director or to amend the article conferring those rights. Normally, the number of extra votes will be sufficient to defeat the other members. If the membership of the company subsequently changes, it may be necessary to amend this type of article to preserve that position. This sort of protection against removal was held to be valid in *Bushell v. Faith* [1970] AC 1099 (see **23.11**).

If it is intended to give some but not all members protection against removal as a director, it is necessary to give those members a different class of shares with different voting rights.

15.6   Voting on a show of hands

Under the common law, voting is conducted on a show of hands unless there are regulations or enactments to the contrary (*R. v. Rector of Birmingham* (1837) 1 Ad. & El. 254). The Act is drafted on the assumption that voting will proceed first by some means other than a poll, and the articles of most companies adopt the common law practice. There is, however, no statutory requirement to do so and a company's articles could provide, for example, that voting shall be conducted by a poll on all substantive resolutions. In the USA, voting at general meetings of listed corporations must be conducted in this way. Some UK listed companies have also adopted this practice recently (e.g. Glaxo SmithKline and BAe).

However, most companies adopt provisions similar to reg. 46 of Table A which provides that a resolution put to the vote at a meeting shall be decided on a show of hands unless before, or on the declaration of the result of, the show of hands a poll is duly demanded.

Under the common law, each member present has one vote on a show of hands regardless of any other factors such as the number of shares held (*Re Horbury Bridge Coal, Iron & Waggon Co.* (1879) 11 Ch. D. 109) or the fact that he or she may be attending in more than one capacity (*Ernest v. Loma Gold Mines* [1897] 1 Ch. 1). Articles usually provide that on a show of hands each member or corporate representative shall have one vote (e.g. reg. 54). Articles do not usually allow proxies to vote on a show of hands, particularly where a member may appoint more than one proxy because this would allow a member represented by more than one proxy to cast more votes on a show of hands than a member present in person.

Voting on a show of hands is clearly not a perfect method of ascertaining the sense of the meeting. It does not reflect the different number of votes that members may be entitled to exercise by virtue of their holding, and does not take into account the votes of members who have appointed a proxy. This does not really matter because members and proxies have a statutory right to demand a poll whereupon all these factors are taken into account. The advantage of taking a vote on a show of hands, rather than voting on a poll, is that it is quicker and more convenient. If all the members present support the resolution, there will be little to be gained from calculating the precise number of votes in favour. Even if the vote is not unanimous, it is advantageous to be able to assume that those who oppose it do not have sufficient votes to defeat the resolution on a poll. It is, of course, open to members who oppose the resolution to demand a poll.

The Combined Code recommends that listed companies should count all proxy votes and, except where a poll is called, should indicate the level of proxies lodged on each resolution, and the balance for and against the resolution, after it has been dealt with on a show of hands (Combined Code, para. C.2.1). In practice, many listed companies make this information available to members attending the meeting on a printed schedule. Some also announce the number of votes tendered by proxy before the show of hands.

15.7   Declaration of result by chairman

At any meeting at which an extraordinary resolution or a special resolution is submitted to be passed, a declaration by the chairman that the resolution is carried is, unless a poll is demanded, conclusive evidence of the fact without proof of the number or proportion of votes recorded in favour or against the resolution (s. 378(4)). For the purposes of any legal proceedings, the minutes would be prima-facie evidence of the declaration made by the chairman. Other evidence would therefore be admissible to show that they were not an accurate record.

Articles usually extend the operation of s. 378(4) to cover declarations made by the chairman in respect of other types of resolution. Reg. 47 of Table A provides:

> **47.** Unless a poll is duly demanded a declaration by the chairman that a resolution has been carried or carried unanimously, or by a particular majority, or lost, or not carried by a particular majority and an entry to that effect in the minutes of the meeting shall be conclusive evidence of the fact without proof of the number or proportion of the votes recorded in favour or against the resolution.

It can be seen that reg. 47 includes an additional requirement that an entry be made in the minutes. This would seem to add nothing to s. 378(4) as the regulation requires both conditions to be true. So, if the chairman had not actually made the declaration recorded in the minutes, evidence to that effect would still be admissible. A declaration actually made by the chairman in good faith will, under s. 378(4) and articles similar to reg. 47, be conclusive and will prevent the question being reopened in legal proceedings. This is so even where there is evidence that the chairman's declaration was wrong, unless there is evidence of fraud or manifest error. At a meeting where there had been confusion as to whether a special resolution and a resolution to adjourn had been carried, it was held that the declaration of the chairman (as recorded in the minutes) precluded any inquiry into the number of shareholders who voted for or against the resolutions and, in the absence of fraud, was conclusive (*Arnot v. United African Lands* [1901] 1 Ch. 518). Similarly, on a petition for a compulsory winding up, the court refused to consider the question of whether an extraordinary resolution had been carried by the requisite majority (*Re Hadleigh Castle Gold Mines* [1900] 2 Ch. 419).

A special resolution to reduce a company's capital was confirmed by the court despite the fact that there was evidence that it was carried by the votes of members not qualified to vote. However, no poll was demanded and it was held that the declaration of the chairman could not be reviewed (*Graham's Morocco Co. Ltd Petitioners*, 1932 SC 269).

The court will, however, intervene where there has been a manifest error. Where a chairman declared the result of a vote on a show of hands to be 6 in favour and 23 against but went on to declare: 'but there are 200 voting by proxy and I declare the resolution carried as required by Act of Parliament', the court was prepared to intervene (*Re Caratal (New) Mines Ltd* [1902] 2 Ch. 498). Buckley J said:

> I am asked to affirm a proposition that if a chairman makes a declaration and in it actually gives the numbers of votes for and against the resolution, which he is bound to recognise, and adds that there are proxies (which in law he cannot regard), and then declares the result is that the statutory majority has been obtained, although the numbers stated by him show that it has not been obtained, the declaration is conclusive. In my judgement that proposition cannot be supported.

15.8 Poll

A poll is a vote conducted by voting papers rather than by a show of hands. The voting rights of members on a poll will be determined by the articles and, in default, by s. 370(6). Generally speaking, members will be entitled to one vote for each share held. This means that members with larger holdings will have a greater say in the result. It is therefore more democratic than a vote on a show of hands.

Under the common law, where the method of voting used at a meeting is a show of hands, any person who is entitled to vote at a meeting may demand a poll (*R. v. Wimbledon Local Board* (1882) QBD 459). This common law rule applies to company meetings unless the articles provide otherwise. In practice, articles frequently modify the conditions that a person must satisfy in order to make a valid demand for a poll. In a large company with many thousands of shares, it would be ludicrous for one member holding only one share to be allowed to demand a poll without the support of other members. On the other hand, it would not be fair if the conditions imposed made it almost impossible for the members to demand a poll. To ensure that this does not happen, the Act provides that a provision in a company's articles will be void in so far as it excludes the right to demand a poll on any question other than a resolution to elect the chairman of the meeting or to adjourn the meeting (s. 373(1)(a)). Table A allows a poll to be demanded on both the election of the chairman and a resolution to adjourn, but requires that a poll so demanded be taken immediately (reg. 51).

15.8.1   Valid demand

Under s. 373(1)(b) a demand for a poll must be capable of being made either:

- by not less than five members having the right to vote at the meeting; or
- by a member or members representing not less than one-tenth of the total voting rights of all the members having the right to vote at that meeting; or
- by a member or members holding shares in the company conferring a right to vote at the meeting, being shares on which an aggregate sum has been paid up equal to not less than one-tenth of the total sum paid up on all the shares conferring that right.

A provision contained in a company's articles will be void in so far as it would have the effect of making ineffective a demand for a poll in accordance with the above conditions. If an article is deemed to be void under s. 373(1)(b), the common law right to demand a poll will apply whereby one member may make a valid demand (*R. v. Wimbledon Local Board* (1882) QBD 459).

A proxy has the right to demand or join in the demand for a poll, and a demand by a person as proxy for a member is deemed to be the same as a demand by the member (s. 373(2)). Thus two or more proxies appointed by the same member cannot defeat a requirement that more than one member must join in a demand for a poll. However, a person appointed as the proxy for at least five members will always be able to demand a poll.

Articles often relax the conditions for a valid demand. For example, reg. 46 of Table A enables a valid demand to be made by two (rather than five) members having the right to vote at the meeting. It has been held that where the articles state that 'members' holding a certain percentage of shares may demand a poll, a single member holding that percentage may demand a poll (*Siemens Bros & Co. v. Burns* [1918] 2 Ch. 324). In this case the company's articles stated in the definitions section (usually the first article) that words in the singular should be taken to include the plural and vice versa. Most articles track the wording of s. 373(1) to avoid any problem in this regard.

In the absence of any provision to the contrary in the articles, joint holders should be counted as a single member for the purposes of demanding a poll (*Cory v. Reindeer Steamship Co.* (1915) 31 TLR 530). Under reg. 46 of Table A only members entitled to vote may join in a demand for a poll. As only the senior of the joint holders present in person or by proxy may vote, only he or she may join in the demand for a poll.

The chairman has no right to direct that a poll be taken unless it is duly demanded or he is given that right by the articles (*Campbell v. Maund* (1836) 5 Ad. & El. 865). Reg. 46 of Table A gives the chairman the right to demand a poll. The chairman may also be entitled to demand a poll in his capacity as a proxy. Where the chairman has the power to call a poll, he must exercise that power if it is necessary to ascertain the true sense of the meeting. For example, where the chairman has been instructed by proxies to vote in a certain way and those votes, if cast, would produce a different result from the one on the vote on a show of hands, he has a duty to demand a poll (*Second Consolidated Trust Ltd v. Ceylon Amalgamated Tea & Rubber Estates Ltd* [1943] 2 All ER 567).

A poll may be demanded either on or before the declaration of the result of a show of hands by any person or persons entitled under the articles to do so. This will usually include the chairman and a specified number of members or proxies (as determined by reference to articles, e.g. reg. 46 of Table A).

15.8.2 Special rules

The Act provides that different rules shall apply when deciding whether a valid demand has been made in certain circumstances. For example, at a class meeting held to consider a variation in the rights of that class, any member of that class, whether present in person or by proxy, may demand a poll (s. 125(6)).

In addition, any member, whether present in person or by proxy, may demand a poll in the following circumstances:

- on a special resolution to confer, revoke or renew authority for an off-market purchase of a company's own shares (s. 164(5));
- on a special resolution to approve a contingent purchase contract relating to the company's own shares (s. 165(2)); and
- on a special resolution approving payment out of capital for the purchase or redemption of the company's own shares (s. 174(3) and (5)).

15.8.3 Withdrawal of demand

Reg. 48 of Table A provides that the demand for a poll may, before the poll is taken, be withdrawn but only with the consent of the chairman. It goes on to say that a demand so withdrawn shall not be taken to have invalidated the result of a show of hands declared before the demand was made. Without such a provision it would be necessary to take another vote on a show of hands because, under the common law, the result of a show of hands ceases to have any effect once a valid demand for a poll has been made (*R. v. Cooper* (1870) LR 5 QB 457).

If a poll is demanded before a vote on a show of hands has been taken and subsequently withdrawn, it is plainly necessary to put the resolution to a vote by a show of hands.

15.8.4   Conduct of poll

Articles usually specify the manner in which a poll is to be conducted or who may determine the manner in which it is to be conducted. Reg. 49 of Table A provides that a poll shall be taken as the chairman directs and that he may appoint scrutineers (who need not be members) and fix a time and place for declaring the result of the poll and that the result of the poll shall be deemed to be the resolution of the meeting at which the poll was demanded.

A poll cannot be taken on a number of resolutions together. In other words, the members must be given an opportunity to vote for or against each resolution separately (*Patent Wood Keg Syndicate v. Pearse* [1909] WN 164). See, however, *Re R.E. Jones Ltd* (1933) 50 TLR 31 where the members agreed to this procedure being used. This does not mean that separate voting papers must be used for each resolution as long as the voting papers allow members to vote for some resolutions and against others (see **Precedent 15.8A**).

Where the articles allow the chairman to determine the method of taking the poll but also require the personal attendance of the voter or the proxy appointed, the chairman has no right to direct that the poll be taken by voting papers to be returned by members through the post (*McMillan v. Le Roi Mining Co. Ltd* [1906] 1 Ch. 331).

Unless the articles specify the length of time for which the poll is to continue, the chairman should not close it so long as votes are still being tendered (*R. v. St Pancras Local Board* (1839) 11 Ad. & El. 356). Where the articles provide that a poll shall be taken 'in such manner as the chairman may direct', the chairman may direct that it be taken immediately (*Re Chillington Iron Co.* (1885) 29 Ch. D. 159). However, where the articles provided for a poll to be taken at a time and place to be fixed by the directors within seven days of the meeting, it was held that the chairman could not direct that a poll be taken immediately (*Re British Flax Producers Co. Ltd* (1889) 60 LT 215).

Reg. 51 avoids these problems by providing that a poll shall be taken either forthwith or at such time and place as the chairman directs as long as this is not more than 30 days after the poll is demanded. However, it also provides that a poll demanded on the election of a chairman or on a question of adjournment shall be taken forthwith.

Where articles require a poll to be taken forthwith (or immediately) this means as soon as practicable (*Jackson v. Hamlyn* [1953] Ch. 577).

Reg. 51 also provides that a demand for a poll shall not prevent the continuance of a meeting for the transaction of any business other than the question on which the poll was demanded and that, if a poll is demanded before the declaration of the result of a show of hands and the demand is duly withdrawn, the meeting shall continue as if the demand had not been made.

15.8.5 Notice of a poll

A poll taken at a later date is deemed to be a continuance of the original meeting. The original meeting is deemed to have been suspended rather than adjourned and it is not necessary to give any notice unless the articles so require (*Shaw v. Tati Concessions Ltd* [1913] 1 Ch. 292). Articles usually contain provisions that specify when notice of a poll must be given. Under Table A, no notice need be given of a poll not taken forthwith if the time and place at which it is to be taken is announced at the meeting at which it is demanded. In any other case at least seven clear days' notice specifying the time and place at which the poll is to be taken must be given to all the members (including those who did not attend the meeting) (reg. 52). If the chairman does not announce the date and time of the poll at the meeting, it follows that it cannot be held for about eight or nine days and then only if proper notice has been given.

15.8.6 Votes on a poll

Under Table A, every member shall have one vote for every share held on a poll (reg. 54). Votes may be given either personally or by proxy (reg. 59). In the case of an equality of votes, whether on a show of hands or on a poll, the chairman shall be entitled to a casting vote in addition to any other vote he may have (reg. 50).

On a poll taken at a meeting of the company or a meeting of any class of members, a member entitled to more than one vote need not, if he or she votes, use all his or her votes or cast all the votes he or she uses in the same way (s. 374).

A member not present at the meeting at which a poll is demanded may vote on a poll taken at a later time or date (*R. v. Wimbledon Local Board* (1882) QBD 459).

15.8.7 Procedure on a poll

The articles will contain regulations governing voting by shareholders on a poll. The regulations governing holders of other securities should be contained in the trust deed constituting the stock. References to articles below should be read accordingly.

Action before the meeting
- Where proxies have given voting instructions, summarise proxy votes in favour of the chairman for each resolution indicating the number of votes for, against and giving the chairman discretion.
- Analyse proxy votes in favour of other persons.
- In the case of a listed company, prepare a schedule of votes

tendered by proxy for and against each resolution for disclosure at the meeting in accordance with the recommendations of para. C.2.1 of the Combined Code.

- Appoint scrutineers (usually employees of the company or its solicitors, registrars or auditors) and arrange for their attendance.
- Prepare voting papers (see **Precedents 15.8A and 15.8B**).
- Draft script for chairman (see **Appendix L, para. 1.1**).
- Ascertain the conditions under which a valid demand may be made and brief chairman accordingly.
- Brief staff and scrutineers.
- Obtain an up-to-date list of members (or if class meeting, members of that class) and annotate which, if any, are not entitled to vote owing to some restriction imposed by the articles.

When a poll is demanded

- If appropriate, chairman may suggest the demand be withdrawn in view of proxy position.
- If not withdrawn, take the names of those making the demand and check against the register of members whether they satisfy the conditions for a valid demand.
- If the demand is not valid or it is withdrawn, the chairman should rule accordingly and proceed with the business:
  - if the demand was made before a vote was taken on a show of hands, the chairman should invite members to vote on the resolution in that manner and declare the result accordingly;
  - if the demand was made after the chairman had declared the result of the vote on a show of hands, the chairman may proceed to the next item of business although it is preferable to restate the result as previously declared before doing so.

If demand valid

- The chairman should advise the meeting of the validity of the demand.
- The chairman should announce when the poll will be held. Depending on the articles and the nature of the business, this may be:
  - immediately;
  - at the conclusion of meeting; or
  - at a later date.
- If the poll is to be held later (i.e. not immediately), the chairman should proceed to next item of business.

Holding a poll

- The chairman should explain the procedure for the taking of the poll (see chairman's script at **Appendix L, para. 1.4**).
- Issue voting papers to all those entitled to vote (see **Precedents 15.8A and 15.8B**).
- The chairman should complete voting forms in respect of proxy votes held by him (see **Precedent 15.8C**).
- Collect completed voting cards.
- Check for completeness of each voting paper.

- Where vote is given by proxy:
  - check that person voting has been validly appointed as a proxy;
  - that proxy has followed member's instruction, if any (see **14.22**).
- Any voting paper not, on the face of it, valid, should be referred to the scrutineers. In cases of doubt the chairman should be asked to make a ruling (see **15.10**).
- Verify holdings with list.
- Eliminate votes given by proxy (including those given by the chairman in that capacity) where the member voted in person on the poll.
- If a member has appointed more than one proxy, ensure that the total number of votes cast does not exceed that member's holding. Refer any problems to the chairman.
- Count the votes for and against.
- Prepare a summary of the votes cast for and against in person and by proxy.
- Scrutineers to sign summary and certify the result of the poll.
- Report the result to the chairman.

Declaration of result of poll

- At the meeting:
  - if poll directed to be taken at a later time, the meeting to be resumed at the appointed time and the result declared;
  - if poll taken immediately, chairman to announce result when other business completed.
- If the resolution is passed, a copy of it may need to be filed at Companies House and, in the case of listed companies, with the UK Listing Authority (see **12.6**).

15.8.8 Result of the poll

It has been held that the date of a resolution passed on a poll is the date on which the result of the poll is ascertained (*Holmes v. Keyes* [1959] Ch. 199). Accordingly, if the date of the resolution is important, it may be necessary to ensure that the result of a poll is declared on the day of the meeting.

Probably the least satisfactory aspect of voting on a poll rather than a show of hands is the fact that the result of the poll is rarely known until after the meeting. The only exception will be where the poll is taken immediately, perhaps because the articles require it to be taken forthwith, e.g. a poll on a resolution to adjourn under Table A. This means that the members present will have no idea whether the resolution has been passed or defeated, let alone how many votes were cast for or against. There is no requirement to notify members of the results of the poll. This is the case even with regard to the members who demanded it. This is not to say that a company should refuse to reveal the results of the poll. The result must be recorded in the minutes and any member may, on payment of the prescribed fee, demand a copy of the minutes (s. 383). In addition, if the resolution is one that must be filed at Companies House, the fact that it has been passed will become a matter of public record (see **12.6**). Listed companies may also need to send copies of the resolution to the UK Listing Authority. The results of a poll may be price-sensitive information and it may therefore be necessary for listed companies to issue an announcement of the result to the markets.

It is good practice for the secretary to notify the result to the members who demanded the poll and, perhaps, to send them a copy of the minutes after they have been signed by the chairman. Some companies advertise the results of any poll in a newspaper.

The company may, if it so desires, inform the members how particular votes were cast. It has been held that this is not confidential information and that the company has a right to the information if the poll is conducted by independent scrutineers (*Haarhaus & Co. GmbH v. Law Debenture Trust Corp. plc* [1988] BCLC 640).

15.9   Chairman's casting vote

The articles may give the chairman a casting vote. Reg. 50 states:

> **50.** In the case of an equality of votes, whether on a show of hands or on a poll, the chairman shall be entitled to a casting vote in addition to any other vote he may have.

The circumstances in which it is reasonable for the chairman to use his casting vote on a show of hands are fairly limited. In order to ascertain the true sense of the meeting, the chairman should exercise his power to demand a poll rather than use his casting vote, particularly where he holds proxies on behalf of the members. A casting vote cannot be used to manufacture a tie.

The chairman should use his casting vote in the best interests of the company. This is, of course, a vague duty and it is unlikely that the chairman will be entirely impartial. In Parliament, the Speaker normally uses his or her casting vote to maintain the *status quo*. This will normally entail voting against the resolution as most resolutions seek to change the *status quo*.

15.10   Objections to qualification of voter

Articles usually provide that objections to the qualification of any voter must be raised at the meeting at which the vote objected to is tendered and that every vote not disallowed at the meeting shall be valid. Objections made in due time are normally required to be referred to the chairman whose decision is final and conclusive (e.g. reg. 58). Such provisions are binding and votes not disallowed cannot be challenged afterwards unless the chairman is guilty of fraud or some other misconduct (*Wall v. London & Northern Assets Corporation* [1898] 2 Ch. 469).

In *Re Bradford Investments plc* [1990] BCC 740, such an article was held not to operate where a person who was not a member of the company had acted as the self-appointed chairman for the purposes of electing a chairman of the meeting.

Articles may also make separate provision regarding counting errors (see example at **Precedent 15.10**).

15.11 Freedom to exercise voting rights

A member has a right to have any votes tendered accepted at a meeting of the company (*Pender v. Lushington* (1877) 6 Ch. D. 70) and a refusal to accept those votes may invalidate the resolution (see, however, reg. 58 on the chairman's power to rule on the validity of votes). A member's vote is a property right which as a general rule can be exercised at that person's complete discretion. In casting their votes members are free to use their own judgement and act in their own interests even though those interests might conflict with the general interests of the company (*Carruth v. Imperial Chemical Industries Ltd* [1937] AC 707).

A director who is also a member can exercise his or her votes against a resolution that the court has ordered the company to effect (*Northern Counties Securities Ltd v. Jackson & Steeple Ltd* [1974] 1 WLR 1133). Walton J said:

> When a director votes as a director for or against any particular resolution in a directors' meeting he is voting as a person under a fiduciary duty to the company for the proposition that the company should take a certain course of action. When a shareholder is voting for or against a particular resolution he is voting as a person owing no fiduciary duty to the company and who is exercising his own right of property to vote as he thinks fit. The fact that the result of the voting at the meeting will bind the company cannot effect the position that in voting he is voting simply in exercise of his property rights.

A member may contract to vote in a certain way or at the direction of a third party, e.g. under a shareholders' agreement. The obligations under any such contract can be enforced by mandatory injunction provided that the contract is for consideration and the member continues to hold the shares (*Greenhalgh v. Mallard* [1943] 2 All ER 214). The company (unless it is a party to the contract) need only be concerned that the person tendering the vote is entitled to do so and not with the obligations of that person to vote in a certain way.

A member may vote in favour of a resolution in which he or she has a financial interest even if he or she is a director of the company (*North West Transportation Co. v. Beatty* (1887) 12 App. Cas. 589 and *East Pant-du United Lead Mining Co. Ltd v. Merryweather* (1864) 2 H & M 254). This rule is, of course, subject to the requirements of ss. 164 and 174 regarding resolutions to approve a contract for the purchase of own shares (see **15.2.2**).

Members must, however, exercise the power to alter the

articles of association in good faith for the benefit of the company as a whole (see **16.4**).

15.12   Encouraging institutional investors to vote

In 1999, the National Association of Pension Funds sponsored the establishment of an independent committee, chaired by Yve Newbold, to examine the process of lodging proxies and shareholder voting at company meetings in the UK. The committee's final report (*Report of the Committee of Inquiry into UK Vote Execution*) made eight recommendations to tackle what it considered to be major flaws in the UK system of vote execution. These were as follows:

- regular and considered voting by institutional investors should be regarded as a fiduciary responsibility;
- the voting policy of institutions and fund managers ought to be specifically covered by agreement;
- the UK's voting system should be modernised;
- companies should actively encourage voting;
- member associations should offer help and guidance;
- company registrars should support electronic voting arrangements;
- voting in the context of stock lending should be re-examined; and
- custodians should actively assist in the voting process.

An informal working group was subsequently established to develop these recommendations further. Towards the end of 2000, the working group published a report, the *Report of the Shareholder Voting Working Group*, which examined in detail how each of the Newbold committee's recommendations could be implemented, and recommended the development of an agreed code of practice for implementation by all parties in the voting process.

In particular, the report recommended the following:

- all listed companies should offer facilities to enable shareholders to use electronic communications to appoint proxies, check that their instructions have been lodged correctly, and change their voting instructions;
- companies should use plain English in communications with shareholders;
- there should be a review to examine ways of enfranchising underlying beneficial owners;
- companies should make wider use of polls;
- votes cast on company resolutions should be published on the company's website (preferably the day following the meeting) and be the subject of a regulatory announcement made as a requirement under the Listing Rules.

16

Shareholder remedies

16.1 Summary

- Shareholders can enforce their rights as members under the articles against the company and against other members. However, the court will refuse to intervene where the breach is deemed to be a mere internal irregularity which could be cured by the majority simply by following the correct procedure (see **16.2**).
- The proper plaintiff in the case of wrongs done to the company is the company itself. The courts will only allow shareholders to bring actions on behalf of the company against the wrongdoers in very limited circumstances. As a general rule the will of the majority is allowed to prevail (see **16.3**).
- Although a company may alter its articles, the alterations must not discriminate unfairly against the minority (see para.16.4).
- Shareholders may apply to the court for relief from conduct that is unfairly prejudicial. The court's remedy in most cases of unfair prejudice will be to order the majority shareholders to purchase the shares of the minority (see **16.5**).
- A member may apply to the court to have the company wound up on just and equitable grounds under s. 122(1)(g) of the Insolvency Act 1986 (see **16.6**). The court may grant such an order even though the company has been run in accordance with the Act and the company's constitution.
- The remedies outlined above tend to be used as a last resort. The Act provides various other means by which shareholders may be able to reconcile their problems (see **16.7**).

16.2 Section 14 contract

The memorandum and articles, when registered, bind the company and its members to the same extent as if they had been signed and sealed by each member and contained covenants on the part of each member to observe all the provisions of the memorandum and articles (s. 14). This provision creates a

contract (known as the 'section 14 contract') between the
company and its members, the terms of which are contained in
the memorandum and articles. However, provisions in the
memorandum or articles that conflict with the requirements of
the Act will not be enforceable because s. 14 is made subject to
other provisions of the Act.

The s. 14 contract differs in a number of ways from normal
contracts. Provision is made in the Act for its terms to be altered
by a special majority (see ss. 4 and 9 on the alteration of the
memorandum and articles by special resolution). The consent of
all the parties is required to vary normal contracts; and although
the courts regard articles as commercial documents which should
be construed so as to give them reasonable business efficacy
(*Holmes v. Keyes* [1959] Ch. 199, 215, per Jenkins LJ), the Court of
Appeal has held that terms cannot be implied into the articles in
order to do so (*Bratton Seymour Service Co. Ltd v. Oxborough* [1992]
BCLC 693).

The company can enforce the s. 14 contract against its
members (*Hickman's case* [1915] 1 Ch. 881) and the members can
enforce it against each other (*Rayfield v. Hands* [1960] Ch. 1).
However, the circumstances in which members can enforce the
contract against the company are limited. First, it has been held
on a number of occasions that members may only enforce
provisions in the articles that confer rights in their capacity as
members. For example, it has been held that a member cannot
enforce a provision in the articles that he or she should be the
company's solicitor (*Eley v. Positive Government Security Life
Assurance Co. Ltd* (1976) 1 Ex. D. 88) but can enforce his or her
right to vote under the articles (*Pender v. Lushington* (1877) 6 Ch.
D. 70). The application of this rule in cases involving shareholder
directors is less certain. In *Browne v. La Trinidad* (1887) 37 Ch. D.
1, the Court of Appeal refused to enforce a provision in the
company's articles that a member should be a director and should
not be removed from office. However, in *Quin & Axtens Ltd v.
Salmon* [1909] AC 442, the court upheld a provision in the articles
giving a director a right to veto certain board resolutions. This is
an exceedingly difficult area of the law and one much loved by
academic writers. For a more detailed analysis of the issues, see
the Law Commission Consultation Paper No. 142, 'Shareholder
Remedies'.

The second major exception for shareholders is that they may
not be able to bring personal actions for breaches that the courts
consider to be mere internal irregularities. As a general rule the
courts impose this restriction where it is clear that even if the
action is allowed, the majority will still get its own way by
following the correct procedures. For example, in *MacDougall v.
Gardiner* (1875) 1 Ch. D. 13, the court refused to declare an
adjournment passed on a show of hands invalid simply because
the chairman had improperly refused to allow a minority
shareholder to demand a poll. Where, however, it is clear that the

breach affected the outcome of the meeting, the courts will allow an action to proceed, e.g. where the chairman improperly excluded some votes cast by a proxy in favour of a resolution that would have been passed had they been accepted (*Oliver v. Dalgleish* [1963] 1 WLR 1274). The internal irregularities exception is founded on the same principles as the rule in *Foss v. Harbottle*, which is dealt with below.

16.3   The rule in *Foss v. Harbottle*

The rule in *Foss v. Harbottle* limits the ability of shareholders to bring actions on behalf of the company (derivative actions) for wrongs done to the company. It is founded on two important principles. The first is that where a wrong is done to a company, only the company can take action against the wrongdoers and not individual members (the proper plaintiff principle). The second is that the will of the majority of the members should generally be allowed to prevail in the running of the company's business. Thus in *Foss v. Harbottle* (1843) 2 Hare 461, the court refused to intervene in a case brought by minority shareholders who alleged that the directors had misapplied the company's property, because the acts complained of were capable of being confirmed by the members and there was nothing to prevent the company from obtaining redress in its corporate capacity.

The rule in *Foss v. Harbottle* is subject to certain important exceptions. These were set out by the Court of Appeal in *Edwards v. Halliwell* [1950] 2 All ER 1064 and restated in *Prudential Assurance Co. Ltd v. Newman Industries (No. 2)* [1982] Ch. 204 as follows:

(1) The proper plaintiff in an action in respect of a wrong alleged to be done to a corporation is, prima facie, the corporation.

(2) Where the alleged wrong is a transaction which might be made binding on the corporation and on all its members by a simple majority of the members, no individual member of the corporation is allowed to maintain an action in respect of that matter because, if the majority confirms the transaction, [the question is at an end]; or if the majority challenges the transaction, there is no valid reason why the company should not sue.

(3) There is no room for the operation of the rule if the alleged wrong is ultra vires the corporation, because the majority of members cannot confirm the transaction.

(4) There is also no room for the operation of the rule if the transaction complained of could be validly done or sanctioned only by a special resolution or the like, because a simple majority cannot confirm a transaction which requires the concurrence of a greater majority.

(5) There is an exception to the rule where what has been

done amounts to fraud and the wrongdoers are themselves in control of the company.

In *Smith v. Croft (No. 2)* [1988] Ch. 114, Knox J went even further by ruling that a shareholder could not bring a derivative action if an 'independent organ' did not want it to proceed. In this case, the wrongdoer controlled about 66% of the voting rights at general meetings and the plaintiffs about 14%. Another shareholder who was judged by Knox J to be independent held about 19% and opposed the action being brought. The plaintiff and this independent shareholder were deemed to constitute an independent organ and Knox J dismissed the action on the basis that this independent organ did not want it to proceed.

Derivative actions are allowed to proceed by virtue of an equitable concession by the Court of Chancery which makes an exception to the general rule that the proper plaintiff in an action seeking redress for a wrong done to the company is the company itself. A member may be prevented from taking advantage of this concession where there is evidence of 'behaviour by the minority shareholder, which, in the eyes of equity, would render it unjust to allow a claim brought by the company at his insistence to succeed' (*Nurcumbe v. Nurcombe* [1985] 1 WLR 370, 378, per Browne-Wilkinson LJ).

Where a derivative action is allowed, the plaintiff must bring the action against the wrongdoer for the benefit of the company rather than his or her own benefit. The company is enjoined as a defendant to ensure that it enforces any judgment.

16.3.1 *Ultra vires* transactions

The exception to the rule in *Foss v. Harbottle* that the majority cannot confirm an act that is *ultra vires* the company (i.e. beyond the capacity of the company as prescribed by the objects clause in the memorandum) is now qualified by s. 35(3) (as amended by the Companies Act 1989). Section 35(3) allows a company to ratify by special resolution acts of the directors that are *ultra vires* the company. It follows, however, that ratification by anything less than a special resolution will still be open to challenge under the third limb of the rule in *Foss v. Harbottle* as restated in *Prudential Assurance Co. Ltd v. Newman Industries (No. 2)*.

Section 35 does not, however, allow a company to ratify transactions that are *ultra vires* because they are illegal (e.g. the giving of financial assistance for the purpose of acquiring shares in the company contrary to the Act) and a shareholder will be able to bring a derivative action against the wrongdoers on behalf of the company in these circumstances (*Smith v. Croft (No. 2)* [1988] Ch. 114).

It should also be noted that s. 35 specifically preserves a shareholder's right to bring a personal action against the company to restrain it from committing an *ultra vires* act.

16.3.2   Special resolution procedures

Members can bring derivative actions to restrain breaches of
special majority procedures (whether they are contained in the
Act or the memorandum or articles) and to prevent the company
from acting on resolutions passed as a result of such breaches. In
Edwards v. Halliwell [1950] 2 All ER 1064, the Court of Appeal
declared a decision by a trade union to increase its membership
fees invalid because a requirement in its constitution that a two-
thirds majority of the members should agree had not been
observed.

16.3.3   Fraud on the minority

Shareholders may bring an action on behalf of the company
where the wrongdoers have committed a fraud on the minority
and control the company. This is an important exception to the
rule in *Foss v. Harbottle*, for without it the courts would not be
able to redress wrongs done by the majority for their own
benefit. The word 'fraud' in this context embraces a wider
equitable meaning than deceit and in reality will be a wrong done
to the company rather than to the minority. Lord Davey defined
fraud in *Burland v. Earle* [1902] AC 83 as embracing all cases
where the wrongdoers 'are endeavouring, directly or indirectly, to
appropriate to themselves money, property or advantages which
belong to the company or in which the other shareholders are
entitled to participate'. It should be noted that this definition does
not embrace situations where the wrongdoers do not benefit.
Neither does it cover negligence on the part of the directors. In
Pavlides v. Jensen [1956] Ch. 565, it was held that a shareholder
could not sue the directors for negligently selling a mine at a
gross undervalue under the fraud on the minority exception to
the rule in *Foss v. Harbottle*. In these circumstances, the proper
course would be for the company to sue the directors and, if the
directors sought to prevent it from doing so for their own benefit,
this would probably constitute a fraud on the minority.

In order to bring an action under the fraud on the minority
exception, a plaintiff must demonstrate that the alleged
wrongdoers control the company. This will be relatively simple
where they own a majority of shares conferring voting rights and
it is not necessary in such circumstances to demonstrate that the
wrongdoers have refused to institute proceedings (*Mason v. Harris*
(1879) 11 Ch. D. 97). However, it has also been held to be
sufficient to demonstrate that the wrongdoers secured with their
votes the passing of a resolution that the company would not
institute proceedings, even if they did not own a majority of the
voting shares (*Cook v. Deeks* [1916] 1 AC 554). In *Prudential
Assurance Co. Ltd v. Newman Industries (No. 2)* [1982] Ch. 204, it
was observed as a dictum that control 'embraces a wide spectrum
extending from an overall absolute majority of votes at one end

to a majority of votes at the other made up of those likely to be cast by the delinquent himself plus those voting with him as a result of influence or apathy'.

It seems that a shareholder may also be prevented from bringing a derivative action under the fraud on the minority exception where an independent organ of the company does not want it to proceed (*Smith v. Croft (No. 2)* [1988] Ch. 114).

16.4 Alteration of articles

The Act allows a company to alter its articles by special resolution (s. 9). However, this power must be exercised by the members in good faith for the benefit of the company as a whole (*Allen v. Gold Reefs of West Africa Ltd* [1900] 1 Ch. 656). In *Greenhalgh v. Ardene Cinemas Ltd* [1951] Ch. 286, Evershed MR said (at p. 291):

> Certain principles, I think, can be safely stated as emerging from the authorities. In the first place, I think it is now plain that 'bona fide for the benefit of the company as a whole' means not two things but one thing. It means that the shareholder must proceed upon what, in his honest opinion, is for the benefit of the company as a whole. The second thing is that the phrase 'the company as a whole' does not ... mean the company as a commercial entity, distinct from the corporators: it means the corporators as a general body. That is to say, the case may be taken of an individual hypothetical member and it may be asked whether what is proposed is, in the honest opinion of those who voted in its favour, for that person's benefit. I think that the matter can, in practice, be more accurately and precisely stated by looking at the converse and saying that a special resolution of this kind would be liable to be impeached if the effect of it were to discriminate between the majority shareholders and the minority shareholders.

If the shareholders have acted honestly in what they believe to be the best interests of the company, the court is unlikely to interfere unless there are no reasonable grounds upon which such a decision could be reached (*Shuttleworth v. Cox Bros. & Co.* [1927] 2 KB 9).

Thus an alteration that gave rights of expropriation at a fair value with respect to the shares of any member who was in business as a competitor was held to be valid even though such a member existed at the time of the alteration (*Sidebottom v. Kershaw, Leese & Co.* [1920] 1 Ch. 154 (CA)). However, an alteration that enabled the majority to require any member (other than a named member) to transfer his or her shares was held to be invalid (*Dafen Tinplate Co. Ltd v. Llanelly Steel Co. (1917) Ltd* [1920] 2 Ch. 124).

An alteration giving a company a lien over fully paid shares for other debts of the holder was held to be valid because it was capable of applying to all fully paid shares, even though at the time the change only adversely affected the position of those who sought to challenge it (*Allen v. Gold Reefs of West Africa Ltd* [1900] 1 Ch. 656).

It should be noted that even though minority shareholders might not succeed under this heading, they could be entitled to relief under the unfair prejudice provision of s. 459.

16.5 Unfairly prejudicial conduct

A member may petition the court for relief from unfairly prejudicial conduct under s. 459. This statutory remedy has removed many of the obstacles that prevented minority shareholders seeking relief under the common law. Any member may petition the court and there is no need to satisfy the requirements of the rule in *Foss v. Harbottle*. Relief under s. 459 is not restricted to minority shareholders although the court will not grant a majority shareholder a remedy if he or she can easily rid himself of the prejudice by using his or her majority shareholding (*Re Baltic Real Estate (No. 2)* [1993] BCLC 246).

Where the court is satisfied that a petition is well founded, it may make any order it thinks fit for giving relief in respect of the matters complained of (s. 461). The order may, for example:

- regulate the conduct of the company's affairs in the future;
- require the company to refrain from doing or continuing an act complained of or to do an act that the petitioner has complained it has omitted to do;
- authorise civil proceedings to be brought in the name of and on behalf of the company by such person or persons and on such terms as the court may direct;
- provide for the purchase of the shares of any members of the company by other members or by the company itself and in the case of a purchase by the company itself, the reduction of the company's capital accordingly; or
- alter the company's memorandum or articles of association.

The court may grant a petitioner relief under s. 459 where the company's affairs are being or have been conducted in a manner that is unfairly prejudicial to the interests of its members generally or some of the members (including at least the petitioner), or where any actual or proposed act or omission of the company (including an act or omission on its behalf) is or would be so prejudicial (s. 459(1)). According to a study undertaken on behalf of the Law Commission for its Consultation Paper No. 142 'Shareholder Remedies', the conduct that most petitioners (over 67%) complain of in cases brought under this heading is exclusion from the management of the company. It also reported that nearly 70% of petitioners seek an order for the purchase of their shares.

For an example of a case on exclusion from the company's management, see *Re Saul D. Harrison & Sons plc* [1995] 1 BCLC 14, where the court held that the petitioner had a legitimate expectation of being able to participate in the management of the company and that his exclusion could therefore be unfairly prejudicial to his interests.

Relief has been given under s. 459 where a member who held 60% of a company's shares voted to allot himself new shares to increase his holding to 96% and reduce the holding of a minority shareholder from 40% to 4% (*Re D.R. Chemicals* (1989) 5 BCC 39). In this case the majority shareholder was ordered to purchase the minority shareholder's 40% holding at a price to be fixed by independent valuation.

Cases have also been brought successfully where there has been a deliberate diversion of the company's business by those in control to another business owned by them, e.g. *Re London School of Electronics Ltd* [1986] Ch. 211.

In *Re a Company (No. 002612 of 1984)* (1986) 2 BCC 99, it was held that a director's remuneration of over £350,000 over a 14-month period was plainly in excess of anything he had earned and was therefore unfairly prejudicial to the petitioner's interests. Excessive remuneration is often linked to the non-payment of dividends. However, the non-payment of dividends could in itself be unfairly prejudicial even though it affects all shareholders equally.

The courts are reluctant to grant relief for mismanagement (*Re Elingdata Ltd* [1991] BCLC 959). However, in *Re Macro (Ipswich) Ltd* [1994] 2 BCLC 354, Arden J granted relief for specific acts of mismanagement which had been repeated over many years and which the respondent had failed to prevent or rectify. A failure to provide information about how the company is being run to a person who has a right to be consulted on major decisions could constitute unfairly prejudicial conduct (*Re R.A. Noble* [1983] BCLC 273).

The Secretary of State may also petition the court for an order if it appears to him or her that a company's affairs are being or have been conducted in a manner that is unfairly prejudicial to the interests of its members or some of its members (s. 460).

16.6 Just and equitable winding up

Shareholders may in certain circumstances petition the court under s. 122(1)(g) of the Insolvency Act 1986 for an order that the company be wound up on just and equitable grounds. Indeed, this is often pleaded in the alternative to a petition under s. 459. The House of Lords has held that a member may petition for a winding up on just and equitable grounds if he or she can show any circumstances affecting him or her in his or her relations with the company or with the other shareholders for which winding up is a just and equitable solution (*Ebrahimi v. Westbourne Galleries Ltd* [1973] AC 360). In that case, the plaintiff and a Mr Nazar formed a private company in 1958 to carry on a business, which they had previously done as equal partners, and were appointed the company's first directors. Shortly afterwards, Nazar's son also became a director and between them Nazar and his son controlled the majority of votes at general meetings. All the company's profits were distributed as directors' remuneration and no dividends were ever paid. At a general meeting in 1969, Mr Ebrahimi was removed as a director by Nazar and his son in accordance with the statutory procedures. Mr Ebrahimi petitioned the court to wind up the company on just and equitable grounds and this was allowed even though Nazar and his son had acted in strict accordance with the Act and the company's articles. Lord Wilberforce explained the meaning of 'just and equitable' by saying:

> The words are a recognition of the fact that a limited company is more than a mere legal entity, with a personality in law of its own: that there is room in company law for recognition of the fact that behind it, or amongst it, there are individuals, with rights, expectations and obligations inter se which are not necessarily submerged in the company structure ... The just and equitable provision does not ... entitle one party to disregard the obligations he assumes by entering a company, nor the court to dispense him from it. It does, as equity always does, enable the court to subject the exercise of legal rights to equitable considerations; considerations, that is, of a personal character arising between one individual and another, which may make it unjust, or inequitable, to insist on legal rights, or to exercise them in a particular way.

The courts have also wound up companies under this heading where:

- it was no longer possible to achieve the purpose for which the company was formed (see *Re Eastern Telegraph Co. Ltd* [1974] 2 All ER 104);
- the company was promoted fraudulently (*Re Thomas Edward Brinsmead & Sons* [1897] 1 Ch. 406, CA); and
- the company was formed for an illegal purpose (*Re The International Securities Corporation Ltd* (1908) 24 TLR 837).

16.7 Other remedies

The remedies outlined above tend to be used as a last resort. The Act provides various other means by which shareholders may be able to reconcile their problems. For example:

- The Secretary of State has wide powers to appoint inspectors to investigate matters, which may have been drawn to his or her attention by a member (ss. 431 and 442). The Secretary of State may, as a result of these investigations, apply for a winding up order under the Insolvency Act 1986 or for an order under Part XVII of the Companies Act 1985.
- Shareholders representing not less than 10% of the total voting rights may require the directors to convene an EGM (s. 368) (see **10.6**).
- Any member may apply to the Secretary of State for an order calling a general meeting where the company is in default of its obligation to hold an AGM (s. 377) (see **10.4**).
- If for any reason it is impracticable to call a meeting of a company, or to conduct the meeting in the manner prescribed by the articles or the Act, any member may apply to the court for an order calling a meeting (s. 371) (see **10.5**).
- Members may require the company to circulate notice of any resolution intended to be moved at the next AGM and require the company to circulate a statement in connection with any business to be proposed at a general meeting (s. 376) (see **11.13**).
- Any member of a private company that has passed an elective resolution to dispense with holding AGMs or to dispense with the laying of accounts or with the annual appointment of auditors may require the company to hold an AGM, to lay the accounts at a general meeting or to convene a meeting to propose that the auditors' appointment be brought to an end (ss. 366A, 253 and 393) (see **Chapter 25**).
- Members who did not vote in favour of the change have a right to apply to the court to cancel a special resolution to alter the company's objects clause or any provision in the memorandum that could have been contained in the articles and for which no provision is made for alteration (ss. 5 and 17).
- Resolutions varying the rights attached to any class of shares may be challenged by members holding not less than 15% of that class who did not vote in favour of the change (s. 127).
- A special resolution passed by a private company approving the giving of financial assistance for the purchase of a company's own shares may be challenged in the court by shareholders holding at least 10% by nominal value of the company's issued share capital who did not vote in favour of the resolution (s. 157).
- Shareholders may by ordinary resolution remove a director before the expiry of his or her term of office (s. 303) (see section 23.11).
- Application may be made to the court for an order that the company's register of members be rectified (s. 359).
- Members have various rights of inspection of company registers and the right to copies of them on payment of a fee.
- A company must send shareholders copies of its annual accounts which must be prepared in accordance with the requirements of the Act (s. 238 and Part VII).

Part III

Running general meetings

This section deals with the organisation of general meetings and draws together practical and legal issues that may arise when the meeting is held. It also includes specific guidance on common items of business.

17

Organising general meetings

17.1 Summary

- This chapter deals with some of the more practical aspects of organising the AGM, although many of the issues raised will also be relevant to other meetings. It includes a checklist for organising AGMs which has been cross-referenced to the relevant paragraphs and chapters in this book (see **17.2**).
- Choosing the right venue for the AGM is an important task. The directors may determine where the meeting will be held, provided that the location is not chosen with the deliberate intention of excluding certain members (see **17.3**).
- The venue should be large enough to accommodate all the members wishing to attend. If not, the meeting will have to be adjourned. The secretary will therefore need to estimate the attendance and be prepared to advise the chairman on the action to take in the event that the room is too small (see **17.4**).
- If members are forced to sit in an uncomfortable environment, they tend to become irritable. Naturally, this is the last thing the chairman and the directors need. Attention to 'hygiene factors' is therefore important. However, shareholders may also complain if the venue is too extravagant, particularly if profits and dividends are down. The final decision will almost always be a compromise between cost, quality, size and availability (see **17.5**).
- Company meetings can be turgid affairs, and it can be difficult to entice members to attend. Various bodies have made recommendations on how the AGM can be improved (see **17.6** and **17.7**).
- Listed companies must be careful at general meetings not to breach the requirements of the Listing Rules on the disclosure of price-sensitive information (see **17.8**).

17.2   Cross-referenced checklist for AGM

Preliminary question for private limited companies (Ltd)

If an elective resolution to dispense with AGM is in force, it is not necessary to hold an AGM unless a member has demanded that an AGM be held. If no such elective resolution is in force, consider passing one (see **25.3**).

Date of meeting

- Calculate last date on which AGM must be held and choose a suitable date or range of possible dates before the last date (see **8.3**).
- Consult chairman and other relevant personnel.
- Fix date and inform relevant company personnel and external advisers, e.g. registrars, auditors, solicitor, broker, PR consultants, etc.
- If a suitable opportunity arrives, inform the members.

Venue

- Calculate likely attendance (see **17.4**).
- Determine other requirements, e.g. location, cost, etc. (see **17.5**).
- Select and visit venues.
- Assess suitability for security purposes (see **20.3**).
- Provisionally book preferred venue.
- Consult chairman.
- If chairman agrees, book venue and obtain confirmation of booking.
- Agree and sign contract.
- Obtain map of venue location.

Other arrangements

- Make arrangements for:
  - catering (if required);
  - security and stewards (see **20.2** and **20.3**);
  - audiovisual equipment (if required);
  - printing of signs for AGM;
  - stage design (if required); and
  - display stands (if required).

Planning the AGM mailing

- Calculate last date notice must be sent out bearing in mind
  - notice requirements (see **11.2**);
  - requirement for clear days' notice (see **11.2**);
  - date notice deemed given if sent by post or electronically (see **11.4**).
- Set date for posting of notice and accounts (preferably before last date).
- If not possible within time limit, consider obtaining consent to short notice (see **11.11**), otherwise change date of AGM.
- Set dates for:

- final draft of notice;
- finalisation of accounts and audit;
- board meeting to approve accounts and convene AGM;
- printing of notice, proxies, circulars, accounts and other documents to go with AGM mailing (inform printers);
- printing of address labels (if by registrar, inform registrar stating where they are to be sent).

Drafting the notice, etc.

- Prepare rough outline of business to be transacted at the AGM (see **8.4**).
- Check whether special notice is required for any resolution, e.g. to remove director or auditors or appoint director over age of 70, etc. (see **11.12**).
- Check type of resolution required for each item of business to be proposed (see **Chapter 12** and **Appendix D**).
- Calculate which (if any) of the directors must retire by rotation (see **23.10**).
- Confirm that auditors are willing to be reappointed (see **23.3**).
- Check whether s. 80 authority needs to be renewed (see **8.4**).
- Include any valid resolutions or statements submitted by members (see **11.13**).
- Draft the AGM notice and circular (see **Precedents**).
- Draft proxy cards (if required) (see **Chapter 14**).
- Draft attendance card (if required) (see **20.2**).
- Draft invitation to members to submit questions in advance (if required) (see **19.6**).

Board meeting to convene AGM and approve results and dividends

- Prepare and send out notice of board meeting including resolutions:
  - to approve report and accounts;
  - to authorise signing of accounts and reports;
  - to recommend a dividend;
  - to convene the AGM and approve business (see **10.2**);
  - to authorise secretary to sign and send out notices, etc.;
  - to recommend the appointment of any directors (if articles require) (see section 23.8 on reg. 76 of Table A);
  - to approve the release of the preliminary announcement (listed plc only);
  - to nominate director to act as chairman of the general meeting in the absence of the chairman of the board (see **18.2**).
- Immediately before meeting check again for any valid members' resolutions and include in papers put to the board (see **11.13**).
- Hold meeting and pass resolutions.
- If problems convening meeting, see **10.3**.

Immediately after the board meeting
- Release preliminary announcement (listed plc only).
- Balance sheet signed by two directors.
- Directors' report signed by director or secretary.
- Auditors' report signed by auditors.
- Notice signed and dated by secretary (see **11.6**).
- Calculate required number of copies of:
  - annual report (including extra copies);
  - notice and proxy cards.
- Final proofs of report and accounts, proxy cards, notice, etc. sent to printers with instructions as to numbers required.
- Directors and relevant employees notified of close period for dealings in company's shares (listed plc only).

Sending out the notice
- Send report and accounts, notice, etc. to persons entitled to receive them (see **23.2**).
- File annual report at Companies House.
- Send report and accounts to others on mailing list kept for that purpose.

Miscellaneous matters
- Make arrangements for the payment of the dividend (if approved).
- Calculate cut-off day and time for valid proxies (see **14.14**) and, if necessary, inform registrars.
- Monitor proxies received.
- If necessary, contact major shareholders to encourage submission of proxies.
- At appropriate time on cut-off date for proxies prepare:
  - schedule of proxies appointed for the use of staff on the registration desk;
  - schedule of voting instructions for the chairman where the member has appointed chairman as proxy.
- Print voting cards and poll cards.

Preparations immediately before AGM
- Arrange for proposers and seconders of resolutions (as required).
- Finalise chairman's agenda/script (see **Appendix L**).
- Prepare AGM briefing document (see **Appendix J**).
- Brief chairman.
- If members were invited to submit questions in advance, prepare answers.
- Rehearse questions and answers.
- Allocate following duties to staff and brief accordingly:
  - registration (see **20.2**);
  - poll (see **15.8**);
  - roving microphone;
  - stewards (see **20.2**).
- Brief staff and rehearse AGM.

- Confirm final arrangements with venue, security staff, registrars, etc.
- Make arrangements for the release of an announcement if it is intended to reveal price-sensitive information at the meeting (listed plc only) (see **17.8**).

Day of the AGM

- Things to take to the meeting:
  - directors' service contracts (see **8.5**);
  - register of directors' interests (see **8.5**);
  - spare copies of report and accounts and notice;
  - chairman's agenda/script (plus copies for other directors who are to propose resolutions);
  - questions and answers script;
  - memorandum and articles of association (indexed);
  - consolidated version of Companies Act 1985 (as amended);
  - a textbook on the law and procedures of meetings;
  - summary of proxies received;
  - original proxy forms and summary sheets;
  - register of members (usually supplied by registrar);
  - attendance sheets for: members, proxies and corporate representatives, and guests (see **19.3**);
  - notepads, pens and pencils;
  - name plates for top table and name badges;
  - reserved seats signs;
  - voting cards;
  - calculator with printed roll for counting votes on a poll;
  - telephone numbers of crucial participants.
- Final briefing of staff.
- Check that quorum present (see **Chapter 13**).
- Open meeting and conduct business.
- Record proceedings.

After the meeting

- Prepare minutes for signature by chairman (see **Chapter 26**).
- Take actions required as a result of resolutions passed.
- Authorise payment of dividend.
- Copy resolutions filed at Companies House (see **12.6**).
- Copy resolutions sent to UK Listing Authority (listed plc only) (see **12.6**).
- Respond to shareholder questions raised at meeting.
- Review the organisation of the AGM.
- Book venue for next AGM.

17.3   Location of meeting

Generally speaking, it is preferable to hold general meetings in the country of incorporation. However, the directors may determine the place at which the meeting shall be held and, in the absence of fraud, their decision cannot be challenged (*Martin v. Walker* (1918) 145 LTJ 377). The directors must therefore exercise their power to select the place of the meeting in the best interests of the company. If they call a meeting to be held at a time and place that clearly restricts the ability of a significant proportion of the members to attend, their decision is liable to challenge (*Cannon v. Trask* (1875) LR 20 Eq. 669).

These rules would not prevent a UK registered company holding a meeting outside the UK if, for example, the majority of its shareholders were resident in the country in which the meeting was to be held or that country was the most convenient for the members as a whole.

17.4 Estimating attendance

Ideally, the venue for the AGM should be capable of accommodating all the members. For private companies with few members, this is relatively easy to arrange. However, for companies with thousands of shareholders, this is impractical. Instead, the company secretary must try to predict the number of members and guests likely to attend. The starting point for this exercise will normally be to examine attendance levels in previous years. If the number of shareholders has increased or decreased significantly, appropriate adjustments should be made.

If the company's results are not as good as expected or it has been the subject of adverse press comment, the proportion of members attending will probably be higher than normal. Numbers will also increase where food and drink or company products are offered for the first time (numbers might not fall quite so dramatically when any such perks are withdrawn – shareholders may attend to complain about the change of policy!). An interesting or unusual venue may also attract more shareholders as may a change of venue to a location that is more accessible.

Whatever figure is finally arrived at, most company secretaries tend to add a little extra for contingency purposes. Preparations for the meeting are usually made a long way in advance and it is sensible to assume that something may subsequently happen that brings shareholders out of the woodwork.

Some companies conduct surveys of a sample of their members in order to estimate the likely attendance. Others ask shareholders to return a reply-paid card if they intend to attend. Such methods usually produce a forecast that is higher than the actual attendance on the day. To this extent, they can be a useful guide to the absolute maximum attendance, particularly for a newly listed company or one that has recently undergone a major change in its shareholder base, e.g. following a takeover or merger. One company, which asked all its members to return a card indicating whether they would attend, found that the responses tallied almost exactly with the actual attendance. However, on analysing the responses, it found that this was because the number of shareholders who said they would attend but did not turn up was practically the same as the number who did not respond but attended on the day.

Having determined the maximum number of members for which accommodation will be provided, additional provision should be made for guests, the press and employees.

17.4.1   Room size

If the estimate of the maximum attendance differs greatly from the normal attendance, the prime consideration may be flexibility. A large room capable of being partitioned off may be preferable to separate overspill rooms which need to be connected by audiovisual links to the main meeting room. Such links are expensive to establish and can be unreliable (see **4.10** and **21.3** for discussion as to their legality where no provision is made in the articles). For an article dealing with overflow arrangements for general meetings, see **Precedent 17.5**.

It is usual for the board of directors to be seated with the chairman, facing the shareholders. Indeed, this is one of the best practice points in ICSA's *Guide to Best Practice for AGMs*. The company secretary will usually be seated on the top table or platform next to the chairman. Some companies also invite the audit partner and the company's solicitor to sit on the top table. Some venues have built-in stage areas and platforms. However, the seating capacity of the room may depend on the size of the platform required. It is becoming increasingly common for each director to have a VDU which is used to display either the running order or information compiled by researchers which may be helpful for the directors when answering questions from shareholders.

What seating arrangement can be provided comfortably (e.g. theatre, classroom or boardroom styles)? Can areas be cordoned off for different classes of members or non-members? Are the chairs comfortable? Will everyone be able to see the top table?

17.5   Other factors influencing the choice of venue

Several other factors will influence the choice of venue and some of these are considered below. It can be useful to produce a checklist of the company's main requirements in order to compare the suitability of the various venues considered. An example of such a checklist can be found at Table 17.1.

17.5.1   Availability

The meeting room(s) should be booked to allow for the possibility that the meeting may take longer than usual. Nothing is likely to annoy shareholders more than for discussion to be cut short because the room has to be vacated. Indeed, the chairman

Table 17.1 Venue checklist

Date or preferred date of meeting   . . . .
Venue required from   time . . . . date . . . .
Venue required until   time . . . . date . . . .

	Main room area	Overspill area	Registration	Refreshments
Maximum capacity				
Top table/platform area				
Rear/front projection				
Exhibition area				
Question points				
Help desks				
Lighting				
Power points				
Noise level				
Heating/air conditioning				
Sound facilities				
Audiovisual links				

Other matters
- Security
- Noticeboards/signposts
- Cloakrooms
- Telephone/fax facilities
- Boardroom
- Licence agreement
- Staff
- Catering requirements
- Cost

may find it necessary to adjourn the meeting in such circumstances which could be both costly and embarrassing. Adequate time must also be allowed to set up the room before the meeting and for taking down any stage designs and displays after the meeting. This may mean booking the room for the day before the meeting and for a few hours after the meeting is due to close.

17.5.2 Terms of licence

Are any of the terms and conditions (e.g. dress codes, security checks, etc.) inconsistent with the company's legal obligations to admit all shareholders (see **20.2**)?

17.5.3 Location

Is the venue easily accessible by road and public transport? Is it in a pleasant and safe area? Does it have access for the disabled?

The ICSA's *Guide to Best Practice for AGMs* recommends that the venue for the AGM should be accessible by attendees who have disabilities, and have facilities for those with poor hearing.

17.5.4   Noise levels

Is the room relatively sound-proof? The most common problem with hotel conference rooms is that they are situated next to the kitchen and catering staff are rarely responsive to requests to keep the noise down. Partitioned rooms should be avoided unless you can afford to reserve the whole suite as it is inevitable that the adjoining section(s) will be hired by people whose activities involve making a great deal of noise. Although the partitions themselves are normally sound-proof, the connecting doors frequently are not. Also check whether the owners intend to do any building, decorating or repairs around the date of the meeting. The venue may look wonderful when you book it. Things could be very different on the day. If possible, obtain a written undertaking that no such work will be carried out on the day.

17.5.5   Lighting, heating and air conditioning

Can the lights, heating and air conditioning be adjusted easily and are they sufficient? In many hotels access to these controls is restricted. If so, will a member of staff be available to make the necessary adjustments?

17.5.6   Registration and help desks

In addition to the main meeting room, the venue will need to have a suitable area for registration. Ideally, it should not be possible for members to gain entry to the meeting room without passing through the registration area. If there is more than one entrance to the venue, the registration area might need to be located immediately outside the entrance to the meeting room. The size of the registration area will depend on the number of members and guests that are expected to attend. It may need to be large enough to accommodate several registration desks and the company's registrars may need power points if they plan to access the register of members using portable computers.

Many companies (particularly those whose private shareholders are potential or captive customers) provide shareholder help desks to deal with members' enquiries about dividends and other issues relating to their personal holdings. Retail and consumer companies often establish separate help desks to deal with enquiries that are customer related. By doing so, members are less likely to raise these issues at the meeting and the chairman is able to refer a member who asks such a question to the relevant help desk. If these facilities are to be provided, they will need to be situated in a prominent position, perhaps in the foyer.

17.5.7   Security

Space may be needed for security checks to be carried out prior to registration to prevent members bringing into the meeting any objects that could be used to disrupt the meeting, e.g. banners, missiles, whistles, klaxons, etc. (see further **20.2** and **20.3**).

17.5.8   Sound system and recordings

Sound equipment may be necessary for the top table and for taking questions from the floor. It should be remembered that the acoustics in an empty room are far better than when it is full of people. If the meeting room is large, it will almost certainly be necessary to provide some means of amplification for shareholders who wish to ask questions during the meeting. This can be done using roving microphones. However, the modern trend is to provide one or more fixed microphones from which shareholders must put questions. If microphones are not provided, the chairman should be briefed to repeat or summarise the questions put from the floor before answering them.

Can the proceedings (including questions from the floor) be recorded so that a transcript can be made? The company may also wish to make arrangements for the proceedings to be videotaped, possibly for transmission on a late night TV slot which shareholders who were unable to attend can record and watch at their leisure.

17.5.9   Refreshments

Where refreshments are provided, they are normally served in a separate room so that the catering staff do not disrupt the meeting. Exhibitions of company products or its history could also be placed in this area or in the main meeting room.

17.5.10   Directors' room

The availability of a meeting or preparation room for the directors and an office for the meeting organisers should also be considered.

17.5.11   Staff

Are the staff friendly and helpful? Do they have sufficient staff to cater for your needs? Will a manager be on hand throughout the meeting to handle any problems?

17.5.12 Toilets and cloakroom facilities

The standard of both the ladies' and the gentlemen's toilets should be checked. Is there anywhere for members to leave their coats and baggage?

17.5.13 Other facilities

The availability of telephone, fax and photocopying facilities may be important to the organisers and to members attending.

17.6 Enhancing the AGM

The purpose of holding AGMs has been called into question on a number of occasions in recent years. This has already resulted in legislation to allow private companies (but not public companies) to dispense with holding AGMs, albeit with safeguards that allow any member to require one to be held (see **Chapter 25**). However, questions have even been raised with regard to listed companies. For example, a committee established by the DTI (under the chairmanship of Paul Myners of Gartmore plc) to examine ways of improving relationships between the City and industry reported that virtually all participants in its consultation exercise viewed the AGM as an expensive waste of time and money (Myners Report, 'Developing a Winning Partnership', 1995). Several factors have probably caused this antipathy towards the AGM to increase in recent years. Probably the most important of these is the increase in the proportion of shares held by institutional investors and the fact that they do not normally attend the meeting, preferring instead to vote by proxy. One of the consequences of this is that the views of private investors who attend the meeting are not as important as they once were. In addition, single-issue pressure groups tend to dominate (and often disrupt) the proceedings of an increasing number of listed companies. This can make it difficult for other shareholders to raise legitimate questions and has undoubtedly caused some shareholders to decide not to attend future meetings. Other reasons given include the constraints imposed by the Listing Rules on the release of price-sensitive information which limit the directors' ability to give meaningful answers to questions raised by shareholders at the meeting (see **17.8**). Companies often complain about the standard of debate and questions raised by shareholders at the meeting. Directors, in particular, complain that many shareholders only seem to attend to complain about the directors' remuneration packages.

Some commentators have called for the AGM to be abolished and for companies to be allowed to conduct postal ballots. One listed company has even included in its articles a provision that would allow it to conduct postal ballots should the law ever be changed. For the moment, however, the weight of opinion still seems to be in favour of maintaining the AGM primarily as a method of holding the directors accountable for their management of the company. Company secretaries often cite as evidence of the AGM's effectiveness the fact that, when taking decisions on certain policies and strategies, directors consider whether they would feel comfortable justifying their proposed course of action at the AGM. The attendance of the press at listed companies' AGMs also means that directors are held accountable to a wider audience.

In an attempt to stimulate new initiatives to enhance the AGM, the Cadbury Committee observed that: 'If too many AGMs are at present an opportunity missed, this is because shareholders do not make the most of them and, in some cases, boards do not encourage them to do so' (Cadbury Report, para. 6.7). Proposals to enhance the AGM have subsequently been made by the Myners Committee in its report *Developing a Winning Partnership*, and the ICSA in its *Guide to Best Practice for AGMs*.

The Myners report made the following recommendations with a view to enhancing the attractiveness of AGMs to institutional investors:

- companies should encourage shareholders to submit questions in advance of the meeting;
- questions specific to an individual, and not of general interest, should be referred to the relevant director for response after the meeting, with the answers subsequently made available to any interested shareholder;
- companies should provide an updated trading statement at the meeting; and
- operational managers should make a presentation at the meeting and be available to answer questions from shareholders outside the formal meeting.

17.7   ICSA's *Guide to Best Practice for AGMs*

In April 1996, the Department of Trade and Industry issued a consultative document, *Shareholder Communications at the AGM*, which asked whether shareholders should have a statutory right to have resolutions circulated free of charge and/or to ask questions at the AGM. The consultative document suggested that some of these issues could be dealt with by the development of best practice by companies. Accordingly, with the encouragement of the DTI, the Institute of Chartered Secretaries and Administrators (ICSA) published a *Guide to Best Practice for AGMs* in September 1996. The recommendations made in the guide have been endorsed by the National Association of Pension Funds, the Association of British Insurers and ProShare. For a summary of recommendations, see **Appendix M**.

17.8 Price-sensitive information

The Listing Rules impose a general obligation on listed companies to disclose certain information which is not public knowledge and which may lead to a substantial movement in the price of their securities (Listing Rules, paras 9.1–10). Such information must always be given to the market as a whole, by an announcement to the Company Announcements Office. Companies are free to use additional media, but selective disclosure of price-sensitive information is not acceptable.

The London Stock Exchange published additional guidance on the application of these rules in 1996, *Guidance on the Dissemination of Price Sensitive Information*. This guidance is still published by the UK Listing Authority although, at the time of writing, it is reported to be preparing a new version. The 1996 guidance includes the following paragraphs on the disclosure of information at general meetings:

> 13. If a meeting is to be held (e.g., with shareholders, analysts or a press conference), companies should consider in advance how to respond to questions designed to elicit price sensitive information. If it is planned to disclose price sensitive information, the information should not be given at the meeting before it is announced to the market.
> 17. Companies are encouraged to make the most of existing opportunities for communicating with investors. In particular, through the annual report, or through the Chairman's address to the AGM, a company may reinforce its corporate messages in non-technical terms and provide indicators of its future direction. While the AGM is an opportunity for investors to discuss with directors issues affecting the company, arrangements must be made for any price sensitive information that is to be discussed at the meeting to be included in an announcement to the Company Announcements Office at or before the time of the meeting.

In order to comply with these requirements, it is usual for listed companies to release a copy of the chairman's address to the Company Announcements Office immediately prior to the meeting, particularly where this includes updated trading information. However, this will not be necessary if the chairman merely recites information already published in the annual report. It may also be necessary to release the text of any presentations to be made by operational managers. As these presentations and the chairman's address will be prepared before the meeting, it will be possible to take advice from the company's brokers on the action that should be taken where there is any doubt, although most listed companies probably err on the side of disclosure these days.

The rules prohibiting the selective disclosure of price-sensitive information also tend to inhibit the ability of directors to answer shareholders' questions at general meetings. Indeed, they are sometimes accused of emasculating one of the main purposes of the AGM, i.e. to enable shareholders to hold the directors accountable for their stewardship of the company. This feeling may have arisen among shareholders because directors often cite the Listing Rules as the reason for not answering certain questions even though commercial confidentiality is probably the primary reason. The acid test in this regard is whether the directors would have answered the question if there were no rules on the release of price-sensitive information. In most cases, the answer would probably be no.

Nevertheless, the Listing Rules do impose limitations on listed companies that are predisposed towards answering shareholders' questions, and the main problem that the directors will face is trying to decide at the meeting whether the answer that they would like to give would constitute price-sensitive information. The *Guidance on the Dissemination of Price Sensitive Information* stresses that it is impossible to define any theoretical percentage movement in a share price that will make a piece of information price sensitive, and points out that no such definition is included in the insider dealing provisions of the Criminal Justice Act 1993. Favourable information could, for example, result in a static share price in a generally falling market. However, the *Guidance* goes on to say:

> 5. However, price sensitive information will potentially have a significant effect on a company's share price. In particular, a company should be able to assess whether an event or information known to the company would have a significant effect on future reported earnings per share, pre-tax profits, borrowings or other potential determinants of the company's share price. The Listing Rules indicate many events which have to be announced to the market because they may be price sensitive. These include dividend announcements, board appointments or departures, profit warnings, share dealings by directors or substantial shareholders, acquisitions and disposals above a certain size, annual and interim results, preliminary results, rights issues and other offers of securities. In other areas judgement will necessarily be required ...
> 6. Companies should remember that, in general, the more specific the information, the greater the risk of it being price sensitive. For that reason, companies should not disclose significant data, least of all financial information such as sales and profit figures, to selected groups rather than to the market as a whole. *Even within these constraints, there is plenty of scope for companies to hold useful dialogue with their shareholders and other interested parties about their prospects, business environment and strategy (particularly in the medium and long term).* [emphasis added]

If, in the course of a general meeting, previously unpublished price-sensitive information is inadvertently disclosed, it will of course be necessary for a listed company to make an announcement to the Company Announcements Office as soon as possible. It should also be noted that the results of resolutions taken at general meetings may in themselves be price-sensitive information, particularly where a resolution has been defeated. Listed companies must send two copies of all resolutions (other than those concerning the Listing Rules definition of ordinary business) to the UK Listing Authority without delay after the relevant meeting (Listing Rules, para. 9.31).

18

Chairman

18.1 Summary

- In view of the importance of the role, it is common for the articles to determine who should chair the meetings rather than allow the members to elect the chairman at each meeting (see **18.2**).
- The members may remove a chairman appointed by them but have limited powers of removal, if any, where the appointment is determined by the articles (see **18.3**).
- The chairman has a duty to ensure that the meeting is properly conducted (see **18.5**), that all shades of opinion are given a fair hearing (see **18.6**) and that the sense of the meeting is properly ascertained and recorded (see **18.7**).
- It is also the chairman's duty to maintain order (see **20.4**).
- See also **Chapter 22** on amendments, **Chapter 21** on adjournment and other procedural motions, and **Appendix L** for examples of a chairman's scripts.

18.2 Appointment of chairman

A general meeting cannot proceed without a chairman for legal and practical reasons. There must be someone to put motions to the meeting, declare the results of voting, and rule on points of order. Articles usually state that the chairman of the board of directors shall chair meetings of the company and make provision for circumstances in which he is not present or is unwilling to act. For example, Table A provides:

> **42.** The chairman, if any, of the board of directors or in his absence some other director nominated by the directors shall preside as chairman of the meeting, but if neither the chairman nor any such other director (if any) be present within fifteen minutes after the time appointed for holding the meeting and willing to act, the directors present shall elect one of their number to be chairman and, if there is only one director present and willing to act, he shall be chairman.

43. If no director is willing to act as chairman, or if no director is present within fifteen minutes after the time appointed for holding the meeting, the members present and entitled to vote shall choose one of their number to be chairman.

Where there is no director present or willing to chair the meeting, articles like reg. 43 of Table A appear to require the members to elect another member to act as chairman. However, the word 'member' must include a proxy where the articles say that proxies can be counted in calculating whether there is a quorum and only proxies are present (*Re Bradford Investments plc* [1990] BCC 740). In the same case, it was held that a person who is neither a member, nor a corporate representative nor a proxy may take the chair at the start of the meeting to preside over the election of a chairman. However, the rulings of such a person will be liable to challenge in the courts irrespective of anything contained in the articles, e.g. on the validity of any votes tendered in the election process.

A person who has legitimately taken the chair in the absence of the chairman may (but need not) vacate it if the chairman subsequently arrives. Any objection to the appointment of a chairman at a meeting should be made immediately as any irregularity in the nomination may be cured by the acquiescence of those present (*Booth v. Arnold* [1985] 1 QB 571).

18.3 Removal of the chairman

A chairman elected by the meeting, e.g. when no director is present or willing to act in that capacity, may be removed by the meeting (*Cornwall v. Woods* (1846) 4 notes of Cases 555). This is normally done by a motion of no confidence in the chair. If such a resolution is proposed, the chairman should step down until the result of the vote is determined.

It is doubtful whether a person who holds office as the chairman by virtue of the articles and his position in the company (e.g. as the chairman of the board or as a director) can be removed by the members. If the chairman did relinquish the chair under pressure from the members, the selection of a replacement would be determined by the articles, and the members would only have power to appoint their own chairman if there was no other person specified by the articles as a potential candidate who was willing or able to act as chairman.

18.4 Chairman's duties

In common law, the person appointed as the chairman of the meeting is deemed to have been given authority by the meeting to regulate its proceedings. As this is a form of delegated authority, the chairman must still act in accordance with the wishes of the majority at the meeting, unless exercising a power conferred by statute or the company's articles of association, or one that the courts have ruled can be exercised by the chairman without reference to the members (e.g. the power to adjourn to restore order).

The chairman has an overriding duty to act in good faith in the best interests of the company and is responsible for:

- the proper conduct of the meeting;
- the preservation of order (see **20.4**);
- ensuring that all shades of opinion are given a fair hearing; and
- ensuring that the sense of the meeting is properly ascertained and recorded.

18.5   Proper conduct of the meeting

The chairman must ensure that the meeting is conducted in accordance with the requirements of the Act, the company's articles of association and any applicable common law rules, and will normally be guided in this respect by the company secretary.

The chairman should not open the meeting before the time specified in the notice and should, as far as possible, ensure that the meeting starts on time and that all the business on the agenda is transacted. The start of the meeting can be delayed in certain circumstances. The most obvious is where there is no quorum, in which case the meeting cannot proceed to business in any case. The chairman can also legitimately delay the meeting to allow members who arrived on time to register and gain admittance (see chairman's scripts at **Appendix L**). As a rule of thumb, it is not advisable to delay the meeting for any longer than 15 to 20 minutes. Problems that take longer than this to sort out should be dealt with by proposing an adjournment immediately after opening the meeting (see **Chapter 21**).

The chairman may rule on any question raised from the floor relating to the conduct of the meeting (*Re Indian Zoedone Co.* (1884) 26 Ch. D. 70). If his decision is challenged, the matter should be put to the meeting and decided by the majority of those present (*Wandsworth and Putney Gas Light Co. v. Wright* (1870) 22 LT 404). The following example serves to demonstrate this process.

At a meeting of a public company, a person begins to ask a question but is interrupted by a member on a point of order. The member informs the chairman that the previous speaker is a proxy and therefore has no right to speak at the meeting, and requests that the chairman make a ruling to that effect. The chairman may think that the proxy should be allowed to speak. However, instead of making a ruling to that effect, he should attempt to gauge the feelings of the members by saying: 'I am minded to allow proxies to speak at this meeting. Does anyone else object to this proposal?' If there is no other opposition from the floor, he may rule that the proxy be allowed to speak. If the member still objects, the chairman should perhaps take a proper vote on the matter. If, however, there is significant opposition from the floor, the chairman would be well advised to drop the proposal or risk being defeated on a vote and losing the confidence of the members. It is rare for such issues to be the subject of a poll, although not impossible.

If the chairman conducts the meeting in a certain way or makes a ruling that is not challenged at the meeting, the members present may be deemed to have acquiesced or consented to that conduct. In *Carruth v. Imperial Chemical Industries Ltd* [1937] AC 707, the directors convened an EGM of the company and two meetings of different classes of shares to be held on the same day and at the same venue to approve a reduction of capital. As one meeting finished, the next meeting was started and each meeting was attended by each of the different classes of member. The resolution of one class of members was challenged on the ground that people who were not members of that class were present at the meeting. The resolution was held to be valid and Lord Russell said:

> There are many matters relating to the conduct of a meeting which lie entirely in the hands of those persons who are present and constitute the meeting. Thus it rests with the meeting to decide whether notices, resolutions, minutes, accounts, and such like shall be read to the meeting or be taken as read; whether representatives of the Press, or any other persons not qualified to be summoned to the meeting, shall be permitted to be present, or if present, shall be permitted to remain; whether and when discussion shall be terminated and a vote taken; whether the meeting shall be adjourned. In all these matters, and they are only instances, the meeting decides, and if necessary a vote must be taken to ascertain the wishes of the majority. If no objection is taken by any constituent of the meeting, the meeting must be taken to be assenting to the course adopted.

The chairman cannot close the meeting until all the business has been dealt with. In *National Dwelling Society Ltd v. Sykes*, the chairman wrongly refused to accept an amendment to a resolution to receive the report and accounts and closed the meeting before all the business had been transacted. The members elected another chairman to transact the unfinished business and adjourned the meeting. It was held that the chairman had acted outside his powers by closing the meeting without its consent before the business had been completed and that the meeting could go on with the business for which it had been convened and appoint another chairman to conduct that business.

See also **Chapter 22** on amendments, **Chapter 21** on

adjournment and other procedural motions, and **Appendix L** for examples of a chairman's scripts.

18.6 Ensuring that all shades of opinion are given a fair hearing

The chairman should seek to ensure that all members who hold different views on a resolution before the meeting are given a fair hearing. To do otherwise would defeat the object of holding the meeting. In particular, the chairman should not curtail the debate unless the minority has had a reasonable opportunity to put its views (*Wall v. London & Northern Assets Corporation Ltd* [1898] 2 Ch. 469). See further **19.5** and **19.6**.

18.7 Ascertaining and recording the sense of the meeting

In *National Dwelling Society Ltd v. Sykes* [1894] 3 Ch. 159, it was held that the chairman has a duty to ensure that 'the sense of the meeting is properly ascertained with regard to any question which is properly before the meeting'. In doing so the chairman should put resolutions to a vote, ensure that the votes are properly counted and declare the results of that vote. In order to prevent issues regarding the precise number of votes cast for and against the resolution being re-opened after the meeting, s. 378(4) provides that, unless a poll is demanded, a chairman's declaration that an extraordinary or special resolution has been carried is conclusive evidence of that fact without proof of the number or proportion of votes. The court has refused to intervene in several cases where questions have been raised as to the validity of the chairman's declaration and has confirmed that the word 'conclusive' means exactly that (see *Arnot v. United African Lands* [1901] 1 Ch. 518; *Re Hadleigh Castle Gold Mines* [1900] 2 Ch. 419; and *Graham's Morocco Co. Ltd, Petitioners*, 1932 SC 269). However, the court has intervened in a case where the chairman put a resolution and declared the result in the following fashion: 'Those in favour ... 6. Those against ... 23 but there are 200 voting by proxy and I declare the resolution carried as required by Act of Parliament.' Buckley J refused to hold that the chairman's declaration was conclusive as it was clear from his declaration that he had acted on a mistaken principle (*Re Caratal (New) Mines Ltd* [1902] 2 Ch. 498).

Articles usually extend the operation of s. 378(4) to other resolutions by stating that a declaration by the chairman that a resolution has been carried or carried unanimously, or by a particular majority, or lost, or not carried by a particular majority and an entry to that effect in the minutes shall be conclusive evidence of that fact without proof of the number or proportion of the votes recorded in favour of or against the resolution (see reg. 47). Although the operation of s. 378(4) is not conditional on an entry having been made in the minutes, the minutes will in any proceedings be prima-facie evidence of the proceedings and therefore of the nature of the chairman's declaration.

Every company is required to produce and keep minutes of all proceedings of general meetings (s. 382(1)). The directors can be fined for any default by the company of the provisions of the Act relating to the maintenance of minutes (s. 382(5), s. 383(4) and s. 722(3)). The chairman can be said to have a special duty in this regard in so far as minutes signed by the chairman of the meeting are prima-facie evidence of the proceedings (s. 382(2)) (see **Chapter 26**).

18.8   Chairman's powers

In addition to making rulings on points of order, the chairman will usually have the power:

- to adjourn the meeting, e.g. reg. 45 (see **20.4** and **Chapter 21**);
- to demand a poll, e.g. reg. 46 (see **15.8**);
- to rule on the validity of votes at general meetings, e.g. reg. 58 (see **15.10**);
- to rule on the validity of an amendment (see **22.5**).

19

Right to attend and speak

19.1 Summary

- The right to attend general meetings goes hand in hand with the right to vote. However, the articles may allow others to attend and the Act gives various people a statutory right to attend (see **19.2** and table at **Appendix E**).
- A record should be kept of the names of the members, proxies and corporate representatives who attend any general meeting (see **19.3**).
- Members entitled to attend and vote at general meetings also have a common law right to speak at the meeting. The Companies Act 1985 gives proxies of members of private companies and all corporate representatives the same rights as members in this regard, but not proxies of members of public companies. Auditors have a statutory right to speak on matters that concern them as auditors. The articles usually give the directors a right to speak even if they are not members (see **19.4**).
- The chairman has a duty to ensure that all shades of opinion are given a fair hearing. However, this does not mean that every member must be allowed to speak on a resolution or that they should be allowed to speak for as long as they want (see **19.5**).
- Members may ask questions at general meetings, but have no right to receive an answer (see **19.6**).

19.2 Right to attend

Company meetings are private meetings and, as such, the company is bound to admit only those who are legally entitled to attend. The right to attend goes hand in hand with the right to vote.

19.2.1   Members and corporate representatives

Voting at general meetings is usually conducted by a show of hands or a poll. Both methods require the presence of the person voting (or their proxy). It follows that in order to exercise their right to vote, the members must also have a right to attend the meeting. However, a member who does not have a right to vote may still have a right to attend the meeting, unless the articles provide otherwise.

Companies whose shares have been admitted to CREST may specify in the notice a time, not more than 48 hours before the time fixed for the meeting, by which a person must be entered on the relevant register of securities in order to have the right to attend and vote at the meeting (see **15.2**).

A member who persistently disrupts the meeting may be ejected (see **20.4**). However, a member who is wrongfully excluded from a meeting, and thereby prevented from voting, may be able to challenge the validity of the proceedings, e.g. a person cannot be excluded merely because they have disrupted previous meetings.

Care should be taken to ensure that a member's right to attend is not prejudiced by the terms and conditions imposed under the licence to use the venue where the meeting is to be held. For example, it would be unwise to choose a venue that imposes a dress code. Some companies have taken powers in their articles that allow them to exclude members who refuse to comply with conditions imposed for the purposes of security, e.g. electronic screening and prohibitions on taking hand baggage into the meeting (see **20.2**).

If the meeting room is not big enough to accommodate all the members who wish to attend, the meeting should be adjourned (see **17.4**).

19.2.2   Joint holders

Where shares are registered in the names of joint holders, each of the joint holders is a member of the company and therefore entitled to attend the meeting, unless the articles provide otherwise. Most articles make special provision for voting by joint holders but do not restrict the right to attend (e.g. reg. 55 of Table A).

19.2.3   Death or bankruptcy

Articles commonly provide that a person who becomes entitled to a share in consequence of the death or bankruptcy of a member shall not be entitled to attend or vote at any meeting of the company or of the holders of any class of shares until he or she has been registered as the holder of the share (e.g. reg. 31 of Table A).

19.2.4   Corporate representatives

Corporate representatives are deemed to have the same rights as individual members by virtue of s. 376. Accordingly, they have the same right to attend as an individual member.

19.2.5   Proxies

Proxies have a statutory right to attend on behalf of those who appointed them (s. 372). If the person who appointed the proxy is not entitled to attend, the proxy will not be entitled to attend. A proxy and the member who appointed the proxy may both attend the meeting. If the member does not vote on a poll, the proxy may do so. If the articles allow members to appoint more than one proxy, each proxy appointed has a right to attend the meeting.

19.2.6   Auditors

A company's auditors have a statutory right to receive notice of any general meeting of the company and to attend and speak at any such meeting on any part of the business that concerns them as auditors (s. 390).

19.2.7   Directors

Directors have no statutory right to attend general meetings, except where a resolution to remove them is to be proposed under s. 303 (s. 304). Directors who are members (or a representative or proxy of a member) will be entitled to attend in that capacity.

Articles usually state that directors who are not members shall be entitled to attend and speak at meetings of the company (e.g. reg. 44). There is some doubt as to whether a director who is not a member could enforce such a right as he or she is not a party to the contract that is deemed to exist between the members and the company by virtue of the articles.

The 1948 Act Table A makes no such provision, presumably because directors were usually required to hold some shares in the company which would give them the right to attend general meetings. A company that proposes to delete an article that imposes a share qualification should perhaps ensure that it also adopts a provision similar to reg. 44 of the 1985 Table A.

A director who is not a member but who is appointed as the chairman of the meeting in accordance with the articles must be deemed to have a right to attend.

19.2.8   Company secretary

The company secretary has no statutory right to attend general meetings. Articles rarely address the subject. However, in view of the role, it would be unusual for the secretary to be excluded from the meeting.

19.2.9 Other classes of member

All members have the right to attend general meetings unless the articles provide otherwise. Where a company has more than one class of shares, it is usual for the articles to specify the rights of each class. For example, preference shareholders are not usually entitled to attend general meetings unless their dividends are in arrears. They will, of course, be entitled to attend meetings of their own class.

19.2.10 Attendance by invitation

The board may invite any other person to attend a meeting of the company. It is normal, for example, for a public company to invite lawyers, specialist advisers, brokers, analysts, press representatives, etc. These invitations are usually issued by the secretary on behalf of the board. The presence at a meeting of persons not entitled to be present or to vote does not invalidate the meeting (*Re Quinn and the National Society's Arbitration* [1921] 2 Ch. 318). However, the meeting and the chairman personally may decide at any time to ask them to leave the meeting. If they refuse, reasonable force may be used to eject them.

Companies should employ some method of ensuring that people attending by invitation cannot vote on any resolution (e.g. by issuing voting cards to the members) or are not counted when a vote is taken (e.g. by placing them in a separate area).

19.3 Record of attendance

A record should be kept of the names of the members, proxies and corporate representatives who attend any general meeting (see **Precedent 19.3**). The record is used primarily to ensure that a quorum is present throughout the proceedings. Totals of the members, corporate representatives and proxies present should be calculated and shown in the minutes. The record of attendance can also be useful in helping to reconcile the votes cast on a poll. In theory, no one should vote on a poll unless they are present either in person or by proxy.

Listed companies usually send each shareholder an attendance card with a unique bar code and require them to produce it on arrival at the meeting. The information on the attendance card is scanned using a light pen and fed into a portable computer which holds details of the register of members. The computer is then able to calculate the number of members present in person or by proxy and to print out a list of attendees. This enables the company to identify whether certain shareholders are present, e.g. institutional investors or members who represent pressure groups.

Regulation 100 of Table A requires the minutes to show the names of the directors present at general meetings.

19.4   Right to speak

The purpose of holding general meetings is to enable the members to reach decisions after debating the issues. If voting was allowed to be conducted without holding a meeting (e.g. by postal ballot) and the members were not unanimously in favour of the proposal, they would have no opportunity to debate the issues and the minority would be deprived of their opportunity to persuade the majority of the merits of its arguments. In practice, the Act does not allow public companies to conduct a ballot of the members without holding a meeting, and only allows private companies to do so if all the members approve the transaction by written resolution. In such circumstances, it is reasonable to assume that no shareholder would wish to make a speech opposing the resolution.

A general meeting is an opportunity for both sides to put their case to the floating voter. Where all or most of the members attend, the debate may have an influence on the final outcome. In practice, the outcome is often determined in advance by the votes given by proxy before the meeting. In the case of listed companies, it is not uncommon for the proxy votes in favour of resolutions proposed by the board to exceed the total number of votes held by all the members actually present at the meeting and the proxy votes cast against the resolution. In other words, even if a speaker persuaded everyone at the meeting to oppose a resolution, it would still be carried on a poll called by the chairman. Nevertheless, this does not mean that the chairman would be justified in curtailing debate on the issues. A member who has appointed a proxy may revoke that proxy by attending the meeting in person and voting. It is also possible for a member to issue new voting instructions any time before the vote is taken. These two factors mean that the outcome will not always be a foregone conclusion.

Members entitled to attend and vote at general meetings also have a common law right to speak at the meeting. Whether a member who is entitled to attend but not to vote is entitled to speak is a moot point. This will be relevant where the articles provide that the vote of the senior joint holder shall be accepted to the exclusion of all others but do not restrict the other joint holders' right to attend meetings of the company. The question may also be relevant for a member who has been disenfranchised for some reason (typically, in the case of listed companies, for failing to respond to a s. 212 notice). In practice, most companies allow members who are entitled to attend to speak even though they are not entitled to vote, and this is undoubtedly the safest course of action.

Corporate representatives are deemed to have the same rights as individual members to speak by virtue of s. 375(2).

All proxies have a statutory right to demand or join in a demand for a poll (ss. 373 and 374). In the case of private companies, proxies appointed by the members to attend and vote on their behalf have the same right to speak as the member who appointed them (s. 372(1)). No such provision is made with regard to proxies of members of public companies. Accordingly, the articles of public companies may specifically confirm or deny the right of proxies to speak. In the absence of any guidance in the articles, the matter is probably one of those that the chairman should decide in accordance with the principles laid down by Lord Russell in *Carruth v. Imperial Chemical Industries Ltd* (see **18.5**). In its *Guide to Best Practice for Annual General Meetings*, the ICSA recommends that chairmen of listed companies should seek the consent of the meeting to proxies speaking and participating in the debate. Some listed companies still prefer not to do so because of the risk of the meeting being hijacked by protesters. In such circumstances, the chairman could just as easily seek the consent of the meeting to revoke the right of proxies to speak.

Although it would be unusual to do so, there is nothing to prevent the articles restricting the rights of members who are entitled to attend and vote from speaking at the meeting. A member's right to speak is a common law right and, as such, is capable of modification by the articles. The Act would not prevent this provided that the restrictions were applied to members rather than being directed at proxies or corporate representatives. Under the Act, proxies of members of private companies only have the same rights as the member who appointed them, and corporate representatives the same rights as the corporation would have if it were an individual member. Accordingly, if the rights of the member were restricted, then the rights of their proxies or corporate representatives would be similarly restricted.

Directors are given a statutory right to speak on a resolution to remove them as directors (s. 304). Apart from this, directors who are not members or a corporate representative or, in the case of private companies, a proxy, do not have a statutory right to speak at meetings. Articles usually give directors who are not members the right to speak (e.g. reg. 44). Where they are silent on the matter, it is possible that the meeting could refuse to allow directors to speak if they are not otherwise qualified to do so. Clearly, this is not something that the members would normally wish to do. In practice, directors will normally be invited by the chairman to speak as and when necessary, and it should be assumed that they may do so unless the meeting objects.

Auditors have a statutory right to speak on matters that concern them as auditors (s. 390(1)). This right is preserved in the case of auditors who have been removed before the expiry of their period of office (s. 391). Resigning auditors have a right to speak at a meeting requisitioned by them to consider the circumstances of their resignation (s. 392A).

19.5   Common law restrictions on the right to speak

The members' right to speak will always be subject to any reasonable limitations imposed by the chairman or the meeting itself. Under the common law, the chairman has a duty to ensure that all shades of opinion on a resolution before the meeting are given a fair hearing. In particular, the chairman should seek to ensure that the minority has had a reasonable opportunity to put its views (*Wall v. London & Northern Assets Corporation Ltd* [1898] 2 Ch. 469). This does not mean that all those who hold those views must be allowed to speak. It will suffice if members representing the range of views on a resolution have been allowed to do so.

The chairman also has a duty to ensure that all the business before the meeting is conducted. In order to facilitate the conduct of the meeting, the chairman may, if the meeting does not object, apply various rules of debate. The most commonly applied is that speakers must confine themselves to the subject of the resolution before the meeting. This is particularly appropriate where a member is speaking on a matter that will be the subject of a subsequent resolution put to the meeting. From a practical point of view, it is normal for the chairman to inform speakers that they will be given an opportunity to raise these matters at the appropriate time and to ask them to keep to the subject of the resolution. It is not so easy to apply this rule where a member wishes to raise a matter that, strictly speaking, is not on the agenda. Here the chairman ought, perhaps, to allow slightly more leeway, particularly if other members want to speak on the same subject. In reality, it is often difficult for the chairman to rule that an issue raised by a member has no connection with the resolution before the meeting. Experienced speakers will normally be able to manufacture a reason that the point they wish to make is relevant and the chairman cannot really decide whether their contribution is relevant without giving them an opportunity to state their case. In such circumstances, it might be advisable for the chairman to allocate time at the end of the meeting to discuss the issues raised.

Another rule of debate which is sometimes applied is that no person other than the proposer of the resolution may speak more than once in connection with it. In the context of general meetings, this may not always be appropriate. For example, members who exercise their right to speak by asking a question ought perhaps to be given an opportunity to comment on any answer given. Ordinarily, there is no reason that a member who has spoken previously should not be allowed to respond to comments made by other speakers, particularly if that member is in the minority. It may, however, be appropriate to apply this rule where there is only limited time available for debate and there are still several members who wish to speak. In addition, there will always come a point where a member has had a reasonable opportunity to make his or her point. The chairman need not allow a member to make the same points over and over again or to speak for an inordinate length of time.

The amount of time that should be made available for debate will vary depending on the nature of the business and the number of people wishing to speak on it. This does not mean that the discussion should be allowed to go on for ever or that everyone who wishes to speak must be allowed to do so. Shortly before closing the debate, the chairman should ask members to refrain from speaking unless they have a different point to make. Although it is not an easy thing to do without causing offence, the chairman should at this point cut short any speaker who is repeating a point made earlier in the debate in order to ensure that those with different views are given a fair hearing. When the chairman considers that a full range of views has been expressed, he may seek to curtail the discussion and put the resolution to a vote. If several members object, the chairman could seek the consent of the meeting by proposing a formal 'closure' motion, i.e. that the question before the meeting be now put to the vote (see further **21.12** and the example script at **Appendix L, para. 1.8**). If the resolution is defeated on a show of hands, the chairman could, if the articles so provide, demand a poll on the question and would be justified in casting votes given to him as proxy in favour of the substantive resolution in favour of the formal closure motion.

19.6   Shareholder questions

In exercising their right to speak, members may ask the chairman or another director to answer a question. Although the chairman and the directors have no legal obligation to respond, it is usual for them to do so in order to explain their point of view and to persuade the members to support the resolution before the meeting. In answering members' questions, directors of listed companies are constrained by the requirements of the Listing Rules on the release of unpublished price-sensitive information. As a result, members often receive prepared answers which rarely expand upon previously published information.

In a consultation document issued in April 1996, a Department of Trade and Industry consultation asked whether shareholders have any difficulties asking questions at AGMs and, if so, whether they should be given statutory rights in this regard ('Shareholder Communications at the Annual General Meeting'). The consultation document recognised that giving shareholders a statutory right to ask questions would make it impossible for the chairman to curtail the debate until all the members had asked their questions. However, it suggested that companies could be required to set aside time at the AGM for shareholders' questions and debate. This proposal would not advance the position of shareholders a great deal. The common law already requires the chairman to give members an opportunity to debate resolutions put to the meeting and to give the minority a fair hearing during that debate. In exercising their right to speak, members may ask questions but have no right to receive an answer, and the DTI's proposal would not affect the members' rights in this regard. If the members were given such a right, the directors might be forced to reveal commercially sensitive or price-sensitive information.

In practice, most companies invite members to ask questions when the meeting considers the report and accounts. Even if the company does not make the accounts the subject of a substantive resolution and simply lays them before the members, the members probably have the same right to speak (and ask questions) because, by doing so, the chairman is putting some business before the meeting upon which there may be a debate. Indeed, it is arguable that the sole purpose of the requirement to lay the accounts at a general meeting is to enable the members to question the directors on their stewardship of the company. No other purpose is served by doing so. If the directors put a resolution to receive or adopt the accounts and it is lost, the accounts will still be the company's statutory accounts. Questions and debate are usually allowed on a broad range of issues when the report and accounts are laid because it is difficult to define the scope of the meeting at that point. Almost any subject raised by a member could have an impact on the financial performance of the company. The chairman would, however, be justified in refusing to allow discussion on a matter that will be raised formally later in the meeting.

The DTI's consultation document conceded that the handling of questions at the AGM was probably a matter that should be dealt with by the development of best practice by companies. Accordingly, the ICSA, with the encouragement of the DTI, produced a *Guide to Best Practice for Annual General Meetings* to address this and several other issues raised in the consultative document. On shareholder questions and debate, the guide recommends that:

- Boards should provide adequate time for shareholder questions at AGMs.
- When moving the adoption or receipt of the accounts, the chairman should allow shareholders to raise questions on any item concerning the company's past performance, its results and its intended future performance. However, the directors need not answer questions that are irrelevant to the company or its business or which could result in the release of commercially sensitive information. Nor should they disclose price-sensitive information unless it can be done in compliance with the Listing

Rules and guidance regarding the release of price-sensitive information.

- Before each resolution is put to the vote, the chairman should explain again its purpose and effect. If necessary, he should elaborate on the information previously provided in the explanatory circular which accompanied the notice of the meeting. He should also invite shareholders to speak.
- Where concerns are raised by a shareholder at the AGM and the chairman undertakes to consider them, the shareholder should subsequently be sent a full report of the action taken.

The guide also suggests that when a particular issue has been raised by a shareholder, the chairman may assist the flow of the meeting by inviting other shareholders who wish to speak on the same subject to do so at that time.

Some listed companies include in the documents sent to shareholders prior to the AGM an invitation to submit questions in advance of the meeting. This enables them to select the most common questions and provide an answer for each one at the meeting. Answers can be given orally by the chairman or the relevant director, or they can be distributed to shareholders in the form of a printed question-and-answer sheet. The latter allows more detailed information to be provided in numerical or graphical form and enables the chairman to refer questioners who raise similar issues at the meeting to the relevant written answer. Although the ICSA urged more companies to invite shareholders to submit questions in advance in its *Guide to Best Practice for Annual General Meetings*, it did not include it as one of its 24 best practice points. It said:

> Of course giving shareholders the opportunity to raise questions in advance of the AGM may not always assuage all their concerns. Questions on broadly the same subject may arrive in 40 or 50 different forms for the company to co-ordinate into a single response. Such a reply may satisfactorily answer most points, but is unlikely to address them all.
>
> We recommend that companies invite shareholders to submit questions in advance, as this makes structuring the AGM more manageable. We leave it to companies to decide how best to convey the invitation. We stress that inviting questions in advance is not to be deployed by companies as a method of manipulating the AGM by requiring written notice of questions; nor is it intended to replace spontaneity at the AGM, which we regard as one of its greatest attributes.

20

Security and disorder

20.1 Summary

- Security is not normally a problem for private companies.
  However, for companies that are in the public eye, it is becoming
  an increasingly important issue. Pressure groups frequently
  disrupt meetings of listed companies in order to gain publicity for
  their cause. In the current political and social environment,
  companies can no longer discount the possibility of terrorist
  attack or the possibility that a member or customer with a grudge
  against the company will behave in a violent manner at the
  meeting. Many companies now invest a considerable amount of
  time and money on security measures to counter these threats.
- The company's first line of defence is, however, the registration
  process. Most listed companies still allow members of the public
  to attend their AGMs without an invitation. However, more and
  more are restricting entry for the purposes of security and require
  people wishing to gain entry to prove their identity (see **20.2**).
- Companies that face disruption need to be prepared to tackle it. A
  security checklist is included at **20.2**.
- Disruption at general meetings is nothing new, and the common
  law has developed various rules that enable the chairman to deal
  with it. A skilful chairman can sometimes avoid undue disruption
  by dealing with dissident members firmly, politely, fairly and with
  good humour. Even if this has no effect on the dissident
  members, it will probably ensure that the chairman retains the
  support of the meeting should further action need to be taken. If
  the dissident members persist in their disorderly conduct to such
  an extent that the meeting is no longer able to transact the
  business before it, the chairman may either order the ejection of
  those who are causing the disorder or adjourn the meeting in an
  attempt to restore order (see **20.4**).

20.2 Security

20.2.1 Proof of identity

A company may refuse to admit members who cannot prove their identity. If it were otherwise the company could be forced to admit two people claiming to be the same person. Most members will have no difficulty satisfying any reasonable request made by the company. This might include the production of a driving licence or some other document showing their name and address. A company should, perhaps, also accept the confirmation of an individual's identity by someone else who is known to the company. It is also arguable that anyone who is able to furnish accurate information about their holding (e.g. full name, address, size of holding, date of purchase of shares, mandate details, etc.) should also be admitted. In cases of doubt, it is probably wise to err on the side of caution as the exclusion of a person entitled to attend and vote could render the meeting liable to challenge.

If proof of identity is required, security and registration staff should be properly briefed. The procedures that should be followed before refusing entry to a person who would be entitled to attend if able to prove their identity should be approved by the chairman. Indeed, it may be preferable to refer difficult cases to the chairman. In cases of doubt, the person could be admitted but asked to sit in a specially allocated area. If that person's vote would have affected the outcome of a show of hands, the chairman may need to make a ruling on the validity of the person's vote. Alternatively, the chairman could demand a poll (if the articles so allow) in the hope that this will resolve the difficulty. This would also enable the company to take further steps to establish the identity of the person claiming to be a member, etc. If the result of the poll is affected by the disputed votes, the chairman will have to make a ruling on their validity. The courts have endorsed the use by the chairman of a 'conditional' casting vote where the validity of some votes had been in doubt and it was not clear whether or not the vote was tied (see **15.10**).

20.2.2 Attendance cards

Some companies send shareholders attendance cards and request that they produce them on arrival in order to gain entry to the meeting. The main advantage of this system is that it helps to speed up the registration process. It does, however, have a number of weaknesses. The first of these is that attendance cards actually facilitate impersonation where no other identity checks are made. In addition, a company cannot refuse to admit members merely because they are unable to produce an attendance card, unless the articles specify this as a condition of entry. Members who cannot produce their attendance cards must be allowed to prove their identity in another way.

20.2.3   Security checks

Some listed companies have taken specific powers in their articles to refuse entry to members who refuse to comply with certain conditions of entry (see **Precedent 20.2**). However, it is submitted that even if the articles do not make specific provision, the company can (and perhaps should where it has reason to suspect trouble) take reasonable security measures.

The chairman has a duty to preserve order at meetings. Security procedures such as screening devices and baggage searches are, it is suggested, a legitimate method of ensuring that the meeting is not disrupted. Many listed companies deliberately hold their meetings at venues that have built-in security screening at the point of entry. Anyone wishing to attend must pass through an electronic screening device and have their baggage inspected. It is submitted that a company can exclude a person who refuses to be screened if the purpose of that screening is to ensure the safety of other members present and to prevent disorder at the meeting. Clearly, it would be irresponsible to admit anyone found in possession of explosives. They should be arrested and handed over to the police. On the other hand, it might be considered unreasonable to exclude a person found in possession of a klaxon or whistle. The correct course of action would be to ask the person to hand over these items for the duration of the meeting.

20.3   Security checklist for AGM

The following checklist is based on material produced by company secretaries of companies whose meetings have been disrupted by protesters and demonstrations.

Planning the meeting
- Make someone responsible for security.
- Identify issues that are likely to be controversial, e.g.
  - any company issues likely to lead to demonstrations;
  - any staff issues likely to lead to demonstrations;
  - any shareholder issues likely to lead to demonstrations;
  - any active shareholder protest groups;
  - any known agitators likely to attend;
  - any historical issues that have arisen at the company's AGM.
- Consider issuing a statement concerning any controversial or difficult issues prior to the AGM to defuse potential protests.
- Notify the local police of security concerns and request their availability.
- Persuade the chairman to rehearse any complications.
- If cameras and tape recorders are not to be allowed in, the notice to shareholders should include this information.
- Be aware of the possibilities for various forms of protest and take appropriate precautions, e.g.

- irrelevant questioning;
- mass sit-in;
- storming the platform;
- handcuffing to immovable objects;
- protests outside the AGM venue;
- abseiling from the roof.

The AGM venue

- Ensure that the company's security staff are involved in selecting the venue.
- Can entry to the venue be controlled with limited access points?
- Consider which access routes to the meeting hall are to be used.
- Is there a clear route for the directors to the meeting hall from the venue of any pre-meeting get-together? Can they enter and leave the room by a separate exit which is easily accessible from the stage?
- Is physical security satisfactory?
- Are there any areas that are always open to the public?
- Who else has booked conference facilities on the same day?
- Does the venue have adequate security procedures, e.g. to deal with bomb alerts?
- Does it have a security manager or other in-house security staff?
- Has the venue hosted AGMs before?
- What are the normal arrangements for dealing with disturbances?
- Where does the venue boundary meet the public highway?
- Is there a tannoy system?
- Does it have a controlled car parking area?
- Is it possible to erect barriers at the venue entrance and reception areas to control the flow of attendees?
- Is the reception area large enough to accommodate all attendees before entering the meeting hall?
- Are the toilets inside the secure area or will attendees need to go through security checks each time they enter the hall?
- Check availability of discreet exits to remove demonstrators.
- Are the seats fixed?
- Are the hand-rails or other fittings removable?
- Are there any balconies or other public areas from which items could be thrown, banners displayed or photographers planted?

Precautions

- Prevent demonstrators erecting banners on the stage by using floral arrangements or guards.
- Thoroughly search the meeting area before commencement of meeting for suspicious objects and then secure until access is opened for the meeting.
- Conduct regular security patrols.
- Consider personal searches, including metal detectors. If detectors or scans are to be used, ensure that trained staff are employed to operate them.
- Consider inspection of baggage and/or barring of baggage from

the meeting hall. If baggage is not allowed in, consider providing clear plastic folders for documents.

- Establish a policy on:
  - cameras and videos;
  - recording equipment;
  - mobile telephones;
  - access for TV/radio crews.
- Display clear notices detailing the items not allowed in the meeting.
- Arrange for secure storage of items not allowed into the meeting.
- Alert venue staff to any person who may be carrying anything unusual.
- Send out invitation cards which must be presented to gain access to the meeting. In the event of failure to produce an invitation, entry to meeting should only be permitted on production of identification, personal verification by a known third party or, for shareholders, identification on the share register.
- Organise a system of security passes for all attendees and staff.
- Rotate the colour of passes each year.
- Prepare a script for the chairman to follow in the event of disruptions, covering ejection of protesters by stewards and/or adjournment of the meeting.
- Use radio microphones to prevent attachment or damage to cables.
- Ensure that radio microphones do not interfere with security radio network and vice versa.
- Use hands-free radios for security guards.
- Have the following equipment available:
  - large bolt cutters;
  - solvent for superglue;
  - smother blankets for smoke bombs;
  - tools to remove handrails.
- Bring spare clothes for chairman in case missiles thrown.
- Consider videoing the proceedings.
- Have paramedics (St John's Ambulance) standing by.

Demonstrators

- Identify known activists.
- Review recent purchases of small numbers of shares, paying particular attention to purchases of one share. Obtain details of purchaser (and, if off-market, the transferor) and obtain background information on them if possible (some registrars have compiled a database of shareholders who are known to be connected with certain groups).
- Alert staff on AGM registration desk of suspects' names.
- Obtain copies of questions if possible.
- Be positive with demonstrators – they will attempt to intimidate or antagonise.
- Consider delaying opening doors to meeting hall until, say, half

an hour before the start of the meeting. This may prevent potential agitators obtaining pole positions.

- Consider refusing entry to any press not authorised by the company's PR department.
- Protest groups often pre-warn the press. The company's PR department may be able to find out whether this has happened from its press contacts.

Staffing

- If necessary, engage additional security staff and ensure that the security staff includes a number of women. Use well-trained staff.
- Arrange protection for chairman, directors and senior executives especially during period of mingling with shareholders.
- If there is risk of violence to the chairman or other speakers, access to the rostrum should be restricted by security staff facing the audience.
- Consider the need to have extra security staff available but hidden in the immediate vicinity of the meeting hall.
- Stewards and security staff should be briefed and given a checklist on the arrangements for, and their powers for dealing with, disturbances.
- Place staff on every door leading to the meeting hall and only allow persons with the requisite pass to enter the hall.
- Arrange for venue's own security staff to be present to help in fire or bomb emergencies.
- Consider how security staff (company's own staff, external staff and AGM venue staff) are to be dressed – high or low profile.
- Clearly identify the role of all staff involved.
- Establish with the venue's management that they will deal with the removal, if necessary, of demonstrators from their property to the public highway boundary.
- If staff demonstrations are anticipated, arrange for an industrial relations manager to be available to meet with staff representatives.
- Use staff as fillers to occupy areas of seating and/or form barriers.

20.4 Preservation of order

The chairman's primary responsibility is to ensure that all the business before the meeting is properly and fairly transacted. This is unlikely to be achieved if the meeting is constantly disrupted by dissident members. The chairman is therefore responsible for the preservation of order at the meeting and should seek to ensure that the meeting is carried out without undue disruption.

A skilful chairman can sometimes avoid undue disruption by dealing with dissident members firmly, politely and fairly and with good humour. Even if this has no effect on the dissident members, it will probably ensure that the chairman retains the support of the meeting should further action need to be taken.

Where it is known that a group of shareholders is likely to

attempt to disrupt the meeting, the chairman may take preventative action before the meeting, e.g. to prevent shareholders entering the hall with klaxons, tape recorders, banners, and any other objects that could be used to disrupt the meeting.

20.4.1   Adjournment to restore order

If there is persistent and violent disorder, the chairman has a right and may even have a duty to adjourn the meeting in order to restore order. In *John v. Rees* [1969] 2 WLR 1294, Megarry J explained this principle as follows:

> The first duty of the chairman of a meeting is to keep order if he can. If there is disorder, his duty, I think, is to make earnest and sustained efforts to restore order, and for this purpose to summon to his aid any officers or others whose assistance is available. If all his efforts are in vain, he should endeavour to put into operation whatever provisions for adjournment there are in the rules, as by obtaining a resolution to adjourn. If this proves impossible, he should exercise his inherent power to adjourn the meeting for a short while, such as 15 minutes, taking due steps to ensure as far as possible that all persons know of this adjournment. If instead of mere disorder there is violence, I think that he should take similar steps, save that the greater the violence the less prolonged should be his efforts to restore order before adjourning. In my judgment, he has not merely a power but a duty to adjourn in this way, in the interests of those who fear for their safety. I am not suggesting that there is a power and a duty to adjourn if the violence consists of no more than a few technical assaults and batteries. Mere pushing and jostling is one thing; it is another when people are put in fear, where there is heavy punching, or the knives are out, so that blood may flow, and there are prospects, or more, of grievous bodily harm. In the latter case the sooner the chairman adjourns the meeting the better. At meetings, as elsewhere, the Queen's Peace must be kept.
>
> If then, the chairman has this inherent power and duty, what limitations, if any, are there upon its exercise? First, I think that the power and duty must be exercised bona fide for the purpose of forwarding and facilitating the meeting, and not for the purpose of interruption or procrastination. Second I think that the adjournment must be for no longer than the necessities appear to dictate. If the adjournment is merely for such period as the chairman considers to be reasonably necessary for the restoration of order, it would be within his power and his duty; a long adjournment would not. One must remember that to attend a meeting may for some mean travelling far and giving up much leisure. An adjournment to

another day when a mere 15 minutes might suffice to restore order may well impose an unjustifiable burden on many; for they must either once more travel far and give up their leisure, or else remain away and lose their chance to speak and vote at the meeting.

20.4.2 Powers of ejection

Members may be expelled from a meeting if they seriously interfere with the business of the meeting. 'The power ... of suspending a member guilty of obstruction or disorderly conduct during the continuance of [a meeting] is ... reasonably necessary for the proper exercise of the functions of any ... assembly' (*Barton v. Taylor* (1886) 11 App. Cas. 197, *per* Lord Selborne at p. 204).

If possible, the chairman should seek the consent of the meeting before ordering that a person be expelled. In practice, it will rarely be possible to take a vote on the matter and the chairman must rely on his innate authority to take action to preserve order at the meeting. Expulsion should only be used as a last resort or in cases of severe disorder. Members should, if possible, be warned of the consequences of their actions. If they continue to disrupt the meeting, they should be given an opportunity to leave the meeting voluntarily. If they refuse to do so, they can be forcibly ejected, although only reasonable force should be used (*Collins v. Renison* (1754) 1 Sayer 138). If unnecessary force is used, the person removed will have a cause of action for assault against the persons responsible (*Doyle v. Falconer* (1866) LR 1 PC 328). This may include the chairman as the person who authorised their removal.

21

Adjournment and other procedural motions

21.1 Summary

- It is not always possible or desirable to transact all the business for which a meeting has been called. In such circumstances, it may be appropriate to adjourn the meeting, i.e. to call a temporary halt to the proceedings with a view to reconvening to deal with the unfinished business at some other time and possibly at some other place.
- The Companies Act 1985 has very little to say on the subject of adjournment. Thus the common law rule that the power to adjourn is vested in the meeting itself will normally apply (see **21.2**).
- The chairman will usually have no power to adjourn unless the articles provide otherwise. The only exceptions to this rule are that the chairman has the power to adjourn to conduct a poll, to restore order, or to facilitate the business of the meeting (see **21.3**).
- Articles usually provide that a meeting will automatically be adjourned if a quorum is not present within a specified period from the time appointed for the start of the meeting (see **21.4**).
- A resolution to adjourn must specify when the adjourned meeting is to be held or who is to decide when the meeting is to be held. The articles may specify that a poll may not be demanded on a resolution to adjourn or that a poll on such a resolution must be taken immediately (see **21.5**).
- The company may need to give notice of an adjourned meeting in certain circumstances (see **21.6**).
- It is not possible for the directors to postpone a meeting once it has been called, unless the articles allow (see **21.7**).
- A proxy submitted for the original meeting will also be valid at any adjournment of that meeting. The articles usually make special provision for the submission of proxies between the original meeting and the adjourned meeting (see **21.8**).

- Procedural motions (formal motions) are used to expedite the business of the meeting (see **21.10** to **21.16**).

21.2   Power to adjourn

Under the common law the right to adjourn any meeting (including a general meeting of a company) is vested in the meeting itself (*Kerr v. Wilkie* (1860) 1 LT 501). If the chairman, contrary to the wishes of the majority, purports to halt the proceedings before the business of the meeting has been completed, the meeting may elect a new chairman and continue to transact the unfinished business (*Stoughton v. Reynolds* (1736) 2 Strange 1044). These basic common law rules are subject to a number of exceptions and are subject to modification by the articles.

21.2.1   Articles

Articles usually contain detailed provisions setting out when, how and by whom general meetings can be adjourned. Regulation 45 of Table A states: 'The chairman may, with the consent of a meeting at which a quorum is present (and shall if so directed by the meeting), adjourn the meeting from time to time and from place to place, but no business shall be transacted at an adjourned meeting other than that business which might properly have been transacted at the meeting had the adjournment not taken place.' This type of article leaves the matter of adjournment in the hands of the meeting. The chairman must adjourn the meeting if a resolution to adjourn is duly passed.

If, however, the articles provide that the chairman may adjourn with the consent of the meeting, and omit the words 'and shall if so directed by the meeting', the chairman can refuse to adjourn despite the fact that a resolution to adjourn has been passed by the meeting (*Salisbury Gold Mining Co. v. Hathorn* [1897] AC 268).

Some articles give the chairman power to adjourn without the consent of the meeting (see example at **Precedent 21.2**). These modifications are usually made in order to clarify the chairman's inherent powers under the common law (see below).

21.3   Chairman's inherent power to adjourn

The chairman has inherent power to adjourn to facilitate the conduct of the meeting. The leading authority on this matter is *R. v. D'Oyly* (1840) 12 Ad. & El. 139, and the following extract from this case sets out the position:

> Setting aside the inconvenience that might arise if a majority of the parishioners could determine the point of adjournment, we think that the person who presides at the meeting is the proper individual to decide this. It is on him that it devolves,

both to preserve order in the meeting, and to regulate the proceedings so as to give all persons entitled a reasonable opportunity of voting. He is to do the acts necessary for those purposes on his own responsibility, and subject to being called upon to answer for his conduct if he has done anything improperly.

21.3.1 To conduct a poll

In *Jackson v. Hamlyn* [1953] Ch. 577 it was held that the chairman's inherent power to adjourn to enable a poll to be conducted survived even though the company's articles stated that the chairman could only adjourn with consent of the meeting. In this case the chairman adjourned the meeting in order to take a poll on a resolution to adjourn the meeting. Quite naturally, those seeking to oppose the resolution to adjourn objected. However, it was held that the chairman had power to stand over the proceedings to another time, since some such power had to exist in order to give effect to the provisions as to polls in the articles. Upjohn J stated that although this standing over was not an adjournment within the meaning of the articles, the chairman had a residual power to take such steps as would in the ordinary usage of the word amount to an adjournment.

Most articles that allow a poll on a resolution to adjourn state that the poll must be taken immediately (see below).

21.3.2 Room too small

The concept of the chairman's inherent or residual power to adjourn in order to facilitate the conduct of the meeting was taken a step further in *Byng v. London Life Association Ltd* [1989] 1 All ER 560. The articles of London Life provided that the chairman may, with the consent of any meeting at which a quorum is present (and shall if so directed by the meeting), adjourn the meeting from time to time and from place to place. The venue for an EGM of the company was not large enough to accommodate the members wishing to attend and communications between the main meeting room and overflow facilities proved to be inadequate. As it was impossible to take a proper vote, the chairman purported to adjourn the meeting himself to an alternative venue later on the same day. The Court of Appeal held that the company's articles did not exclude the chairman's inherent power to adjourn the meeting where it proved to be impossible to ascertain the wishes of the meeting. However, the chairman's inherent power was only exercisable for the purpose of giving members a proper opportunity to debate and vote on the resolutions before the meeting. On the facts of this case the chairman's decision to adjourn the meeting to the Café Royal later in the day was held to be unreasonable and declared invalid because it did not achieve this purpose. The chairman did not properly take into account the fact that a significant proportion of the members who had attended the original meeting would not be able to attend the adjourned meeting and would therefore be unable to vote because the company's articles required proxies to be delivered 48 hours before the meeting. Browne-Wilkinson V-C suggested that the correct course of action in this case would have been either to abandon the meeting or to adjourn it *sine die* and to give 21 days' notice of a fresh meeting to be held, say, a month later. He added:

> The chairman's decision will not be declared invalid unless on the facts which he knew or ought to have known he failed to take into account all the relevant factors, took into account irrelevant factors or reached a conclusion which no reasonable chairman, properly directing himself as to his duties, could have reached, i.e. the test is the same as that applicable on judicial review in accordance with the principles of *Associated Provincial Picture Houses Ltd v. Wednesbury Corp.* [1947] 2 All ER 680.

As a result of this case, some companies have modified their articles to give the chairman complete discretion to adjourn to another time or place without the consent of the meeting where it appears to him that it is likely to be impracticable to hold or continue to hold the meeting because of the number of members or their proxies present or wishing to attend (see example at **Precedent 21.2**). Most listed companies also make specific provision in their articles for overflow arrangements at general meetings (see **Precedent 17.5**).

21.3.3 Adjournment to restore order

The chairman has a right to adjourn if there is persistent and violent disorder, but for no longer than is necessary to restore order (*John v. Rees* [1969] 2 WLR 1294) (see **20.4**).

21.4 Automatic adjournment where no quorum

Articles usually provide that a meeting will be automatically adjourned if a quorum is not present shortly after the time appointed for the commencement of the meeting. Table A provides:

> **41.** If such a quorum is not present within half an hour from the time appointed for the meeting, or if during a meeting such a quorum ceases to be present, the meeting shall stand adjourned to the same day in the next week at the same time and place or to such time and place as the directors may determine.

This type of provision is necessary in order to avoid having to call a new meeting. Strictly speaking there is no meeting unless a quorum is present and therefore nothing to adjourn.

21.5 Resolution to adjourn

A formal resolution to adjourn the meeting must be proposed and passed by the meeting. The resolution can be proposed by the chairman or a member from the floor. For example scripts, see **Appendix L**.

A meeting may be adjourned for as short or long a period as is necessary. If the purpose of the adjournment is to restore order, 15 minutes may suffice. On the other hand, an indefinite adjournment may be appropriate where it is not known when the unfinished business can be dealt with, in which case the meeting is said to have been adjourned *sine die*. If an adjournment is not planned or expected, the company is not likely to have made arrangements to reserve a venue for the adjourned meeting. In these circumstances the original meeting may have to be adjourned to a time and place to be determined by the directors.

21.5.1 Poll on a resolution to adjourn

Section 371 provides members with a statutory right to demand a poll. However, s. 373(1) specifically allows a company's articles to exclude that right on a resolution to adjourn. Most articles (including Table A) do not do so but provide that a poll called on a resolution to adjourn shall be taken forthwith (e.g. reg. 51). If the right to demand a poll on a resolution to adjourn is excluded, a dissident minority may be able to obstruct the will of the majority by packing the meeting and proposing a long adjournment to prevent a poll being conducted on a resolution to which they are opposed. Under reg. 46 of Table A, the chairman would be entitled to demand a poll on the question of adjournment which would be taken forthwith (reg. 51). The chairman would normally cast those proxies that he holds in favour of the substantive resolution against the resolution to adjourn.

21.6 Notice of adjourned meeting

Under the common law, there is no need to give notice of an adjourned meeting if the resolution to adjourn specifies the time and place at which the meeting is to be held. This rule obviously does not apply where the meeting is adjourned indefinitely (*sine die*) or to a time and place to be specified by the chairman or the directors.

Articles usually modify this rule by requiring notice to be given of any meeting that is adjourned for longer than a specified period. Regulation 45 of Table A states:

> **45.** .... When a meeting is adjourned for fourteen days or more, at least seven days' notice shall be given specifying the time and place of the adjourned meeting and the general

nature of the business to be transacted. Otherwise it shall not be necessary to give any such notice.

21.7 Postponement

Once a meeting has been duly called, it is not possible to postpone it unless the articles so provide. Thus the meeting should be held at the appointed time and place. If the chairman and the directors fail to attend, the members present can elect their own chairman and proceed to transact the business of the meeting (*Smith v. Paringa Mines Ltd* [1906] 2 Ch. 193). If nobody attends or there is no quorum, the meeting will normally be adjourned automatically under the articles (see **21.4**). The correct procedure is therefore to open the meeting in the normal way and, if appropriate, to adjourn it to another time or place or, if the purpose of the meeting is redundant, to close it after passing a resolution not to put any of the business to a vote.

The immediate adjournment procedure was used by two major listed companies in the 1990s after their AGM venues were destroyed by a terrorist bomb in London. Both companies advertised the change of venue in national newspapers prior to the meeting and posted staff at access points to the original venue to direct members to the new venue. The chairman and sufficient members to form a quorum held a meeting as close as possible to the original venue at the appointed hour and immediately adjourned to the new venue. Had there been any contentious business at either meeting, the safest course of action might have been to adjourn the meeting for longer and to give notice to the members in accordance with the articles. To prevent any problems in this regard, some companies now include articles that allow the directors to postpone and change the place of the meeting (see example article at **Precedent 21.7**).

21.8 Attendance, voting and proxies at adjourned meetings

A member who was not present at the original meeting may attend and vote at the adjourned meeting (*R. v. D'Oyly* (1840) 12 Ad. & El. 139). An instrument of proxy deposited in time for the original meeting is also valid for any adjournment of that meeting on the basis that the adjourned meeting is merely a continuation of the original meeting (*Scadding v. Lorrant* (1851) 3 HLC 418).

Proxies submitted after the deadline for the original meeting are not valid for the adjourned meeting unless the articles make provision to that effect (*McLaren v. Thomson* [1917] 2 Ch. 261). Most articles (e.g. reg. 62 of Table A) provide that a proxy lodged at least 48 hours before an adjourned meeting will be valid for that meeting. Instruments of proxy usually state that the appointment is made in respect of the original meeting 'and any adjournment thereof'. An instrument in this form submitted the appropriate number of hours before the adjourned meeting would be valid even though it was not submitted in time for the original meeting.

21.9 Date of resolution passed at an adjourned meeting

Where a resolution is passed at an adjourned meeting, it is treated for all purposes as having been passed on the date on which it is in fact passed, and not on any earlier date (s. 381).

21.10 Procedural motions

Procedural motions (formal motions) are used to expedite the business of the meeting. The terminology used to describe these motions is often old-fashioned and obscure. There is no magic or mystery in the use of this terminology. Provided that the intention of the motion is clear, there is little to be gained from insisting that it be used.

As procedural motions relate to the conduct, rather than the business, of the meeting, no prior notice is required or, indeed, could be given. The chairman or any member entitled to vote and speak at the meeting may propose a formal motion. The word 'member' includes a joint holder or a corporate representative for these purposes. It is not clear whether proxies can propose formal motions even where they have the right to speak. Should a proxy who has the right to speak attempt to do so, it may be advisable for the chairman to ask whether a member is prepared to propose the motion. If none is prepared to do so, the chairman might be able to persuade the proxy to withdraw the proposal due to lack of support. Failing that, the chairman could propose the motion on the proxy's behalf.

21.11 Motion 'that the chairman leave the chair'

This is a variant of the motion to adjourn. If carried, it takes effect *sine die* (until further notice), or, in the case of a regularly recurring meeting, until the date of the next regular meeting. No amendment of such a motion is possible.

21.12 Motion 'that the question be now put' (the closure)

A closure motion (traditionally referred to as 'the closure') is a simple way of curtailing the debate. The chairman or any member may simply propose 'that the question be now put' or words to that effect. The motion need not be seconded although it is unlikely that it would be carried if a seconder could not be found. No debate need be allowed on the motion, although it might be difficult to prevent objections from those who still wish to speak on the question before the meeting. The chairman may, it is suggested, refuse to put the motion to the vote on the ground that it is an infringement of the rights of the majority. However, if, acting in good faith, the chairman allows it to be put, the court will not intervene (*Wall v. London & Northern Assets Corporation* [1898] 2 Ch. 469). If a closure motion is carried, the question before the meeting must be put to the vote immediately. See **Appendix L** for a chairman's script for a closure motion.

21.13 Motion 'that the meeting proceed to the next business' (next business)

The object of this motion is to delay or preclude a decision by the meeting on the main question. It can be put at any time during discussion or during the discussion of an amendment. If the motion is carried, no further discussion or decision on the substantive question before the meeting should be allowed at the meeting (or any adjournment thereof) as its effect is to remove the question from the scope of the meeting. The question can only be considered again if it is proposed at a subsequent meeting. If it is rejected, discussion on the main issue may continue.

21.14 Motion 'that the question be not now put' (previous question)

The motion 'that the question be not now put' differs slightly from a motion 'to proceed to the next business' in that it may be moved only during the discussion on the main question before the meeting and not while an amendment is being considered. Discussion is normally allowed before putting the motion to a vote. If the motion is lost, it is normal to put the question before the meeting to an immediate vote although the chairman could allow debate to continue if it is clear that several members still wish to speak.

This motion is known as the 'previous question' because it gives rise to an issue that must be decided before the main question. It is probably the least common of the formal motions as substantially the same effect can be achieved by a motion to proceed to the next business.

21.15 Motion 'that the question lie on the table'

The effect of this motion is that the question is put aside for the time being. It can, however, be restored if the meeting so desires. A more modern form of words might be 'that consideration of the question before the meeting be postponed until such time as the meeting wishes to reopen discussion'.

21.16 Motion 'that the matter be referred back to ...'

This motion is used to refer back for further investigation or inquiry a matter that has arisen from the recommendations of another body or committee. Psychologically, it is obviously preferable to do this rather than to reject a proposal outright.

22

Amendments

22.1 Summary

- Dealing with amendments is one of the most difficult duties of the chairman. Unless the articles require prior notice of amendments to be given, the chairman will have to decide at the meeting whether to allow the proposed amendment to be put to the meeting.
- If the chairman wrongly refuses to admit an amendment the resolution will be invalid (see **22.2**).
- Amendments are only allowed to extraordinary, special and elective resolutions in very restricted circumstances (see **22.3**).
- The position is not clear with regard to ordinary resolutions that require special notice (see **22.4**).
- However, for other ordinary resolutions, the answer will depend on a variety of factors (see **22.5**).
- Special problems can arise with regard to amendments on proposals to appoint directors (see **22.6**).
- Procedural rules may need to be followed where a series of amendments are put on the same resolution (see **22.7**).
- Many companies now adopt articles on amendments (see **22.8**).

22.2 Consequences of wrongly refusing to submit

If the chairman wrongly refuses to submit an amendment to the meeting and the original resolution is passed, it will be invalid. It makes no difference whether the mover of the amendment contested the chairman's ruling or left the meeting (*Henderson v. Bank of Australasia* (1890) 45 Ch. D. 330). Articles sometimes provide that substantive resolutions shall not be invalidated by any error in good faith on the part of the chairman in ruling an amendment out of order (see **22.8**).

22.3 Amendment of extraordinary, special and elective resolutions

Extraordinary, special and elective resolutions may only be amended in very limited circumstances. In *Re Moorgate Mercantile Holdings Ltd* [1980] 1 All ER 40, Slade J established the following principles:

1. If a notice of the intention to propose a special resolution is to be a valid notice, it must identify the intended resolution by specifying either the text or the entire substance of the resolution that it is intended to propose. In the case of a notice of intention to propose a special resolution, nothing is achieved by the addition of such words as 'with such amendments and alterations as shall be determined on at such meeting'.

2. If a special resolution is to be validly passed, the resolution as passed must be the same resolution as that identified in the preceding notice; the phrase the resolution in (s. 378(2)) means the aforesaid resolution.

3. A resolution as passed can properly be regarded as 'the resolution' identified in a preceding notice, even though:

(a) it departs in some respects from the text of a resolution set out in such notice (for example by correcting those grammatical or clerical errors which can be corrected as a matter of construction, or by reducing the words to more formal language); or

(b) it is reduced into the form of a new text, which was not included in the notice, provided only that in either case there is no departure from the substance.

4. However, in deciding whether there is complete identity between the substance of a resolution passed and the substance of an intended resolution as notified, there is no room for the court to apply the de minimis principle or a 'limit of tolerance'. The substance must be identical. Otherwise the condition precedent to the validity of a special resolution as passed, which is imposed by (s. 378(2)), namely that notice has been given 'specifying the intention to propose the resolution as a special resolution' is not satisfied.

5. It necessarily follows from the above propositions that an amendment to the previously circulated text of a special resolution can be properly be put to and voted on at a meeting if, but only if, the amendment involves no departure from the substance of the circulated text, in the sense indicated in propositions (3) and (4) above.

6. References to notices in the above propositions are intended to include references to circulars accompanying notices. In those cases where notices are so accompanied, the notices and circulars can and should, in my judgment ordinarily be treated as one document.

7. All the above propositions may be subject to modification where all the members or a class of members, of a company unanimously agree to waive their rights to notice under (s. 378(2)), see *Re Pearce, Duff & Co Ltd* and *Re Duomatic Ltd* [1969] 1 All ER 161.

The Act makes similar provision with regard to the notice required to be given to the members of extraordinary and elective resolutions. Accordingly, the same principles will apply to amendments of such resolutions.

In *Re Willaire Systems* [1987] BCLC 67, it was held that where a special resolution for the reduction of a company's capital contained an error (the number of shares was said to be 14,926,580 instead of 14,926,583), the court could confirm the reduction on terms that corrected the error provided that it was so insignificant that no one could be thought to be prejudiced by its correction and the way in which it was to be corrected was clear. This case is probably an example of an amendment that could have been made at the meeting in order to rectify a minor clerical error (see also *Re European Home Products plc* [1988] 4 BCC 779).

To eliminate any uncertainty with regard to amendments, companies sometimes adopt an article that disallows any amendment of extraordinary and special resolutions (see **22.8**).

22.4   Resolutions requiring special notice

It is arguable that the rules on amending extraordinary and special resolutions also apply to resolutions requiring special notice. The wording of s. 379(2) (resolutions requiring special notice) is similar to that of s. 378 (extraordinary and special resolutions) in so far as the company is required to give its members notice of 'any such resolution'. It is submitted therefore that the substance of such resolutions should not be amended and that an amendment should only be accepted to rectify a clerical error (see above).

22.5   Amendment of ordinary resolutions

An amendment to an ordinary resolution must be put to the vote unless it is:

- outside the scope of the notice of the meeting;
- irrelevant in so far as it bears no relation to the original motion or subject matter;
- redundant because its effect is simply to negate the resolution or to propose something that has already been resolved by the meeting;
- incompatible with a decision previously made by the meeting;

- vexatious, i.e. its sole purpose is to obstruct the transaction of business; or
- rejected by the chairman under a discretion granted by the articles.

22.5.1 Outside the scope of the notice

Amendments must be within the scope of the notice of meeting. The meeting may transact any business that is within the 'general nature' of the business set out in the notice. In deciding what the 'general nature' of the business in the notice is, the test is what a reasonable shareholder reading the resolution would consider the business to be. The courts normally adopt a practical approach and, where there is any ambiguity, apply a restrictive interpretation, so as to protect the absent shareholder. A guide endorsed by the courts is that an amendment should not be allowed if it would have affected a member's decision to attend. For example, a resolution authorising the directors to allot shares could be amended to reduce the number they may allot, but not to increase it.

In *Betts & Co. Ltd v. MacNaghten* [1910] 1 Ch. 430, it was held that the notice of meeting, which set out the names of the proposed directors, was sufficient to enable unnamed directors to be elected in place of or in addition to the named directors, because on reading the notice a reasonable shareholder would realise that those nominated might not be elected and therefore that others could be put up in their place. In this case the notice stated that the meeting was to consider resolutions 'with such amendments and alterations as shall be determined upon at such meeting'. These words could be considered redundant as it can be assumed that resolutions might be amended at the meeting.

In *Choppington Collieries Ltd v. Johnson* [1944] 1 All ER 762, the Court of Appeal held that a notice that referred to the election of directors but which also stated that only one director was retiring and offering himself for re-election was wide enough to permit the election of directors, up to the maximum allowed by the articles. The court's decision was based on the general nature of the phrase in the notice 'to elect directors' which a shareholder might reasonably interpret as contemplating the appointment of more than one director. In this and other cases, the courts have emphasised that the question of the scope of the notice of meeting will turn on the construction of the notice in any given case.

22.5.2 Ordinary and special business

Articles sometimes distinguish between 'ordinary' and 'special' business (e.g. reg. 52 of the 1948 Table A). Matters specified in the articles as 'ordinary' business may be considered at an AGM without prior notice having been given. These usually include:

- declaration of a dividend;
- consideration of the report and accounts;
- election of directors in the place of those retiring; and
- appointment and remuneration of the auditors.

In effect notice is deemed to have been given of any of these matters. Thus any resolution or amendment to any resolution on these matters will be within the scope of the notice of the AGM. By default, any other business will be deemed to be 'special' business and, as such, the notice must specify the general nature of that business for it to be within the scope of the notice.

The 1985 version of Table A requires the notice of general meetings to specify 'the general nature of the business to be transacted' (reg. 38). In other words, all business is treated in the same way as special business.

22.5.3 Other reasons for rejecting amendments

An amendment need not be allowed if its effect is to negate the original resolution. The chairman should refuse to put such an amendment and point out that those who support it can achieve the same result by voting against the original resolution. For example, an amendment may be proposed to a resolution authorising the board to fix the remuneration of the auditors which imposes a maximum sum. But if the amendment proposes a limit of 1p, it effectively negates the resolution to authorise the board to fix the remuneration.

The chairman can reject amendments if they seek to re-open business already settled at the meeting or they are incompatible with a previous decision of the meeting. The chairman may sometimes do so where the proposed amendment is either obstructive, vexatious, dilatory or irrelevant; for example, where the proposer is merely attempting to obstruct the conduct of the business by proposing a series of amendments.

22.6 Amending a resolution to appoint directors

Amendments to resolutions to appoint directors are probably the most common as shareholders often seek to propose a new person as a director, whether in place of or in addition to a nominated director. Unfortunately, this area is beset with difficulties. The principles outlined above in respect of ordinary resolutions apply and the basic question that must be considered is whether the amendment is within the scope of the notice. Before addressing this point, the chairman should, however, check the following points which may prevent the amendment being put.

- Articles normally fix (or determine the method of fixing) the maximum number of directors that may be appointed. If that maximum would be exceeded by passing the amendment, it can be rejected.

- Articles usually require notice to be given to the company of the intention to propose someone as a director who is not recommended by the board, e.g. reg. 76 of Table A which requires notice to be given by a member not less than 14 nor more than 35 clear days before the date appointed for the meeting together with the particulars which would, if that person was appointed, be required to be included in the company's register of directors together with notice executed by that person of his or her willingness to be appointed. Assuming that the company receives no such notice from a member entitled to vote 14 clear days before the meeting, no one other than a director retiring at the meeting or a person recommended by the board would be eligible for election as a director at the meeting.

- The articles may require prior notice to be given to the company of any amendments to be proposed at the meeting. If no such notice has been given, the chairman may reject the amendment.

22.7 Procedure on an amendment

An amendment may be moved at any time after discussion on the original motion has been invited by the chairman and before the motion has been put to the vote. For an example of a chairman's script for dealing with an amendment proposed from the floor, see **Appendix L**. It is not necessary for an amendment to be seconded unless the articles so provide (*Re Horbury Bridge Coal, Iron & Waggon Co.* (1879) 11 Ch. D. 109).

An amendment may alter the original motion by making deletions, additions or insertions. The proposal must be carefully drafted and, if necessary, the chairman should assist the proposers in giving proper effect to their proposal.

For example, on a resolution 'to appoint ABC as auditors until the next annual general meeting at which accounts are laid and to authorise the directors to fix their annual remuneration' the following amendment might be proposed: 'THAT the motion before the meeting be amended by deleting the word "annual" and adding after the word "remuneration" the words "provided that the amount paid as remuneration shall not exceed £25,000"'.

22.7.1 Order in which amendments taken

A properly moved amendment must be considered and put to the meeting before the original motion. It is normal for discussion to be restricted to the amendment itself. If it is carried, the chairman should read out the amended motion and invite discussion on it before putting it to the vote. If more than one amendment is proposed to the same motion, each amendment should be considered in the order in which it affects the motion.

For example, on a motion 'to appoint ABC as auditors until the next general meeting at which accounts are laid and to authorise the directors to fix their remuneration' an amendment proposing to delete 'ABC' and to insert 'BCD' should be taken before an amendment proposing to limit the amount that the directors are authorised to pay as remuneration for the auditors.

An amendment to an amendment may be proposed before the principal amendment is put to the vote. In these circumstances, the secondary amendment must be taken first. If it is carried, it must be embodied in the principal amendment which should be read to the meeting before discussion is invited.

22.8 Articles on amendments

Some companies have articles that provide that no amendment shall be considered (except at the discretion of the chairman) unless prior notice in writing of the proposed amendment has been given to the company (see example at **Precedent 22.8A**). This enables the chairman to take legal advice before the meeting as to whether the amendment should be accepted.

Articles may also provide that substantive resolutions shall not be invalidated by any error in good faith on the part of the chairman in ruling an amendment out of order (see **Precedent 22.8B**). The effect of such articles has not been tested. However, it is fairly obvious that the courts could intervene if the chairman had not acted with scrupulous fairness.

23

Dealing with common items of business

23.1 Summary

- This chapter outlines the procedures for dealing with some of the more common items of business at the AGM, as follows:
  - laying of the report and accounts (see **23.2**);
  - appointment of auditors (see **23.3**);
  - resignation of auditors (see **23.4**);
  - removal of auditors (see **23.5**);
  - auditors' remuneration (see **23.6**);
  - dividends (see **23.7**);
  - appointment of directors (see **23.8**);
  - appointment of a director over the age of 70 (see **23.9**);
  - retirement by rotation (see **23.10**);
  - removal of directors (see **23.11**).

23.2 Report and accounts

The Act requires the directors of every limited company to prepare the following:

- a balance sheet and a profit and loss account (s. 226);
- if it is a parent company, group accounts (s. 227);
- a directors' report (s. 234).

The auditors must also make a report on the accounts to the shareholders which forms part of the statutory accounts and reports ('the accounts'), copies of which must be filed with Companies House and sent to the members. The directors must also lay the accounts before the company in general meeting (s. 241) unless the company is a private company and has passed an elective resolution to dispense with this requirement.

23.2.1 Approved by the board of directors

The annual accounts and the directors' report must be approved by the board of directors. The balance sheet must be signed on behalf of the board by one director (s. 233(1)) and the directors' report by the secretary or a director (s. 234A(1)). The auditors' report must state the name of the auditors and be signed by them (s. 236). The copy of the accounts and reports delivered to the registrar must be an original signed copy. The copy laid before a general meeting and any copies that are circulated, published or issued need not be signed but must state the name(s) of the person(s) who signed the balance sheet and the directors' report on behalf of the board and the name(s) of the auditors who signed the auditors' report.

The order of events for approving and signing the accounts is therefore as follows:

- Board of directors approves the accounts (including, if a parent company, its own profit and loss accounts (which are not usually published)) and the directors' report.
- Board of directors authorises a director to sign the balance sheet and the secretary or a director to sign the directors' report.
- The director authorised by the board signs the balance sheet and the secretary (or director) signs the directors' report in at least three copies of the accounts.
- The auditors then sign the auditors' report in all three copies, retaining one copy and returning the other two to the company.
- One of the returned copies is delivered to the Registrar of Companies.
- The other is kept in the company's archives.

23.2.2 Time for laying and delivering

The accounts must be laid before a general meeting and delivered to the Registrar within ten months of the accounting reference date (year end) for private companies or seven months in the case of a public company (s. 244). They do not need to be laid before they are delivered to the Registrar. A company carrying on business or having interests outside the UK can claim a three-month extension by giving notice in the prescribed form before the end of the period allowed for laying and delivering accounts. However, the period allowed for laying and delivering accounts is reduced for newly incorporated companies whose first accounts cover more than 12 months (s. 244(2)).

If the accounts are not laid within the appropriate period, every person who immediately before the end of that period was a director of the company is guilty of an offence and liable to a fine and, for continued contravention, to a daily default fine (s. 241(2)).

Listed companies must publish their accounts as soon as

possible after they are approved and, in any event, within not less than six months of their year end (Listing Rules, para. 12.42(e)). Publication is not the same as laying or delivering for which the usual time limits apply. Publication is the act of issuing, publishing or sending out copies of the accounts. If a listed company needs to obtain an extension to the period for laying and delivering accounts from the Registrar, it will also need to obtain an extension from the UK Listing Authority of the time limit for publication.

23.2.3 Persons entitled to receive copies of the accounts and reports

A copy of the report and accounts must be sent at least 21 days before the date of the meeting at which they are to be laid to the following:

- every member of the company;
- every debenture holder; and
- every person who is entitled to receive notice of general meetings (s. 238(1)).

Copies need not be sent to the following:

- a member or debenture holder who is not entitled to receive notice and whose address is not known to the company (if the member is entitled to receive notice but the company does not know the current address, the copy should be sent to the last known address);
- joint holders of shares or debentures who are not entitled to receive notice of general meetings unless none of the joint holders is entitled to receive notice, in which case at least one of the joint holders must be sent a copy.

Where copies of the accounts are sent out over a period of days (perhaps because of the sheer scale of the operation) they are deemed to have been sent on the last of those days (s. 238(6)). If copies of the accounts and reports are not sent in accordance with the above requirements, the company and every officer of it in default is liable to a fine (s. 238(5)). However, if copies of the accounts and reports are sent less than 21 days before the date of the meeting at which they are to be laid, they will be deemed to have been duly sent if it is so agreed by all the members entitled to attend and vote at the meeting (s. 238(4)) (see **Precedent 23.2A**). This is useful if the general meeting at which accounts are to be laid is held at short notice. It is arguable that accounts can be laid in accordance with s. 241 even though copies have not been sent to the members in compliance with the requirements of s. 238. There is no direct link between s. 241 and s. 238. The only consequence of a failure to comply with s. 238 would therefore seem to be that the directors may be liable to a fine (see below, however, with regard to electronic communications).

23.2.4 Electronic communications

Instead of sending a paper copy of the accounts, a company may now:

- use electronic communications to send the accounts and reports in full to any person who has agreed to accept service in this manner and has provided an 'address' for that purpose (s. 238(4A)); or
- if the person entitled to receive a copy of the accounts agrees, notify him or her in an agreed manner that the accounts have been published on a website and leave it up to him or her whether to view it or download them (s. 238(4B)).

A company may take advantage of these provisions notwithstanding anything to the contrary contained in its articles. Both options require the agreement of both parties, i.e. the company and the person entitled to receive a copy of the accounts. It should be noted that members will not necessarily be the only people entitled to receive a copy of the accounts and that electronic communications can be used to send the accounts to anyone entitled to receive a copy provided that they have agreed to accept service in this manner (see **2.5** regarding the meaning of electronic communications and **2.6** for guidance on matters that will need to be considered before using electronic communications for these purposes).

23.2.5 Sending the full accounts using electronic communications

If a company and its members wish to use the method provided for by s. 238(4A), the company must send the full accounts electronically. Bearing in mind the size of the accounts and the fact that other documents may need to be sent at the same time (e.g. the notice of AGM, circulars and proxy forms), the electronic files could become very large. This would not matter a great deal if the files were sent on a CD-ROM or other electronic storage media. It might, however, cause consternation among members who had elected to receive these documents by e-mail. Attention will also need to be paid to the format in which the documents are to be sent and whether members will be able to read or view them.

These factors are likely to make this method of electronic communication impractical and unpopular for all but the most simple documents.

23.2.6 Publishing the accounts on a website

If a person entitled to be sent a copy of the accounts agrees, the company may satisfy the requirements of the Act by notifying them (in an agreed manner) that the accounts have been made available on a website (s. 238(4B)). The notification given by the company in these circumstances must be given in the manner agreed between the company and the person concerned. This could be in writing or by electronic communications. Irrespective of the manner in which it is given, the notification must specify the address of the website, the place on that website where the accounts may be accessed; and how they may be accessed.

Where this method of notification is used instead of sending full accounts through the post or electronically, the accounts will be treated as sent not less than 21 days before the meeting if, and only if:

- they are published on the website throughout the period beginning at least 21 days before the meeting and ending with the conclusion of the meeting; and
- the notification is given not less than 21 days before the meeting (s. 238(4C)).

However, s. 238(4D) provides that failure to publish the accounts throughout this period will not invalidate the proceedings of a meeting if the failure was wholly attributable to circumstances that it would not be reasonable to have expected the company to prevent or avoid. Rather worryingly, it does not protect a company or its officers from any offence that may as a consequence have been committed; and although s. 238 does not specifically state that other failures will invalidate any part of the proceedings of a meeting, this is clearly a distinct possibility with regard to the laying of accounts, where the failure occurred at some time during the 21-day period before the meeting and the members have not consented to receive the accounts at short notice. The conditions that must be satisfied to come within the ambit of the exception for publication failures are fairly onerous, and should any failure occur during the period it may be difficult to state conclusively whether or not the accounts can be laid. Companies that adopt this method of notification should perhaps take extra precautions to avoid failures (for example, by making the accounts available on more than one website, each hosted by different servers, and notifying members of the address of each of these sites).

23.2.7 Summary financial statements

Listed companies may send a summary financial statement instead of the full report and accounts, if a member agrees (s. 251). Provision is made in s. 251 and the Companies (Summary Financial Statement) Regulations 1995 to enable a company to use electronic communications for these purposes. The conditions that must be satisfied in this regard are almost identical to those for the full report and accounts.

23.2.8   Notice

The notice of the general meeting must refer to the laying of the report and accounts unless they are to be laid at an AGM and the articles specify this as ordinary business (see reg. 52 of the 1948 Act Table A). There is little to commend this practice and it is only likely to confuse shareholders. In practice, most companies set out the nature of the business in the normal manner (see **Precedent 23.2B**).

In its *Guide to Best Practice for Annual General Meetings*, the ICSA recommends that the resolution to receive or adopt the accounts should be separate from any resolution to approve the payment of the final dividend recommended by the directors.

23.2.9   Procedure at the meeting

Although s. 241 does not require a resolution to receive the report and accounts to be put to the meeting, it is normal to do so as this is the standard way of putting business before the meeting. The requirement to lay the accounts is merely a device to ensure that the shareholders are given an opportunity to question the directors about the company's performance and the directors' own performance as managers of the company. The wording of the resolution should not give the impression that the accounts and reports can be rejected or that they will not be laid if the members vote against the resolution. If a resolution on the accounts is lost, it does not alter the fact that they are the company's report and accounts or that they have been laid in accordance with s. 241. Thus words such as 'to approve the accounts and reports' and 'to lay the accounts and reports' should be avoided. If a resolution to receive the accounts is defeated, it is normally interpreted as a vote of no confidence in the directors although they would not be under any obligation to resign.

The ICSA's *Guide to Best Practice for Annual General Meetings* recommends that when moving the adoption or receipt of the accounts, the chairman should allow shareholders to raise questions on any item concerning the company's past performance, its results and its intended future performance. However, the directors need not answer questions that are irrelevant to the company or its business or which could result in the release of commercially sensitive information. Nor should they disclose price-sensitive information unless it can be done in compliance with the Listing Rules and guidance regarding the release of price-sensitive information. The ICSA also recommends that where concerns are raised by a shareholder at the AGM and the chairman undertakes to consider them, the shareholder should subsequently be sent a full report of the action taken.

23.2.10   Accounts not ready for AGM

It is not uncommon (particularly for private companies with a 31 March year end and a December AGM) for the accounts not to be ready in time for the AGM. One of the most frequently asked questions in these circumstances is whether it is possible to send out notices and hold the AGM and then to adjourn it until such time as the accounts have been prepared and sent to shareholders. If the adjourned meeting is held within the period for laying of accounts, there would seem to be no objection to this procedure. The requirement is merely that the accounts be laid at a general meeting within the period. If, however, the adjourned meeting is held after the end of the ten-month period for laying and delivering, an offence will still be committed under s. 241. Laying the accounts in this manner would, however, prevent the accumulation of any daily default fines.

23.3   Appointment of auditors

A company must appoint auditors unless it is:

- a dormant company and has resolved not to appoint auditors (s. 249AA and s. 388A); or
- is exempt as a small company from the audit requirements and not therefore obliged to appoint auditors (s. 249A and s. 388A).

23.3.1   Appointment of first auditors

The directors may appoint the first auditors at any time before the first general meeting at which accounts are laid (see **Precedent 23.3A**). Auditors so appointed hold office until the conclusion of that meeting (s. 385(3)). If the directors fail to appoint the first auditors, the company in general meeting may do so (s. 385(4)) (see **Precedent 23.3B**).

23.3.2   Periodic reappointment

Auditors must be appointed or reappointed at each general meeting at which accounts are laid (s. 385(2)). Special procedures apply where an auditor other than the retiring auditor is being appointed (see **23.4**). A private company that already has auditors may elect to dispense with their annual reappointment (see further **25.5**). A private company that has passed an elective resolution to dispense with the laying of accounts but not to dispense with the annual appointment of auditors, must appoint or reappoint auditors at a general meeting of the company held within 28 days from the date the accounts are sent to members (s. 385A).

The resolution to appoint auditors is usually passed after the accounts have been laid. The resolution should be worded so that the auditors are appointed until the conclusion of the next general meeting at which accounts are laid rather than for a year or until the conclusion of the next AGM (see **Precedent 23.3C**).

23.3.3 Appointment by Secretary of State in default

If no auditors are appointed, reappointed or deemed to be reappointed before the end of the time for appointing auditors, the company must notify the Secretary of State who may appoint a person to fill the vacancy (s. 387) and fix their remuneration (s. 390A).

23.3.4 Casual vacancies

A casual vacancy can be caused by the resignation or death of the existing auditor. The board of directors, or the company in general meeting, may fill any such vacancy in the office of auditor (s. 388(1)). Special notice must be given of a resolution at a general meeting to fill a casual vacancy or to reappoint as auditor a person appointed by the directors to fill a casual vacancy (s. 388(3)). On receipt of notice of the intended resolution the company must send a copy of it to the person proposed to be appointed and, if the casual vacancy was caused by the resignation of an auditor, to the auditor who resigned (see below).

23.4 Resignation of auditors

Auditors may resign by notice in writing to the registered office of the company. The notice should be accompanied by a statement as to whether there are any circumstances connected with the resignation that the auditors consider should be brought to the attention of the members or creditors. Within 14 days of receipt of the notice of resignation, the company must file a copy of the notice (but not of the accompanying statement) with Companies House (s. 392).

23.4.1 Statement of circumstances

If the auditors' statement is of circumstances that they consider should be brought to the attention of the members or creditors:

- the company must within 14 days of the deposit of the statement send a copy of it to every person entitled under s. 238 to receive copies of the report and accounts or make an application to the court to restrain publication of that statement (in which case it must notify the auditors of the application);
- unless they are notified within 21 days of the deposit that an application to restrain publication has been made, the auditors must within a further seven days (i.e. 28 days from the date of deposit) file a copy of the statement with Companies House (s. 394).

23.4.2   Rights of resigning auditors

Where the resigning auditors have deposited with their notice of resignation a statement that they consider should be brought to the attention of the members, they may deposit a requisition calling on the directors to convene an EGM of the company to consider their explanation of the circumstances and require the company to circulate to the members a written statement of the circumstances before that meeting (s. 392A). They may, alternatively, require the company to circulate such a statement before any general meeting at which their term of office would have expired or at which it is proposed to fill the vacancy caused by their resignation. The company must comply with any such demands and state in the notice of meeting (possibly as a note) that representations have been made by the auditors. The resigning auditors have a right to receive notice of and to attend and speak at any such meetings. If their representations are received too late for circulation, the auditors may require that they be read out at the meeting. The court may relieve the company of these obligations if it is satisfied that the auditors are using the provisions to secure needless publicity for a defamatory matter.

23.5   Removal of auditors

Where a company wishes to change its auditors, it is normal to approach the existing auditors to see whether they would be prepared to resign voluntarily or agree not to seek reappointment. If they agree to resign, the procedures outlined above would apply and the directors could then appoint new auditors to fill the resulting casual vacancy. If the change is not urgent, it can be left until the next general meeting at which accounts are laid. If the matter is urgent, perhaps because relations have irretrievably broken down, a general meeting could be held to remove the auditors by ordinary resolution before the end of their term of office.

Special notice (see **11.12**) must be given by a member to the company of any resolution to remove the auditors or to appoint as auditors anyone other than the retiring auditors (s. 391). On receipt of notice of the intended resolution, the company must immediately send a copy of it to the proposed auditors and the existing auditors.

The existing auditors may make written representations to the company on the proposed resolution and demand that they be circulated to the members. The company must comply with such a demand and state in the notice of meeting that representations have been made. If the representations are not circulated to the members for any reason, the auditors may require them to be read out at the meeting. The court may relieve the company of these obligations if it is satisfied that the auditors are using the provisions to secure needless publicity for a defamatory matter.

As the auditors who are to be removed or not reappointed will still be the company's auditors at the start of the general meeting, they are entitled to receive notice, attend and speak at the meeting.

An auditor who is removed or not reappointed must also make a statement as to the circumstances connected with his or her removal or non-reappointment (s. 394).

23.6   Remuneration of auditors

The remuneration of auditors appointed by the directors as first auditors or to fill a casual vacancy must be fixed by the directors (s. 390A(2)).

The remuneration of auditors appointed (or reappointed) by the company in general meeting must be fixed by the company in general meeting or in such manner as the company in general meeting may determine (s. 390A(1)). This is usually done at the same time as the appointment by authorising the directors to fix their remuneration (see **Precedent 23.3C**). Although s. 390A(1) envisages that the members themselves may fix the auditors' remuneration, this is not normally a practicable solution. It will normally be difficult to predict the precise audit costs for the forthcoming year, not least because remuneration is deemed to include any of the auditors' expenses paid by the company (s. 390A(4)). The members may only be able to fix the remuneration after the audit is complete. This is unlikely to be acceptable to the auditors as the members may not approve payment of the full amount.

While an elective resolution dispensing with the annual appointment of auditors is in force under s. 386, the auditors are deemed to have been reappointed each year. This can cause complications with respect to the method of fixing their remuneration (see further **25.5**).

23.7   Dividends

23.7.1   Final dividend

Most articles provide that dividends must be declared by an ordinary resolution of the company in general meeting and that no dividend may exceed the amount recommended by the directors (e.g. reg. 102). Dividends can only be paid out of profits available for distribution (ss. 263 to 281). In recommending the final dividend, the directors must ensure that there are sufficient funds available for distribution. It is therefore usual for the resolution to declare a dividend to be proposed at the general meeting at which the accounts have been laid. The wording of the notice with regard to dividends is usually very simple, mainly because the detailed information regarding dividends must be included in the directors' report (see **Precedents 23.7A to C**).

The ICSA's *Guide to Best Practice for Annual General Meetings* recommends that the resolution to receive or adopt the accounts should be separate from any resolution to approve the payment of the final dividend recommended by the directors.

23.7.2 Interim dividend

Articles usually also provide that the directors may pay interim dividends without reference to the members (e.g. reg. 103) (see **Precedent 23.7D**). The directors should not pay a dividend unless it is clear that sufficient funds are available for distribution as dividends.

23.8 Appointment of directors

Articles usually contain detailed procedures on the appointment of directors. Any natural or legal person may be appointed as a director. A company may be appointed as a director of another company. The method of appointment and the body or person authorised to make the appointment may differ according to the type of appointment being made. Table 23.1 shows the position under the 1985 Table A. These provisions are frequently modified and it is essential to check the articles very carefully.

23.8.1 Procedure for appointment of directors

- Check articles for the method of appointment (see Table 23.1 if Table A applies).
- If additional appointment, check that it will not cause the number of directors to exceed any maximum prescribed by the articles.

Table 23.1 Methods of appointing directors under the 1985 Table A

Type of appointment	Appointed by	Source
First directors	Subscribers to the memorandum	CA 1985, s. 10
Additional directors	Board of directors	reg. 79
	Members	regs 76 to 78
Appointments to fill a casual vacancy	Board of directors	reg. 79
	Members	regs 76 to 78
Reappointment following retirement by rotation	Members	regs 72 to 75 and 78
Reappointment following retirement at first AGM after appointment	Members	regs 72, 78 and 79
Alternate directors	Directors	regs 65 to 69

- Check articles for age limits. In the case of a plc or a subsidiary of a plc, if nothing in articles, special notice required to appoint person aged 70 or over (see further **23.9**).
- Check articles for share qualifications.
- Obtain approval for the appointment at a board meeting or, as the case may be, at a general meeting (if a private company, members' approval may be obtained by written resolution).
- Submit completed Form 288a to Companies House within 14 days of appointment ensuring that the new director has signed the consent to act.
- Enter details of the new director in the register of directors, including any former name, usual residential address, nationality, business occupation, particulars of past and present directorships and date of birth (s. 289).
- Remind director of any share qualification required by the articles.
- Remind director to disclose any interest in shares and debentures of the company.
- Request director to give general notice of any interest in contracts or proposed contracts with the company.
- Notify the company's bankers as appropriate.
- Obtain details of the director's PAYE coding and NI number and instructions as to method of payment of remuneration.
- If appropriate, settle terms of service agreement (not to exceed five years without shareholder approval) and issue terms of reference or letter of appointment.

23.8.2 Minimum and maximum number

The Companies Act 1985 provides that every private company (whether limited by shares, limited by guarantee or unlimited) must have at least one director and that every public company formed after 1 November 1929 must have at least two (s. 282). Public companies formed before 1 November 1929 need only one director. Articles may require a higher number than the statutory minimum but not a lower number.

Articles may also specify the maximum number of directors who may be appointed or provide a mechanism for determining such a limit. Any appointment that would cause the number of directors to exceed that maximum will be invalid.

Reg. 64 of Table A provides that the number of directors shall not be subject to any maximum unless the members determine otherwise by ordinary resolution. This is a rather ungainly provision. It is easy to imagine circumstances where the existence of a limit imposed by ordinary resolution might be forgotten as such a resolution does not operate to amend the articles and can only be proved by reference to the minutes of the meeting at which it was passed. It is better to fix a maximum by amending the relevant article. If, however, a maximum is imposed or changed by ordinary resolution under reg. 64, it is advisable to make a note referring to that resolution on the master copy of the articles. It may also be a good idea to make a note that no such resolution has ever been passed if, indeed, that is the case. Reg. 64 can also cause problems if the members vote to impose a maximum that is less than the number of directors currently holding office. It is doubtful whether such a resolution would have the effect of removing any of the directors unless special notice was given of a resolution to remove one or more of those directors in accordance with s. 303. Such a resolution would, however, be effective in preventing any future appointments or reappointments in breach of the maximum.

23.8.3 First directors

Before a company can be registered, the subscribers to the memorandum (i.e. the people who will become the company's first members) must provide the Registrar of Companies with the name(s) and details of the first director(s) on Form 10. The form must be signed by the people nominated as directors to show that they are willing to act in that capacity. On incorporation, the people named as directors on Form 10 are deemed to have been appointed and no further action is required (s. 13(5)). It is, however, standard practice to note in the minutes of the first board meeting the method by which they were appointed (see **Precedents 4.6B and 4.6C**). There is nothing to prevent the subscribers nominating themselves as the first directors.

If the articles require the directors to hold shares in the company, the Act provides that they will cease to be directors if they do not satisfy that requirement within two months or such shorter time as the articles may specify (s. 291). The articles may also require the directors to satisfy other qualifications or provide for their removal from office on the happening of certain events.

If the subscribers wish to appoint a sole director of a private company, it will be necessary to appoint two initially or to modify regs 64, 89 and 90 of Table A as they are drafted on the basis that there will be a minimum of two directors in the first instance.

23.8.4 Subsequent appointments

Subsequent appointments must be made in accordance with the procedures laid down in the company's articles of association and the requirements of the Companies Act 1985. The Act only interferes by providing:

- that a director must comply within a certain period with any article requiring him or her to hold shares in the company (s. 291);
- that a motion for the appointment of two or more persons as directors by a single resolution at a general meeting of a public company shall not be valid unless the meeting agrees

unanimously to a proposal that the resolution be proposed in that manner (s. 292);

- special procedures for the appointment by a public company or one of its subsidiaries of a director aged 70 or more (s. 293) (see **23.9**); and
- that details of appointments of directors must be entered in a register by the company and notified to Companies House, although failure to do so does not invalidate the appointment (ss. 288 to 290).

All other questions relating to the appointment of directors must be resolved by reference to the articles. This is one of the areas where the Table A procedures are most likely to be modified and a careful examination of the articles will be necessary to ensure that the correct procedures are followed. If the articles make no provision for the appointment of directors, appointments must be made by the members in general meeting.

23.8.5   Appointment by the directors

Under Table A the board may appoint new directors either to fill vacancies or as additional directors (subject to any maximum fixed in accordance with the articles) (reg. 79). A vacancy arises where an existing director has died, resigned or become disqualified. Such appointments must be made by the directors at a properly constituted meeting of the board or, if the articles allow, by written resolution. See **Precedents 23.8A and B** for examples of board resolutions appointing directors.

Under Table A, directors appointed by the board must retire at the AGM following their appointment and offer themselves for election by the members (reg. 79). Not less than seven and no more than 28 days before the meeting the company must give notice of any person retiring in this manner who is recommended by the directors for appointment or reappointment. The notice must include the details that would be required to be included in the register of directors if that person was appointed or reappointed (reg. 77). The purpose of this provision is to ensure that the directors cannot propose a person for appointment or reappointment without giving the members prior notice of his or her details, e.g. by including in the notice of the meeting an item of business to elect directors without naming them. If the company fails to give notice in accordance with reg. 77 the appointment will be invalid. If the members resolve not to reappoint a director, the director ceases to hold office at the conclusion of the AGM. Directors retiring in this manner are not taken into account in determining the directors who are to retire by rotation at the meeting (see **23.10**).

A private company may, of course, dispense with AGMs under the elective regime (see **Chapter 25**). If for any reason an AGM is subsequently held, directors appointed under reg. 79 while the election was in force should retire at that meeting and offer themselves for re-election.

23.8.6 Common modifications to reg. 79

Reg. 79 applies in respect of vacancies and appointments of additional directors. However, articles sometimes allow the directors to make appointments to fill casual vacancies only. In these circumstances, the directors may only appoint a person to replace a director who has died, resigned or been disqualified from acting as a director. They may not fill any vacancy that arises by virtue of the procedures on rotation of directors or any vacancy that arises because an appointment made for a fixed period has ceased, e.g. an appointment for fixed term of one year or an appointment that ceases at the conclusion of the next AGM (*York Tramways Co. v. Willows* (1882) 8 QBD 685}.

Where the articles restrict the powers of the directors to filling casual vacancies, the members retain the power to appoint additional directors.

23.8.7 Appointment by the members

If the articles give the directors power to fill casual vacancies and appoint additional directors, the members will have no power to do so unless the articles make specific provision to that effect. Under Table A, the members can also appoint directors to fill casual vacancies or as additional directors by ordinary resolution at a general meeting (subject to any maximum) (reg. 78). However, they must give the company prior notice of their intention to propose a person as a director who is not recommended by the board, not less than 14 days and not more than 35 days before the date of the meeting. The notice given to the company must include the details that would be required to be included in the register of directors if that person was appointed and notice signed by the person nominated of his or her willingness to act as a director (reg. 76). The purpose of reg. 76 is to prevent the members from relying on the inclusion in the notice of the meeting of an item of business to elect or re-elect directors in order to propose a person not recommended by the directors. It should be noted, however, that the fact that a member has given notice in accordance with reg. 76 does not guarantee that the proposal will be within the scope of the notice of the meeting (see **22.5**).

Not less than seven and not more than 28 days before the meeting, the company must give notice to every person who is entitled to receive notice of the meeting of any person in respect of whom notice has been given to the company of the intention to propose him or her at the meeting for appointment or reappointment as a director in accordance with reg. 76. The notice given by the company must include the details that would be required to be included in the register of directors (reg. 77).

Most companies' articles include a provision similar to reg. 76 requiring members to notify the company of their intention to propose as a director someone not recommended by the directors. The Listing Rules used to require listed companies to adopt an article similar to reg. 76 but did not (and still do not) require them to adopt an article similar to reg. 77. Accordingly, most listed companies still have an article similar to reg. 76 but very few have anything like reg. 77.

Under reg. 76, the members may notify the company of their intention to propose a person as a director as little as 14 days before the meeting, i.e. after the notice calling the meeting has been sent. In order to comply with the requirements of reg. 77 in these circumstances, the company would have to do a second mailing to its members. The purpose of reg. 77 is to ensure that the members have advance warning that a person not recommended by the board is to be proposed as a director at the meeting and act accordingly, e.g. by attending the meeting or by appointing proxies to vote for or against the resolution. Giving notice in this manner enables the board to mobilise opposition to the appointment. In practice, listed companies tend to rely on the fact that the chairman controls sufficient proxy votes to defeat any such resolution.

Although it is clear that a resolution of the members in general meeting to appoint a person as a director not recommended by the board will be invalid if the members have not complied with the requirement to give the company prior notice in accordance with reg. 76, it is not clear whether such an appointment would be invalid if the company fails to give notice to the members in accordance with reg. 77. Also, it is not clear whether the company, by giving notice in accordance with reg. 77, automatically brings the resolution to be proposed by the members within the scope of the notice of the meeting, e.g. where the reg. 77 notice was not sent within the normal period of notice for AGMs (21 clear days) or EGMs (14 clear days) and the resolution is not within the scope of the notice of the meeting already sent to members. With these difficulties in mind, it is hardly surprising that reg. 77 is rarely adopted by listed companies.

A number of points should be noted with regard to the above regulations:

- although they do not apply to the reappointment of a director retiring by rotation, they do to a director appointed by the directors to fill a casual vacancy or as an additional director who is required to retire at the AGM next following his or her appointment;
- notice must be given to the members in accordance with reg. 77 in respect of any person recommended by the directors;

- a valid resolution of the board of directors will be required for a person to qualify as being recommended by the directors;
- two conditions must be satisfied for a person to be proposed who is not recommended by the directors, namely notice must be given to the company in accordance with reg. 76 (see **Precedent 23.8C**) and the company must give notice to the members in accordance with reg. 77 (see **Precedent 23.8D**).

23.8.8   1948 Act Table A

The 1948 Act Table A provisions are much simpler and are commonly adopted by public companies in preference to the 1985 Table A provisions. Reg. 93 of the 1948 Table A provides:

> **93.** No person other than a director retiring at the meeting shall unless recommended by the directors be eligible for election to the office of director at any general meeting unless not less than three nor more than twenty-one days before the date appointed for the meeting there shall have been left at the registered office of the company notice in writing, signed by a member duly qualified to attend and vote at the meeting for which such notice is given, of his intention to propose such person for election, and also notice in writing signed by that person of his willingness to be elected.

Reg. 93 does not apply to any director retiring at the meeting whether by rotation or otherwise. Although a member is still required to give notice to the company, there is no corresponding requirement for the company to give notice to the members.

Under reg. 97 of the 1948 Act Table A, the members may by ordinary resolution appoint another person in place of a director who has been removed from office and, without prejudice to the powers of the directors (essentially the same as under the 1985 Table A), appoint any person to be a director either to fill a casual vacancy or as an additional director. There is no corresponding requirement for the members to give notice of their intention to propose such a resolution.

23.8.9   Other methods of appointment

Other methods of appointment can be adopted. Articles sometimes provide that directors may be appointed or removed from office by notice in writing signed by members holding a majority of the voting shares. This method is most likely to be used by subsidiary companies as it enables the parent company to make appointments without having to hold a meeting of the subsidiary.

A variation on this theme can be useful for joint venture companies where each of the partners in the joint venture is given the right to appoint a fixed number of directors (and replace them with others) by giving notice in writing. This can be achieved by having different classes of shares with each class having separate rights to appoint a fixed number of directors.

The articles of small owner-managed companies are frequently modified to ensure that the founders retain the right to participate in their management. Some amendment may be necessary even where all the company's shares are held equally by two people who are both appointed as directors. This is because under reg. 50 of Table A, the chairman of the general meeting has a casting vote and could therefore appoint and remove directors against the wishes of the other member to gain management control. The simplest solution in these circumstances is to amend the articles to exclude that part of reg. 50 that gives the chairman a casting vote. For a person holding less than 50% of the company's shares more elaborate protection is necessary. The articles could be amended so that an extraordinary or special resolution is required (i.e. a majority of 75%) to appoint new directors. The major problem for a minority shareholder, however, is the fact that the members in general meeting have a statutory right to remove a director from office by ordinary resolution (s. 303). There are a number of ways in which this problem can be overcome (see further **23.11** on the removal of directors) and it goes without saying that a minority shareholder should ensure that appropriate measures are taken before becoming a shareholder.

23.9 Directors' age limits

The purpose of the following provisions on directors' age limits is to enable shareholders to remove a director or to prevent the appointment of a director who has reached the age of 70. The statutory rules only apply to public companies and their subsidiaries. There is no statutory age limit in respect of private companies except where the company is a subsidiary of a public company. Table A is also silent on the matter. The following procedures can therefore be ignored by private companies unless they are a subsidiary of a public company or their articles have been amended so as to include similar age restrictions.

For directors of public companies and their subsidiaries, s. 293 sets a notional age limit of 70. It is notional because a person who has reached that age may still be appointed or reappointed as a director as long as the procedures laid down by that section are followed. In addition, the articles of a public company or any of its subsidiaries may override these statutory rules (see example article at **Precedent 23.9C**).

Section 293 provides that a person who has reached the age of 70 may not be appointed as a director unless the appointment is approved by an ordinary resolution of the members in general meeting. Thus, the directors cannot appoint a person who has reached the age of 70 to fill a casual vacancy or as an additional director unless the articles make specific provision to that effect.

A director of a public company or any of its subsidiaries who reaches the age of 70 while in office must retire at the conclusion of the AGM next following his or her 70th birthday, although the members may by ordinary resolution reappoint a director retiring under these rules.

Special notice must be given of the resolution (either to appoint or to reappoint the director) in accordance with s. 379 (see **11.12**). The notice given by the member to the company (see **Precedent 23.9A**) and the notice given by the company to its members (see **Precedent 23.9B**) must state the age of the person to whom the resolution relates.

Where a director retires under these rules, any provision for the automatic reappointment of retiring directors in default of another appointment (e.g. reg. 75) does not apply and if, at the meeting at which the director retires, the vacancy is not filled, it may be filled as a casual vacancy (e.g. by the directors under reg. 79) (s. 293(4)).

23.9.1 Effect on retirement by rotation

A retirement under s. 293 is ignored for the purposes of determining the order and timing of rotation of directors provided that the retiring director is reappointed or a person is appointed in place of the director so retiring (s. 293(6)). For example, if a public company has six directors, one of whom (A) reaches the age of 70 in the third year, the following order would apply:

Year 1: A and B retire and are reappointed
Year 2: C and D retire and are reappointed
Year 3: A, E and F retire and are reappointed
Year 4: A and B retire and are reappointed

In the above example, if G was appointed in place of A in year 3, G would have to retire again in year 4 (i.e. when the person replaced would have retired if still in office).

23.9.2 Age limits in articles

If a private company, which is not a subsidiary, has any rules on age limits in its articles, those rules will apply irrespective of anything in s. 293 as the statutory rules apply only to public companies and their subsidiaries. The articles of a public company or its subsidiary may exclude either in whole or in part the effect of the statutory age limits (s. 293(7)).

23.10 Retirement by rotation of directors

Although Table A makes provision for directors to retire by rotation, there is nothing in the Act to prevent a company from deleting these requirements or adopting different rules. The standard Table A provisions often cause more trouble than they are worth for owner-managed private companies. They are, of course, also totally superfluous for subsidiaries and joint venture companies. Particular attention should be paid to the articles of any company bought 'off the shelf' from a company registration agent. These often contain non-standard provisions on retirement which may, for example, require the board to determine when an appointment is made whether the director is to be subject to the retirement provisions. If no decision is taken at the time of the appointment, the assumption will often be that the director will be subject to the retirement provisions.

The Combined Code on Corporate Governance recommends that all directors of listed companies should retire and offer themselves for re-election at least once every three years (see below). Although the Code does not have the force of law, most listed companies now comply with this recommendation in respect of both executive and non-executive directors.

23.10.1   1985 Table A

The basic provisions on rotation in Table A are as follows:

> **73.** At the first AGM all the directors shall retire from office, and at every subsequent AGM one-third of the directors who are subject to retirement by rotation or, if their number is not three or a multiple of three, the number nearest to one third shall retire from office; but, if there is only one director who is subject to retirement by rotation, he shall retire.
> **74.** Subject to the provisions of the Act, the directors to retire by rotation shall be those who have served longest in office since their last appointment or reappointment, but as between persons who became or were last reappointed directors on the same day those to retire shall (unless they otherwise agree among themselves) be determined by lot.
> **75.** If the company, at the meeting at which a director retires by rotation, does not fill the vacancy the retiring director shall, if willing to act, be deemed to have been reappointed unless at the meeting it is resolved not to fill the vacancy or unless a resolution for the reappointment of the director is put to the meeting and lost.

23.10.2   Number to retire

In order to determine who must retire each year, it is necessary first to determine which directors are subject to retirement by rotation. Under reg. 84 of Table A, the executive directors are not subject to retirement by rotation. If all the directors hold some executive office, the rotation provisions will not apply.

Most articles provide that the number nearest to one-third of the directors subject to retirement by rotation shall retire. The normal rounding-up and rounding-down rules should be applied when calculating the number of directors who must retire unless the articles state that the number nearest to, but not exceeding, one-third shall retire, in which case the figure must always be rounded down.

Under reg. 73 of the 1985 Table A, it is clear that even where only one director is subject to retirement by rotation, that person must retire at each AGM. The same is true where the articles follow reg. 89 of 1948 Table A by providing that the 'number nearest one-third' shall retire (*Re New Cedos Engineering Co. Ltd* [1994] 1 BCLC 797, 810). In both cases, one person must retire at each AGM if two directors are subject to retirement by rotation. However, if the articles provide that 'the number nearest to, but not exceeding, one-third' shall retire and the number of directors subject to retirement by rotation is two or less, then no directors need to retire (*Re Moseley & Sons Ltd* [1939] Ch. 719).

23.10.3 Who is to retire?

The directors to retire by rotation will normally be those who have served longest since their last appointment or reappointment. Articles normally provide that, where the number who must retire is less than the number who are eligible under this rule because they were appointed or last reappointed on the same day, the selection of those to retire is to be determined by lot, unless they otherwise agree among themselves (in which case their unanimous agreement is required with respect to the decision or the method of reaching that decision). A lot may be performed by the drawing of straws or some other similar method of chance. It has been held that where the articles state that the matter is to be settled by ballot, this also means by lot rather than by any method of voting (*Eyre v. Milton Proprietary* [1936] Ch. 244). This case is also authority for the fact that temporary directors (e.g. those appointed by the directors under reg. 79 and who must therefore automatically retire at the next

Table 23.2 Retirement of directors

Number of directors subject to retirement by rotation	*Number to retire at each AGM*	
	1948 and 1985 Table A	*'Nearest to, but not exceeding one-third'*
One	1	0
Two	1	0
Three	1	1
Four	1	1
Five	2	1
Six	2	2

following AGM) should not be included when calculating how many directors should retire under the rotation provisions.

23.10.4   Combined Code recommendations

The Combined Code on Corporate Governance recommends that all directors should be subject to election by shareholders at the first opportunity after their appointment, and to re-election thereafter at intervals of no more than three years. It also recommends that the names of directors submitted for election or re-election should be accompanied by sufficient biographical details to enable shareholders to take an informed decision on their election (Combined Code, para. A.6.2).

In order to ensure compliance with this recommendation, it is necessary for listed companies to adopt articles that differ from Table A in a number of respects. First, Table A exempts executive directors from retirement by rotation. Second, under the formula adopted by Table A, it is possible that a director may not become eligible for re-election every three years. Most listed companies have solved this problem by retaining the usual formula that one-third of the directors are to retire at each AGM and by adding a proviso to ensure that no director can hold office for more than three years without retiring (see example article at **Precedent 23.10**). Considerable caution should be exercised before encouraging directors to retire before their allotted time where the articles make no specific provision in this regard.

23.10.5   Notice and proxy forms

Unless the articles specify the re-election of directors retiring by rotation as ordinary business, it will be necessary to indicate the general nature of the business in the notice. This can be done simply by stating as an item of business 'to re-elect directors retiring by rotation'. However, it is more usual to include a

Table 23.3 Example of retirement by rotation under 1985 Table A (all directors subject to rotation)

Event	AGM	Directors to retire
A, B, C and D appointed as first directors on formation	First AGM	A, B, C and D (under reg. 73)
	Second AGM	C (drawn by lot between A, B, C and D)
	Third AGM	B (drawn by lot between A, B and D)
Board appoints E as additional director	Fourth AGM	A and D (under regs 73 and 74) and E (under reg. 79)
	Fifth AGM	B and C (under regs 73 and 74)
	Sixth AGM	A and E (by lot between A, D and E)

separate resolution for each director who will be retiring by rotation and seeking re-election at the meeting. The ICSA's *Guide to Best Practice for Annual General Meetings* recommends that directors standing for re-election to the board should be named in the notice and form of proxy. The Combined Code recommends that the names of directors submitted for election or re-election should be accompanied by sufficient biographical details to enable shareholders to take an informed decision on their election. The ICSA's *Guide to Best Practice for Annual General Meetings* expands upon this by recommending that a brief description of the relevant directors should be given, including their ages, their relevant experience (not merely a list of other directorships they hold), the dates that they were first appointed to the board, and details of any board committees to which they belong. This could be done in any circular that accompanies the notice or in the directors' report if the accounts are sent to the members with the notice.

Listed companies must send proxy cards to members which allow them to indicate how their proxy should vote on every resolution (other than procedural resolutions) which will be put to the meeting (Listing Rules, para. 13.28). Where the number of retiring directors standing for re-election exceeds five, the proxy form may give shareholders the opportunity to vote for or against the re-election of the retiring directors as a whole but must also allow votes to be cast for or against the re-election of the retiring directors individually (Listing Rules, para. 13.29). The Act provides that a motion for the appointment of two or more persons as directors by a single resolution at a general meeting of a public company shall not be valid unless the meeting agrees unanimously to a proposal that the resolution be proposed in that manner (s. 292).

23.10.6 Failure to hold an AGM

If a company fails to hold an AGM, the directors who were due to retire at that meeting will be deemed to have retired at the end of the year in which the AGM was due to be held. In *Re Consolidated Nickel Mines Ltd* [1914] 1 Ch. 883, the company's articles of association provided that a general meeting should be held once in every year and that at the ordinary meeting (AGM) in 1906 all the directors should retire from office. No such meeting was held or called. It was held that the directors vacated office on 31 December 1906, i.e. the last day on which the ordinary meeting for that year could have been held. This decision was followed in *Re Zinotty Properties Ltd* [1984] 3 All ER 754 in a case concerning an article based on reg. 89 of the 1948 Table A. There is no reason to suppose that the result in these cases would have been any different if the article in question had been art. 73 of the 1985 Table A.

23.10.7   Position under elective regime

Re Consolidated Nickel Mines and *Re Zinotty Properties* were, however, both decided at a time when all companies were required by statute to hold AGMs. The question arises therefore as to what rules apply to a private company that has elected, pursuant to ss. 366A and 381A of the Companies Act 1985, to dispense with AGMs if its articles also require the directors to retire by rotation at the AGM. In *Re Zinotty Properties*, Mervyn Davies J stated that the fact that the company had no directors was a consequence of the company never having held AGMs coupled with the operation of reg. 89 of the 1948 Act Table A and the company's article 16. Reg. 89 provides:

> **89.** At the first annual general meeting of the company all the directors shall retire from office and at the annual general meeting in every subsequent year one-third of the directors for the time being, or, if their number is not three or a multiple of three, then the number nearest one-third, shall retire from office.

The company's art. 16 read: 'In clause 89 of Table A the words "all the directors shall retire from office" shall be deleted.' Mervyn Davies J seemed to indicate that the existence of an article such as reg. 89 was sufficient on its own to cause this result. This was undoubtedly correct at the time as all companies were required by law to hold AGMs. However, in view of the fact that private companies can now dispense with AGMs, this may not always be true today.

An elective resolution to dispense with holding AGMs is not passed as an amendment to the articles. However, it is well established that the unanimous agreement of the members can have the same effect as an amendment to the articles (*Cane v. Jones* [1981] 1 All ER 533). It could be argued that an elective resolution, being a unanimous resolution of the members, has the same effect. Thus, it might have the effect of amending any provision in the articles that is inconsistent with its purpose, e.g. a provision that requires the company to hold an AGM each year, e.g. reg. 47 (and, by implication, reg. 89) of the 1948 Act Table A (the 1985 version of Table A does not include any such provision).

Even if an elective resolution does not amend any article that is inconsistent with its purpose, it must at least suspend its operation while it is in force. This distinction is irrelevant with respect to any article that requires the company to hold AGMs as this would be a statutory requirement if the elective resolution was revoked. However, it is a crucial point in relation to retirement by rotation as it determines whether the retirement provisions would operate if an AGM is subsequently held for any reason. In the author's view, an elective resolution should be viewed as merely suspending the operation of any article that is inconsistent with its purpose, although it has to be said that reg.

73 of the 1985 Act Table A is more conducive to this solution than, for example, reg. 89 of the 1948 Act Table A which seems to imply that an AGM must be held each year (reg. 73 merely provides that certain directors shall retire at the first AGM and at every subsequent AGM).

23.10.8 Wrong directors retire

A problem that commonly arises because of a miscalculation or a lack of understanding of the articles is that the wrong directors retire at the meeting. The situation with regard to a person who should have retired depends on the articles. Such a person will cease to be a director at the conclusion of the AGM unless the articles include a saving provision similar to art. 75 of Table A:

> **75.** If the company, at the meeting at which a director retires by rotation, does not fill the vacancy the retiring director shall, if willing to act, be deemed to have been reappointed unless at the meeting it is resolved not to fill the vacancy or unless a resolution for the appointment of the director is put to the meeting and lost.

The words 'at a meeting at which a director retires by rotation' should not be interpreted as requiring any action on the part of the director. A director who is due to retire by rotation will be deemed to have retired at that meeting. Thus a vacancy will exist even though another director retired at the meeting and, provided that the other conditions of the relevant article are satisfied, the director will be deemed to have been reappointed.

The position with regard to any director who retired by mistake is complicated by the fact that the articles commonly restrict the ability of the members to appoint or reappoint directors, e.g. reg. 77 of the 1985 Table A. A director who retires earlier than is necessary does not do so by rotation under the articles. Thus any conditions in the articles on appointments by the members must be satisfied otherwise the appointment will be invalid. If the reappointment can be deemed to have been recommended by the directors, it would be valid under reg. 77 of Table A.

23.10.9 Meeting held but no resolution put

Articles such as reg. 75 of Table A also save the situation where an AGM is held but no resolution is put to the meeting with respect to rotation, except where the meeting has resolved not to fill the vacancy. Thus, if the company fails by mistake or otherwise to put forward resolutions to deal with rotation at the meeting, the directors will be deemed to be reappointed. Although this type of article may be necessary to save the situation where a genuine mistake is made, it is hardly conducive

to good corporate governance in so far as it allows a director to
be reappointed without the approval of the members.

23.11 Removal of directors from office

The statutory rules on removal of directors apply to public and
private companies alike and cannot be excluded by the articles.
The articles may, however, provide an additional method of
removal, e.g. by extraordinary resolution. If so, the members may
use the statutory procedures or the additional method provided
by the articles to remove a director.

The statutory procedures on removal are designed primarily to
ensure that a simple majority of the members have the power to
remove a director. This is a crucial safeguard for the members
who would otherwise have little or no control over the directors.
The statutory procedures also ensure that directors are given a
fair chance to defend themselves against any proposal to remove
them as directors. Directors are not normally afforded similar
rights where an additional procedure is provided by the articles,
e.g. removal by extraordinary resolution.

Section 303 provides that the members in general meeting may
by ordinary resolution remove a director provided that special
notice of that resolution has been given in accordance with s. 379
(see **Precedents 23.11A** and **23.11B**). This statutory power
applies notwithstanding anything in the company's articles or in
any agreement between the company and the director. Special
notice is also required with respect to any resolution to appoint at
the same meeting another person instead of a director removed
under these statutory powers.

23.11.1 Director's right to protest removal (s. 304)

On receipt of a valid notice from a member, the company must
immediately send a copy of it to the director concerned (see
Precedent 23.11C) who is entitled to speak on the resolution at
the meeting, whether or not he or she is a member of the
company (s. 304(1)).

If the director makes written representations to the company in
connection with the resolution and requests their notification to
the members, the company must, unless the representations are
received too late for it to do so:

1. state in any notice of the resolution given to members that
   representations have been made; and
2. send a copy of the director's representations to every member
   entitled to receive notice of the meeting (s. 304(2)).

Special notice may be served on the company up to 28 days
before the meeting. The company may not have time to wait for
the director to make representations if it is to meet its 21-day

deadline for giving notice of the resolution to the members. If notice of the resolution has already been given or if there is not sufficient time to have the notice reprinted, the company need not comply with para. (1) above. However, even if notice of the resolution has already been sent, the company must still send a copy of the director's representations to each member (and bear the cost of doing so) unless it is impossible to deliver them to the members before the meeting.

If, for any reason, a copy of the director's representations is not sent to the members, the director may require them to be read out at the meeting. In these circumstances, the director still has a right to speak on the resolution at the meeting (s. 304(4)).

The company or any other person who claims to be aggrieved may apply to the court for an order that the director's representations should not be sent to members or read out at the meeting on the grounds that the director is abusing the rights conferred by s. 304 to secure needless publicity for defamatory matter (s. 304(4)).

It is possible to avoid the effect of s. 303. In *Bushell v. Faith* [1970] AC 1099, the articles of a company with three equal shareholders provided that in the event of a resolution being proposed at any general meeting of the company for the removal from office of any director, any shares held by that director shall on a poll in respect of such resolution carry the right to three votes per share. When two of the shareholders tried to remove Faith as a director he was therefore able to defeat the resolution by demanding a poll. It was held by the House of Lords that the article was valid and did not infringe s. 303. That section simply provides that a director may be removed by ordinary resolution. It does not prevent the articles giving a member weighted voting rights.

Part IV

Avoiding general meetings

Companies often view the requirement to hold general meetings as an unnecessary administrative burden. Many prepare minutes of meetings that have not actually taken place. This practice is known as holding a 'paper meeting', a name that gives it a false aura of legality. In fact, as no meeting has legally been held, the transactions recorded in the minutes are liable to challenge. In reality, a paper meeting may be no better than no meeting at all.

Decisions taken outside formal meetings may, however, sometimes be validated under the common law rule of unanimous consent. As its name implies, this rule only applies where all the members have approved the transaction. Although it is not necessary for the members to agree in writing, minutes of a paper meeting signed by all the members would be sufficient evidence for these purposes. However, the common law rule is subject to other limitations, and it is not always safe to rely on it (see **Chapter 24**).

It is not necessary for a private company to take these risks in any case. The Companies Act 1985 allows private companies to:

- pass resolutions without holding meetings, i.e. by written resolution (see **Chapter 24**); and
- dispense with the AGM (and other related formalities) under an elective regime (see **Chapter 25**).

24

Written resolutions and unanimous consent

24.1 Summary

- The Act makes special provision for private companies to act by written resolution (see **24.2**).
- Articles commonly make provision for the members to act by written resolution (see **24.3**).
- Under the common law, if all the members who would have been entitled to vote at a general meeting unanimously approve a proposal that they could have transacted at a meeting, it does not matter whether a formal resolution was put to the vote or that the requirements as to notice were not complied with or that the members did not give their assent at a meeting at which they were all present (see **24.4**).

24.2 Statutory written resolutions

A private company may be able to avoid holding a general meeting (or a class meeting) by using the statutory procedure for written resolutions set out in ss. 381A to 381C of the Act. The resolution must be signed by (or on behalf of) all the members who would have been entitled to vote at a general meeting (or class meeting) at the date of the resolution. This is a stringent requirement. One member can prevent the resolution being passed by written resolution by refusing to sign. This does not mean that the resolution cannot be passed at all. It could still be passed at a general meeting (or class meeting) if the necessary majority can be obtained.

A resolution agreed to as a written resolution in accordance with s. 381A has effect as if it was passed by the company in general meeting (or a meeting of the relevant class of members) and any reference in any statute to a meeting at which a resolution is passed or to members voting in favour of a resolution shall be construed accordingly (s. 381A(4)).

24.2.1 Resolutions that may be passed as written resolutions

Any matter that a private company may do by a resolution at a general meeting (or at a meeting of any class of members) may be done by written resolution (s. 381A). This includes anything required by statute or the company's articles to be done by an ordinary, extraordinary, special or elective resolution. The only exception to this rule is that a written resolution cannot be used to pass:

- a resolution under s. 303 removing a director before the expiry of his or her period of office; and
- a resolution under s. 391 removing an auditor before the expiry of his or her term of office (s. 381A(7) and Part 1 of Schedule 15A).

It is not possible to hold an AGM by written resolution. The Act requires a meeting to be held (s. 366). It should also be noted that a written resolution cannot be used to lay the accounts. In order to comply with the requirements of s. 241, a general meeting must be held. Strictly speaking, it is not necessary for the members to approve or adopt the accounts to comply with s. 241 (although it is common practice to put such a resolution to the meeting). A company that lays its accounts at a general meeting will have complied with s. 241 even if the accounts are not approved by the members, either because a vote on a resolution to adopt them was lost or no such resolution was put to the meeting. It is, of course, open to a private company to dispense with holding AGMs and the laying of the accounts by passing an elective resolution to that effect (see **Chapter 25**).

24.2.2 Special rules for certain resolutions passed as written resolutions

Part II of Schedule 15A lists a number of resolutions which cannot be passed as a written resolution unless the company has furnished members with certain documents or information. If such a resolution is to be proposed as a written resolution, the relevant documents must be sent with or attached to the copy of the written resolution given to each member to sign. A copy must also be sent to the company's auditors (s. 390(2)(a)). Matters subject to these special rules are as follows:

- a resolution under s. 95(2) regarding disapplication of pre-emption rights;
- a resolution giving approval under s. 155(4) or (5) for financial assistance for purchase of company's own shares or those of holding company;
- a resolution conferring authority to make an off-market purchase of the company's own shares under s. 164(2);
- a resolution conferring authority to vary a contract for an off-market purchase of the company's own shares under s. 164(7);

- a resolution varying, revoking or renewing any authority under s. 164(3);
- a resolution giving approval under s. 173(2) for the redemption or purchase of company's own shares out of capital;
- a resolution approving any such term as is mentioned in s. 319(1) (director's contract of employment for more than five years); and
- a resolution under s. 337(3)(a) to fund a director's expenditure in performing his or her duties.

24.2.3 No notice required

A written resolution may be used to pass a resolution without complying with the requirements as to notice which would apply if it were proposed at a general meeting. Effectively, no notice need be given and there is no need for the members to sign any form of consent to short notice. This is logical because, by signing the written resolution, the members effectively indicate their consent to the use of a procedure that does not require prior notice to be given.

24.2.4 Form of written resolution

To pass a written resolution, a copy of the full text of the resolution must be signed by or on behalf of all the members who at the date of the resolution would be entitled to attend and vote at a general meeting (or meeting of the relevant class of members). It is not necessary for the members' signatures to be on a single document. The members may sign separate documents provided that each document accurately states the terms of the resolution (s. 381A(2)). In practice, this means that the wording of the resolution on each document should be identical. The form of words that precede the substantive resolution should make it clear that the resolution is being proposed as a written resolution under the statutory procedures (see **Precedent 24.2A** for a members resolution, **Precedent 24.2B** for a written resolution of a class of members).

24.2.5 Copy to auditors

If a director or secretary of a company knows that it is proposed to seek agreement to a resolution in accordance with s. 381A and knows the terms of the resolution, he or she shall, if the company has auditors, secure that a copy of the resolution is sent to them (see **Precedent 24.2C**) or that they are otherwise notified of its contents, at or before the time the resolution is supplied to a member for signature (s. 381B(1)). Failure to do so does not affect the validity of any resolution (s. 381B(4)). However, the directors and the secretary will be liable to a fine unless they can prove that the circumstances were such that it was not practicable to comply with this requirement or that they believed on reasonable grounds that a copy of the resolution had been sent to the company's auditors or that the auditors had otherwise been informed of its contents.

Section 381B used to require a copy of any intended written resolution to be sent to the company's auditors. It also provided that the resolution would not be effective unless and until:

- the auditors notify the company that the resolution does not concern them as auditors or that, although it does concern them as auditors, it need not be considered by the company in general meeting (or by a meeting of the relevant class of members); or
- a period of seven days has elapsed since the auditors received the copy of the resolution and they have not given notice that in their opinion the resolution should be considered at a general or class meeting (s. 381B).

These requirements were repealed by the Deregulation (Resolutions of Private Companies) Order 1996 which substituted a new s. 381B in the Act.

24.2.6   Company with no auditors

The new s. 381B only imposes a duty on the directors and secretary to send a copy of a proposed written resolution to the auditors where the company has auditors. A company may not have auditors because it is a new company which has not yet appointed auditors or it is a dormant company which has dispensed with the appointment of auditors under s. 250. This has clarified a failing of the old s. 381B which made no provision for companies without auditors.

24.2.7   Date written resolution passed

A written resolution will be regarded as passed on the date on which the resolution is signed by (or on behalf of) the last member to sign (s. 381A(3) and (5) as amended by the Deregulation (Resolutions of Private Companies) Order 1996). Previously, a written resolution was not effective unless and until the auditors had notified the company that the resolution need not be considered at a general meeting (or class meeting) or had failed to respond within seven days of receipt of a copy of the resolution.

24.2.8   Filing requirements

The requirement to file copies of certain resolutions at Companies House applies even though they have been passed as written resolutions (see **12.6**).

24.2.9   Record of written resolution

A record of any written resolution (and of the signatures) must be entered in the company's minute book for general meetings. Any such record signed by a director or the secretary is evidence of the passing of the resolution (s. 382A) (see **Precedent 24.3**).

24.2.10   Single member company

The statutory procedures for written resolutions will be particularly useful for private limited companies with only one member. Before the procedures were amended, it was often quicker to pass a resolution at a general meeting called at short notice than to use the written resolution procedures because of the need to wait up to seven days after the auditors received their copy of the resolution before it took effect. However, there is now nothing to be gained from holding a formal meeting of the sole member and written resolutions will almost certainly become the standard method of decision-making. The directors and the secretary should, of course, send a copy of the proposed resolution to the auditors before the sole member signs it or ensure that they are notified in some other way of its contents.

24.3   Written resolutions under powers in articles of association

Many companies' articles contain a clause that provides a procedure for written resolutions of the members. For example, reg. 53 of Table A states:

> **53.** A resolution in writing executed by or on behalf of each member who would have been entitled to vote upon it if it had been proposed at a general meeting at which he was present shall be as effectual as if it had been passed at a general meeting duly convened and held and may consist of several instruments in the like form executed by or on behalf of one or more members.

Section 381C states that the statutory procedures for written resolutions have effect notwithstanding any provision of the company's memorandum or articles, but do not prejudice any power conferred by any such provision. This means that a private company may pass a written resolution in accordance with ss. 381A to 381B even if its articles require a meeting to be held. It may also mean that a private company can pass a written resolution in accordance with the statutory procedures or in accordance with any valid provision in its memorandum or articles of association.

As the statutory procedures have now been relaxed, there will usually be little to be gained from using the procedures specified by the articles. Indeed, it is probably safer to use the statutory procedures. There has always been a question mark over the validity of written resolutions passed in accordance with the articles where the Act requires notice of the resolution to be accompanied by other documents (see above) or special notice of the resolution is required. These matters are dealt with under the statutory procedures, although it is not possible under those procedures to pass a resolution to remove a director or the auditors before the conclusion of their period of office. It should also be noted that articles like reg. 53 of Table A merely restate the position under the common law as to informal agreement. The only difference is that the agreement of the members to the resolution under provisions contained in the articles must be evidenced in writing. It probably follows that any provision in the Act that defeats the common law rule will also defeat a provision in the articles (see **24.4**).

Public companies cannot pass written resolutions under ss. 381A to 381C. However, many have a provision in their articles similar to reg. 53 of Table A, in which case the same caveats will apply to the use of those procedures. In practice, it is virtually impossible for most public companies to secure the agreement of all their members to a proposal and this question will only be of interest to those that are closely held.

24.3.1   Signature by a smaller proportion of members

The Act requires special, extraordinary and elective resolutions and resolutions requiring special notice to be passed at general meetings. Even where it requires something to be done by ordinary resolution, it often specifies that this must be done at a general meeting, e.g. s. 80 (authority to allot shares) and s. 385 (annual appointment of auditors). The common law rule on informal consent is that the members must comply with the requirements of the Act unless all those who are entitled to vote at a general meeting have assented to the proposal (see *EBM Co. Ltd v. Dominion Bank* [1937] 3 All ER 555). Articles on written resolutions can be viewed as a slightly more formal codification of this rule. The articles cannot exclude the operation of the Act unless the Act allows. The articles could not therefore provide a procedure for written resolutions that does not require the agreement of all the members entitled to vote at a general meeting (e.g. require the signature of members holding only 90% of the voting shares). The fact that s. 381C now states that the statutory procedures for written resolutions do not prejudice any power conferred by the articles in that regard, does not mean that any provision in the articles will be valid. All it means is that any provision that was valid before the statutory procedures were introduced will still be valid. The only possible exception to this principle would be on a resolution to approve something that was not required to be done in a particular way by the Act but by the articles, e.g. the appointment of directors or the issue of instructions by the members to the directors. In fact, articles of joint venture companies often provide for a type of written resolution procedure for the appointment of directors by each of the members. In such cases, a member holding less than 50% of the shares may be able to appoint a specified number of directors by giving notice in writing to the company.

24.4   Unanimous consent rule

Under the common law rule of unanimous consent, the members may act informally without holding a meeting if they unanimously approve the transaction in some other manner, whether in writing or orally. In *Re Express Engineering Works Ltd* [1920] 1 Ch. 466, five directors, who were the only shareholders of the company, resolved at a board meeting to purchase some property from a syndicate in which they each had an interest. The company's articles disqualified directors from voting on any contract in which they were interested. The liquidator subsequently sought to have the transaction set aside on the basis that the directors were precluded from voting and that the members were only capable of acting at a properly constituted general meeting. The Court of Appeal held that although the meeting was referred to in the minutes as a board meeting, the unanimous informal consent of the five as the members of the company was capable of binding the company.

Provided all the members assent and the transaction is within the company's powers, the members may assent at different times (*Parker & Cooper v. Reading* [1926] Ch. 975).

In *Cane v. Jones* [1981] 1 All ER 533, it was held that an agreement signed by all the shareholders that the chairman should cease to be entitled to use his casting vote, had the same effect as a special resolution altering the articles to that effect, and it was immaterial that the statutory obligation to file such resolutions had not been complied with.

The fact that the informal consent of members must be unanimous was emphasised in *EBM Co. Ltd v. Dominion Bank* [1937] 3 All ER 555. In this case, there were five shareholders, three of whom held over 99% of the shares. The other two shareholders had one share each. A resolution of the three major shareholders was held not to bind the company in relation to security given to a bank for a loan despite the fact that the other two holdings were insignificant.

24.4.1   Exceptions

Generally speaking, it is not a good idea to rely on the unanimous consent rule as a routine method of decision making. It is, for example, infinitely preferable for a private company to act by written resolution in accordance with the statutory provisions (see **24.2**). The courts tend to apply the rule to rectify defects in the decision-making process in owner-managed companies that arise out of ignorance of the proper procedures. They also tend not to look too kindly on its deliberate use. For example, the courts will not apply the rule so as to enable the members to do something they would not have been able to do at a meeting (*Re New Cedos Engineering Co. Ltd* [1994] 1 BCLC 797).

In addition, they will not necessarily apply the rule where legislation requires certain formalities to be carried out in order for the resolution to be effective. The general approach of the courts in this regard appears to be that the rule will not apply where these formalities cannot be waived by the current members or where the formalities are designed to protect third parties. However, it is not always easy to predict how the courts will apply these general principles.

In *Re Duomatic Ltd* [1969] 1 All ER 161, directors' salaries were paid without being authorised by a resolution of the shareholders as required by the articles. It was held that the agreement of the two directors who held all the voting shares amounted to an informal ratification of the payment of unauthorised salaries even though they had never constituted themselves as a shareholders' meeting. The fact that they had not informed or sought the agreement of the sole holder of the company's preference shares had no bearing because all that was required was the unanimous agreement of the members entitled to vote. However, the court came to a different conclusion in the same case in relation to a payment made to a director for loss of office because statute required particulars of the proposed payment to be disclosed to the members and no such disclosure had taken place with regard to the preference shareholder.

It has been held that the principle does not apply to approval of a contract for a purchase of shares under s. 164 (*R.W. Peak (Kings Lynn) Ltd* [1998] 1 BCLC 193) and doubt has been expressed whether the principle would apply in relation to a resolution to approve a substantial property transaction with a director under s. 320 (*Demite Ltd v. Protec Health Ltd* [1998] BCC 638). In *Re Barry Artist plc* [1985] BCLC 283, the court confirmed a reduction in capital which had been agreed informally by all the members with 'great reluctance' and warned that this procedure would not be accepted in future reductions.

By contrast, in *Atlas Wright (Europe) Ltd v. Wright* [1999] 2 BCLC 301, the principle was applied to uphold approval of a service agreement under s. 319. And, in *Re Torvale Group Ltd* [1999] 2 BCLC 605, it was applied to prevent a transaction from exceeding a limitation of directors' powers and being voidable under s. 322A.

24.5   Single member companies

The sole member of a private limited company may, of course, make a decision that binds the company without holding a formal meeting at any time. The Act provides that where a sole member takes any decision that may be taken by the company in general meeting, he or she shall (unless the decision is taken by way of written resolution) provide the company with a written record of that decision (s. 382B(1)) (see **Precedent 24.5**). A sole member who fails to comply with this requirement will be liable to a fine (s. 382B(2)). However, failure to comply will not invalidate the decision of the sole member (s. 382B(3)).

Whether it is advisable for the sole member to adopt this informal method for all purposes is open to question. The consultative document which preceded the regulations amending the Act in 1992 stated that s. 382B was intended to deal with the types of decision the courts have held may be taken by the members unanimously without the need for a formal meeting of the company or a written resolution. It would seem, therefore, that informal decisions should not be used for matters such as a reduction of capital where the Act specifies formalities. Informal decisions can, however, be used for passing ordinary resolutions and, it seems, changing the articles.

It will always be safer for the sole member of a private limited company to make decisions using the statutory procedures for written resolutions and there is no real advantage in using the informal arrangements in view of the recent amendments to the statutory procedures (see **24.2**).

25

Elective regime

25.1 Summary

- A private company may elect to dispense with the AGM and other related formalities. This must be done by passing an elective resolution in accordance with the requirements of s. 379A (see **25.2**).
- A private company can pass an elective resolution to:
  - dispense with holding AGMs (s. 366A) (see **25.3**);
  - dispense with the laying of accounts and reports before general meetings (s. 252) (see **25.4**);
  - dispense with the annual appointment of auditors (s. 386) (see **25.5**);
  - extend the period for which the general meeting may authorise the directors to allot shares under s. 80 of CA 1985 (s. 80A) (see **25.6**); or
  - reduce the majority required to authorise short notice of meetings (s. 369(4) and s. 378(3)) (see **25.7**).

25.2 Elective resolutions

It is possible to pass an elective resolution relating to some or all of the above dispensations. However, there is very little to be gained from dispensing with AGMs without electing to dispense with the requirement to lay the accounts or the annual appointment of auditors. In these circumstances, a general meeting would need to be held each year to comply with these requirements. On the other hand, it may not be necessary to extend the period for which the general meeting may authorise the directors to allot shares in order to avoid holding general meetings. Authority (if it is required) can already be granted for up to five years. Similarly, reducing from 95% to 90% the majority required to authorise short notice of meetings may be pointless if each member of the company holds more than 10% of the shares.

The procedural requirements for passing an elective resolution to dispense with any of the above requirements are set out in s. 379A of the Companies Act 1985. The resolution will not be effective unless it is agreed to at a general meeting, in person or by proxy, by all the members entitled to attend and vote at the meeting. It should be stressed that this means all the members and not just those who attend the meeting. If one member fails to vote, the resolution will not be valid. This is clearly an onerous requirement. The majority required to pass other types of resolution is based on a percentage of those actually voting.

At least 21 days' notice must be given in writing or by electronic communications of the intention to propose such a resolution as an elective resolution at a general meeting of the company and the terms of the resolution must be given in full in the notice of the meeting. Formerly, it was not possible to pass an elective resolution at short notice. This has now been changed by the Deregulation (Resolutions of Private Companies) Order 1996 which inserted a new subsection 2A in s. 379A which provides that an elective resolution shall be effective notwithstanding the fact that less than 21 days' notice in writing of the meeting has been given if all the members entitled to attend and vote at the meeting so agree.

25.2.1 Passing an elective resolution by written resolution

Even if all the members support a proposal to pass an elective resolution, it may be difficult to bring them all together at a meeting to approve the resolution. Fortunately, it is possible to pass an elective resolution without holding a meeting using the statutory procedures for written resolutions set out in ss. 381A to 381C (see above and **Precedent 25.2A**). No notice need be given when passing a resolution in this manner. Therefore it is not necessary for the members to consent to short notice.

25.2.2 Revocation of elective resolution

Circumstances may change after the company passes an elective resolution which may cause a member to wish to reverse the decision permanently or to suspend its operation. The members may at any time revoke an elective resolution by passing an ordinary resolution to that effect at a general meeting of the company (s. 379(3)) (see **Precedent 25.2B**). A number of other safeguards exist to protect the interest of members of a company that has elected to dispense with the holding of AGMs, the laying of accounts and the annual reappointment of auditors (see below). These safeguards can be invoked by any member and have the effect of temporarily suspending the operation of the elective resolution.

25.2.3   Filing requirement

A copy of any elective resolution (and any subsequent ordinary resolution to revoke it) must be sent to the Registrar of Companies within 15 days of it being passed. It used to be necessary for a private company to state whether an elective resolution is in force to dispense with AGMs or to dispense with the laying of accounts on its annual return. However, this requirement has now been abolished.

25.3   Dispensing with the AGM

An elective resolution under s. 366A to dispense with AGMs (see **Precedent 25.3A**) has effect for the year in which it was made and subsequent years. However, it will have no effect on any liability already incurred for failing to hold an AGM in the time allowed. In other words, the elective resolution must be passed before the AGM becomes due or an offence will have been committed.

25.3.1   Notice requiring AGM

If an elective resolution to dispense with AGMs is in force (and an AGM has not been held in that year), any member may require a meeting to be held by giving notice to the company not later than three months before the end of the year (see **Precedent 25.3B**). A company that receives such a notice on any date between 1 January and 30 September must hold an AGM before the end of the year. If it fails to do so, the default provisions of s. 366(4) will apply. It should be noted that in such circumstances the elective resolution continues to be in force. Thus, the company would not need to hold an AGM in the following year unless required to do so again under these procedures or the elective resolution has subsequently been revoked in accordance with s. 379A(3) by an ordinary resolution of the company in general meeting.

If an elective resolution dispensing with AGMs is revoked by passing an ordinary resolution to that effect, the company must hold an AGM before the end of the calendar year in which the ordinary resolution was passed unless it was passed after 30 September, in which case it must start holding AGMs the following year (s. 366A(5)).

Where an elective resolution is in force to dispense with AGMs, members may now exercise their right to require the company to hold an AGM by sending an electronic notification to an address specified for that purpose by or on behalf of the company (s. 366A(3A)). If the company does not specify an address for this purpose, the notice must be given in writing (see **2.5** regarding the meaning of electronic communications).

25.4   Dispensing with the laying of accounts

If a resolution to dispense with AGMs is to serve any practical purpose, it should be accompanied by a resolution to dispense with the laying of accounts before the members in general meeting, otherwise a general meeting will need to be called each year to lay the accounts (see **Precedent 25.4A**). An election under s. 252 to dispense with the laying of accounts and reports has effect in relation to the accounts and reports of the financial year in which the resolution was passed and subsequent financial years. Thus, if the company has not already done so, it must still lay the accounts of the previous financial year before the company in general meeting. To avoid confusion among the members, it is probably best to propose this and any other elective resolutions at the meeting (preferably the AGM) at which accounts for the previous financial year are laid.

A company that has elected to dispense with the laying of accounts and reports must still prepare accounts and send copies to anyone entitled to receive them under s. 238. Copies must be sent not less than 28 days before the end of the period allowed for laying and delivering accounts and reports, i.e. for a private company, ten months less 28 days after the end of the company's accounting reference period. They must be accompanied, in the case of accounts sent to members of the company, by a notice informing them of their right to require the laying of the accounts and reports before a general meeting (s. 253(1)) (see **Precedent 25.4B**).

25.4.1   Member may require accounts to be laid

While an elective resolution dispensing with the laying of accounts is in force any member may require the company to hold a general meeting for the purpose of laying the accounts and reports (s. 253(2)). A member must deposit at the company's registered office notice in writing to that effect (see **Precedent 25.4C**) 'before the end of the period of 28 days beginning with the day on which the accounts are sent out', e.g. if the accounts were sent out on 1 July, not later than 29 July. If, within 21 days of the date of deposit of the notice, the directors do not proceed to convene a general meeting to be held within three months of the date of deposit, the person who deposited the notice may convene a meeting. In such circumstances, the member who convenes the meeting is entitled to recover from the company any reasonable expenses incurred and the company can recoup these from any outstanding or future fees or other remuneration due to the directors.

Where an elective resolution is in force to dispense with the laying of accounts, the members or the auditors may now exercise their right to require the company to lay the accounts by sending an electronic notification to an address specified for that purpose by or on behalf of the company (s. 253(2A)). If the company does not specify an address for this purpose, the notice must be given in writing (see **2.5** regarding the meaning of electronic communications).

Copies of the accounts sent to members must be accompanied by a notice informing them of their rights under s. 253(2).

25.5 Dispensing with the requirement to appoint auditors annually

Under s. 385, auditors must be appointed at the general meeting at which accounts are laid (normally the AGM). Clearly, it is impossible to comply with this requirement if the company has passed an elective resolution dispensing with the requirement to lay the report and accounts. In those circumstances, s. 385A applies and the company must appoint auditors at a general meeting held within 28 days of the date on which copies of the company's annual accounts for the previous year are sent to members. Thus a company that has elected to dispense with AGMs and the laying of the accounts and reports, but not the requirement to appoint auditors annually, must hold a meeting to appoint auditors shortly after sending its accounts to the members. This requirement would, to say the least, be unduly burdensome and it would be unusual for a company not to take advantage also of s. 386 which allows a private company to elect to dispense with the requirement to appoint auditors annually (see **Precedent 25.5A**).

When a resolution is passed to dispense with the annual appointment of auditors, the company's auditors are deemed to have been reappointed for each succeeding financial year on the expiry of the time for appointing auditors. If the election is revoked in accordance with s. 379A, the auditors holding office at that time continue to hold office until either the conclusion of the next general meeting of the company at which accounts are laid or, if an elective resolution is still in force dispensing with the requirement to lay accounts, the expiry of the period for appointing auditors.

25.5.1 Termination of appointment of auditors not appointed annually

Usually, members have an opportunity to vote against the reappointment of the auditors at the general meeting at which accounts are laid. If the majority are opposed to their reappointment, the auditors will be removed. It should be noted that this gives the members an opportunity each year to remove the auditors without having to comply with the requirements as to special notice. Special notice is required where the auditors being proposed for appointment are not the same as those appointed previously by the members.

Where an elective resolution not to appoint auditors annually is in force, the Act provides a special procedure which allows members to vote not to reappoint auditors who would otherwise be reappointed automatically. In such circumstances, any member of the company may deposit notice in writing at the company's registered office proposing that the appointment of the company's auditors be 'brought to an end'. No member may deposit more than one such notice in any financial year of the company (s. 393(1)). On receipt of such a notice, the directors have a duty to convene a general meeting of the company for a date not more than 28 days after the date on which the notice was given, and to propose at that meeting a resolution in a form enabling the company to decide whether the appointment of the company's auditors should be 'brought to an end'.

If the decision of the company at the meeting is that the appointment of the auditors should be 'brought to an end', the auditors shall not be deemed to be reappointed when next they would be and, if the notice was deposited within the period immediately following the distribution of the accounts (i.e. the period beginning with the day on which copies of the company's annual accounts are sent to the members under s. 238 and ending 14 days after that day), any deemed reappointment for the financial year following that to which those accounts relate which has already occurred shall cease to have effect (s. 393(2)).

If the directors fail to convene a meeting in accordance with these requirements within 14 days of the date of the deposit, the member (or members) who deposited the notice may convene the meeting themselves for a date which must be no later than three months after the date of deposit (s. 393(4)). They must convene the meeting in the same manner as that in which meetings are to be convened by directors (s. 393(5)) and are entitled to be paid any reasonable expenses they incur in doing so (s. 393(6)).

This section does not prevent a member requisitioning a meeting to propose a resolution to remove the auditors in accordance with s. 391. Special notice of such a resolution must be given. The resolution proposed at a meeting requisitioned under s. 393 need only be framed so that the auditors' appointment shall be brought to an end when they would next be deemed reappointed, etc. (e.g. to propose that the appointment of the company's auditors be brought to an end in accordance with the provisions of s. 393).

The directors could propose a resolution to remove the auditors immediately. However, to do so, they would have to comply with the requirements of s. 390. The notice given by the member under s. 393 does not constitute the first limb of the special notice requirements of s. 379.

25.5.2 Resignation of auditors while elective resolution in force

If an auditor resigns while the elective regime is in force, the directors may fill the vacancy under s. 388(1). The new auditor will, it seems, be automatically reappointed from year to year by virtue of s. 386(2). Alternatively the appointment could be effected by a resolution of the members under s. 388(1). This would, however, require special notice of the resolution under s. 388(3). An EGM could be called to deal with the matter or the resolution could be passed as a written resolution under s. 381A.

25.5.3   Auditors' remuneration

Under s. 390A, the remuneration of auditors appointed by the directors as first auditors or to fill a casual vacancy must be fixed by the directors. When auditors are appointed (or reappointed) by the company in general meeting, their remuneration must be fixed by the company in general meeting or in such manner as the company in general meeting may determine. However, while an elective resolution dispensing with the annual appointment of auditors is in force under s. 386, the auditors are deemed to have been reappointed each year. Section 386 does not say who, if anyone, should be assumed to have reappointed them and s. 390A does not state how the auditors' remuneration should be fixed while the resolution is in force.

It is recommended that immediately after passing a resolution to dispense with the annual appointment of auditors, a resolution be passed authorising the directors to fix the remuneration of the auditors until such time as a resolution to appoint auditors is proposed at a general meeting of the company (see **Precedent 25.4B**). This may be necessary where the company in general meeting has been in the habit of fixing the auditors' remuneration itself or placing a cap on the amount that can be paid to the auditors or the previous resolution regarding auditors' remuneration was expressed in such a manner that it relates only to the financial year in which it was passed.

25.6   Extending the period of the directors' authority to allot shares

The directors cannot allot new shares unless they have been given authority to do so in accordance with the requirements of s. 80. Under s. 80(4), the maximum period for which authority can be given is five years. If required, this authority is usually renewed at the AGM. In normal circumstances, it follows that a private company that has dispensed with AGMs and wishes to renew the directors' authority would need to call a general meeting. It can, however, avoid doing so by passing an elective resolution in accordance with s. 379A stating that the provisions of s. 80A shall apply, instead of the provisions of s. 80(4) and (5), in relation to the giving or renewal of authority to allot shares (see **Precedent 25.6A**). The provisions of s. 80A allow authority to be given to the directors by ordinary resolution for an indefinite period or for a fixed period longer than the five-year maximum allowed under s. 80 (see **Precedent 25.6B**).

In order to extend the period in this manner, it is therefore necessary to pass two resolutions in the following order:

- an elective resolution stating that the provisions of s. 80A shall apply, instead of the provisions of s. 80(4) and (5), in relation to the giving or renewal of authority to allot shares; and
- an ordinary resolution authorising the directors to allot shares or other securities, specifying the maximum amount of shares or other securities that may be allotted under it and the period to which the authority relates.

Any authority given in this manner (including an authority contained in the articles) may be revoked or varied by an ordinary resolution of the company in general meeting (s. 80A(3)).

25.7 Election as to the majority required to authorise short notice of a meeting

This is perhaps the least useful of the dispensations available to private companies. It allows the majority required to authorise the holding of an EGM at short notice to be reduced from 95% to as low as 90% (s. 369(4)) and allows the majority required to authorise a special resolution to be proposed at short notice to be similarly reduced (see **Precedent 25.7**).

No advantage will be gained from passing an elective resolution along these lines if each shareholder owns more than 10% of the voting shares. In these circumstances, the agreement of all the members would still be required to hold a meeting at short notice because a majority of 90% could not be achieved if any member withheld consent. It must also be doubtful whether a member or members holding between 5% and 10% of the shares would vote in favour of a resolution that clearly undermines their rights. Nevertheless, there may be occasions when these relaxations may be helpful, e.g. where the company's shares are held in different names but are beneficially owned by the same person.

The elective resolution must specify the percentage that is to be substituted for the percentage in the two relevant sections. This percentage may be any figure that is less than 95% but not lower than 90%.

Part V

Minutes

The Act requires minutes to be kept of general meetings and meetings of directors. Although this may, at times, seem a burdensome requirement, it is the company that stands to benefit if it is done properly. This is because minutes signed by the chairman are deemed to be evidence of the proceedings. In other words, if the company produces a set of minutes signed by the chairman, those minutes are taken as evidence that the meeting actually took place properly and as evidence of the decisions taken at that meeting. Unless other evidence to the contrary is submitted during legal proceedings, the company will not need to tender any other evidence in support of the minutes.

Because the primary purpose of the minutes is to provide evidence of the decisions taken, it is essential that minutes accurately record those decisions. As a rule of thumb, this means that they should contain sufficient information to enable a person who did not attend to ascertain what decisions were taken.

26

Minutes

26.1 Summary

- Directors have a statutory duty to ensure that minutes are kept of general meetings and meetings of directors (see **26.2**).
- It is not necessary for them to take or prepare the minutes themselves. This job normally falls to the company secretary (see **26.3**).
- Minutes should be kept securely in a minute book (see **26.4**).
- They are part of the statutory records of the company and must be retained permanently (see **26.5**).
- Minutes signed by the chairman will be prima-facie evidence of the proceedings at that meeting (see **26.6** and **26.7**).
- Once they have been signed they should not be amended (see **26.8**).
- Minutes of general meetings must be made available for inspection by the members and the auditors. Members do not have a right to inspect the minutes of board meetings (see **26.10**).
- Minutes should contain certain basic information and provide an accurate record of the proceedings. There are many ways of doing this and the style adopted will depend on the use to which they are put and the preferences of the directors and secretary (see **26.11**).
- Special rules apply to members' written resolutions (see **26.12**) and decisions taken by the sole member of a single member company (see **26.13**).

26.2 General duty to prepare and keep

Every company is required to produce and keep minutes of all proceedings at general meetings and meetings of directors and managers (s. 382(1)). The term 'general meetings' includes AGMs, EGMs and class meetings. See s. 259 of the Insolvency Act and rule 5.22 of the Insolvency Rules for meetings in insolvency.

It is logical to assume that the phrase 'meetings of directors' in

s. 382(1) includes committees of the board. However, in *Guinness plc v. Saunders* [1988] 2 All ER 940, the Court of Appeal held in relation to disclosure by directors of interests in contracts in accordance with s. 317 that 'a meeting of directors' does not include a committee of the board. It should be noted that for the purposes of s. 382, the phrase used is 'meetings of directors' and not 'a meeting of directors' as in s. 317. This, it is suggested, is sufficient to enable any court to distinguish the interpretation of the Court of Appeal, quite apart from the different context in which the words appear. In any case, most articles (including reg. 100 of Table A) state explicitly that the directors should keep minutes of committees of directors. In practice, where power to bind the company has been delegated to a committee, it will be necessary to keep minutes as evidence that transactions have been duly authorised. The requirement to keep minutes of committees of directors will apply even where a committee of only one director has been appointed. In this case, the minutes may take the form of a written record of decisions taken, signed by the director concerned.

26.3   Who should take the minutes?

Preparing minutes of company meetings is one of the company secretary's core duties. If the company secretary is not available, it normally falls to the deputy or assistant secretary to undertake the task. Although not good practice, there is nothing to prevent someone else performing these functions. The report of the Cadbury Committee states at para. 4.25: 'It should be standard practice for the company secretary to administer, attend and prepare minutes of board proceedings.' The ICSA's *Code on Good Boardroom Practice* also states:

> **9.** The company secretary should be responsible to the chairman for the proper administration of meetings of the company, the board and any committees thereof. To carry out this responsibility the company secretary should be entitled to be present at (or represented at) and prepare (or arrange for the preparation of) minutes of the proceedings of all such meetings.

The company secretary and the directors can be fined for any default by the company of the provisions of the Act relating to the maintenance of minutes (s. 382(5), s. 383(4) and s. 722(3)). Although the directors are responsible for ensuring that minutes are kept, it is difficult for anyone to contribute to the business of the meeting if they are also required to record the proceedings. It could also be argued that they lack the impartiality that the secretary can provide when drafting the minutes.

It is quite common for company secretaries to use an assistant to help take notes of the proceedings. This allows them to concentrate more on their advisory role during the meeting. It is also increasingly common for a recording of the meeting to be made to assist in the preparation of the minutes. This can be particularly helpful at AGMs where it is often difficult for the secretary to record all the names of speakers from the floor, and sometimes difficult to understand the meaning of their questions or statements. It should also be noted that transcripts and recordings of meetings can be called in evidence during legal proceedings to rebut the evidence of the minutes, and would have to be disclosed during the discovery process prior to those proceedings.

26.4   Minute books

Section 382 requires minutes to be entered in books kept for that purpose. However, s. 722 provides that any minute book required by the Act to be kept by the company may be kept either by making entries in bound books or 'by recording the entries in any other manner', provided in the latter case that adequate precautions are taken for guarding against falsification and for facilitating their discovery. Thus minutes may be typed or processed using a computer and included in a loose-leaf folder or pasted into a bound book.

26.4.1   Computerised records

According to s. 723, the words 'in any other manner' in s. 722(1) can include computer records provided that they are capable of being reproduced in a legible form. If minutes are kept on a computer they must still be signed by the chairman to be treated as evidence of the proceedings under s. 382(2). Any doubts over the admissibility of electronic signatures for these purposes have been removed by the Electronic Communications Act 2000 (see **2.8**). Accordingly, the chairman could apply his electronic signature to a file containing the minutes which could then be stored on a computer. As the security of the technique used to apply the electronic signature could have a bearing on the weight the courts give to the minutes, it would be preferable for the chairman to use the most modern cryptographic techniques to do this (see **2.8**).

Different considerations arise where it is proposed, for example, to scan manually signed minutes for retention in computerised form and to destroy the original paper copies. Where this is done, the electronic image may ultimately need to be tendered in evidence in court, as secondary evidence of the signature of the minutes and of their contents. To ensure that it is acceptable as evidence in this regard, it will be essential to follow the British Standards Institute's *Code of Practice for Legal Admissibility of Information Stored on Electronic Document Management Systems*.

If minutes are kept in computerised form, they must still be capable of being reproduced in legible form. This probably sounds simpler than it is in reality. The minutes must still be capable of being reproduced in legible form not just today but in 20 or 30 years' time. Ideally, whenever new computer systems or software are adopted, checks should be carried out to ensure that the files containing the minutes can still be read. If not, it may be possible to convert them into a readable format. However, if this is not possible (doing so could compromise the electronic signature), it may be necessary to retain the old hardware and software for ever.

26.4.2   Guarding against falsification

Minutes may not be acceptable as evidence if inadequate precautions have been taken to guard against falsification. In a judgment prior to the current legislation, a loose-leaf minute book was rejected on the basis that 'anyone wishing to do so . . . can take a number of leaves out and substitute any number of other leaves. It is a thing with which anyone disposed to be dishonest can easily tamper' (*Heart of Oaks Assurance Co. Ltd v. James Flower & Sons* [1936] 1 Ch. 76). Although the law now allows loose-leaf minute books, their content could easily be challenged if it could be proved that the security measures taken to guard against falsification were inadequate. In a more recent case, purported minutes of a directors' meeting were rejected as prima-facie evidence of the proceedings because it was impossible to tell from the document who had chaired the meeting or who had signed them (no other evidence was submitted on the matter), and because the document had never been kept in a minute book (*POW Services v. Clare* [1995] 2 BCLC 435).

Some or all of the following safeguards should be adopted where minutes are kept in minute books:

- sequential numbering of the minutes of each type of meeting, e.g. if the last minute of the first meeting of directors is numbered minute 20, the first minute of the second meeting of directors should be numbered minute 21 and so on;
- the chairman should initial every page;
- pages should be numbered sequentially on specially printed paper;
- when pasted into bound books, the chairman's signature and initials should start on the printed sheet and run on to the bound page;
- the minute book should be kept in a safe (preferably fireproof) with restricted access;
- a lockable binder should be used, particularly for minutes kept in a loose-leaf folder; and
- minutes of general meetings and board meetings should be kept in separate books or folders to prevent members (who are entitled

to inspect the minutes of general meetings) from gaining access to the minutes of meetings of directors and managers.

If copies of signed minutes are kept on microfiche or on a computerised document imaging system, the company should, at the very least, comply with the recommendations of the British Standards Institute for retaining documents in that form.

26.5 Retention of minutes

Minutes should be retained permanently, i.e. for at least the life of the company and possibly beyond in view of the provisions of s. 653(2) and reg. 32 of the Insolvency Regulations 1986. It is arguable whether it is necessary to keep the original signed copies if they have been microfilmed or recorded using a document imaging system (see **26.4**). However, most companies still do so.

26.6 Signature by chairman

Companies are given considerable leeway in the methods that they can adopt for approving the minutes and the ICSA's *Code on Good Boardroom Practice* recommends that boards should establish written procedures with regard to minutes of board meetings. Although minutes that have not been signed by the chairman may be admissible as evidence of the proceedings, they will certainly not be accorded the same weight.

26.6.1 General meetings

It is standard practice for the minutes of general meetings to be signed shortly after the meeting by the person who acted as the chairman of the meeting. This is often done at the first available board meeting so as to allow the other directors to make any comments but also so that an entry may be made in the board minutes to the effect that they were duly signed. If this procedure is followed, it is not necessary to seek the approval of the members at the next general meeting nor, indeed, to refer to the minutes of the previous meetings at all.

If the person who acted as the chairman of the meeting is unable or unwilling to sign the minutes, they should be signed by the chairman of the next general meeting.

If it is not possible to adopt this procedure, then the minutes should be read at the next general meeting (they cannot be taken as read unless all the members have received a copy) and a resolution put to the meeting that they be approved.

26.6.2 Meetings of directors

Board minutes are usually distributed in draft form to the directors for comment and signed by the chairman of the next succeeding board meeting. They are often included in the agenda papers for the meeting at which they are to be approved, particularly if any changes have been made to the first draft as a consequence of comments by directors. At the meeting, the minutes are usually taken as read and a motion is put recommending their adoption as a true and accurate record of the proceedings of the meeting to which they refer. If approved, they should be signed immediately by the chairman who need not have been present at the original meeting.

The chairman may, however, sign the minutes before the next succeeding meeting of the board and need not necessarily give the other directors an opportunity to comment on them. This will rarely be necessary and any chairman who follows this procedure should be prepared to explain to his fellow directors why he departed from the usual practice and expect to have the minutes scrutinised more closely than might normally be the case. If this procedure is followed and the directors disagree with the chairman's interpretation of the proceedings, they could pass a resolution to that effect which would be recorded in the minutes of that meeting. The minutes that were the subject of the disagreement should not be altered although it might be sensible for the secretary to make a marginal note in the original minutes cross-referring to the subsequent decision.

In the unlikely event that the chairman refuses to sign the minutes, it should be recorded in the minutes of the next meeting that they were approved as a true record by the other directors who were present at the original meeting, if that was the case.

26.7 Evidence

Minutes are evidence of the proceedings of the relevant meeting once they have been signed by the chairman of that meeting or by the chairman of the next succeeding meeting (s. 382(2)). However, they are only prima-facie (on their face) evidence of the proceedings (*Re Indian Zoedone Co.* (1884) 26 Ch. D. 70). Other evidence is admissible to show that they are not an accurate record (*Re Llanharry Hematite Iron Ore Co., Roney's Case* (1864) 4 De G.J. & Sm. 426) even if the articles state that they are to be taken as conclusive evidence without further proof (*Kerr v. Mottram* [1940] Ch. 657 and *Re Caratal (New) Mines Ltd* [1902] 2 Ch. 498).

26.8 Amendment

Alterations can be made to the minutes before they have been signed as an accurate record by the chairman. The directors may wish to amend the company secretary's original draft and may request the chairman to amend the draft that is put before them at the next board meeting. Once the minutes have been included in the papers for a board meeting, best practice dictates that they should be amended by longhand or typed entries on the original copy and each amendment should be initialled by the chairman before signing the minutes themselves. It may not be practical to follow precisely the same procedures where the minutes are to be kept on a computer and signed by the chairman electronically.

Alterations should not be made after the minutes have been signed by the chairman. If the directors present at a subsequent meeting disagree with a decision taken at a previous meeting that is properly recorded in signed minutes, they should pass a further resolution rescinding or amending their previous decision which should be recorded in the minutes of that meeting. Similarly, if it is discovered after the minutes have been signed that they are inaccurate, a further resolution should be passed and recorded in the minutes of the meeting at which the inaccuracy was raised.

Details that were not available at the meeting should not be inserted in the minutes, e.g. the date of a call (*Re Cawley & Co.* (1889) 42 Ch. D. 209). However, resolutions can be framed so that they allow a director or the secretary to action a matter that is contingent upon further details being available.

26.9   Record of attendance

There is no need to keep a separate record of attendance at either general or board meetings unless the articles so provide (see, for example, reg. 86 of the 1948 Act Table A). However, it is important to include sufficient details in the minutes to show that a quorum was present or, in the case of meetings of directors, that a disinterested quorum was present. It should also be clear from the minutes who chaired the meeting. This is normally done by adding the words 'chairman' or 'in the chair' next to the name of the relevant director. If someone other than a director chairs a general meeting, this should also be apparent from the minute referring to the election of the chairman.

Reg. 100 of Table A requires the names of the directors present at meetings (including general meetings) to be included in the minutes of that meeting. If a director attends for only part of a meeting, this should be recorded in the minutes, normally by annotating the list of directors present with the words such as 'for minutes 23 to 34 only'. By doing so, it should be clear whether or not a disinterested quorum was present throughout the meeting.

Although it is not necessary to record in the minutes of general meetings the names of the members present at the meeting, it is essential to record the numbers present. As reg. 100 of Table A requires the names of the directors present at general meetings to be recorded in the minutes (whether or not they are also members), care should be taken not to include the directors who are also members in the number of other members present.

26.10   Inspection of minutes

26.10.1   General meetings

The minutes of general meetings (s. 383(1)) and written resolutions agreed by the members (s. 382A(3)) must be kept at the company's registered office and be open to inspection by members of the company without charge. Inspection should be allowed for a minimum of two hours between 9am and 5pm on each business day (Companies (Inspection and Copying of Register, Indices and Documents) Regulations 1991 (SI 1991/1998)). Creditors and members of the public have no rights of inspection.

Members are entitled to be provided with copies of minutes of general meetings within seven days of making a request. The company may make a small charge to cover administrative expenses subject to a maximum established by statutory instrument (currently 10p per 100 words). In practice, companies rarely levy the charge unless a member requests a large number of copies.

If the company wrongly refuses to allow an inspection or fails to provide copies of the minutes within the proper time, it and any responsible officer can be fined. In such circumstances, the court may order an immediate inspection or direct that the desired copies be sent.

Members are entitled to be accompanied by an adviser when they inspect the minutes of general meetings (*McCrusker v. McRae*, 1966 SC 253).

26.10.2   Meetings of directors

It is standard practice to distribute copies of the minutes to the directors before the next meeting or with the papers for the next succeeding meeting. In addition, however, directors have a common law right to inspect the minutes and to be accompanied by an adviser when they do so (*McCrusker v. McRae*, 1966 SC 253).

Members, creditors and members of the public are not entitled to inspect nor to take copies of the minutes of meetings of directors or managers.

26.10.3   By auditors

The auditors have a right of access to all books and such information and explanations necessary for the performance of their duties as auditors. This includes the minutes of general meetings, board meetings and any committees of the board. The auditors' letter of engagement will normally make some reference to the obligation of the company to make these records available for inspection.

26.11   Content and style

Different people often have different views about what took place at a meeting. These views tend to become even more polarised as those present become blessed with the benefit of hindsight. There is little point holding formal meetings if no one can remember what was decided at the meeting. The decisions taken must be recorded and those present should confirm that the record properly reflects what was decided. Preparing minutes is therefore an essential part of the decision-making process. It is also something of an art.

The secretary is expected to be psychic. Matters are decided without being expressed verbally. Individuals signal their agreement by gestures that would tax the most experienced auctioneer. Issues are discussed that no one expects to be included in the minutes. The chairman does not follow the order of the agenda. The meeting will spend hours on trivial matters which are expected to be minuted in great detail and then gallop through the most important items. Despite all this, the secretary is expected to make sense of the meeting and produce in a timely manner (i.e. by tomorrow morning) an accurate and clear set of minutes. To cap it all, although everyone expects the minutes to record what they said in great detail, they also expect them to be concise.

The art of preparing minutes is not simply doing so concisely, accurately and clearly in the shortest possible time, although achieving these objectives requires a degree of aptitude. It is knowing when to sacrifice or adapt these principles. Egos must be soothed. Detailed explanations may sometimes be required. On other occasions, brevity will be the only way to avoid opening old wounds.

Thus, although certain conventions are normally followed, the presentational style can be tailored. The preferences of the chairman will usually be the most influential. What can never be compromised, however, is the principle that the minutes should contain an accurate record of the decisions taken.

Although the minutes should represent a true and accurate record of the proceedings of the meeting, it is neither necessary, nor is it desirable, to include a transcript of the proceedings. According to ICSA's *Code of Good Boardroom Practice* (1991), they should 'record the decisions taken and provide sufficient background to those decisions'. Many different styles of presentation may be adopted provided that the minutes include the following basic elements:

- name of the company;
- type of meeting, e.g. AGM or audit committee;
- place where the meeting was held;
- day and date of the meeting (it is not necessary to include the time);

- names and/or numbers present (see **26.9**);
- record of the proceedings; and
- chairman's signature.

The record of the proceedings should include the text of any resolutions put to the meeting and the result of any vote. It should also include a record of any amendments and procedural resolutions proposed at the meeting and the results of any vote on them. Any rulings made by the chairman should be recorded, e.g. on a demand for a poll. If a resolution is passed on a show of hands it is only necessary to state that the chairman declared the resolution carried. If a poll is called and taken, the number of votes for and against should be included in the minutes together with a statement as to whether the resolution was or was not carried (see **Precedent 26.11A**).

All papers presented at the meeting should be clearly identified in the minutes (see minute 77 of **Precedent 26.11C**) and retained for reference. In the interests of brevity, it is possible to refer in the minutes to papers presented at the meeting that contain the detailed proposals, rather than reproduce the proposals in full. Any such document should be initialled by the chairman for the purpose of identification and the minutes should record that fact. However, it should be noted that minutes are not user-friendly at the best of times and it will not help matters if readers have to make continuous reference to other documents in order to discern what decisions were taken. In addition, documents that are essential in order to understand the record of decisions taken in the minutes should be retained in the same way and for as long as the minutes themselves.

26.12   Written resolutions

Where a written resolution is agreed to in accordance with s. 381A, a record of the resolution (and of the signatures) should be entered in the minute book in the same way as minutes of proceedings at general meetings (s. 382A(1)) (see **Precedent 26.3**). Any such record, if purporting to be signed by a director of the company or the company secretary, is evidence of the proceedings in agreeing to the resolution. Where a record is made in accordance with s. 382A, until the contrary is proved, the requirements of the Act with respect to those proceedings are deemed to be complied with (s. 382A(2)).

26.13   Informal decisions by a sole member

Where a private company has only one member and that member takes any decision that may be taken by the company in general meeting and which has effect as if agreed by the company in general meeting, he or she shall (unless that decision is taken by way of a written resolution) provide the company with a written record of that decision (s. 382B) (see **Precedent 24.5**). Failure to do so renders the sole member liable to a fine but does not invalidate the decision (s. 382B(2) and (3)).

Precedents

The precedents are numbered according to the main section in the text to which they relate.

List of precedents contained in this chapter

Chapter 2: Electronic Communications

P. 2.7 **Form allowing members to elect to receive documents via electronic communications**

Following recent changes to the law, you may now elect to receive documents such as the AGM notice and the company's annual report and accounts by electronic communications instead of in paper form through the post. The options available to you are set out below. If you would like us to use one of these methods to send you company documents, you should complete the attached form and return it to us using the envelope provided. [You may also register your choice via our web site at [address]. If you do so, you will be asked to provide the identification number printed at the top of this form.]

If you would like to continue receiving company documents in paper form through the post, you need take no further action. [However, you may request the company to continue sending documents by post and notify you by e-mail when documents such as the AGM notice have been published on the company's web site.]

Documents that we may send using your chosen option
You may [may not] elect to receive documents in different ways, [although you may elect to receive notifications regarding publication on our web site and continue to receive the documents in paper form through the post].

If you make an election using this form, we may use that method to send you the following documents, if you are entitled to receive a copy of that document:

- the notice of any general meeting (including the AGM);
- the notice of any general meeting of the holders of any class of shares;
- the notice of any meeting of holders of other securities;
- any document or circular which is issued at the same time as any of the above notices (including any proxy forms);
- the company's annual report and accounts and any documents, reports, notices that are required to be contained in it or sent with it under applicable rules and regulations;
- (if applicable), the company's summary financial statement;
- any notice we are required to serve on you pursuant to the company's articles or the Companies Acts;
- any document we are required by the Financial Service Authority, in its capacity as the UK Listing Authority, to send you; and
- general correspondence and company literature.

The available options
- **Via e-mail**
  If you choose this option, we will send you the documents in full by e-mail or as an e-mail attachment to the e-mail address notified by you for these purposes.

- **Notification of availability on our web site**

  If you choose this method, we will send you an e-mail (or, if you choose, a notification by post) informing you when the documents have been published on our web site. The notification will also tell you the address of the web site and how to find the information on the web site. Unless you opt to continue to receive the relevant documents in paper form through the post, it will then be up to you whether to access the web site and view the documents. The documents on the web site will be made available in commonly used formats. You will, however, need to have access to the internet in order to access them. If you choose to be notified by e-mail, we will send the e-mail to the address notified by you for these purposes.

- **Fax**

  If you choose this option we will send the documents by fax to a fax number supplied by you for these purposes.

Please read the following notes before making your election.
If you choose an option which requires the company to use an electronic address such as an e-mail address, you will need to inform us of the address you wish us to use and notify us whenever that address changes. You may inform us of such changes by [ ]. If you choose an option which requires the company to send any document or notification through the post, we will only use your registered address.

If we are aware that an electronic transmission has failed, we will make at least one more attempt to send it. If that attempt fails, we will notify you by post that we have tried without apparent success to send you a document via your chosen method. If possible, we will also send you a copy of that document by post. However, this may not always be possible, and the company will be deemed under the articles to have fulfilled its obligations to serve the document or notice on you at the first attempt, even though it failed.

The election you make and the contact details you provide will be used by us until you give us different instructions.

We may decide to send you certain documents through the post even though you have elected to receive them in some other manner. You should therefore continue to inform us of any change to your postal address.

We will take all reasonable precautions to ensure that no viruses are present in any communications sent electronically. However, we cannot accept any liability for any loss or damage arising from the opening or use of any e-mail or attachments.

I agree to accept, in the manner indicated below, and until such time as I notify the company otherwise, service of any notice or document which the company may be required to send me in compliance with any statutory or regulatory requirement, or in compliance with any obligation imposed by the Financial Services

Authority in its capacity as the UK Listing Authority, or in compliance with the company's articles of association, or in compliance with any other applicable rules or regulations.

PLEASE TICK ONLY ONE OF OPTIONS A, B OR C

☐ **Option A: Notification of publication on our web site**
If you select this option we will send you a notification when the relevant documents are published on our web site. We will send the notification in the manner which you select and to the address or number which you provide.
Please tick one of the following to indicate the method you would like us to use to send the notification and provide an e-mail address or fax number as appropriate.
☐ Notification sent by e-mail to _____
☐ Notification sent by fax to _____
☐ Notification sent by post to my/our registered address

☐ **Option B: By sending the documents in full to the following e-mail address**

Data Protection Statement
A. The identity of the Data Controller
[The Company] is a Data Controller for the purposes of the Data Protection Act 1998. This means that it is responsible for making decisions about how your personal data will be processed and how it may be used.
B. Use of your personal data
The company will record any election you make on this form and any information which you provide that is necessary for the company to give effect to that election. The data will be used to determine what methods the company may use to serve documents and notices on you and the address that should be used for that purpose. The company will use any e-mail address you supply only to send company documents connected with your election.
The company will disclose to [its registrars], some or all of the data you provide. The registrars will use that data solely for the purposes of distributing documents connected with your election. In addition, the company will receive certain administrative data from its registrars, which it has created for the purposes of carrying out its function as registrar and which relates to your shareholding.
C. Security of your personal data
The company has put in place appropriate technical and organisational measures to prevent the unauthorised or unlawful processing of your personal data. These include restricted access to databases that contain personal data, access restricted by password authentication and training of personnel on the rules of data protection and obligations of confidentiality.

D. Updating your personal data
Under the Data Protection Act you have the right to be told what personal data the company holds about you and to request that it be updated. This may be done by contacting: [name and address].

Chapter 3: Directors

P. 3.3A **Extract from directors' service agreement**

The director shall exercise such powers and functions and perform such duties in relation to the company or any of its subsidiaries and associates as may from time to time be vested in or assigned to him by the board and shall comply with all directions from time to time given to him by the board (or anyone authorised by the board) and with all rules and regulations from time to time laid down by the company concerning employees.

P. 3.3B **Board minute of resolution to appoint managing director**

There was produced a draft of a service contract between the company and [name] appointing [name] as managing director of the company with effect from [date], on the terms and conditions set out in the service contract.

It was resolved:
THAT [name] be appointed managing director of the company with effect from [date] on the terms set out in the service contract produced at the meeting and that the chairman be authorised to sign the service agreement on behalf of the company.

Chapter 4: Board Meetings

P. 4.5 **Notice of board meeting**

XYZ LIMITED

[Address]
[Date]

To the directors of XYZ Limited

Notice of board meeting
A meeting of the directors of the company will be held at [place] on [date] at [time].

[Signature]
Secretary
By order of the chairman

P. 4.6A   Example of notice of board meeting including the agenda

XYZ LIMITED

A board meeting will be held at [place] on [date] at [time]

AGENDA

1. *Minutes*
    To approve the minutes of the board meeting held on 24 August 1996 (board paper no. 09/96/01).

2. *Management Accounts*
    To consider the management accounts for August 1996 (board paper no. 09/96/02).

3. *Appointment of Directors*
    To consider the recommendations of the nomination committee on the appointment of non-executive directors (board paper no. 09/96/03).

4. *Charitable Donation*
    To consider and, if thought fit, to approve the following charitable donations:

5. *Date of Next Meeting*
    To note that the next meeting will be held on 26 October 1996 at 299 Kingsdown Place at 10.30am.

. . . .
Secretary

P. 4.6B   Agenda for first board meeting (private company)

XYZ LIMITED
Agenda for board meeting to be held at [place] on [date] at [time]

1. To produce the certificate of incorporation and a copy of the memorandum and articles of association as registered.
2. To note that the first directors of the company named by the subscribers in the documents delivered to the Registrar of Companies with the memorandum of association are: [names].
3. To consider and, if thought fit, resolve that [name of director] be appointed chairman of the board.
4. To note that [name] was named by the subscribers as secretary in the documents delivered to the Registrar of Companies and to consider and, if thought fit, resolve:
    THAT the appointment of [name] as secretary be confirmed at a salary payable from [date] at the rate of [amount] per annum, such appointment being terminable by [period] notice in writing given by either party to the other at any time.
5. To consider and, if thought fit, resolve:

THAT the situation of the company's registered office shown in the documents delivered with the memorandum to the Registrar of Companies (namely, [address]) be confirmed.

6. To consider and, if thought fit, resolve:
THAT the seal, of which an impression is affixed in the margin hereof, be adopted as the common seal of the company.

7. To consider opening a bank account with [name of bank] and, if thought fit, resolve:
[Resolutions in accordance with bank's printed form for opening an account.]

8. To consider and, if thought fit, resolve:
THAT [name] be appointed auditors of the company to hold office until the conclusion of the first general meeting at which accounts are laid before the company.

9. To produce and read to the meeting notices given by the directors pursuant to section 317(3) of the Companies Act 1985.

10. To produce forms of application for 98 shares of £1 each in the capital of the company, together with cheques for a total of £100, being payment in full for the said shares and the two shares taken by the subscribers to the memorandum of association.
To consider and, if thought fit, resolve:

(a) THAT 49 shares of £1 each, fully paid and numbered 3 to 51 inclusive, be allotted to [applicant 1];

(b) THAT 49 shares of £1 each, fully paid and numbered 52 to 100 inclusive, be allotted to [applicant 2];

(c) THAT the undermentioned share certificates drawn in respect of subscribers' shares and the allotments made by resolutions (a) and (b) above be approved and that the common seal be affixed thereto:

No. 1 [applicant 1]   50 shares numbered 1 to 50 inclusive
No. 2 [applicant 2]   50 shares numbered 51 to 100 inclusive

11. To consider and, if thought fit, resolve:
THAT all the shares of the company shall henceforth cease to bear distinguishing numbers.

12. To consider fixing dates for future board meetings.

P. 4.6C   Minutes of first board meeting (private company)

XYZ LIMITED

Minutes of board meeting held at [place] on [date] at [time]

1. There were produced the certificate of incorporation and a copy of the memorandum and articles of association as registered.

2. It was noted that the first directors of the company named by the subscribers in the documents delivered to the Registrar of Companies with the memorandum of association are: [names].

3. It was resolved:
THAT [name of director] be appointed chairman of the board.

4. It was noted that [name] was named by the subscribers as secretary in the documents delivered to the Registrar of Companies and resolved:

THAT the appointment of [name] as secretary be confirmed at a salary payable from [date] at the rate of [amount] per annum, such appointment being terminable by [period] notice in writing given by either party to the other at any time.

5. It was resolved:
THAT the situation of the company's registered office shown in the documents delivered with the memorandum to the Registrar of Companies (namely, [address]) be confirmed.

6. It was resolved:
THAT the seal, of which an impression is affixed in the margin hereof, be adopted as the common seal of the company.

7. It was resolved:
THAT a bank account be opened with [name of bank] and ... [resolutions in accordance with bank's printed form for opening an account].

8. It was resolved:
THAT [name] be appointed auditors of the company to hold office until the conclusion of the first general meeting at which accounts are laid before the company.

9. There were produced and read to the meeting notices given by [names of directors] pursuant to section 317(3) of the Companies Act 1985.

10. There were produced forms of application for 98 shares of £1 each in the capital of the company, together with cheques for a total of £100, being payment in full for the said shares and the two shares taken by the subscribers to the memorandum of association.
It was resolved:

(a) THAT 49 shares of £1 each, fully paid and numbered 3 to 51 inclusive, be allotted to [applicant 1];

(b) THAT 49 shares of £1 each, fully paid and numbered 52 to 100 inclusive, be allotted to [applicant 2];

(c) THAT the undermentioned share certificates drawn in respect of subscribers' shares and the allotments made by resolutions (a) and (b) above be approved and that the common seal be affixed thereto:

No. 1 [applicant 1] 50 shares numbered 1 to 50 inclusive
No. 2 [applicant 2] 50 shares numbered 51 to 100 inclusive

11. It was resolved:
THAT all the shares of the company shall henceforth cease to bear distinguishing numbers.

12. It was resolved that the next meeting of the board of directors would be held at [place] on [date] at [time].

[Signed]
[Chairman]

P. 4.6D Agenda for board meeting of public company

XYZ PLC

Agenda for board meeting to be held at [place] on [date] at [time]

1.   The chairman to sign the minutes of the board meeting held on [date] and the committee meeting held on [date], copies having been circulated to the directors.

2.   To produce transfer audit reports dated [date] from the company's registrars and to resolve:

(a)   THAT share transfers Nos. ... to ... inclusive and loan stock transfers Nos. ... to ... inclusive be approved.

(b)   THAT the sealing and issue of share certificates Nos. ... to ... inclusive and loan stock certificates Nos. ... to ... inclusive be confirmed.

3.   To produce the seal book and resolve:
      THAT the affixing of the common seal of the company to the documents set out against items Nos. ... to ... inclusive in the seal book be confirmed.

4.   To produce and consider:

(a)   a list of bank balances as at [date]

(b)   cash flow statements for the period to [date]

(c)   financial statement as at [date].

5.   To produce and consider a proof print of the report of the directors and the accounts for the year ended [date], and a draft of the chairman's statement and operating and financial review to be circulated with the report and accounts.
      To consider and, if thought fit, resolve:

(a)   THAT, with reference to minute No. [ ] of the annual general meeting held on [date], the remuneration of the auditors be fixed at [amount].

(b)   THAT the report of the directors, the chairman's statement, the operating and financial review and the accounts for the year ended [date], including the final dividend of [ ]p per share recommended therein (making a total dividend of [ ]p per share for the year) be approved and that, subject to approval by the company in general meeting, such dividend be paid on [date] to shareholders registered at the close of business on [date].

(c)   THAT the signature of the balance sheet by two directors on behalf of the board be authorised.

(d)   THAT the signature of the directors' report by the secretary be authorised.

(e)   THAT the annual general meeting of the company be convened and held at [place] on [date] at [time] to transact the ordinary business of the company and that the secretary be authorised to issue notices accordingly, together with a form of proxy in accordance with the proof print submitted to and approved by this meeting.

(f)   THAT [the company's bankers] be requested to open dividend account No. [ ] in the name of the company and be authorised to honour warrants dated [date], drawn on the said account bearing the facsimile or autographic signature of the secretary without other signature thereto.

6.   To consider and, if thought fit, resolve:
      THAT the secretary be authorised to release forthwith to the

London Stock Exchange and to the company's press agents a preliminary announcement of the results of the year ended [date].

P. 4.8A   Board resolution to fix quorum for meetings of directors

THAT the quorum necessary for the transaction of the business of the directors be fixed at three.

P. 4.8B   Article allowing interested directors to vote and be counted in quorum

A director may vote at a meeting of directors or any committee of directors on any contract or arrangement in which he is interested and on any incidental matter, and a director who is so interested shall be counted in calculating whether a quorum exists for that item of business[; and Regulation 94 of Table A shall be modified accordingly].

P. 4.8C   Article allowing sole director to act

The quorum for the transaction of business of the directors may be fixed by the directors and unless so fixed at any other number shall be two; but if and so long as there is a sole director, he may exercise all the powers and authorities vested in the directors by these Articles [and Table A; and Regulation 89 of Table A shall be modified accordingly]. A person who holds office only as an alternate director shall, if his appointor is not present, be counted in the quorum.

P. 4.10   Article allowing directors attending meetings by telephone to be counted in the quorum

The quorum necessary for the transaction of business of the Board may be fixed from time to time by the Board and unless so fixed at any other number shall be three. For the purposes of these Articles any Director who is able (directly or by telephonic communication) to speak and be heard by each of the other Directors present or deemed to be present at any meeting of the Board, shall be deemed to be present in person at such meeting and shall be entitled to vote or be counted in the quorum accordingly. Such meeting shall be deemed to take place where the largest group of those participating is assembled, or, if there is no such group, where the chairman of the meeting then is, and the word 'meeting' shall be construed accordingly.

P. 4.11A   Form of appointment of alternate director

Pursuant to article [no.] of the articles of association of [name of company] and subject to the approval of the board of [name of company], I [name of director making appointment] being a director of [name of company] hereby appoint [name of person to be appointed as alternate] to be my alternate director.

P. 4.11B   Resolution approving appointment of alternate director

There was produced a form of appointment dated [date] by which [name of director] appoints [name of alternate] to be his alternate director.
It was resolved THAT the appointment by [name of director] of [name of alternate] to be his alternate director be approved.

P. 4.11C   Form of revocation of appointment of alternate director

Pursuant to article [no.] of the articles of association of [name of company], I hereby revoke the appointment dated [date] of [name of alternate appointed] as my alternate director.

P. 4.11D   Board minute noting revocation of appointment of alternate director

A form of revocation dated [date] by which [name of director] revokes the appointment of [name of alternate] as his alternate was produced and noted.

Chapter 5: Committees of Directors

P. 5.2A   Board resolution to appoint committee

THAT, pursuant to article [no.] of the company's articles of association, A, B, and C (any two of whom shall be a quorum) be appointed a committee with power to . . .

P. 5.2B   Board resolution to appoint committee

THAT, pursuant to article [no.] of the company's articles of association, any two directors be appointed a committee to take such action and to complete all documents necessary for [reason].

P. 5.10   Written resolution of committee of one director

XYZ LIMITED
Pursuant to the authority given by article [no.] of the company's articles of association, I, the undersigned, being the sole member of a committee established by the board of directors on [date] to [short description of purpose], hereby resolve:
THAT . . . . .
[Date]
[Signature]

P. 5.11 Specimen terms of reference of an audit committee

Constitution
1. The Board hereby resolves to establish a Committee of the Board to be known as the Audit Committee.

Membership
2. The Committee shall be appointed by the Board from amongst the non-executive directors of the Company and shall consist of not less than three members. A quorum shall be two members.
3. The chairman of the committee shall be appointed by the Board.

Attendance at meetings
4. The Finance Director, the Head of Internal Audit, and a representative of the external auditors shall normally attend meetings. Other Board members shall also have the right of attendance. However, at least once a year the Committee shall meet with the external auditors without executive Board members present.
5. The Company secretary shall be the Secretary of the Committee.

Frequency of meetings
6. Meetings shall be held not less than twice a year. The external auditors may request a meeting if they consider that one is necessary.

Authority
7. The Committee is authorised by the Board to investigate any activity within its terms of reference. It is authorised to seek any information it requires from any employee and all employees are directed to co-operate with any request made by the Committee.
8. The Committee is authorised by the Board to obtain outside legal or other independent professional advice and to secure the attendance of outsiders with relevant experience and expertise if it considers necessary.

Duties
9. The duties of the Committee shall be:
(a) to consider the appointment of the external auditor, the audit fee, and any question of resignation or dismissal;
(b) to discuss with the external auditor before the audit commences the nature and scope of the audit, and ensure co-ordination where more than one audit firm is involved;
(c) to review the half-year and annual financial statements before submission to the Board, focusing particularly on:
(i) any changes in accounting policies and practices
(ii) major judgemental areas
(iii) significant adjustments resulting from the audit
(iv) the going concern assumption
(v) compliance with accounting standards
(vi) compliance with stock exchange and legal requirements;
(d) to discuss problems and reservations arising from the interim and final audits, and any matters the auditor may wish to discuss (in the absence of management where necessary);
(e) to review the auditor's management letter and management's response;

(f) to review the Company's statement on internal control systems prior to endorsement by the Board;

(g) to review the internal audit programme, ensure co-ordination between internal and external auditors, and ensure that the internal audit function is adequately resourced and has appropriate standing within the Company;

(h) to consider the major findings of internal investigations and management's response;

(i) to consider other topics as defined by the Board.

Reporting procedures

10. The Secretary shall circulate minutes of meetings of the Committee to all members of the Board.

P. 5.13 Specimen terms of reference for nomination committee

Constitution

1. The Board hereby resolves to establish a Committee of the Board to be known as the Nomination Committee.

Membership

2. The Committee shall comprise three Directors appointed by the Board, the majority of whom must be non-executive directors. A quorum shall be two members.

3. The Chairman of the Committee shall be appointed by the Board.

Frequency of meetings

4. The Committee shall meet at least once a year.

Powers

5. The Committee shall have the power to employ the services of such advisers as it deems necessary to fulfil its responsibilities.

Duties

6. The duties of the Committee shall be:

(a) to nominate candidates for the approval of the Board to fill vacancies on the board of directors;

(b) to consider and make recommendations to the Board at least annually on its composition and balance.

Reporting procedures

7. The company secretary shall act as secretary to the Committee and shall keep an appropriate record of its proceedings.

Chapter 6: Directors' Written Resolutions and Informal Consent

P. 6.2A Written resolution of the directors

XYZ LIMITED

Pursuant to the authority given by article [no.] of the company's articles of association, we, the undersigned, being all the directors of XYZ Limited [entitled to receive notice of a meeting of directors], hereby resolve:

THAT . . . . .

[Date]

[Signatures]

P. 6.2B **Article allowing electronic/written resolutions approved by 90% of directors**

A resolution in writing signed or approved by fax or by any electronic system or by telephone and subsequently confirmed in writing or by fax or by electronic systems by not less than 90% of the directors for the time being in the United Kingdom and entitled to vote thereon shall be as valid and effectual as a resolution duly passed at a meeting of the directors and may consist of several documents or other such forms of approval in the like form each signed or so approved by one or more directors.

Chapter 9: Class Meetings

P. 9.4 **Notice of class meeting**

XYZ Limited
Notice is hereby given that a separate meeting of the holders of the six per cent £1 preference shares in the capital of the company will be held on [date] at [place] at [time] to propose the following resolution as an extraordinary resolution:

THAT this separate class meeting of the holders of the six per cent £1 preference shares in the capital of the company hereby sanctions [resolution being sanctioned] and hereby sanctions any variation, modification or abrogation of the rights and privileges attached or belonging to the six per cent £1 preference shares effected thereby or necessary to give effect thereto.
By order of the Board
[Signature]
Secretary
[Registered office address]
[Date]

Notes:
Holders of six per cent preference shares in the company are entitled to attend and vote at this meeting or to appoint a proxy to attend and vote in their stead. A proxy need not be a member of the company.

Chapter 10: Calling General Meetings

P. 10.2A **Minute of board resolution convening annual general meeting**

It was resolved:

THAT the Annual General Meeting of the Company be convened and held at [place] on [date] at [time] for the following purposes:

1. To receive the accounts and the reports of the directors and auditors for the financial year ending [date].

2. To re-appoint ABC as auditors until the conclusion of the next meeting at which accounts are laid and to authorise the directors to fix their remuneration.

3. To authorise the directors to allot shares pursuant to section 80 of the Companies Act 1985.

THAT the secretary be authorised to sign the notice on behalf of the Board and to issue notices accordingly, together with a form of proxy in accordance with the proof print submitted to and approved by this meeting.

P. 10.2B   Minute of board resolution convening extraordinary general meeting

It was resolved:

THAT an Extraordinary General Meeting of the Company be convened and held at [place] on [date] at [time] for the following purpose:

1. To increase the share capital of the Company.

THAT the Secretary be authorised to sign the notice on behalf of the Board and to issue notices accordingly, together with a form of proxy in accordance with the proof print submitted to and approved by this meeting.

P. 10.6A   Members' requisition for extraordinary general meeting

The Directors
XYZ p.l.c.

We the undersigned, being members of XYZ p.l.c. holding in the aggregate [number] ordinary shares of £1 each out of the issued and paid-up capital of [number] ordinary shares of £1 each, require you, pursuant to section 368 of the Companies Act 1985, to convene an extraordinary general meeting of the company for the purpose of considering the following resolutions, which will be proposed as ordinary resolutions:

1. THAT [name] be appointed a director of the company.

2. THAT the share capital of the company be increased to £[amount] by the creation of [number] additional ordinary shares of £1 each.

[Signatures]   [Addresses]
[Date]
[Note: If (unusually) the company's articles provide a more relaxed regime for a members' requisition and the members are unable to meet the statutory requirements, the wording of the requisition should refer to the relevant article.]

P. 10.6B **Notice of requisitioned meeting given by requisitionists**

XYZ p.l.c.

NOTICE IS HEREBY GIVEN that, pursuant to a requisition dated [date] made in accordance with the provisions of section 368 of the Companies Act 1985, and deposited at the registered office of the company on [date of deposit], an Extraordinary General Meeting of the company will be held at [place] on [date], at [time] for the purpose of considering the following resolutions, which will be proposed as ordinary resolutions:

RESOLUTIONS

1. THAT [name] be appointed a director of the company.
2. THAT the share capital of the company be increased to £[amount] by the creation of [number] additional ordinary shares of £1 each.

A member entitled to attend and vote at the meeting is entitled to appoint one or more proxies to attend and vote instead of him. A proxy need not also be a member.

[Signatures and names]   [Addresses]

[Date]

Chapter 11: Notice of General Meetings

P. 11.5A **Notice of annual general meeting of public limited company**

XYZ PLC

Notice is hereby given that the annual general meeting of XYZ PLC (the Company) will be held at [place] on [date] at [time] for the following purposes:

Resolutions – ordinary business
1. To receive the report of the Directors and the audited accounts for the year ended [year end].
2. To re-elect the following Directors:
[Name]
[Name]
3. To reappoint [name of auditors] as auditors and authorise the Directors to determine their remuneration.
Resolutions – special business
4. To consider and, if thought fit, to pass the following resolution as a Special Resolution:
THAT the authority and power conferred on the Directors by Article [No.] (Authority to allot securities) of the Articles of Association of the Company be and they are hereby renewed for the period expiring on the date of the annual general meeting of the Company to be held in [year + 1] and that:
(a) for the purposes of Article [No.], the prescribed amount for the above period shall be £[amount 1] and
(b) for the purposes of the proviso to Article [No.], the aggregate

nominal amount of equity securities allotted wholly for cash during such period, otherwise than as mentioned in such proviso, shall not exceed £[amount 2].

By order of the Board
ABC Delta, Secretary
[Registered office address]
[date]

Notes
1. A member entitled to attend and vote at the meeting is entitled to appoint a proxy or more than one proxy to attend and vote instead of him. A proxy need not be a member.
2. To be entitled to attend and vote at the meeting (and for the purpose of the determination by the company of the number of votes they may cast), members must be entered on the company's register of members by [time and date not more than 48 hours before the time fixed for the meeting] ('the specified time'). If the meeting is adjourned to a time not more than 48 hours after the specified time for the original meeting, that time will also apply for the purpose of determining the entitlement of members to attend and vote (and for the purpose of determining the number of votes they may cast) at the adjourned meeting. If the meeting is adjourned for a longer period, to be entitled to attend and vote at the adjourned meeting (and for the purpose of the determination by the company of the number of votes they may cast), members must be entered on the company's register of members [number of hours] before the time fixed for the adjourned meeting or, if the Company gives notice of the adjourned meeting, the time specified in that notice.
See **Precedent 26.11A** for the minutes of the above meeting.

P. 11.5B   Notice of extraordinary general meeting

XYZ Limited
Notice is hereby given that an extraordinary general meeting of XYZ Limited will be held at [place] on [date] at [time] for the purpose of considering and, if thought fit, passing the following resolution as a special resolution:
SPECIAL RESOLUTION
THAT the name of the company be changed to '[name] Limited'.

By order of the Board
[Name]
Secretary
[Registered office address]
[Date]

Note:
A member entitled to attend and vote at the meeting is entitled to

appoint a proxy to attend and vote instead of him. A proxy need not be a member.

P. 11.7   **Regulations 50 and 52 of the 1948 Act Table A regarding ordinary business**

50. An Annual General Meeting and a Meeting called for the passing of a Special Resolution shall be called by twenty-one days' notice in writing at the least, and a Meeting of the Company other than an Annual General Meeting or a Meeting for the passing of a Special Resolution shall be called by fourteen days' notice in writing at the least. The notice shall be exclusive of the day on which it is served or deemed to be served and of the day for which it is given, and shall specify the place, the day and the hour of meeting and, in case of special business, the general nature of that business, and shall be given, in manner hereinafter mentioned or in such other manner, if any, as may be prescribed by the Company in General Meeting, to such persons as are, under the regulations of the Company, entitled to receive such notices from the Company:
Provided that a Meeting of the Company shall, notwithstanding that it is called by shorter notice than that specified in this regulation, be deemed to have been duly called if it is so agreed—
   (a) in the case of a Meeting called as the Annual General Meeting, by all the Members entitled to attend and vote thereat; and
   (b) in the case of any other Meeting, by a majority in number of the Members having a right to attend and vote at the Meeting, being a majority together holding not less than 95 per cent. in nominal value of the Shares giving that right.

52. All business shall be deemed special that is transacted at an Extraordinary General Meeting, and also all that is transacted at an Annual General Meeting, with the exception of declaring a dividend, the consideration of the accounts, balance sheets, and the reports of the Directors and Auditors, the election of Directors in the place of those retiring and the appointment of, and the fixing of the remuneration of, the Auditors.

P. 11.11A   **Consent to short notice of an annual general meeting**

We, the undersigned, all the members for the time being of XYZ Limited, and having a right to attend and vote at the annual general meeting of the company to be held on [date], hereby agree:
(a) to accept shorter notice of the said meeting than the period of notice prescribed by section 369(2)(a) of the Companies Act 1985; and
(b) to accept copies of the company's accounts less than 21 days

before the date of the said meeting as required by section 238(1) of the Companies Act 1985.

Dated this .... day of .... 20......

[Signatures]

P. 11.11B   Consent to short notice of an extraordinary general meeting

We, the undersigned, being a majority in number of the members together holding not less than 95 per cent of the share capital of XYZ Limited having a right to attend and vote at the meeting referred to below, hereby agree to an extraordinary general meeting of the company being held on [date], notwithstanding that shorter notice has been given of the said meeting than the period of notice prescribed by section 369(2) of the Companies Act 1985.

Dated this .... day of .... 20......

[Signatures]

P. 11.11C   Consent to short notice of an extraordinary general meeting to pass a special resolution

We, the undersigned, being a majority in number of the members together holding not less than 95 per cent of the share capital of XYZ Limited having a right to attend and vote at the meeting referred to below, hereby agree to an extraordinary general meeting of the company being held on [date], for the purpose of considering the special resolution set out in the notice of the said meeting notwithstanding that less than twenty-one days' notice of the meeting has been given.

Dated this .... day of .... 20......

[Signatures]

P. 11.12A   Special notice from member to company

To: The directors,
XYZ plc
[Registered Office]
I hereby give notice, pursuant to section 379 and section [293 / 303 / 388 / 391A] of the Companies Act 1985, of my intention to propose the following resolution as an ordinary resolution at the next [annual/extraordinary] general meeting of the company:

   ORDINARY RESOLUTION
   [Text of resolution]

[Signed]   [Address]
[Date]

P. 11.12B   Notice of resolution requiring special notice

To consider and, if thought fit, to pass as an ordinary resolution the following resolution for which special notice has been given in accordance with section 379 of the Companies Act 1985: THAT . . . .

P. 11.13A Requisition of resolution [and supporting statement] under section 376 of the Companies Act 1985

The Directors
XYZ plc
[Registered office address]
We the undersigned being members of XYZ plc representing not less than one-twentieth of the total voting rights of all the members having at the date hereof a right to vote at the next annual general meeting of the company, hereby require you to give to the members entitled to receive notice of the next annual general meeting notice of the following resolution, which it is intended to move thereat as an ordinary resolution [, and to circulate to the members entitled to have notice of the meeting sent to them the annexed statement with respect to the matter referred to in the proposed resolution]:

ORDINARY RESOLUTION
[Text of resolution]

[STATEMENT IN SUPPORT]
[Text of statement of not more than 1,000 words]

[Signed]   [Address]
[Date]

P. 11.13B Requisition for circulation of statement under section 376 of the Companies Act 1985

The Directors
XYZ plc
[Registered office address]
We the undersigned being members of XYZ plc representing not less than one-twentieth of the total voting rights of all the members having at the date hereof a right to vote at the annual general meeting/extraordinary general meeting of the company convened for [insert date of meeting], hereby require you to circulate to the members entitled to have notice of the meeting sent to them the following statement with respect of the resolution set out in the notice of the said meeting:

STATEMENT
[Text of statement of not more than 1,000 words]

[Signed]   [Address]
[Date]

P. 11.13 C   Requisitioned resolution in notice of annual general meeting

To consider the following resolution intended to be moved at the meeting as a special resolution, notice of which is given by the company pursuant to section 376 of the Companies Act 1985 on the requisition of certain members:

SPECIAL RESOLUTION

[Text of resolution]

P. 11.13 D   Notice of requisitioned resolution

XYZ plc

NOTICE OF RESOLUTION

Notice is hereby given, upon the requisition of certain members pursuant to section 376 of the Companies Act, that the company has been advised of an intention to move the following resolution as an extraordinary resolution at the annual general meeting of the company to be held on [date] at [place] at [time]:

EXTRAORDINARY RESOLUTION

[Text of resolution]

By order of the board upon a requisition pursuant to section 376 of the Companies Act 1985
By Order of the Board
[Signed]
Secretary

Chapter 12: Resolutions

See also **P. 24.2D** for a certified copy of a members' written resolution.

P. 12.6   Copy resolution for filing with Registrar of Companies

[Company Number]

THE COMPANIES ACT 1985
AND
THE COMPANIES ACT 1989

COMPANY LIMITED BY SHARES

[NAME OF COMPANY]

At an [annual/extraordinary] general meeting of the members of the above-named company held at [place] on [date] the following resolutions were duly passed:

As SPECIAL RESOLUTIONS
[Resolutions]

As ORDINARY RESOLUTIONS
[Resolutions]

As EXTRAORDINARY RESOLUTIONS
[Resolutions]

Chairman/Secretary

Chapter 13: Quorum

P. 13.4 Example of article on failure to obtain a quorum at a general meeting

If within fifteen minutes from the time appointed for a general meeting (or such longer time not exceeding one hour as the chairman of the meeting may determine to wait) a quorum is not present, the meeting, if convened on the requisition of members, shall be dissolved. In any other case it shall stand adjourned to such other day and at such other time and place as may have been specified for the purpose in the notice or (if not so specified) as the chairman of the meeting may determine; in the latter case, not less than seven days' notice of the adjourned meeting shall be given in like manner as in the case of the original meeting. If at such adjourned meeting a quorum is not present within fifteen minutes from the time appointed for holding the meeting, the members present in person or by proxy and entitled to vote at such meeting shall be a quorum.

Chapter 14: Proxies and Corporate Representatives

P. 14.4A Example article on authority of corporate representatives

Any corporation which is a member of the company may by resolution of its directors or other governing body authorise such person as it thinks fit to act as its representative at any meeting of the company, and any person so authorised shall be entitled to exercise the same powers on behalf of the corporation which he represents as that corporation could exercise if it were an individual member of the company, but such representative may be required to produce evidence of such authorisation on admission or at any time during the meeting or in connection with the exercise of any right in respect of such meeting, including without limitation participation in a poll on any resolution. Any such authorisation in writing purporting to be signed by an officer of or other person duly authorised for the purpose by the said corporation shall be conclusive evidence of the authority of the representative to act on behalf of the corporation.

P. 14.4B   Board minute appointing corporate representative

It was resolved:

THAT [name] or, failing him, [name] or, failing her, [name] be appointed, pursuant to section 375 of the Companies Act 1985, to act as the company's representative at any meeting of the members or creditors of other companies in which the company is or may become interested as a member or creditor.

P. 14.11   Example of article allowing electronic proxies

An appointment of a proxy shall be in any usual or common form or in any other form which the directors may prescribe or accept and, in the case of an instrument in writing:

(a) in the case of an individual shall be signed by the appointor or by his attorney; and

(b) in the case of a corporation shall be either given under its common seal or executed in any manner prescribed by the Statutes to have the same effect as if given under the common seal of the corporation or signed on its behalf by an attorney or duly authorised officer of the corporation.

The directors may, but shall not be bound to, require evidence of the authority of any such attorney or officer. The signature on such instrument need not be witnessed.

An appointment of a proxy may be contained in an electronic communication in accordance with these articles, authenticated or executed in such manner as is specified by the directors.

P. 14.13   Two-way proxy which complies with the Listing Rules

XYZ plc

Form of appointment of proxy

I/We, [name of member/names of joint holders], of [address/addresses], being a member/members of the above-named company, hereby appoint the chairman of the meeting* or [name of proxy] of [address of proxy] as my/our proxy to vote in my/our name[s] and on my/our behalf at the annual/extraordinary general meeting of the company to be held on [date], and at any adjournment thereof.

[*Delete if it is desired to appoint any other person and insert his or her name and address in the space provided.]

I/We hereby authorise and instruct the proxy to vote on the resolutions to be proposed at such meeting as indicated in the boxes below. Unless otherwise directed, the proxy will vote or abstain from voting as he or she thinks fit. Should any resolutions, other than those specified, be proposed at the meeting, the proxy may vote thereon as he or she thinks fit.

Resolutions	For	Against

1. Ordinary Resolution to receive the report and accounts

2. Ordinary Resolution to declare a dividend

3. Ordinary resolution to reappoint AC&B as auditors and to authorise the directors to fix their remuneration

4. Ordinary resolution to re-elect [name] as a director

5. Ordinary resolution to authorise directors to allot shares

6. Special resolution to alter articles of association

[Date]
[Signature]

Notes:

1. To be effective this form must be lodged at the offices of the Company's Registrars, [address], not later than [48] hours before the time of the meeting together, if appropriate, with the power of attorney or other authority under which it is signed or a notarially certified copy of such power or authority.
2. In the case of a corporation this proxy should be given under its common seal or should be signed on its behalf by an attorney or officer so authorised and the words 'authorised signatory' added under the signature.
3. In the case of joint holders the vote of the senior who tenders a vote, whether in person or by proxy, will be accepted to the exclusion of the votes of the other holders. For this purpose seniority is determined by the order in which the names stand in the register of members in respect of the joint holding.
4. A proxy need not be a member of the company.

P. 14.19 Example article on non-revocation of proxies

A vote given in accordance with the terms of an instrument of proxy shall be valid, notwithstanding the previous death or insanity of the principal or revocation of the proxy, or of the authority under which the proxy was executed, or the transfer of the share in respect of which the proxy is given, provided that no intimation in writing of such death, insanity, revocation or transfer shall have been received by the Company at the Office (or other place in the United Kingdom specified pursuant to Article [No.]) before the commencement of the meetings or adjourned meeting at which the proxy is used.

Chapter 15: Voting

P. 15.4A **Example of article which removes voting and other rights where a call is unpaid**

No member shall, unless the Board otherwise determines, be entitled to vote at a General Meeting either personally or by proxy, or to exercise any privilege as a member unless all calls or other sums presently payable by him in respect of shares in the Company have been paid.

P. 15.4B **Example of plc article removing voting rights for failure to respond to a s. 212 notice**

Without prejudice to any other rights or remedies of the company where, in respect of any shares in the company ('the default shares', which expression shall include any further shares which are allotted or issued in respect of such shares), any holder of such shares or other person appearing to be interested in such shares fails to comply with any notice (in this article called a 'statutory notice') given to that holder or other person by the company pursuant to Part VI of the Companies Act 1985 or, in purported compliance with such a statutory notice, makes a statement which is false in a material particular, then not earlier than fourteen days after the service of such statutory notice, the directors may serve upon such holder a notice (in this Article called a 'disenfranchisement notice') stating that the default shares and, if the Directors so determine, any other shares held by the holder shall from the service of the disenfranchisement notice confer on him, and on any transferee to which any such shares are transferred other than pursuant to an approved transfer, no right to attend or vote, in person or by proxy, either at any general meeting of the company or at any separate general meeting of the holders of the shares of the relevant class or to exercise any other right conferred by membership in relation to any such meeting.

P. 15.5 **Specimen article giving enhanced voting rights**

(a) Subject to sub-paragraphs 2 and 3 below, on a show of hands every member who (being an individual) is present in person or (being a corporation) is present by a duly authorised representative, not being himself a member, shall have one vote and on a poll every member shall have one vote for every share of which he is the holder.
(b) If at any general meeting a poll is duly demanded on a resolution to remove a director from office, the director named in the resolution shall be entitled to [number] votes for each share of which he is the holder.
(c) If at any general meeting a poll is duly demanded on a resolution to delete or amend the provisions of this article, every

director shall have [number] votes for each share of which he is the holder if voting against such a resolution.

P. 15.8A   **Voting card for use by members and corporate representatives on a poll**

VOTING CARD
For the [Annual/Extraordinary] General Meeting of
XYZ PLC
held on [date]
(To be used as instructed by the chairman)

Name of shareholder. . . . .
    (In Block Capitals)
Signature. . . . .
Number of shares held . . . .

                                For   Against
Resolution 1

Resolution 2

Resolution 3

Notes
1. Please record your votes by placing an X in the appropriate column above.
2. It is not necessary to complete the number of shares held, provided the vote is being given in respect of the entire holding.
3. If you wish to cast some of your votes for and some against a resolution, you may do so by indicating the number of votes cast for and against in the appropriate columns.

P. 15.8B   **Voting card for use by proxies on a poll**

VOTING CARD
For the [Annual/Extraordinary] General Meeting of
XYZ PLC
held on [date]
(To be used as instructed by the chairman)

Name of proxy . . . .
    (In Block Capitals)
Signature of proxy. . . . .
Name of shareholder represented . . . .
    (In Block Capitals)
Number of shares represented by proxy . . . .

                                For   Against
Resolution 1

Resolution 2

Resolution 3

Notes
1. Please record your votes by placing an X in the appropriate column above.
2. It is not necessary to complete the number of shares held, provided the vote is being given in respect of the entire holding.
3. If you wish to cast some of your votes for and some against a resolution, you may do so by indicating the number of votes cast for and against in the appropriate columns.
4. If you represent more than one member (other than members who hold shares jointly), you should complete a separate voting card in respect of each holding.

P. 15.8C   Voting card for use by chairman on a poll

CHAIRMAN'S VOTING CARD
For the [Annual/Extraordinary] General Meeting of
XYZ PLC
held on [date]

Signature of chairman of meeting . . . .

See attached sheet for names and holdings of shareholders represented.

Number of votes
For   Against

Resolution 1

Resolution 2

Resolution 3

P. 15.10   Example article on votes counted in error

If any votes shall be counted which ought not to have been counted or might have been rejected, the error shall not vitiate the resolution unless it be pointed out at the same meeting, or at any adjournment thereof, and not in that case unless it shall in the opinion of the Chairman of the meeting be of sufficient magnitude to vitiate the resolution.

Chapter 17: Organising General Meetings

P. 17.5   Article dealing with overflow arrangements at general meetings

(A) The Board may make arrangements for simultaneous

attendance and participation in General Meetings by members
and proxies entitled to attend such meetings at places other than
the place specified in the Notice convening the meeting ('the
specified place').

(B) Any arrangements for simultaneous attendance at other places
shall operate so that any members and proxies excluded from
attendance at the specified place are able to attend at one or more
of the other places. For the purposes of all other provisions of
these Articles any such meeting shall be treated as being held and
taking place at the specified place.

(C) The right of any member or proxy otherwise entitled to
attend a General Meeting at the specified place shall be subject to
any arrangements that the Board may at its discretion make from
time to time (whether before or after the date of the Notice
convening the meeting) for facilitating the organisation and
administration of any General Meeting by requiring any such
person (selected on such basis as the Board may at its discretion
decide) to attend the meeting at one or more of the other places.

Chapter 19: Right to Attend and Speak

P. 19.3   Attendance sheet (members)

XYZ PLC
Members present at the annual general meeting held on [date]
NAME (IN BLOCK CAPITALS)   SIGNATURE
[Names]   [Signatures]

Chapter 20: Security and Disorder

P. 20.2   Article allowing security checks at general meetings

The chairman of a meeting, or the company secretary, can take
any action they consider appropriate for:
- the safety of people attending a general meeting;
- proper and orderly conduct at a general meeting; or
- the meeting to reflect the wishes of the majority.

For example, they can require any people to prove who they are,
they can carry out security searches, and stop certain things being
taken into the meeting. They can refuse to allow any person into
a meeting, or can arrange for any person who refuses to comply
with any requirements imposed under this Article to be removed
from a meeting.

[**Note:** this article is written in plain English]

Chapter 21: Adjournment and Other Procedural Motions

P. 21.2   Article giving the chairman power to adjourn

The Chairman of a General Meeting may, with the consent of any
meeting at which a quorum is present (and shall if so directed by

the meeting) adjourn the meeting from time to time (or *sine die*) and from place to place, but no business shall be transacted at any adjourned meeting except business left unfinished at the meeting from which the adjournment took place. If it appears to the Chairman of the meeting that it is likely to be impracticable to hold or continue the meeting because of the number of members or their proxies present or wishing to attend or that an adjournment is otherwise necessary so that the business of the meeting may be properly conducted, he may without the need for such consent adjourn the meeting to such other time and place as he may determine (or *sine die*). When a meeting is adjourned *sine die* the time and place of the adjourned meeting shall be fixed by the Board. When a meeting is adjourned for thirty days or more or *sine die*, notice of the adjourned meeting shall be given as in the case of the original meeting. Save as expressly provided by these Articles it shall not be necessary to give any notice of an adjournment or of the business to be transacted at an adjourned meeting.

P. 21.7 Article giving the directors power to postpone or change the place of a meeting

If the directors consider that it is impractical, or undesirable, to hold a general meeting on the date or at the time or place stated in the notice of the meeting, they may change the place or postpone the meeting or do both. In such circumstances and if it is practical, the company shall announce the date, time and place of the adjourned meeting by advertisement in at least two United Kingdom national newspapers. It shall not be necessary to give notice of the adjourned meeting. The directors shall take reasonable steps to ensure that a member trying to attend the meeting at the original date, time and place is informed of the new arrangements. If a meeting is adjourned in this way, proxies may be lodged in accordance with the provision of article [no.] until 48 hours before the adjourned meeting. The directors may also change the place of or postpone the adjourned meeting, or do both, under this article.

Chapter 22: Amendments

P. 22.8A Example of article requiring prior notice of amendments

Amendments can be proposed to any type of resolution if the amendments are only clerical amendments to correct an obvious error. No other amendments to any *special* or *extraordinary resolution* can be proposed or voted on. In the case of an *ordinary resolution* any amendments to the resolution can be proposed and voted on (even if they are more than clerical amendments made to correct an obvious error), but such amendments can only be proposed and voted on if written notice of the proposed amendment and the intention to propose the amendment is delivered to the Registered Office at least 48 hours before the time fixed for the meeting or *adjourned* meeting.

P. 22.8B   Example of article on validity of amendments

If an amendment shall be proposed to any resolution under consideration but shall in good faith be ruled out by the Chairman of the meeting the proceedings on the substantive resolution shall not be invalidated by any error in such ruling. In the case of a resolution duly proposed as a Special or Extraordinary resolution no amendment thereto (other than a mere clerical amendment to correct a manifest error) may in any event be considered or voted upon.

Chapter 23: Dealing with Common Items of Business

P. 23.2A   Agreement to accept accounts less than 21 days before general meeting

We, the undersigned, being all the members of XYZ Limited entitled to attend and vote at the [annual/extraordinary] general meeting, convened for [date of meeting], hereby agree that copies of the documents required to be sent to us in accordance with section 238 of the Companies Act 1985 not later than twenty-one days before the date of the said meeting shall be deemed to have been duly sent notwithstanding that they are sent less than twenty-one days before the date of the meeting.
[Date]
[Signatures]

P. 23.2B   Notice of AGM re laying of accounts

To receive the accounts and reports of the directors and the auditors for the year ended [date].

P. 23.3A   Board resolution to appoint first auditors

THAT [name of auditors] be appointed auditors of the company to hold office until the conclusion of the first general meeting at which accounts are laid before the company.

P. 23.3B   Resolution of company to appoint first auditors

THAT [name of auditors] be appointed auditors of the company to hold office until the conclusion of the first general meeting at which accounts are laid before the company [and that their remuneration be fixed by the directors].

P. 23.3C Resolution to reappoint auditors at general meeting

THAT [name of auditors] be reappointed auditors of the company until the conclusion of the next general meeting at which accounts are laid before the company [and that their remuneration be fixed by the directors].

P. 23.5A Resolution of general meeting for removal of auditors

THAT [name of auditors] be removed from office as auditors of the company with immediate effect [and that [name of new auditors] be appointed auditors of the company in their place to hold office until the conclusion of the next general meeting at which accounts are laid and that their remuneration be fixed by the directors].

P. 23.5B Resolution of general meeting for appointment of auditors other than retiring auditors

THAT [name of auditors] be appointed auditors of the company in place of the retiring auditors to hold office until the conclusion of the next general meeting at which accounts are laid before the company and that their remuneration be fixed by the directors.

P. 23.7A Directors' report re dividends

An interim dividend of 5p per share has been paid and the directors recommend a final dividend of 9p per share in respect of the year ended [date], making a total for the year of 14p per share. The proposed dividend will, if approved at the annual general meeting, be paid on [date] to shareholders on the register at the close of business on [date].

P. 23.7B Notice of resolution to declare a dividend

To declare a dividend.

P. 23.7C Minute of resolution to declare a dividend

It was resolved:
THAT a final dividend of 9p per 25p ordinary share in respect of the year ended [date] be declared payable on [date] to shareholders registered at the close of business on [date].

P. 23.7D Directors' resolution to pay an interim dividend

It was resolved:
THAT an interim dividend for the year ended [date] of 7p per share on the ordinary shares of 25p each be paid on [date] to shareholders registered at the close of business on [date].

P. 23.8A Board resolution to fill a casual vacancy

THAT [name of new director] be appointed a director of the company in the place of [name of former director] with effect from [date] and shall hold office until the next annual general meeting.

P. 23.8B Board resolution to appoint an additional director

THAT [name of new director] be appointed a director of the company with effect from [date] and shall hold office until the next annual general meeting.

P. 23.8C Appointment of additional director by sole continuing director

XYZ LIMITED

Pursuant to the authority given by regulation 90 of Table A in The Companies (Tables A to F) Regulations 1985 (which regulation is incorporated in the company's articles of association), I, [name], the sole continuing director of the company, hereby appoint [name of person to be appointed] to be a director of the company to fill the vacancy caused by [circumstances, e.g. death or resignation] of [name].

[Date]
[Signature]

P. 23.8D Notice given by member to the company of intention to propose person (not recommended by the directors) for appointment or reappointment as a director

To the Directors
XYZ Ltd

Pursuant to reg. 76 of Table A, I hereby give notice of my intention to propose [name] for election as a director at the annual general meeting of the company to be held on [date]. The particulars regarding [name] which would, if he were so appointed or reappointed, be required to be included in the company's register of directors are set out below.

[Particulars]
[Signature]
[Date]

I, [name], hereby give notice that I am willing, if elected, to act as a director of XYZ Ltd.

[Signature]
[Date]

P. 23.8E   Notice given by company to members in accordance with reg. 77 of resolution to appoint director not retiring by rotation

To elect [name] as a director (see Note 1).
Note 1: [Particulars which would be required to be included in the register of directors.]

P. 23.9A   Special notice to company to comply with s. 293

The Directors
XYZ Limited
I hereby give notice pursuant to sections 293 and 379 of the Companies Act 1985 of my intention to propose the following resolution as an ordinary resolution at the next annual general meeting of the company:

THAT Mrs S. Brown, who has attained the age of 70 years, be re-elected a director of the company.

[Signature]
[Address]   [Date]

P. 23.9B   Notice given by company to its members to comply with s. 293

To re-elect Mrs S. Brown a director of the company, special notice having been given to the company pursuant to sections 293 and 379 of the Companies Act 1985 of the intention to propose the following resolution as an ordinary resolution:

THAT Mrs S. Brown, who has attained the age of 70 years, be re-elected a director of the company.

P. 23.9C   Plc article disapplying directors' age limits

No person shall be disqualified from being appointed a Director in accordance with these Articles by reason of having attained the age of seventy years or any other age, nor shall special notice or other special formality be required on that account. No Director shall vacate his office by reason only of his age.

P. 23.10   Retirement by rotation article to comply with Combined Code

(A) At each annual general meeting:
    (a) any director who was elected or last re-elected a director at or before the annual general meeting held in the third calendar year before the current year shall retire by rotation; and
    (b) such further directors (other than any directors who, pursuant to article [no.], are not then subject to retirement by rotation) shall retire by rotation as would bring the

number retiring by rotation up to one-third of the number of directors in office at the date of the notice of the meeting (or, if their number is not a multiple of three, the number nearest to but not greater than one-third).

(B) The directors to retire by rotation at any general meeting shall exclude any directors who, pursuant to article [No.], are not then subject to retirement by rotation, but shall include (so far as necessary to obtain the number required) any director who is due to retire at the meeting by reason of age or who wishes to retire and not to offer himself for re-election. Any further directors so to retire shall be those of the other directors who have been longest in office since their election or last re-election and so that as between persons who were last elected or re-elected directors on the same day those to retire shall in the absence of agreement be selected by lot. A retiring director shall be eligible for re-election.

(C) The company at the meeting at which a director retires under any provision of these articles may by ordinary resolution fill the office being vacated by electing thereto the retiring director or some other person eligible for election.

(D) The retirement shall not have effect until the conclusion of the meeting except where a resolution is passed to elect some other person in place of the retiring director or a resolution is put to the meeting and lost. Accordingly a retiring director who is re-elected or deemed to have been re-elected will continue in office without a break.

P. 23.11A Special notice to company to remove director

The Directors
XYZ Limited
I hereby give notice pursuant to sections 303 and 379 of the Companies Act 1985 of my intention to propose the following resolution as an ordinary resolution at the next annual general meeting of the company:

THAT Mrs S. Brown be removed from office as a director of the company.

[Signature]
[Address]   [Date]

P. 23.11B Notice given by the company to its members

Special notice has been given to the company in accordance with sections 303 and 379 of the Companies Act 1985 of the intention to propose the following resolution as an ordinary resolution:

THAT Mrs S. Brown be removed from office as a director of the company.

P. 23.11C **Letter from company accompanying copy of notice sent to the director concerned**

Dear Mrs Brown,

Please find enclosed a copy of a notice received by the company from Mr Brown (a member of the company) stating that he intends at the next general meeting of the company to propose a resolution to remove you as a director of the company.

Yours sincerely,

[Secretary]

[Copy of notice enclosed]

Chapter 24: Written Resolutions and Unanimous Consent

P. 24.2A **Written resolution (members)**

XYZ LIMITED

Pursuant to Section 381A of the Companies Act 1989, we the undersigned being all the members of the company who at the date of this resolution are entitled to vote at a general meeting of the company, hereby resolve:

THAT . . . .

[Signatures and dates]*

* The date of the resolution is the date when it was signed by the last member to sign.

P. 24.2B **Written resolution (class of members)**

XYZ Limited

Pursuant to Section 381A of the Companies Act 1989, we the undersigned being all the members of the company who at the date of this resolution are entitled to vote at a meeting of the holders of the [description of class] of the company, hereby resolve:

THAT . . . .

[Signatures and dates]*

* The date of the resolution is the date when it was signed by the last member to sign.

P. 24.2C **Letter to auditors to accompany copy of statutory written resolution**

To: the Auditors

We enclose a copy of a resolution which it is proposed to be agreed as a written resolution of the company pursuant to Section 381A of the Companies Act 1985 ('the Act'). This copy is being sent to you in accordance with the requirements of Section 381B of the Act.

Yours faithfully,

[Signature]
Secretary
On behalf of XYZ Limited

P. 24.2D   **Certified copy of a members' written resolution for filing at Companies House**

[Company Number]
THE COMPANIES ACT 1985
AND
THE COMPANIES ACT 1989
RESOLUTION
OF
XYZ LIMITED

On the .... day of .... 20..., the following RESOLUTION IN WRITING (such resolution to have effect as a [special] resolution) was duly passed by all the members of the Company who were at the date thereof entitled to attend and vote at a general meeting of the Company pursuant to section 381A, Companies Act 1985 (as amended):

THAT   [Text of resolution]

[Signed]
Secretary

P. 24.3   **Record of a written resolution**

Record of a written resolution of XYZ LIMITED
The following resolution(s) was/were passed as a written resolution on [date] being the date of the last signature.

A copy of the resolution was delivered to the auditors on [date].

The signatories to the resolution were:
[Names of directors]

[Signature]
[Director/Secretary]
[Date]

P. 24.5   **Written record of decision by sole member of a company**

XYZ LIMITED
Written record under s. 382B of the Companies Act 1985 (as amended) of a decision (which may be taken by the company in general meeting) taken by the sole member on [date].

The following resolution, having effect as an [ordinary] resolution, was approved on the above date by the undersigned sole member of the company:

THAT . . . .

[Signature]
[Date]

Chapter 25: Elective Regime

P. 25.2A   Written resolution to dispense with the AGM

XYZ LIMITED

Pursuant to Section 381A of the Companies Act 1985 we the undersigned, being all the members of the company who at the date of this resolution are entitled to attend and vote at general meetings of the company, hereby unanimously resolve as an elective resolution in accordance with Section 379A of the Companies Act 1985 (the Act):

THAT the company hereby elects:
(1) pursuant to Section 252 of the Act, to dispense with the laying of accounts and reports before the company in general meeting;
(2) pursuant to Section 366A of the Act, to dispense with the holding of annual general meetings;
(3) pursuant to Section 386 of the Act, to dispense with the obligation to appoint auditors annually; and

[Members' signatures and date signed]

P. 25.2B   Ordinary resolution to revoke an elective resolution

THAT pursuant to Section 379A of the Companies Act 1985, the company hereby revokes the elective resolution passed on [date] [purpose of resolution].

P. 25.3A   Elective resolution to dispense with AGM

To resolve as an elective resolution in accordance with Section 379A of the Companies Act 1985:
THAT pursuant to Section 366A of the Companies Act 1985, the company elects to dispense with the holding of annual general meetings.

P. 25.3B   Notice by member to company requiring annual general meeting while elective resolution is in force

To: The Directors   [Date]
XYZ Ltd
[Registered Office]
As a member of the company I hereby give notice, pursuant to section 366A(3) of the Companies Act 1985, that I require the company to hold an annual general meeting for the year ending 20..... notwithstanding that an elective resolution to dispense with the holding of annual general meetings is in force.

[Signature]
[Name and address]

P. 25.4A   **Elective resolution to dispense with laying of accounts and report**

To resolve as an elective resolution in accordance with Section 379A of the Companies Act 1985:
THAT pursuant to Section 252 of the Companies Act 1985, the company elects to dispense with the laying of accounts and reports before the company in general meeting.

P. 25.4B   **Notice to members in annual report and accounts informing them of their rights under s. 253(2)**

An elective resolution dispensing with the requirement to lay the accounts and reports at a general meeting of the company is currently in force. This means that the accounts and reports for the year ended . . . . . 20.... (enclosed with this notice) will not be laid at a general meeting, unless a member of the company requires a general meeting to be held for this purpose.

Under s. 253 of the Companies Act 1985 any member may require the company to hold a general meeting for the purpose of laying the accounts and reports by giving notice in writing to that effect to the company at its registered office (addressed to the secretary) within 28 days of the date of this notice.
[Dated]

P. 25.4C   **Notice to company from member requiring general meeting to be held for the purpose of laying accounts and reports**

To: The Directors   [Date]
XYZ Ltd
[Registered Office]
As a member of the company I hereby give notice, pursuant to section 253(2) of the Companies Act 1985, that I require a general meeting of the company to be held for the purpose of laying the accounts and reports of the company for the year ending 20.....
[Signature]
[Name and address]

P. 25.5A   **Elective resolution to dispense with appointment of auditors annually**

To resolve as an elective resolution in accordance with Section 379A of the Companies Act 1985:
THAT pursuant to Section 386 of the Companies Act 1985, the company elects to dispense with the obligation to appoint auditors annually.

P. 25.5B   **Ordinary resolution authorising the directors to fix the remuneration of auditors while an elective resolution dispensing with their annual appointment is in force**

THAT the directors be authorised to fix the remuneration of the auditors until such time as a resolution to appoint auditors is passed at a general meeting of the company.

P. 25.6A   **Elective resolution electing that the provisions of s. 80A apply in relation to the giving or renewal of authority to allot shares**

To resolve as an elective resolution in accordance with Section 379A of the Companies Act 1985 ('the Act'):
THAT in relation to the giving or renewal of authority under Section 80 of the Act, the provisions of Section 80A of the Act shall apply, instead of the provisions of Section 80(4) and 80(5) of the Act, after the passing of this resolution.

P. 25.6B   **Ordinary resolution authorising the directors to allot shares for an indefinite period**

THAT the directors be generally and unconditionally authorised, pursuant to Section 80 of the Companies Act 1985, to exercise for an indefinite period any power of the company to allot and grant rights to subscribe for or to convert securities into shares of the company up to a maximum nominal amount equal to the nominal amount of the authorised but unissued share capital at the date of the passing of this resolution.

P. 25.7   **Elective resolution to reduce the majority required to authorise short notice of meetings**

To resolve as an elective resolution in accordance with Section 379A of the Companies Act 1985 ('the Act'):
THAT pursuant to Sections 369(4) and 378(3) of the Act, that the provisions of those Sections shall have effect in relation to the company as if for the references to 95 per cent in those provisions there was substituted references to 90 per cent.

Chapter 26: Minutes

See also precedents for **Chapter 4**.

P. 26.11A   **Minutes of annual general meeting of public limited company**

Minutes of the annual general meeting of XYZ PLC held on [date] at [place]

Present: [Name of director], Chairman
[Names of other directors]

[Number] members
[Number] proxies representing [number] members

In attendance   Secretary

34. The chairman opened the meeting at 11.00 a.m.

35. The chairman proposed and the meeting agreed to take the notice of the meeting as read.

36. [Name] representing [name of auditors] read the report of the auditors to the members.

Resolution 1
37. The chairman proposed THAT the report of the Directors and the audited accounts for the year ended [date], now laid before the meeting, be received.
After dealing with questions, the chairman put the resolution to the meeting and declared it carried.

Resolution 2
38. The chairman proposed THAT [name 1], a director retiring by rotation, be re-elected a director of the company.
The resolution was put to the meeting and the chairman declared it carried.

Resolution 3
39. The chairman proposed THAT [name 2], a director retiring by rotation, be re-elected a director of the company.
During the discussion of this proposal, [name], a proxy for a member of the company opposed to the reappointment of [name 2], attempted to make a speech in breach of article [No.] of the company's articles of association. Despite repeated warnings from the chairman, the proxy refused to be quiet. To general acclamation, the chairman warned him that if he did not comply he would be asked to leave the meeting. The proxy continued to speak in a highly aggressive manner. Accordingly, the chairman ordered him to leave the meeting. The proxy ignored the chairman's order and advanced towards the stage in a threatening manner. The chairman ordered the stewards to remove him from the meeting and he was removed following a brief struggle.
After dealing with further questions, the chairman put the resolution to the meeting and declared it carried.

Resolution 4
40. The chairman proposed THAT [name of auditors] be reappointed as auditors to hold office until the conclusion of the next general meeting at which accounts are laid before the company and that their remuneration be determined by the directors.

The resolution was put to the meeting and the chairman declared it carried.

[Name], a member of the company holding [number] shares, demanded a poll. The chairman ruled that the member was not able to satisfy the requirements of article [No.] of the company's articles of association and that the demand was therefore invalid, and confirmed that the resolution had been carried.

Resolution 5

41. The chairman proposed as a special resolution:

THAT the authority and power conferred on the Directors by Article [No.] (Authority to allot securities) of the Articles of Association of the Company be renewed for the period expiring on the date of the annual general meeting of the Company to be held in [year + 1] and that:

a) for the purposes of Article [No.], the prescribed amount for the above period shall be [amount 1] and

b) for the purposes of the proviso to Article [No.], the aggregate nominal amount of equity securities allotted wholly for cash during such period, otherwise than as mentioned in such proviso, shall not exceed [amount 2].

[Name], a member of the company, proposed an amendment the effect of which would have been to substitute [amount 3] as the prescribed amount for the purposes of Article [No.]. The chairman ruled the amendment out of order and explained that it was not possible to amend the substance of a special resolution. After further discussion, the chairman put the resolution to the meeting and declared it carried.

[Name], a member of the company, and [name], a proxy representing a member of the company, demanded a poll on the resolution. The chairman informed the meeting that the demand was valid and that a poll would be held immediately at which representatives of the company's auditors would act as scrutineers. After the chairman informed the meeting of the poll procedures, voting papers were issued and collected by the company's registrars.

The results of the poll were as follows:
For: 13,567,342
Against: 1,003,231

42. The chairman closed the meeting.

[Signed]
Chairman

P. 26.11B   Minutes of general meeting of a single member company

XYZ LIMITED

Minutes of an extraordinary general meeting held at [place] on [date]

Present: Mr XYZ (Chairman)

In attendance: C. Sec. (Company Secretary)

The chairman proposed as a [special] resolution:

THAT . . . .

After declaring an interest in the resolution to the extent that [nature of interest] this was passed by the sole member of the company as a [special] resolution of the company.

[Signature]

Chairman

P. 26.11C   Minutes of board meeting of a public company

EXAMPLE PLC

Minutes of a meeting of the BOARD OF DIRECTORS held on [date] at 27 Fitzwilliam Place, London W1.

Present:	Julian Gold	Director (in the chair)
	Susan Silver	Director
	Richard Wood	Director
	Samuel Johnson	Director (for minutes 74 to 79 only)
	George Hawkins	Director
In attendance:	Alan Scribe	Secretary

72. The chairman signed the minutes of the board meeting held on [date], copies having been circulated to the directors.

73. Subsequent to a recommendation by the Nomination Committee it was resolved:

THAT Mr Andrew de Chancery be and is hereby appointed a director of the company and shall hold office until the next annual general meeting.

74. Mr George Hawkins joined the meeting.

75. It was resolved:

THAT pursuant to article [No.] of the company's articles of association, any two directors be appointed a committee to take any actions and to complete all documents necessary to purchase the freehold on 27 Fitzwilliam Place, London W1.

76. There were produced and considered:

(a) group management accounts made up to 30th September 1994 (Board paper 94/10);

(b) predicted cash flow statement for the six months to 30th April 1995 (Board paper 94/11).

It was resolved:

THAT the company's bankers be approached by Richard Wood to negotiate an increase in the company's overdraft facilities to £2,000,000 to cover the cash shortfall predicted to arise between [date] and [date].

77. There was produced and discussed a paper prepared by Susan Silver entitled 'Going greener' (Board paper 94/12), on the company's environmental policy. It was resolved:

THAT no decision could be made to implement the proposals in the paper without detailed costings. The chairman requested Susan Silver to resubmit the proposals at the next board meeting together with a schedule of the projected costs of implementing each of the recommendations for each of the company's subsidiaries.

78. The chairman stated that the next meeting of the board of directors would be held on [date] at Fitzwilliam Place.

79. There being no further business the meeting was closed.

[Signature]

Chairman

Appendix A

Companies Act 1985 provisions on meetings

The following provisions include all amendments made up to the end of January 2001.

CHAPTER II
CLASS RIGHTS

125. Variation of class rights

(1) This section is concerned with the variation of the rights attached to any class of shares in a company whose share capital is divided into shares of different classes.

(2) Where the rights are attached to a class of shares otherwise than by the company's memorandum, and the company's articles do not contain provision with respect to the variation of the rights, those rights may be varied if, but only if –

    (a) the holders of three-quarters in nominal value of the issued shares of that class consent in writing to the variation; or

    (b) an extraordinary resolution passed at a separate general meeting of the holders of that class sanctions the variation;

and any requirement (howsoever expressed) in relation to the variation of those rights is complied with to the extent that it is not comprised in paragraphs (a) and (b) above.

(3) Where –

    (a) the rights are attached to a class of shares by the memorandum or otherwise;

    (b) the memorandum or articles contain provision for the variation of those rights; and

    (c) the variation of those rights is connected with the giving, variation, revocation or renewal of an authority for allotment under section 80 or with a reduction of the company's share capital under section 135;

those rights shall not be varied unless –

    (i) the condition mentioned in subsection (2)(a) or (b) above is satisfied; and

    (ii) any requirement of the memorandum or articles in relation to the variation of rights of that class is complied with to the extent that it is not comprised in that condition.

(4) If the rights are attached to a class of shares in the company by the memorandum or otherwise and –
  (a) where they are so attached by the memorandum, the articles contain provision with respect to their variation which had been included in the articles at the time of the company's original incorporation; or
  (b) where they are so attached otherwise, the articles contain such provision (whenever first so included), and in either case the variation is not connected as mentioned in subsection (3)(c), those rights may only be varied in accordance with that provision of the articles.

(5) If the rights are attached to a class of shares by the memorandum, and the memorandum and articles do not contain provision with respect to the variation of those rights, those rights may be varied if all the members of the company agree to the variation.

(6) The provisions of section 369 (length of notice for calling company meetings), section 370 (general provisions as to meetings and votes) and sections 376 and 377 (circulation of members' resolutions) and the provisions of the articles relating to general meetings shall, so far as applicable, apply in relation to any meeting of shareholders required by this section or otherwise to take place in connection with the variation of the rights attached to a class of shares, and shall so apply with the necessary modifications and subject to the following provisions, namely –

  (a) the necessary quorum at any such meeting other than an adjourned meeting shall be two persons holding or representing by proxy at least one-third in nominal value of the issued shares of the class in question and at an adjourned meeting one person holding shares of the class in question or his proxy;
  (b) any holder of shares of the class in question present in person or by proxy may demand a poll.

(7) Any alteration of a provision contained in a company's articles for the variation of the rights attached to a class of shares, or the insertion of any such provision into the articles, is itself to be treated as a variation of those rights.

(8) In this section and (except where the context otherwise requires) in any provision for the variation of the rights attached to a class of shares contained in a company's memorandum or articles, references to the variation of those rights are to be read as including references to their abrogation.

126. Savings for court's powers under other provisions

Nothing in subsections (2) to (5) of section 125 derogates from the powers of the court under the following sections of this Act, namely –

sections 4 to 6 (company resolution to alter objects),
section 54 (litigated objection to public company becoming
private by re-registration),
section 425 (court control of company compromising with
members and creditors),
section 427 (company reconstruction or amalgamation),
sections 459 to 461 (protection of minorities).

127. Shareholders' right to object to variation

(1) This section applies if, in the case of a company whose share
capital is divided into different classes of shares –
(a) provision is made by the memorandum or articles for
authorising the variation of the rights attached to any class of
shares in the company subject to –
(i) the consent of any specified proportion of the holders of
the issued shares of that class, or
(ii) the sanction of a resolution passed at a separate meeting
of the holders of those shares, and in pursuance of that
provision the rights attached to any such class of shares
are at any time varied; or
(b) the rights attached to any class of shares in the company are
varied under section 125(2).

(2) The holders of not less in the aggregate than 15 per cent of the
issued shares of the class in question (being persons who did not
consent to or vote in favour of the resolution for the variation),
may apply to the court to have the variation cancelled; and if
such an application is made, the variation has no effect unless and
until it is confirmed by the court.

(3) Application to the court must be made within 21 days after the
date on which the consent was given or the resolution was passed
(as the case may be), and may be made on behalf of the
shareholders entitled to make the application by such one or more
of their number as they may appoint in writing for the purpose.

(4) The court, after hearing the applicant and any other persons who
apply to the court to be heard and appear to the court to be
interested in the application, may, if satisfied having regard to all
the circumstances of the case, that the variation would unfairly
prejudice the shareholders of the class represented by the
applicant, disallow the variation and shall, if not satisfied, confirm
it. The decision of the court on any such application is final.

(5) The company shall within 15 days after the making of an order
by the court on such an application forward a copy of the order
to the registrar of companies; and if default is made in complying
with this provision, the company and every officer of it who is in
default is liable to a fine and, for continued contravention, to a
daily default fine.

(6) 'Variation', in this section, includes abrogation; and 'varied' is to
be construed accordingly.

128. Registration of particulars of special rights

(1) If a company allots shares with rights which are not stated in its memorandum or articles, or in any resolution or agreement which is required by section 380 to be sent to the registrar of companies, the company shall deliver to the registrar of companies, within one month from allotting the shares, a statement in the prescribed form containing particulars of those rights.

(2) This does not apply if the shares are in all respects uniform with shares previously allotted; and shares are not for this purpose to be treated as different from shares previously allotted by reason only that the former do not carry the same rights to dividends as the latter during the 12 months immediately following the former's allotment.

(3) Where the rights attached to any shares are varied otherwise than by an amendment of the company's memorandum or articles or by a resolution or agreement subject to section 380, the company shall within one month from the date on which the variation is made deliver to the registrar of companies a statement in the prescribed form containing particulars of the variation.

(4) Where a company (otherwise than by any such amendment, resolution or agreement as is mentioned above) assigns a name or other designation, or a new name or other designation, to any class of its shares, it shall within one month from doing so deliver to the registrar of companies a notice in the prescribed form giving particulars of the name or designation so assigned.

(5) If a company fails to comply with this section, the company and every officer of it who is in default is liable to a fine and, for continued contravention, to a daily default fine.

129. Registration of newly created class rights

(1) If a company not having a share capital creates a class of members with rights which are not stated in its memorandum or articles or in a resolution or agreement to which section 380 applies, the company shall deliver to the registrar of companies within one month from the date on which the new class is created a statement in the prescribed form containing particulars of the rights attached to that class.

(2) If the rights of any class of members of the company are varied otherwise than by an amendment of the memorandum or articles or by a resolution or agreement subject to section 380, the company shall within one month from the date on which the variation is made deliver to the registrar of companies a statement in the prescribed form containing particulars of the variation.

(3) If a company (otherwise than by any such amendment, resolution or agreement as is mentioned above) assigns a name or other designation, or a new name or other designation, to any class of its members, it shall within one month from doing so deliver to

the registrar of companies a notice in the prescribed form giving particulars of the name or designation so assigned.

(4) If a company fails to comply with this section, the company and every officer of it who is in default is liable to a fine and, for continued contravention, to a daily default fine.

ACCOUNTS AND AUDIT

238. Persons entitled to receive copies of accounts and reports

(1) A copy of the company's annual accounts, together with a copy of the directors' report for that financial year and of the auditors' report on those accounts, shall be sent to –
(a) every member of the company,
(b) every holder of the company's debentures, and
(c) every person who is entitled to receive notice of general meetings, not less than 21 days before the date of the meeting at which copies of those documents are to be laid in accordance with section 241.

(2) Copies need not be sent –
(a) to a person who is not entitled to receive notices of general meetings and of whose address the company is unaware, or
(b) to more than one of the joint holders of shares or debentures none of whom is entitled to receive such notices, or
(c) in the case of joint holders of shares or debentures some of whom are, and some not, entitled to receive such notices, to those who are not so entitled.

(3) In the case of a company not having a share capital, copies need not be sent to anyone who is not entitled to receive notices of general meetings of the company.

(4) If copies are sent less than 21 days before the date of the meeting, they shall, notwithstanding that fact, be deemed to have been duly sent, if it is so agreed by all the members entitled to attend and vote at the meeting.

(4A) References in this section to sending any person copies of a company's annual accounts, of the directors' report and of the auditors' report include references to using electronic communications for sending copies of those documents to such address as may from time to time be notified to the company by that person for that purpose.
(b) where the company and the person to whom they are to be sent so agree, publishing the accounts and reports on a web site or sites for the period specified in subsection (4B) below, and notifying that person in a manner agreed with him for that purpose that they have been so published and of the address of each web site.

(4B) For the purpose of this section copies of those documents are also to be treated as sent to a person where –
(a) the company and that person have agreed to his having access

to the documents on a web site (instead of their being sent to him);

(b) the documents are documents to which that agreement applies; and

(c) that person is notified, in a manner for the time being agreed for the purpose between him and the company, of –
   (i) the publication of the documents on a web site;
   (ii) the address of that web-site; and
   (iii) the place on that web site where the documents may be accessed, and how they may be accessed.

(4C) For the purposes of this section documents treated in accordance with subsection (4B) as sent to any person are to be treated as sent to him not less than 21 days before the date of a meeting if, and only if –

(a) the documents are published on the web site throughout a period beginning at least 21 days before the date of the meeting and ending with the conclusion of the meeting; and

(b) the notification given for the purposes of paragraph (c) of that subsection is given not less than 21 days before the date of the meeting.

(4D) Nothing in subsection (4C) shall invalidate the proceedings of a meeting where –

(a) any documents that are required to be published as mentioned in paragraph (a) of that subsection are published for a part, but not all, of the period mentioned in that paragraph; and

(b) the failure to publish those documents throughout that period is wholly attributable to circumstances which it would not be reasonable to have expected the company to prevent or avoid.

(4D) A company may, notwithstanding any provision to the contrary in its articles, take advantage of any of subsections (4A) to (4D).

(5) If default is made in complying with this section, the company and every officer of it who is in default is guilty of an offence and liable to a fine.

(6) Where copies are sent out under this section over a period of days, references elsewhere in this Act to the day on which copies are sent out shall be construed as references to the last day of that period.

MEETINGS AND RESOLUTIONS

366. Annual General Meeting

(1) Every company shall in each year hold a general meeting as its annual general meeting in addition to any other meetings in that year, and shall specify the meeting as such in the notices calling it.

(2) However, so long as a company holds its first annual general meeting within 18 months of its incorporation, it need not hold it in the year of its incorporation or in the following year.

(3)   Not more than 15 months shall elapse between the date of one annual general meeting and that of the next.

(4)   If default is made in holding a meeting in accordance with this section, the company and every officer of it who is in default shall be liable to a fine.

366A. Election by private company to dispense with annual general meetings

(1)   A private company may elect (by elective resolution in accordance with section 379A) to dispense with the holding of annual general meetings.

(2)   An election has effect for the year in which it is made and subsequent years, but does not affect any liability already incurred by reason of default in holding an annual general meeting.

(3)   In any year in which an annual general meeting would be required to be held but for the election, and in which no such meeting has been held, any member of the company may, by notice to the company not later than three months before the end of the year, require the holding of an annual general meeting in that year.

(3A)   The power of a member under subsection (3) to require the holding of an annual general meeting is exercisable not only by the giving of a notice but also by the transmission to the company at such address as may for the time being be specified for the purpose by or on behalf of the company of an electronic communication containing the requirement.

(4)   If such a notice is given or electronic communication is transmitted, the provisions of section 366(1) and (4) apply with respect to the calling of the meeting and the consequences of default.

(5)   If the election ceases to have effect, the company is not obliged under section 366 to hold an annual general meeting in that year if, when the election ceases to have effect, less than three months of the year remains. This does not affect any obligation of the company to hold an annual general meeting in that year in pursuance of a notice given or electronic communication transmitted under subsection (3).

(5A)   In this section, 'address' includes any number or address used for the purposes of electronic communications.

367. Secretary of State's power to call meeting in default

(1)   If default is made in holding a meeting in accordance with section 366, the Secretary of State may, on the application of any member of the company, call or direct the calling of, a general meeting of the company and give such ancillary or consequential directions as he thinks expedient, including directions modifying or supplementing, in relation to the calling, holding and conduct of the meeting, the operation of the company's articles.

(2)   The directions that may be given under subsection (1) include a

direction that one member of the company present in person or by proxy shall be deemed to constitute a meeting.

(3) If default is made in complying with directions of Secretary of State under subsection (1), the company and every officer of it who is in default is liable to a fine.

(4) A general meeting held under this section shall, subject to any directions of the Secretary of State, be deemed to be an annual general meeting of the company; but, where a meeting so held is not in the year in which the default in holding the company's annual general meeting occurred, the meeting so held shall not be treated as the annual general meeting for the year in which it is held unless at that meeting the company resolves that it be so treated.

(5) Where a company so resolves, a copy of the resolution shall within 15 days after its passing, be forwarded to the registrar of companies and recorded by him; and if default is made in complying with this subsection, the company and every officer of it who is in default is liable to a fine and, for continued contravention, to a daily default fine.

368. Extraordinary general meeting on members' request

(1) The directors of a company shall, on a members' requisition, forthwith proceed duly to convene an extraordinary general meeting of the company.

This applies notwithstanding anything in the company's articles.

(2) A members' requisition is a requisition of –

(a) members of the company holding at the date of the deposit of the requisition not less than one-tenth of such of the paid-up capital of the company as at that date carries the right of voting at general meetings of the company; or

(b) in the case of a company not having a share capital, members of it representing not less than one tenth of the total voting rights of all the members having at the date of deposit of the requisition a right to vote at general meetings.

(3) The requisition must state the objects of the meeting, and must be signed by the requisitionists and deposited at the registered office of the company, and may consist of several documents in like form each signed by one or more requisitionists.

(4) If the directors do not within 21 days from the date of deposit of the requisition duly convene a meeting, the requisitionists, or any of them representing more than one half of the total voting rights of all of them, may themselves convene a meeting, but any meeting so convened shall not be held after the expiration of three months from that date.

(5) A meeting convened under this section by requisitionists shall be convened in the same manner, as nearly as possible, as that in which meetings are to be convened by directors.

(6) Any reasonable expenses incurred by the requisitionists by reason

of the failure of the directors duly to convene a meeting shall be repaid to the requisitionists by the company out of any sums due or to become due from the company by way of fees or other remuneration in respect of their services to such of the directors as were in default.

(7) In the case of a meeting at which a resolution is to be proposed as a special resolution, the directors are deemed not to have duly convened the meeting if the do not give the notice required for special resolutions by section 378(2).

(8) The directors are deemed not to have duly convened a meeting if they convene a meeting for a date more than 28 days after the date of the notice convening the meeting.

369. Length of notice for calling meetings

(1) A provision of a company's articles is void in so far as it provides for the calling of a meeting of the company (other than an adjourned meeting) by a shorter notice than –

(a) in the case of the annual general meeting, 21 days' notice in writing; and

(b) in the case of a meeting other than an annual general meeting or a meeting for the passing of a special resolution –
   (i) 7 days' notice in writing in the case of an unlimited company; and
   (ii) otherwise, 14 days' notice in writing.

(2) Save in so far as the articles of a company make other provision in that behalf (not being a provision avoided by subsection (1)), a meeting of the company (other than an adjourned meeting) may be called –

(a) in the case of the annual general meeting, 21 days' notice in writing; and

(b) in the case of a meeting other than an annual general meeting or a meeting for the passing of a special resolution –
   (i) 7 days' notice in writing in the case of an unlimited company; and
   (ii) otherwise, 14 days' notice in writing.

(3) Notwithstanding that a meeting is called by shorter notice than that specified in subsection (2) or in the company's articles (as the case may be), it is deemed to have been duly called if it is so agreed –

(a) in the case of a meeting called as the annual general meeting, by all the members entitled to attend and vote at it; and

(b) otherwise, by the requisite majority.

(4) The requisite majority for this purpose is a majority in number of the members having a right to attend and vote at the meeting, being a majority –

(a) together holding not less than 95 per cent in nominal value of the shares giving a right to attend and vote at the meeting; or

(b) in the case of a company not having a share capital, together representing not less than 95 per cent of the total voting rights at that meeting of all the members.

A private company may elect (by elective resolution in accordance with section 379A) that the above provisions shall have effect in relation to the company as if for the references to 95 per cent there were substituted references to such lesser percentage, but not less than 90 per cent, as may be specified in the resolution or subsequently determined by the company in general meeting.

(4A) For the purposes of this section the cases in which notice in writing of a meeting is to be taken as given to a person include any case in which notice of the meeting is sent using electronic communications to such address as may for the time being be notified by that person to the company for that purpose.

(4B) For the purposes of this section a notice in writing of a meeting is also to be treated as given to a person where –

(a) the company and that person have agreed that notices of meetings required to be given to that person may instead be accessed by him on a web site;

(b) the meeting is a meeting to which that agreement applies;

(c) that person is notified, in a manner for the time being agreed between him and the company for the purpose, of–

   (i) the publication of the notice on a web site;

   (ii) the address of that web site; and

   (iii) the place on that web site where the notice may be accessed, and how it may be accessed;

and

(d) the notice continues to be published on that web site throughout the period beginning with the giving of that notification and ending with the conclusion of the meeting;

and for the purposes of this section a notice treated in accordance with this subsection as given to any person is to be treated as so given at the time of the notification mentioned in paragraph (c).

(4C) A notification given for the purposes of subsection (4B)(c) must –

(a) state that it concerns a notice of a company meeting served in accordance with this Act,

(b) specify the place, date and time of the meeting, and

(c) state whether the meeting is to be an annual or extraordinary general meeting.

(4D) Nothing in subsection (4B) shall invalidate the proceedings of a meeting where –

(a) any notice that is required to be published as mentioned in paragraph (d) of that subsection is published for a part, but not all, of the period mentioned in that paragraph; and

(b) the failure to publish that notice throughout that period is wholly attributable to circumstances which it would not be reasonable to have expected the company to prevent or avoid.

(4E) A company may, notwithstanding any provision to the contrary in a company's articles, take advantage of any of subsections (4A) to (4D).

(4F) In so far as the articles of the company do not provide for notices and notifications to be served using electronic communications, the provisions of Table A (as for the time being in force) as to such service shall apply.

(4G) In this section, 'address' includes any number or address used for the purposes of electronic communications.'

370. General provisions as to meetings and votes

(1) The following provisions have effect in so far as the articles of the company do not make provision in that behalf.

(2) Notice of the meeting of the company shall be served on every member of it in the manner in which notices are required to be served by Table A (as for the time being in force).

(3) Two or more members holding not less that one-tenth of the issued share capital or, if the company does not have a share capital, not less than 5 per cent in number of the members of the company may call a meeting.

(4) Two members personally present are a quorum.

(5) Any member elected by the members present at the meeting may be chairman of it.

(6) In the case of a company originally having a share capital, every member has one vote in respect of each share or each £10 of stock held by him; and in any other case every member has one vote.

370A. Quorum at a meeting of the sole member

Notwithstanding any provision to the contrary in the articles of a private company limited by shares or by guarantee having only one member, one member present in person or by proxy shall be a quorum.

371. Power of court to order meeting

(1) If for any reason it is impracticable to call a meeting of a company in any manner in which meetings of that company may be called, or to conduct the meeting in manner prescribed by the articles or this Act, the court may either of its own motion or on the application –
(a) of any director of the company, or
(b) of any member of the company who would be entitled to vote at the meeting,
order a meeting to be called, held and conducted in any manner the court thinks fit.

(2) Where such an order is made, the court may give such ancillary or consequential directions as it thinks expedient; and these may include a direction that one member of the company present in person or by proxy be deemed to constitute a meeting.

(3) A meeting called, held and conducted in accordance with an order under subsection (1) is deemed for all purposes a meeting of the company duly called, held and conducted.

372. Proxies

(1) Any member of a company entitled to attend and vote at a meeting of it is entitled to appoint another person (whether a member or not) as his proxy to attend and vote instead of him; and in the case of a private company a proxy appointed to attend and vote instead of a member has also the same right as the member to speak at the meeting.

(2) But, unless the articles otherwise provide –

(a) subsection (1) does not apply in the case of a company not having a share capital; and

(b) a member of a private company is not entitled to appoint more than one proxy to attend on the same occasion; and

(c) a proxy is not entitled to vote except on a poll.

(2A) The appointment of a proxy may, notwithstanding any provision to the contrary in a company's articles, be contained in an electronic communication sent to such address as may be notified by or on behalf of the company for that purpose.

(2B) In so far as the articles of the company do not make other provision in that behalf, the appointment of a proxy may be contained in an electronic communication in accordance with the provisions of Table A (as for the time being in force).

(3) In the case of a company having a share capital, in every notice calling a meeting of the company there shall appear with reasonable prominence a statement that a member entitled to attend and vote is entitled to appoint a proxy or, where that is allowed, one or more proxies to attend and vote instead of him, and that a proxy need not also be a member.

(4) If default is made in complying with subsection (3) as respects any meeting, every officer of the company who is in default is liable to a fine.

(5) A provision contained in a company's articles is void in so far as it would have the effect of requiring the appointment of a proxy or any document necessary to show the validity of, or otherwise relating to, the appointment of a proxy, to be received by the company or any other person more than 48 hours before a meeting or adjourned meeting in order that the appointment may be effective.

(6) If for the purpose of any meeting of a company invitations to appoint as proxy a person or one of a number of persons specified in the invitations are issued at the company's expense to some only of the members entitled to be sent a notice of the meeting and to vote at it by proxy, then every officer of the company who knowingly and wilfully authorises or permits their issue in that manner is liable to a fine.

However, an officer is not so liable by reason only of the issue to a member at his request of a form of appointment naming the proxy, or of a list of persons willing to act as proxy, if the form or list is available on request to every member entitled to vote at the meeting by proxy.

(6A) In this section, 'address' includes any number or address used for the purposes of electronic communications.

(7) This section applies to meetings of any class of members of a company as it applies to general meetings of the company.

373. Right to demand a poll

(1) A provision contained in a company's articles is void in so far as it would have the effect either –

(a) of excluding the right to demand a poll at a general meeting on any question other than the election of the chairman of the meeting or the adjournment of the meeting; or

(b) of making ineffective the demand for a poll on any such question which is made either –

    (i) by not less than 5 members having the right to vote at the meeting; or

    (ii) by a member or members representing not less than one-tenth of the total voting rights of all the members having the right to vote at the meeting; or

    (iii) by a member or members holding shares in the company conferring the right to vote at the meeting, being shares on which an aggregate sum has been paid up equal to not less than one-tenth of the total sum paid up on all the shares conferring that right.

(2) The appointment of a proxy to vote at a meeting of a company is deemed also to confer authority to demand or join in demanding a poll; and for the purposes of subsection (1) a demand by a person as proxy for a member is the same as a demand by a member.

374. Voting on a poll

On a poll taken at a meeting of a company or a meeting of any class of members of a company, a member entitled to more than one vote need not, if he votes, use all his votes or cast all the votes he uses in the same way.

375. Representation of corporations at meetings

(1) A corporation, whether or not a company within the meaning of this Act, may –

(a) if it is a member of another corporation, being such a company, by resolution of its directors or other governing body authorise such persons as it thinks fit to act as its representative at any meeting of the company or at any meeting of any class of members of the company;

(b) if it is a creditor (including a holder of debentures) of another corporation, being such a company, by resolution of its directors or other governing body authorise such persons as it thinks fit to act as its representative at any meeting of creditors of the company held in pursuance of this Act or of rules made under it, or in pursuance of the provisions contained in any debenture or trust deed, as the case may be.

(2) A person so authorised is entitled to exercise the same powers on behalf of the corporation which he represents as that corporation could exercise if it were an individual shareholder, creditor or debenture-holder of the other company.

376. Circulation of members' resolutions

(1) Subject to the section next following, it is the duty of a company, on the requisition in writing of such members as is specified below and (unless the company otherwise resolves) at the expense of the requisitionists –

(a) to give to members of the company entitled to receive notice of the next annual general meeting notice of any resolution which may properly be moved and is entitled to be moved at the meeting;

(b) to circulate to members entitled to have notice of any general meeting sent to them any statement of not more than 1,000 words with respect to the matter referred to in any proposed resolution or the business to be dealt with at that meeting.

(2) The number of members necessary for a requisition under subsection (1) is –

(a) any number of members representing not less than one-twentieth of the total voting rights of all the members having at the date of the requisition a right to vote at the meeting to which the requisition relates; or

(b) not less than 100 members holding shares in the company on which there has been paid up an average sum, per member, of not less than £100.

(3) Notice of any such resolution shall be given, and any such statement shall be circulated, to members of the company entitled to have notice of the meeting sent to them, by serving a copy of the resolution or statement on each such member in any manner permitted for service of notice of the meeting.

(4) Notice of any such resolution shall be given to any other member of the company by giving notice of the general effect of the resolution in any other manner permitted for giving him notice of meetings of the company.

(5) For compliance with subsections (3) and (4), the copy must be served, or notice to the effect of the resolution be given (as the case may be) in the same manner and (as far as practicable) at the same time as the notice of the meeting; and where it is not practicable for it to be served or given at the same time, it must be served or given as soon as practicable thereafter.

(6)   The business which may be dealt with at an annual general meeting includes any resolution of which notice is given in accordance with this section; and for the purposes of this subsection notice is deemed to have been so given notwithstanding the accidental omission, in giving it, of one or more members. This has effect notwithstanding anything in the company's articles.

(7)   In the event of default in complying with this section, every officer of the company who is in default is liable to a fine.

377. In certain cases, compliance with s 376 not required

(1)   A company is not bound under section 376 to give notice of a resolution or to circulate a statement unless –

    (a) a copy of the requisition signed by the requisitionists (or two or more copies which between them contain the signatures of all the requisitionists) is deposited at the registered office of the company –

        (i) in the case of a requisition requiring notice of a resolution, not less than 6 weeks before the meeting, and

        (ii) otherwise, not less than a week before the meeting; and

    (b) there is deposited or tendered with the requisition a sum reasonably sufficient to meet the company's expenses in giving effect to it.

(2)   But if, after a copy of a requisition requiring notice of a resolution has been deposited at the company's registered office, an annual general meeting is called for a date 6 weeks or less after the copy has been deposited, the copy (though not deposited within the time required by subsection (1)) is deemed properly deposited for the purposes of that subsection.

(3)   The company is also not bound under section 376 to circulate a statement if, on the application either of the company or of any other person who claims to be aggrieved, the court is satisfied that the rights conferred by that section are being abused to secure needless publicity for defamatory matter; and the court may order the company's costs on such application to be paid in whole or in part by the requisitionists, notwithstanding that they are not parties to the application.

378. Extraordinary and special resolutions

(1)   A resolution is an extraordinary resolution when it has been passed by a majority of not less than three-fourths of such members as (being entitled to do so) vote in person or, where proxies are allowed, by proxy, at a general meeting of which notice specifying the intention to propose the resolution as an extraordinary resolution has been duly given.

(2)   A resolution is a special resolution when it has been passed by such a majority as is required for the passing of an extraordinary resolution and at a general meeting of which not less than 21 days' notice, specifying the intention to propose the resolution as a special resolution, has been duly given.

(3) If it is so agreed by a majority in number of the members having the right to attend and vote at such a meeting, being a majority –

   (a) together holding not less than 95 per cent in nominal value of the shares giving that right; or
   (b) in the case of a company not having a share capital, together representing not less than 95 per cent of the total voting rights at that meeting of all the members,

   a resolution may be proposed and passed as a special resolution at a meeting of which less than 21 days' notice has been given. A private company may elect (by elective resolution in accordance with section 379A) that the above provisions shall have effect in relation to the company as if for the references to 95 per cent there were substituted references to such lesser percentage, but not less than 90 per cent, as may be specified in the resolution or subsequently determined by the company in general meeting

(4) At any meeting at which an extraordinary resolution or a special resolution is submitted to be passed, a declaration by the chairman that the resolution is carried is, unless a poll is demanded, conclusive evidence of the fact without proof of the number or proportion of the votes recorded in favour of or against the resolution.

(5) In computing the majority on a poll demanded on the question that an extraordinary resolution or a special resolution be passed, reference is to be had to the number of votes cast for and against the resolution.

(6) For the purposes of this section, notice of a meeting is deemed duly given, and the meeting duly held, when the notice is given and the meeting held in the manner provided by this Act or the company's articles.

379. Resolution requiring special notice

(1) Where by any provision of this Act special notice is required of a resolution, the resolution is not effective unless notice of the intention to move it has been given to the company at least 28 days before the meeting at which it is moved.

(2) The company shall give its members notice of any such resolution at the same time and in the same manner as it gives notice of the meeting or, if that is not practicable, shall give them notice either by advertisement in a newspaper having an appropriate circulation or in any other mode allowed by the company's articles, at least 21 days before the meeting.

(3) If after notice of the intention to move such a resolution has been given to the company, a meeting is called for a date 28 days or less after the notice has been given, the notice is deemed properly given, though not given within the time required.

379A. Elective resolution of private company

(1)   An election by a private company for the purposes of –

    (a) section 80A (election as to duration of authority to allot shares),

    (b) section 252 (election to dispense with laying of accounts and reports before general meeting),

    (c) section 366A (election to dispense with holding annual general meeting),

    (d) section 369(4) or 378(3) (election as to majority required to authorise short notice of meetings), or

    (e) section 386 (election to dispense with appointment of auditors annually),

shall be made by resolution of the company in general meeting in accordance with this section.

Such a resolution is referred to in this Act as an 'elective resolution'.

(2)   An elective resolution is not effective unless –

    (a) at least 21 days' notice in writing is given of the meeting, stating that an elective resolution is to be proposed and stating the terms of that resolution, and

    (b) the resolution is agreed to at the meeting, in person or by proxy, by all the members entitled to attend and vote at the meeting.

(2A)   An elective resolution is effective notwithstanding the fact that less than 21 days' notice in writing of the meeting is given if all the members entitled to attend and vote at the meeting so agree.

(2B)   For the purposes of this section, notice in writing of the meeting is to be taken as given to a person where notice of the meeting is sent using electronic communications to such address as may for the time being be notified by that person to the company for that purpose.

(2C)   For the purposes of this section a notice in writing of the meeting is also to be treated as given to a person where –

    (a) the company and that person have agreed that notices of meetings required to be given to that person may instead be accessed by him on a web site;

    (b) the meeting is a meeting to which that agreement applies;

    (c) that person is notified, in a manner for the time being agreed between him and the company for the purpose, of –

        (i)   the publication of the notice on a web site;

        (ii) the address of that web site; and

        (iii) the place on that web site where the notice may be accessed, and how it may be accessed; and

    (d) the notice continues to be published on that web site throughout the period beginning with the giving of that notification and ending with the conclusion of the meeting; and for the purposes of this section a notice treated in accordance with this subsection as given to any person is to be treated as so given at the time of the notification mentioned in paragraph (c).

(2D) A notification given for the purposes of subsection (2C)(c) must –
   (a) state that it concerns a notice of a company meeting at which an elective resolution is to be proposed, and
   (b) specify the place, date and time of the meeting.

(2E) Nothing in subsection (2C) shall invalidate the proceedings of a meeting where –
   (a) any notice that is required to be published as mentioned in paragraph (d) of that subsection is published for a part, but not all, of the period mentioned in that paragraph; and
   (b) the failure to publish that notice throughout that period is wholly attributable to circumstances which it would not be reasonable to have expected the company to prevent or avoid.

(2F) In so far as the articles of the company do not provide for notices and notifications to be served using electronic communications, the provisions of Table A (as for the time being in force) as to such service shall apply.'

(3) The company may revoke an elective resolution by passing an ordinary resolution to that effect.

(4) An elective resolution shall cease to have effect if the company is registered as a public company.

(5) An elective resolution may be passed or revoked in accordance with this section, and the provisions referred to in subsections (1) and (2B) to (2E) have effect, notwithstanding any contrary provision in the company's articles of association.

(5A) In this section, 'address' includes any number or address used for the purposes of electronic communications.

380. Registration, etc of resolutions and agreements

(1) A copy of every resolution or agreement to which this section applies shall, within 15 days after it is passed or made, be forwarded to the registrar of companies and recorded by him; and must be either a printed copy or else a copy in some other form approved by the registrar.

(2) Where articles have been registered, a copy of every such resolution or agreement for the time being in force shall be embodied in or annexed to every copy of the articles issued after the passing of the resolution or the making of the agreement.

(3) Where articles have not been registered, a printed copy of every such resolution or agreement shall be forwarded to any member at his request on payment of 5 pence or such lesser sum as the company may direct.

(4) This section applies to –
   (a) special resolutions;
   (b) extraordinary resolutions;
   (bb) an elective resolution or a resolution revoking such a resolution;

(c) resolutions or agreements which have been agreed to by all the members of a company but which, if not so agreed to, would not have been effective for their purpose unless (as the case may be) they had been passed as special resolutions or as extraordinary resolutions;

(d) resolutions or agreements which have been agreed to by all the members of some class of shareholders but which, if not so agreed to, would not have been effective for their purpose unless (as the case may be) they had been passed by some particular majority or otherwise in some particular manner, and all resolutions or agreements which effectively bind all the members of any class of shareholders though not agreed to by all those members.

(e) a resolution passed by the directors of a company in compliance with a direction under section 31(2) (change of name on Secretary of State's direction);

(f) a resolution of a company to give, vary, revoke or renew an authority to the directors for the purposes of section 80 (allotment of relevant securities);

(g) a resolution of the directors passed under section 147(2) (alteration of memorandum on company ceasing to be a public company, following acquisition of its own shares);

(h) a resolution conferring, varying, revoking or renewing authority under section 166 (market purchase of company's own shares);

(j) a resolution for voluntary winding up, passed under section 84(1)(a) of the Insolvency Act;

(k) a resolution passed by the directors of an old public company, under section 2(1) of the Consequential Provisions Act, that the company should be re-registered as a public company;

(l) a resolution of the directors passed by virtue of regulation 16(2) of the Uncertificated Securities Regulations 1995 (which allow title to a company's shares to be evidenced and transferred without written instrument); and

(m) a resolution of a company passed by virtue of regulation 16(6) of the Uncertificated Securities Regulations 1995 (which prevents or reverses a resolution of the directors under regulation 16(2) of those Regulations).

(5) If a company fails to comply with subsection (1), the company and every officer of it who is in default is liable to a fine and, for continued contravention, to a daily default fine.

(6) If a company fails to comply with subsection (2) or (3), the company and every officer of it who is in default is liable to a fine.

(7) For the purposes of subsections (5) and (6), a liquidator of a company is deemed an officer of it.

381. Resolution passed at an adjourned meeting
Where a resolution is passed at an adjourned meeting of –
(a) a company;

(b) the holders of any class of shares in a company;
(c) the directors of a company;
the resolution is for all purposes to be treated as having been passed on the date on which it was in fact passed, and is not to be deemed passed on any earlier date.

381A. Written resolutions of private companies

(1) Anything which in the case of a private company may be done –
(a) by resolution of the company in general meeting, or
(b) by resolution of a meeting of any class of members of a company, may be done, without a meeting and without previous notice being required, by resolution in writing signed by or on behalf of all the members of the company who at the date of the resolution would be entitled to attend and vote at such a meeting.

(2) The signatures need not be on a single document provided each is on a document which accurately states the terms of the resolution.

(3) The date of the resolution means when the resolution is signed by or on behalf of the last member to sign.

(4) A resolution agreed to in accordance with this section has effect as if passed –
(i) by the company in general meeting, or
(ii) by a meeting of the relevant class of members of the company, as the case may be; and any reference in any enactment to a meeting at which a resolution is passed or to members voting in favour of a resolution shall be construed accordingly.

(5) Any reference in any enactment to the date of passing of a resolution is, in relation to a resolution agreed in accordance with this section, a reference to the date of the resolution.

(6) A resolution may be agreed to in accordance with this section which would otherwise be required to be passed as a special, extraordinary or elective resolution; and any reference in any enactment to a special extraordinary or elective resolution includes such a resolution.

(7) This section has effect subject to the exceptions specified in Part I of Schedule 15A; and in relation to certain descriptions of resolutions under this section the procedural requirements of this Act have effect with the adaptations specified in Part II of that Schedule.

381B. Duty to notify auditors of proposed written resolution

(1) If a director or secretary of a company –
(a) knows that it is proposed to seek agreement to a resolution in accordance with section 381A, and
(b) knows the terms of the resolution, he shall, if the company has auditors, secure that a copy of the resolution is sent to them or that they are otherwise notified of its contents, at or before the time the resolution is supplied to a member for signature.

(2)   A person who fails to comply with subsection (1) is liable to a fine.

(3)   In any proceedings for a offence under this section it is a defence for the accused to prove –

(a) that the circumstances were such that it was not practicable for him to comply with subsection (1), or

(b) that he believed on reasonable grounds that a copy of the resolution had been sent to the company's auditors or that they had otherwise been informed of its contents.

(4)   Nothing in this section affects the validity of any resolution.

381C. Written resolutions: supplementary provisions

(1)   Sections 381A and 381B have effect notwithstanding any provision of the company's memorandum or articles, but do not prejudice any power conferred by any such provision.

(2)   Nothing in those sections affects any enactment or rule of law as to –

(a) things done otherwise than by passing a resolution, or

(b) cases in which a resolution is treated as having been passed, or a person is precluded from alleging that a resolution has not been duly passed.

382. Minutes of meetings

(1)   Every company shall cause minutes of all proceedings of general meetings, all proceedings at meetings of its directors and, where there are managers, all proceedings at meetings of its managers to be entered in books kept for that purpose.

(2)   Any such minute, if purporting to be signed by the chairman of the meeting at which the proceedings were had, or by the chairman of the next succeeding meeting, is evidence of the proceedings.

(3)   Where a shadow director by means of a notice required by section 317(8) declares an interest in a contract or a proposed contract, this section applies –

(a) if it is a specific notice under paragraph (a) of that subsection, as if the declaration had been made at the meeting there referred to, and

(b) otherwise, as if it had been made at the meeting of directors next following the giving of the notice; and the making of the declaration is in either case deemed to form part of the proceedings at the meeting.

(4)   Where minutes have been made in accordance with this section of the proceedings at any general meeting of the company or meeting of directors or managers, the, until the contrary is proved, the meeting is deemed duly held and convened, and all proceedings had at the meeting to have been duly had; and all appointments of directors, managers or liquidators are deemed valid.

(5)   If a company fails to comply with subsection (1), the company and every officer of it who is in default is liable to a fine and, for continued contravention, to a daily default fine.

382A. Recording of written resolutions

(1) Where a written resolution is agreed to in accordance with section 381A which has effect as if agreed by the company in general meeting, the company shall cause a record of the resolution (and of the signatures) to be entered in a book in the same way as minutes of proceedings of a general meeting of the company.

(2) Any such record, if purporting to be signed by a director of the company or by the company secretary, is evidence of the proceedings in agreeing to the resolution; and where a record is made in accordance with this section, then, until the contrary is proved, the requirements of this Act with respect to those proceedings shall be deemed to be complied with.

(3) Section 352(5) (penalties) applies in relation to failure to comply with subsection (1) above as it applies in relation to a failure to comply with subsection (1) of that section; and section 383 (inspection of minute books) applies in relation to a record made in accordance with this section as it applies in relation to minutes of a general meeting.

382B. Recording of decisions by the sole member

(1) Where a private company limited by shares or by guarantee has only one member and he takes any decision which may be taken by the company in general meeting and which has effect as if agreed by the company in general meeting, he shall (unless that decision is taken by way of a written resolution) provide the company with a written record of that decision.

(2) If the sole member fails to comply with subsection (1) he shall be liable to a fine.

(3) Failure by the sole member to comply with subsection (1) shall not affect the validity of any decision referred to in that subsection.

383. Inspection of minute books

(1) The books containing the minutes of proceedings of any general meeting of a company held on or after 1st November 1929 shall be kept at the company's registered office, and ... be open to the inspection of any member without charge.

(2) ...

(3) Any member shall be entitled [on payment of such fee as may be prescribed] to be furnished, within 7 days after he has made a request in that behalf to the company, with a copy of any such minutes as are referred to above, ...

(4) If an inspection required under this section is refused or if a copy required under this section is not sent within the proper time, the company and every officer of it who is in default is liable in respect of each offence to a fine.

(5) In the case of any such refusal or default, the court may by order compel an immediate inspection of the books in respect of all proceedings of general meetings, or direct that copies required be sent to the persons requiring them.

PART XXV

MISCELLANEOUS AND SUPPLEMENTARY PROVISIONS

722. Form of company registers, etc

(1)   Any register, index, minute book or accounting records required by the Companies Acts to be kept by a company may be kept either by making entries in bound books or by recording the matters in question in any other manner.

(2)   Where any such register, index, minute book or accounting record is not kept by making entries in a bound book, but by some other means, adequate precautions shall be taken for guarding against falsification and facilitating its discovery.

(3)   If default is made in complying with subsection (2), the company and every officer of it who is in default is liable to a fine and, for continued contravention, to a daily default fine.

723. Use of computers for company records

(1)   The power conferred on a company by section 722(1) to keep a register or other record by recording the matters in question otherwise than by making entries in bound books includes the power to keep the register or other record by recording those matters otherwise than in a legible form, so long as the recording is capable of being reproduced in a legible form.

(2)   Any provision of an instrument made by a company before 12th February 1979 which requires a register of holders of the company's debentures to be kept in legible form is to be read as requiring the register to be kept in a legible or non-legible form.

(3)   If any such register or other record of the company as is mentioned in section 722(1), or a register of holders of company debentures, is kept by the company by recording the matters in question otherwise than in a legible form, any duty imposed on the company by this Act to allow inspection of, or to furnish a copy of, the register or other record or any part of it is to be treated as a duty to allow inspection of, or to furnish, a reproduction of the recording or of the relevant part of it in a legible form.

(4)   The Secretary of State may by regulations in a statutory instrument make such provision in addition to subsection (3) as he considers appropriate in connection with such registers or other records as are mentioned in that subsection, and are kept as so mentioned; and the regulations may make modifications of provisions of this Act relating to such registers or other records.

(5)   A statutory instrument under subsection (4) is subject to annulment in pursuance of a resolution of either House of Parliament.

SCHEDULE 15A

Section 381A(7)

WRITTEN RESOLUTIONS OF PRIVATE COMPANIES

PART I

EXCEPTIONS

1. Section 381A does not apply to –

    (a) a resolution under section 303 removing a director before the expiration of his period of office, or
    (b) a resolution under section 391 removing an auditor before the expiration of his term of office.

PART II

ADAPTATION OF PROCEDURAL REQUIREMENTS

Introductory

2.-(1) In this Part of this schedule (which adapts certain requirements of this Act in relation to proceedings under section 381A) –

    (a) a 'written resolution' means a resolution agreed to, or proposed to be agreed to, in accordance with that section, and
    (b) a 'relevant member' means a member by whom, or on whose behalf, the resolution is required to be signed in accordance with that section.

   (2) A written resolution is not effective if any of the requirements of this Part of this Schedule is not complied with.

Section 95 (disapplication of pre-emption rights)

3.-(1) The following adaptations have effect in relation to a written resolution under section 95(2) (disapplication of pre-emption rights), or renewing a resolution under that provision.
   (2) So much of section 95(5) as requires the circulation of a written statement by the directors with a notice of meeting does not apply, but such a statement must be supplied to him for signature.
   (3) Section 95(6) (offences) applies in relation to the inclusion in any such statement of matter which is misleading, false or deceptive in a material particular.

Section 155 (financial assistance for purchase of company's own shares or those of holding company)

4. In relation to a written resolution giving approval under section 155(4) or (5) (financial assistance for purchase of company's own shares or those of holding company), section 157(4)(a) (documents to be available at meeting) does not apply, but the documents referred to in that provision must be supplied to each relevant member at or before the time at which the resolution is supplied to him for signature.

Sections 164, 165 and 167 (authority for off-market purchase or contingent purchase contract of company's own shares)

5.-(1) The following adaptations have effect in relation to a written resolution –

(a) conferring authority to make an off-market purchase of the company's own shares under section 164(2),

(b) conferring authority to vary a contract for an off-market purchase of the company's own shares under section 164(7), or

(c) varying, revoking or renewing any such authority under section 164(3).

(2) Section 164(5) (resolution ineffective if passed by exercise of voting rights by member holding shares to which the resolution relates) does not apply; but for the purposes of section 381A(1) a member holding shares to which the resolution relates shall not be regarded as a member who would be entitled to attend and vote.

(3) Section 164(6) (documents to be available at the company's registered office and at meeting) does not apply, but the documents referred to in that provision and, where that provision applies by virtue of section 164(7), the further documents referred to in that provision must be supplied to each relevant member at or before the time at which the resolution is supplied to him for signature.

(4) The above adaptations also have effect in relation to a written resolution in relation to which the provisions of section 164(3) to (7) apply by virtue of –

(a) section 165(2) (authority for contingent purchase contract), or

(b) section 167(2) (approval of release of rights under contract approved under section 164 or 165).

Section 173 (approval for payment out of capital)

6.-(1) The following adaptations have effect in relation to a written resolution giving approval under section 173(2) (redemption or purchase of company's own shares out of capital).

(2) Section 174(2) (resolution ineffective if passed by exercise of voting rights by member holding shares to which resolution relates) does not apply; but for the purposes of section 381A(1) a member holding shares to which the resolution relates shall not be regarded as a member who would be entitled to attend and vote.

(3) Section 174(4) documents to be available at meeting) does not apply, but the documents referred to in that provision must be supplied to each relevant member at or before the time at which the resolution is supplied to him for signature.

Section 319 (approval of director's service contracts)

7.   In relation to a written resolution approving any such term as is mentioned in section 319(1) (director's contract of employment for more than five years), section 319(5) (documents to be made available at company's registered office and at meeting) does not apply, but the documents referred to in that provision must be supplied to each relevant member at or before the time at which the resolution is supplied to him for signature.

Section 337 (funding of director's expenditure in performing duties)

8.   In relation to a written resolution giving approval under section 337(3)(a) (funding a director's expenditure in performing his duties), the requirement of that provision that certain matters be disclosed at the meeting at which the resolution is passed does not apply, but those matters must be disclosed to each relevant member at or before the time at which the resolution is supplied to him for signature.

Appendix B

Companies Act 1985 Table A (as amended)

The 1985 Table A is contained in the Companies (Tables A to F) Regulations 1985. These regulations were amended on 22 December 2000 by the Companies Act 1985 (Electronic Communications) Order 2000. The amendments made by the Order have been incorporated in the following text and are highlighted in italics. Where necessary, the text of the unamended version of the 1985 Table A is given by way of notes. Companies which adopted the 1985 Table A prior to 22 December 2000 will need to refer to these notes. However, if a company whose articles make no provision for electronic communications, takes advantage of the new statutory procedures (see **Chapter 2**), it must in certain circumstances comply with the relevant provisions of the amended Table A, even though they do not form part of its articles.

TABLE A

REGULATIONS FOR MANAGEMENT
OF A COMPANY LIMITED BY SHARES

INTERPRETATION

1. In these regulations –
'the Act' means the Companies Act 1985 including any statutory modification or re-enactment thereof for the time being in force.
'the articles' means the articles of the company.
'clear days' in relation to the period of notice means that period excluding the day when the notice is given or deemed to be given and the day for which it is given or on which it is to take effect.
[*'communication' means the same as in the Electronic Communications Act 2000,*
'electronic communication' means the same as in the Electronic Communications Act 2000][1]
'executed' includes any mode of execution.

---

[1] The italicised words were inserted by the Schedule 1 of the Companies Act 1985 (Electronic Communications) Order 2000 on 22 December 2000. Prior to that date Table A did not include a definition of an 'electronic communication' or a 'communication'.

'office' means the registered office of the company.

'the holder' in relation to shares means the member whose name is entered in the register of members as the holder of the shares.

'the seal' means the common seal of the company.

'secretary' means the secretary of the company or any person appointed to perform the duties of the secretary of the company, including a joint, assistant or deputy secretary.

'the United Kingdom' means Great Britain and Northern Ireland. Unless the context otherwise requires, words or expressions contained in these regulations bear the same meaning as in the Act but excluding any statutory modification thereof not in force when these regulations become binding on the company.

SHARE CAPITAL

2. Subject to the provisions of the Act and without prejudice to the rights attached to any existing shares, any share may be issued with such rights or restrictions as the company may by ordinary resolution determine.

3. Subject to the provisions of the Act, shares may be issued which are to be redeemed or are to be held liable to be redeemed at the option of the company or the holder on such terms and in such manner as may be provided by the articles.

4. The company may exercise the powers of paying commissions conferred by the Act. Subject to the provisions of the Act, any such commissions may be satisfied by the payment of cash or by the allotment of fully or partly paid shares or partly in one way and partly in the other.

5. Except as required by law, no person shall be recognised by the company as holding a share upon any trust and (except as otherwise provided by the articles or by law) the company shall not be bound by or recognise any interest in any share except an absolute right to the entirety thereof in the holder.

SHARE CERTIFICATES

6. Every member, upon becoming the holder of any shares, shall be entitled without payment to one certificate for all the shares of each class held by him (and, upon transferring part of his holding of shares of any class, to a certificate for the balance of such holding) or several certificates each for one or more of his shares upon payment for every certificate after the first of such reasonable sum as the directors may determine. Every certificate shall be sealed with the seal and shall specify the number, class and respective amounts paid thereon. The company shall not be bound to issue more than one certificate for shares held jointly by several persons and delivery of a certificate to one joint holder shall be sufficient delivery to all of them.

7. If a share certificate is defaced, worn-out, lost or destroyed, it may be renewed on such terms (if any) as to evidence and indemnity and payment of the expenses reasonably incurred by the company in investigating evidence as the directors may determine but otherwise free of charge, and (in the case of defacement or wearing-out) on delivery up of the old certificate.

LIEN

8. The company shall have a first and paramount lien on every share (not being a fully paid share) for all moneys (whether presently payable or not) payable at a fixed time or called in respect of that share. The directors may at any time declare any share to be wholly or in part exempt from the provisions of this regulation. The company's lien on a share shall extend to any amount payable in respect of it.

9. The company may sell in such manner as the directors determine any shares on which the company has a lien if a sum in respect of which the lien exists is presently payable and is not paid within fourteen clear days after notice has been given to the holder of the share or to the person entitled to it in consequence of the death or bankruptcy of the holder, demanding payment and stating that if the notice is not complied with the shares may be sold.

10. To give effect to a sale the directors may authorise some person to execute an instrument of transfer of the shares sold to, or in accordance with the directions of, the purchaser. The title of the transferee to the shares shall not be affected by any irregularity in or invalidity of the proceedings in reference to the sale.

11. The net proceeds of the sale, after payment of the costs, shall be applied in payment of so much of the sum for which the lien exists as is presently payable, and any residue shall (upon surrender to the company for cancellation of the certificate for the shares sold and subject to a like lien for any moneys not presently payable as existed upon the shares before the sale) be paid to the person entitled to the shares at the date of the sale.

CALLS ON SHARES AND FORFEITURE

12. Subject to the terms of allotment, the directors may make calls upon the members in respect of any moneys unpaid on their shares (whether in respect of nominal value or premium) and each member shall (subject to receiving at least fourteen clear days' notice specifying when and where payment is to be made) pay to the company as required by the notice the amount called on his shares. A call may be required to be paid by instalments. A call may, before receipt by the company of any sum due thereunder, be revoked in whole or part and payment of a call may be postponed in whole or part. A person upon whom a call

is made shall remain liable for calls made upon him notwithstanding the subsequent transfer of the shares in respect whereof the call was made.

13.   A call shall be deemed to have been made at the time when the resolution of the directors authorising the call was passed.

14.   The joint holders of a share shall be jointly and severally liable to pay all calls in respect thereof.

15.   If a call remains unpaid after it has become due and payable the person from whom it is due and payable shall pay interest on the amount unpaid from the day it became due and payable until it is paid at the rate fixed by the terms of allotment of the share or in the notice of the call or, if no rate is fixed, at the appropriate rate (as defined by the Act) but the directors may waive payment of the interest wholly or in part.

16.   An amount payable in respect of a share on allotment or at any fixed date, whether in respect of nominal value or premium or as an instalment of a call, shall be deemed to be a call and if it is not paid the provisions of the articles shall apply as if the amount had become due and payable by virtue of a call.

17.   Subject to the terms of allotment, the directors may make arrangements on the issue of shares for a difference between the holders in the amounts and times of payment of calls on their shares.

18.   If a call remains unpaid after it has become due and payable the directors may give to the person from whom it is due not less than fourteen clear days' notice requiring payment of the amount unpaid together with any interest which may have accrued. The notice shall name the place where payment is to be made and shall state that if the notice is not complied with the shares in respect of which the call was made will be liable to be forfeited.

19.   If the notice is not complied with any share in respect of which it was given may, before the payment required by the notice has been made, be forfeited by a resolution of the directors and the forfeiture shall include all dividends or other moneys payable in respect of the forfeited shares and not paid before the forfeiture.

20.   Subject to the provisions of the Act, a forfeited share may be sold, re-allotted or otherwise disposed of on such terms and in such manner as the directors determine either to the person who was before the forfeiture the holder or to any other person and at any time before sale, re-allotment or other disposition, the forfeiture may be cancelled on such terms as the directors think fit. Where for the purposes of its disposal a forfeited share is to be

transferred to any person the directors may authorise some person to execute an instrument of transfer of the shares to that person.

21. A person any of whose shares have been forfeited shall cease to be a member in respect of them and shall surrender to the company for cancellation the certificate for the shares forfeited but shall remain liable to the company for all moneys which at the date of forfeiture were presently payable by him to the company in respect of those shares with interest at the rate at which interest was payable on those moneys before the forfeiture or, if no interest was so payable, at the appropriate rate (as defined by the Act) from the date of forfeiture until payment but the directors may waive payment wholly or in part or enforce payment without any allowance for the value of the shares at the time of forfeiture or for any consideration received on their disposal.

22. A statutory declaration by a director or the secretary that a share has been forfeited on a specified date shall be conclusive evidence of the facts stated in it as against all persons claiming to be entitled to the share and the declaration shall (subject to the execution of an instrument of transfer if necessary) constitute a good title to the share and the person to whom the share is disposed of shall not be bound to see to the application of the consideration, if any, nor shall his title to the share be affected by any irregularity in or invalidity of the proceedings in reference to the forfeiture or disposal of the share.

TRANSFER OF SHARES

23. The instrument of transfer of a share may be in any usual form or in any other form which the directors may approve and shall be executed by or on behalf of the transferor and, unless the share is fully paid, by or on behalf of the transferee.

24. The directors may refuse to register the transfer of a share which is not fully paid to a person of whom they do not approve and they may refuse to register the transfer of a share on which the company has a lien. They may also refuse to register a transfer unless –
   (a) it is lodged at the office or at such other place as the directors may appoint and is accompanied by the certificate for the shares to which it relates and such other evidence as the directors may reasonably require to show the right of the transferor to make the transfer;
   (b) it is in respect of only one class of shares; and
   (c) it is in favour of not more than four transferees.

25. If the directors refuse to register a transfer of a share, they shall within two months after the date on which the transfer was

lodged with the company send to the transferee notice of the refusal.

26. The registration of transfers of shares or of transfers of any class of shares may be suspended at such times and for such periods (not exceeding thirty days in any year) as the directors may determine.

27. No fee shall be charged for the registration of any instrument of transfer or other document relating to or affecting the title to any share.

28. The company shall be entitled to retain any instrument of transfer which is registered, but any instrument of transfer which the directors refuse to register shall be returned to the person lodging it when notice of the refusal is given.

TRANSMISSION OF SHARES

29. If a member dies the survivor or survivors where he was a joint holder, and his personal representatives where he was a sole holder or the only survivor of joint holders, shall be the persons recognised by the company as having any title to his interest; but nothing herein contained shall release the estate of a deceased member from any liability in respect of any share which had been jointly held by him.

30. A person becoming entitled to a share in consequence of the death or bankruptcy of a member may, upon such evidence being produced as the directors may properly require, elect either to become the holder of the share or to have some other person nominated by him registered as the transferee. If he elects to become the holder he shall give notice to the company to that effect. If he elects to have another person registered he shall execute an instrument of transfer of the share to that person. All the articles relating o the transfer of shares shall apply to the notice or instrument of transfer as if it were an instrument of transfer executed by the member and the death or bankruptcy of the member had not occurred.

31. A person becoming entitled to a share in consequence of the death or bankruptcy of a member shall have the rights to which he would be entitled if he were the holder of the share, except that he shall not, before being registered as the holder of the share, be entitled in respect of it to attend or vote at any meeting of the company or at any separate meeting of the holders of any class of shares in the company.

ALTERATION OF SHARE CAPITAL

32. The company may by ordinary resolution –
    (a) increase its share capital by new shares of such amount as the resolution prescribes;

(b) consolidate and divide all or any of its share capital into shares of larger amount than its existing shares;

(c) subject to the provisions of the Act, sub-divide its shares, or any of them, into shares of smaller amount and the resolution may determine that, as between the shares resulting from the sub-division, any of them may have any preference or advantage as compared with the others; and

(d) cancel shares which, at the date of the passing of the resolution, have not been taken or agreed to be taken by any person and diminish the amount of its share capital by the amount of the shares so cancelled.

33. Whenever as a result of a consolidation of shares any members would become entitled to fractions of a share, the directors may, on behalf of those members, sell the shares representing the fractions for the best price reasonably obtainable to any person (including, subject to the provisions of the Act, the company) and distribute the net proceeds of sale in due proportion among those members, and the directors may authorise some person to execute an instrument of transfer of the shares to, or in accordance with the directions of, the purchaser. The transferee shall not be bound to see to the application of the purchase money nor shall his title to the shares be affected by any irregularity in or invalidity of the proceedings in reference to the sale.

34. Subject to the provisions of the Act, the company may by special resolution reduce its share capital, any capital redemption reserve and any share premium account in any way.

PURCHASE OF OWN SHARES

35. Subject to the provisions of the Act, the company may purchase its own shares (including any redeemable shares) and, if it is a private company, make a payment in respect of the redemption or purchase of its own shares otherwise than out of distributable profits of the company or the proceeds of a fresh issue of shares.

GENERAL MEETINGS

36. All general meetings other than annual general meetings shall be called extraordinary general meetings.

37. The directors may call general meetings and, on the requisition of members pursuant to the provisions of the Act, shall forthwith proceed to convene an extraordinary general meeting for a date not later than eight weeks after receipt of the requisition. If there are not within the United Kingdom sufficient directors to call a general meeting, any director or any member of the company may call a general meeting.

NOTICE OF GENERAL MEETINGS

38. An annual general meeting and an extraordinary general meeting

called for the passing of a special resolution or a resolution appointing a person as a director shall be called by at least twenty-one clear days' notice. All other extraordinary general meetings shall be called by at least fourteen clear days' notice but a general meeting may be called by shorter notice if it is so agreed –

(a) in the case of an annual general meeting, by all the members entitled to attend and vote thereat; and

(b) in the case of any other meeting by a majority in number of the members having a right to attend and vote being a majority together holding not less than ninety-five per cent in the nominal value of the shares giving that right.

The notice shall specify the time and place of the meeting and the general nature of the business to be transacted and, in the case of an annual general meeting, shall specify the meeting as such. Subject to the provisions of the articles and to any restriction imposed on any shares, the notice shall be given to all members, to all person entitled to a share in consequence of the death or bankruptcy of a member and to the directors and auditors.

39.   The accidental omission to give notice of a meeting to, or the non-receipt of notice of a meeting by, any person entitled to receive notice shall not invalidate the proceedings at that meeting.

PROCEEDINGS AT GENERAL MEETINGS

40.   No business shall be transacted at any meeting unless a quorum is present. Two persons entitled to vote upon the business to be transacted, each being a member or a proxy for a member or a duly authorised representative of a corporation, shall be a quorum.

41.   If such a quorum is not present within half an hour from the time appointed for the meeting, or if during a meeting such a quorum ceases to be present, the meeting shall stand adjourned to the same day in the next week at the same time and place or to such time and place as the directors may determine.

42.   The chairman, if any, of the board of directors or in his absence some other director nominated by the directors shall preside as chairman of the meeting, but if neither the chairman nor any such other director (if any) be present within fifteen minutes after the time appointed for holding the meeting and willing to act, the directors present shall elect one of their number to be chairman and, if there is only one director present and willing to act, he shall be chairman.

43.   If no director is willing to act as chairman, or if no director is present within fifteen minutes after the time appointed for holding the meeting, the members present and entitled to vote shall choose one of their number to be chairman.

44.   A director shall, notwithstanding that he is not a member, be entitled to attend and speak at any general meeting and at any separate meeting of the holders of any class of shares in the company.

45.   The chairman may, with the consent of a meeting at which a quorum is present (and shall if so directed by the meeting), adjourn the meeting from time to time and from place to place, but no business shall be transacted at an adjourned meeting other than that business which might properly have been transacted at the meeting had the adjournment not taken place. When a meeting is adjourned for fourteen days or more, at least seven days' notice shall be given specifying the time and place of the adjourned meeting and the general nature of the business to be transacted. Otherwise it shall not be necessary to give any such notice.

46.   A resolution put to the vote of a meeting shall be decided on a show of hands unless before, or on the declaration of the result of, the show of hands a poll is duly demanded. Subject to the provisions of the Act, a poll may be demanded –
       (a) by the chairman; or
       (b) by at least two members having the right to vote at the meeting; or
       (c) by a member or members representing not less than one-tenth of the total voting rights of all the members having the right to vote at the meeting; or
       (d) by a member or members holding shares conferring a right to vote at the meeting being shares on which an aggregate sum has been paid up equal to not less than one-tenth of the total sum paid up on all the shares conferring that right; and a demand by a person as proxy for a member shall be the same as a demand by the member.

47.   Unless a poll is duly demanded a declaration by the chairman that a resolution has been carried unanimously, or by a particular majority, or lost, or not carried by a particular majority and an entry to that effect in the minutes of the meeting shall be conclusive evidence of the fact without proof of the number or proportion of the votes recorded in favour or against the resolution.

48.   The demand for a poll may, before the poll is taken, be withdrawn but only with the consent of the chairman and a demand so withdrawn shall not be taken to have invalidated the result of a show of hands declared before the demand was made.

49.   A poll shall be taken as the chairman directs and he may appoint scrutineers (who need not be members) and fix a time and place for declaring the result of the poll. The result of the poll shall be

deemed to be the resolution of the meeting at which the poll was demanded.

50.   In the case of an equality of votes, whether on a show of hands or on a poll, the chairman shall be entitled to a casting vote in addition to any other vote he may have.

51.   A poll demanded on the election of a chairman or on a question of adjournment shall be taken forthwith. A poll demanded on any other question shall be taken either forthwith or at such time and place as the chairman directs not being more than thirty days after the poll is demanded. The demand for a poll shall not prevent the continuance of a meeting for the transaction of any business other than the question on which the poll was demanded. If a poll is demanded before the declaration of the result of a show of hands and the demand is duly withdrawn, the meeting shall continue as if the demand had not been made.

52.   No notice need be given of a poll not taken forthwith if the time and place at which it is to be taken are announced at the meeting at which it is demanded. In any other case at least seven clear days' notice shall be given specifying the time and place at which the poll is to be taken.

53.   A resolution in writing executed by or on behalf of each member who would have been entitled to vote upon it if it had been proposed at a general meeting at which he was present shall be as effectual as if it had been passed at a general meeting duly convened and held and may consist of several instruments in the like form executed by or on behalf of one or more members.

VOTES OF MEMBERS

54.   Subject to any rights or restrictions attached to any shares, on a show of hands every member who (being an individual) is present in person or (being a corporation) present by a duly authorised representative, not being himself a member entitled to vote, shall have one vote and on a poll every member shall have one vote for every share of which he is the holder.

55.   In the case of joint holders the vote of the senior who tenders a vote, whether in person or by proxy, shall be accepted to the exclusion of the votes of the other joint holders; and seniority shall be determined by the order in which the names of the holders stand in the register of members.

56.   A member in respect of whom an order has been made by any court having jurisdiction (whether in the UK or elsewhere) in matters concerning mental disorder may vote, whether on a show of hands or on a poll, by his receiver, curator bonis or other person authorised in that behalf appointed by that court, and any such

receiver, curator bonis or other person may, on a poll, vote by proxy. Evidence to the satisfaction of the directors of the authority of the person claiming to exercise the right to vote shall be deposited at the office, or at such other place as is specified in accordance with the articles for the deposit of instruments of proxy, not less than 48 hours before the time appointed for holding the meeting or adjourned meeting at which the right to vote is to be exercised and in default the right to vote shall not be exercisable.

57. No member shall vote at any general meeting or at any separate meeting of the holders of any class of shares in the company, either in person or by proxy, in respect of any share held by him unless all moneys presently payable by him in respect of that share have been paid.

58. No objection shall be raised to the qualification of any voter except at the meeting or adjourned meeting at which the vote objected to is tendered, and every vote not disallowed at the meeting shall be valid. Any objection made in due time shall be referred to the chairman whose decision shall be final and conclusive.

59. On a poll votes may be given either personally or by proxy. A member may appoint more than one proxy to attend on the same occasion.

60. *The appointment of a proxy shall be executed by or on behalf of the appointor and shall be in the following form (or in a form as near thereto as circumstances allow or in any other form which is usual or which the directors may approve) –[2]*
   ‘   PLC/Limited
   I/We,   , of   , being a member/members of the above-named company, hereby appoint   of   ,
   or failing him,   of , as my/our proxy to vote in my/our name[s] and on my/our behalf at the annual/extraordinary general meeting of the company to be held on   19   , and at any adjournment thereof.
   Signed on   19   .’

61. Where it is desired to afford members an opportunity of instructing the proxy how he shall act the *appointment of*[3] a proxy

---

[2] Regulation 60 was amended by Schedule 1 of the Companies Act 1985 (Electronic Communications) Order 2000 on 22 December 2000. Prior to that date it read as follows: ‘An instrument appointing a proxy shall be in writing, executed by or on behalf of the appointor and shall be in the following form ...’.

[3] The words ‘appointment of’ were inserted in reg. 61 by Schedule 1 of the Companies Act 1985 (Electronic Communications) Order 2000 on 22 December 2000. Prior to that date it read as follows: ‘Where it is desired to afford members an opportunity of instructing the proxy how he shall act the instrument appointing a proxy ...’

shall be in the following form (or in a form as near thereto as circumstances allow or in any other form which is usual or which the directors may approve) –

'   PLC/Limited
I/We,   , of   , being a member/members of the above-named company, hereby appoint   of
, or failing him, of   , as my/our proxy to vote in my/our name[s] and on my/our behalf at the annual/extraordinary general meeting of the company to be held on   19   , and at any adjournment thereof.
This form is to be used in respect of the resolutions mentioned below as follows:
Resolution No 1 *for *against
Resolution No 2 *for *against.
*Strike out whichever is not desired.
Unless otherwise instructed, the proxy may vote as he thinks fit or abstain from voting.
Signed this day   of   19   .'

62.   *The appointment of a proxy and any authority under which it is executed or a copy of such authority certified notarially or in some other way approved by the directors may –*

(a) *in the case of an instrument in writing, be deposited at the office or such other place within the United Kingdom as is specified in the notice convening the meeting or in any instrument of proxy sent out by the company in relation to the meeting not less than 48 hours before the time for holding the meeting or adjourned meeting at which the person named in the instrument proposes to vote; or*

(aa) *in the case of an appointment contained in an electronic communication, where an address has been specified for the purpose of receiving electronic communications –*

   (i) *in the notice convening the meeting, or*

   (ii) *in any instrument of proxy sent out by the company in relation to the meeting, or*

   (iii) *in any invitation contained in an electronic communication to appoint a proxy issued by the company in relation to the meeting,*

be received at such address not less than 48 hours before the time for holding the meeting or adjourned meeting at which the person named in the appointment proposes to vote;

(b) *in the case of a poll taken more than 48 hours after it is demanded, be deposited or received as aforesaid after the poll has been demanded and not less than 24 hours before the time appointed for the taking of the poll; or*

(c) *where the poll is not taken forthwith but is taken not more than 48 hours after it was demanded, be delivered at the meeting at which the poll was demanded to the chairman or to the secretary or to any director;*

and an appointment of proxy which is not deposited, delivered or received in a manner so permitted shall be invalid. In this regulation and the next, 'address', in relation to electronic communications,

*includes any number or address used for the purposes of such
communications.*][4]

63.   A vote given or poll demanded by proxy or by the duly authorised
      representative of a corporation shall be valid notwithstanding the
      previous determination of the authority of the person voting or
      demanding a poll unless notice of the determination was received
      by the company at the office or at such other place at which the
      instrument of proxy was duly deposited *or, where the appointment of
      the proxy was contained in an electronic communication, at the address
      at which the appointment was duly received* before the
      commencement of the meeting or adjourned meeting at which the
      vote is given or the poll demanded or (in the case of a poll taken
      otherwise than on the same day as the meeting or adjourned
      meeting) the time appointed for taking the poll.[5]

NUMBER OF DIRECTORS

64.   Unless otherwise determined by ordinary resolution, the number
      of directors (other than alternate directors) shall not be subject to
      any maximum but shall be not less than two.

ALTERNATE DIRECTORS

65.   Any director (other than an alternate director) may appoint any
      other director, or any other person approved by resolution of the
      directors and willing to act, to be an alternate director and may
      remove from office an alternate director so appointed by him.

---

[4] Regulation 62 was amended by Schedule 1 of the Companies Act 1985
(Electronic Communications) Order 2000 on 22 December 2000. Prior to
that date it read as follows: 'The instrument appointing a proxy and any
authority under which it is executed or a copy of such authority certified
notarially or in some other way approved by the directors may –
(a) be deposited at the office or such other place within the United
    Kingdom as is specified in the notice convening the meeting or in any
    instrument of proxy sent out by the company in relation to the
    meeting not less than 48 hours before the time for holding the
    meeting or adjourned meeting at which the person named in the
    instrument proposes to vote; or
(b) in the case of a poll taken more than 48 hours after it is demanded,
    be deposited as aforesaid after the poll has been demanded and not
    less than 24 hours before the time appointed for the taking of the
    poll; or
(c) where the poll is not taken forthwith but is taken not more than 48
    hours after it was demanded, be delivered at the meeting at which the
    poll was demanded to the chairman or to the secretary or to any
    director;
and an instrument of proxy which is not deposited or delivered in a
manner so permitted shall be invalid.'
[5] The words in italics in reg. 63 were inserted by Schedule 1 of the
Companies Act 1985 (Electronic Communications) Order 2000 on 22
December 2000.

66.   An alternate director shall be entitled to receive notice of all meetings of directors and of all meetings of committees of directors of which his appointor is a member, to attend and vote at any such meeting at which the director appointing him is not personally present, and generally to perform all the functions of his appointor as a director in his absence but shall not be entitled to receive any remuneration from the company for his services as an alternate director. But it shall not be necessary to give notice of such a meeting to alternate director who is absent from the United Kingdom.

67.   An alternate director shall cease to be an alternate director if his appointor ceases to be a director; but if a director retires by rotation or otherwise but is reappointed or deemed to have been reappointed at the meeting at which he retires, any appointment of an alternate director made by him which was in force immediately prior to his retirement shall continue after his reappointment.

68.   Any appointment or removal of an alternate director shall be by notice to the company signed by the director making or revoking the appointment or in any other manner approved by the directors.

69.   Save as otherwise provided in the articles, an alternate director shall be deemed for all purposes to be a director and shall alone be responsible for his own acts and defaults and he shall not be deemed to be the agent of the director appointing him.

POWERS OF DIRECTORS

70.   Subject to the provisions of the Act, the memorandum and the articles and to any directions given by special resolution, the business of the company shall be managed by the directors who may exercise all the powers of the company. No alteration of the memorandum or articles and no such direction shall invalidate any prior act of the directors which would have been valid if that alteration had not been made or that direction had not been given. The powers given by this regulation shall not be limited by any special power given to the directors by the articles and a meeting of directors at which a quorum is present may exercise all powers exercisable by the directors.

71.   The directors may, by power of attorney or otherwise, appoint any person to be the agent of the company for such purposes and on such conditions as they determine, including authority for the agent to delegate all or any of his powers.

DELEGATION OF DIRECTORS' POWERS

72.   The directors may delegate any of their powers to any committee consisting of one or more directors. They may also delegate to

any managing director or any director holding any other executive office such of their powers as they consider desirable to be exercised by him. Any such delegation may be made subject to any conditions the directors may impose, and either collaterally with or to the exclusion of their own powers and may be revoked or altered. Subject to any such conditions, the proceedings of a committee with two or more members shall be governed by the articles regulating the proceedings of directors so far as they are capable of applying.

APPOINTMENT AND RETIREMENT OF DIRECTORS

73. At the first annual general meeting all the directors shall retire from office, and at every subsequent annual general meeting one-third of the directors who are subject to retirement by rotation or, if their number is not three or a multiple of three, the number nearest to one third shall retire from office; but, if there is only one director who is subject to retirement by rotation, he shall retire.

74. Subject to the provisions of the Act, the directors to retire by rotation shall be those who have served longest in office since their last appointment or reappointment, but as between persons who became or were last reappointed directors on the same day those to retire shall (unless they otherwise agree among themselves) be determined by lot.

75. If the company, at the meeting at which a director retires by rotation, does not fill the vacancy the retiring director shall, if willing to act, be deemed to have been reappointed unless at the meeting it is resolved not to fill the vacancy or unless a resolution for the reappointment of the director is put to the meeting and lost.

76. No person other than a director retiring by rotation shall be appointed or reappointed a director at any general meeting unless –
  (a) he is recommended by the directors; or
  (b) not less than fourteen nor more than thirty-five clear days before the date appointed for the meeting, notice executed by a member qualified to vote at the meeting has been given to the company of the intention to propose that person for appointment or reappointment stating the particulars which would, if he were so appointed or reappointed, be required to be included in the company's register of directors together with notice executed by that person of his willingness to be appointed or reappointed.

77. Not less than seven nor more than twenty-eight clear days before the date appointed for holding a general meeting notice shall be given to all who are entitled to receive notice of the meeting of

any person (other than a director retiring by rotation at the meeting) who is recommended by the directors for appointment or reappointment as a director at the meeting or in respect of whom notice has been duly given to the company of the intention to propose him at the meeting for appointment or reappointment as a director. The notice shall give particulars of that person which would, if he were so appointed or reappointed, be required to be included in the company's register of directors.

78. Subject as aforesaid, the company may by ordinary resolution appoint a person who is willing to act to be a director either to fill a vacancy or as an additional director and may also determine the rotation in which any additional directors are to retire.

79. The directors may appoint a person who is willing to act to be director, either to fill a vacancy or as an additional director, provided that the appointment does not cause the number of directors to exceed the number fixed by or in accordance with the articles as the maximum number of directors. A director so appointed shall hold office only until the next following annual general meeting and shall not be taken into account in determining the directors who are to retire by rotation at the meeting. If not reappointed at such annual general meeting, he shall vacate office at the conclusion thereof.

80. Subject as aforesaid, a director who retires at an annual general meeting may, if willing to act, be reappointed. If he is not reappointed, he shall retain office until the meeting appoints someone in his place, or if it does not do so, until the end of the meeting.

DISQUALIFICATION AND REMOVAL OF DIRECTORS

81. The office of director shall be vacated if –
   (a) he ceases to be a director by virtue of any provision of the Act or becomes prohibited by law from being a director; or
   (b) he becomes bankrupt or makes any arrangement or composition with his creditors generally; or
   (c) he is, or may be, suffering from mental disorder and either –
      (i) he is admitted to hospital in pursuance of an application for treatment under the Mental Health Act 1983 or, in Scotland, an application for admission under the Mental Health (Scotland) Act 1960, or
      (ii) an order is made by a court having jurisdiction (whether in the United Kingdom or elsewhere) in matters concerning mental disorder for his detention or for the appointment of a receiver, curator bonis or other person to exercise powers with respect to his property or affairs; or
   (d) he resigns his office by notice to the company; or

(e) he shall for more than six consecutive months have been absent without permission of the directors from meetings of the directors held during that period and the directors resolve that his office be vacated.

REMUNERATION OF DIRECTORS

82. The directors shall be entitled to such remuneration as the company may by ordinary resolution determine and, unless the resolution provides otherwise, the remuneration shall be deemed to accrue from day to day.

DIRECTORS' EXPENSES

83. The directors may be paid all travelling, hotel, and other expenses properly incurred by them in connection with their attendance at meetings of directors or committees of directors or general meetings or separate meetings of the holders of any class of shares or of debentures of the company or otherwise connection with the discharge of their duties.

DIRECTORS' APPOINTMENTS
AND INTERESTS

84. Subject to the provisions of the Act, the directors may appoint one or more of their number to the office of managing director or to any other executive office under the company and may enter into an agreement or arrangement with any director for his employment by the company or for the provision by him of any services outside the scope of the ordinary duties of a director. Any such appointment, agreement or arrangement may be made on such terms as the directors determine and they may remunerate any such director for his services as they think fit. Any appointment of a director to an executive office shall terminate if he ceases to be a director but without prejudice to any claim for damages for breach of the contract of service between the director and the company. A managing director and a director holding any other executive office shall not be subject to retirement by rotation.

85. Subject to the provisions of the Act, and provided that he has disclosed to the directors the nature and extent of any material interest of his, a director notwithstanding his office –
    (a) may be a party to, or otherwise interested in, any transaction or arrangement with the company or in which the company is otherwise interested;
    (b) may be a director or other officer of, or employed by, or party to any transaction or arrangement with, or otherwise interested in, any body corporate promoted by the company or in which the company is otherwise interested; and
    (c) shall not, by reason of his office, be accountable to the company for any benefit which he derives from any such office or employment or from any such transaction or arrangement or from any interest in any such body corporate

and no such transaction or arrangement shall be liable to be avoided on the ground of any such interest or benefit.

86. For the purposes of regulation 85 –
(a) a general notice given to the directors that a director is to be regarded as having an interest of the nature and extent specified in the notice in any transactions or arrangement in which a specified person or class of persons is interested shall be deemed to be a disclosure that the director has an interest in any such transaction of the nature and extent so specified; and
(b) an interest of which a director has no knowledge and of which it is unreasonable to expect him to have knowledge shall not be treated as an interest of his.

DIRECTOR'S GRATUITIES AND PENSIONS

87. The directors may provide benefits, whether by payment of gratuities or pensions or by insurance or otherwise, for any director who has held but no longer holds any executive office or employment with the company or with any body corporate which is or has been a subsidiary of the company or a predecessor in business of the company or of any such subsidiary, and for any member of his family (including a spouse and a former spouse) or any person who is or was dependent upon him, and may (as well before as after he ceases to hold such office or employment) contribute to any fund and pay premiums for the purchase of any such benefit.

PROCEEDINGS OF DIRECTORS

88. Subject to the provisions of the articles, the directors may regulate their proceedings as they think fit. A director may, and the secretary at the request of a director shall, call a meeting of the directors. It shall not be necessary to give notice of a meeting to a director who is absent from the United Kingdom. Questions arising at a meeting shall be decided by a majority of votes. In the case of an equality of votes, the chairman shall have a second or casting vote. A director who is also an alternate director shall be entitled in the absence of his appointor to a separate vote on behalf of his appointor in addition to his own vote.

89. The quorum for the transaction of business of the directors may be fixed by the directors and unless so fixed at any other number shall be two. A person who holds office only as an alternate director shall, if his appointor is not present, be counted in the quorum.

90. The continuing directors or a sole continuing director may act notwithstanding any vacancies in their number, but, if the number of directors is less than the number fixed as the quorum, the continuing directors or director may act only for the purpose of filling vacancies or of calling a general meeting.

91. The directors may appoint one of their number to be the chairman of the board of directors and may at any time remove him from that office. Unless he is unwilling to do so, the director so appointed shall preside at every meeting of directors at which he is present. But if there is no director holding that office, or if the director holding it is unwilling to preside or is nor present within five minutes after the time appointed for the meeting, the directors present may appoint one of their number to be chairman of the meeting.

92. All acts done by a meeting of directors, or of a committee of directors, or by a person acting as a director shall, notwithstanding that it be afterwards discovered that there was a defect in the appointment of any director or that any of them were disqualified from holding office, or had vacated office, or were not entitled to vote, be as valid as if every such person had been duly appointed and was qualified and had continued to be a director and had been entitled to vote.

93. A resolution signed in writing by all the directors entitled to receive notice of a meeting of directors or of a committee of directors shall be as valid and effectual as if it had been passed at a meeting of directors or (as the case may be) a committee of directors duly convened and held and may consist of several documents in the like form each signed by one or more directors; but a resolution signed by an alternate director need not also be signed by his appointor and, if it is signed by a director who has appointed an alternate director, it need not be signed by the alternate in that capacity.

94. Save as otherwise provided by the articles, a director shall not vote at a meeting of directors or a committee of directors on any resolution concerning a matter in which he has, directly or indirectly, an interest or duty which is material and which conflicts or may conflict with the interests of the company unless his interest or duty arises only because the case falls within one or more of the following paragraphs –
     (a) the resolution relates to the giving to him of a guarantee, security, or indemnity in respect of money lent to, or an obligation incurred by him for the benefit of, the company or any of its subsidiaries;
     (b) the resolution relates to the giving to a third party of a guarantee, security, or indemnity in respect of an obligation the company or any of its subsidiaries for which the director has assumed responsibility in whole or in part and whether alone or jointly with others under a guarantee or indemnity or by the giving of security;
     (c) his interest arises by virtue of his subscribing or agreeing to subscribe for any shares, debentures or other securities of the company or any of its subsidiaries, or by virtue of his being,

or intending to become, a participant in the underwriting or sub-underwriting of an offer of any such shares, debentures or other securities by the company or any of its subsidiaries for subscription, purchase or exchange;

(d) the resolution relates in any way to a retirement benefits scheme which has been approved, or is conditional upon approval, by the Board of Inland Revenue for taxation purposes.

For the purposes of this regulation, an interest of a person who is, for any purpose of the Act (excluding any statutory modification thereof not in force when this regulation becomes binding on the company), connected with a director shall be treated as an interest of the director and, in relation to an alternate director, an interest of his appointor shall be treated as an interest of the alternate director without prejudice to any interest which the alternate director has otherwise.

95. A director shall not be counted in the quorum present at a meeting in relation to a resolution on which he is not entitled to vote.

96. The company may by ordinary resolution suspend or relax to any extent, either generally or in respect of any particular matter, any provision of the articles prohibiting a director from voting at a meeting of directors or of a committee of directors.

97. Where proposals are under consideration concerning the appointment of two or more directors to offices or employments with the company or any body corporate in which the company is interested the proposals may be divided and considered in relation to each director separately and (provided he is not for another reason precluded from voting) each of the directors concerned shall be entitled to vote and be counted in the quorum in respect of each resolution except that concerning his own appointment.

98. If a question arises at a meeting of directors or of a committee of directors as to the right of a director to vote, the question may, before the conclusion of the meeting, be referred to the chairman of the meeting and his ruling in relation to any director other than himself shall be final and conclusive.

SECRETARY

99. Subject to the provisions of the Act, the secretary shall be appointed by the directors for such term, at such remuneration and upon such conditions as they may think fit; and any secretary so appointed may be removed by them.

MINUTES

100. The directors shall cause minutes to be made in books kept for the purpose –

(a) of all appointments of officers made by the directors; and
(b) of all proceedings at meetings of the company, of the holders of any class of shares in the company, and of the directors, and of committees of directors, including the names of the directors present at each such meeting.

THE SEAL

101. The seal shall only be used by the authority of the directors or of a committee of directors authorised by the directors. The directors may determine who shall sign any instrument to which the seal is affixed and unless otherwise so determined it shall be signed by a director and by the secretary or by a second director.

DIVIDENDS

102. Subject to the provisions of the Act, the company may by ordinary resolution declare dividends in accordance with the respective rights of members, but no dividend shall exceed the amount recommended by the directors.

103. Subject to the provisions of the Act, the directors may pay interim dividends if it appears to them that they are justified by the profits of the company available for distribution. If the share capital is divided into different classes, the directors may pay interim dividends on shares which confer deferred or non-preferred rights with regard to dividend as well as on shares which confer preferential rights with regard to dividend, but no interim dividend shall be paid on shares carrying deferred or non-preferred rights if, at the time of payment, any preferential dividend is in arrear. The directors may also pay at intervals settled by them any dividend payable at a fixed rate if it appears to them that the profits available for distribution justify the payment. Provided the directors act in good faith they shall not incur any liability to the holders of shares conferring preferred rights for any loss they may suffer by the lawful payment of an interim dividend on any shares having deferred or non-preferred rights.

104. Except as otherwise provided by the rights attached to shares, all dividends shall be declared and paid according to the amounts paid up on the shares on which the dividend is paid. All dividends shall be apportioned and paid proportionately to the amounts paid up on the shares during any portion or portions of the period in respect of which the dividend is paid; but, if any share is issued on terms providing that it shall rank for dividend from a particular date, that share shall rank for dividend accordingly.

105. A general meeting declaring a dividend may, upon the recommendation of the directors, direct that it shall be satisfied

wholly or partly by the distribution of assets and, where any difficulty arises in regard to the distribution, the directors may settle the same and in particular may issue fractional certificates and fix the value for distribution of any assets and may determine that cash shall be paid to any member upon the footing of the value so fixed in order to adjust the rights of members and may vest assets in trustees.

106.   Any dividend or other moneys payable in respect of a share may be paid by cheque sent by post to the registered address of the person entitled or, if two or more persons are the holders of the share or are jointly entitled to it by reason of the death or bankruptcy of the holder, to the registered address of that one of those persons who is first named on the register of members or to such person and to such address as the person or person entitled may in writing direct. Every cheque shall be made payable to the order of the person or persons entitled or to such other person as the person or persons entitled may in writing direct and payment of the cheque shall be a good discharge to the company. Any joint holder or other person jointly entitled to a share as aforesaid may give receipts for any dividend or other moneys payable in respect of the share.

107.   No dividend or other moneys payable in respect of a share shall bear interest against the company unless otherwise provided by the rights attached to the share.

108.   Any dividend which has remained unclaimed for twelve years from the date when it became due for payment shall, if the directors so resolve, be forfeited and cease to remain owing by the company.

ACCOUNTS

109.   No member shall (as such) have any right of inspecting any accounting records or other book or document of the company except as conferred by statute or authorised by the directors or by ordinary resolution of the company.

CAPITALISATION OF PROFITS

110.   The directors may with the authority of an ordinary resolution of the company –
   (a) subject as hereinafter provided, resolve to capitalise any undivided profits of the company not required for paying any preferential dividend (whether or not they are available for distribution) or any sum standing to the credit of the company's share premium account or capital redemption reserve;
   (b) appropriate the sum resolved to be capitalised to the members who would have been entitled to it if it were

distributed by way of dividend and in the same proportion and apply such sum on their behalf either in or towards paying up the amounts, if any, for the time being unpaid on any shares held by them respectively, or in paying up in full unissued shares or debentures of the company of a nominal amount equal to that sum, and allot the shares or debentures credited as fully paid to those members, or as they may direct, in those proportions, or partly in one way and partly in the other: but the share premium account, the capital redemption reserve, and any profits which are not available for distribution may, for the purposes of this regulation, only be applied in paying up unissued shares to be allotted members credited as fully paid;

(c) make such provision by the issue of fractional certificates or by payment in cash or otherwise as they determine in the case of shares or debentures becoming distributable under this regulation in fractions; and

(d) authorise any person to enter on behalf of all members concerned into an agreement with the company providing for the allotment to them respectively, credited as fully paid, of any shares or debentures to which they are entitled upon such capitalisation, any agreement made under such authority being binding on all such members.

NOTICES

111.   *Any notice to be given to or by any person pursuant to the articles (other than a notice calling a meeting of the directors) shall be in writing or shall be given using electronic communications to an address for the time being notified for that purpose to the person giving the notice.*
In this regulation, 'address', in relation to electronic communications, includes any number or address used for the purposes of such communications.[6]

112.   The company may give any notice to a member either personally or by sending it by post in a prepaid envelope addressed to the member at his registered address *or by leaving it at that address or by giving it using electronic communications to an address for the time being notified to the company by the member.* In the case of joint holders of a share, all notices shall be given to the joint holder whose name stands first in the register of members in respect of the joint holding and notice so given shall be sufficient notice to all the joint holders. A member whose registered address is not within the United Kingdom and who gives to the company an

---

[6] Regulation 111 was amended by Schedule 1 of the Companies Act 1985 (Electronic Communications) Order 2000 on 22 December 2000. Prior to that date it read as follows: 'Any notice to be given to or by any person pursuant to the articles shall be in writing except that notice calling a meeting of directors need not be in writing.'

address within the United Kingdom at which notices may be given to him, *or an address to which notices may be sent by electronic communications,* shall be entitled to have notices given to him at that address, but otherwise no such member shall be entitled to receive any notice from the company. *In this regulation and the next, 'address', in relation to electronic communications, includes any number or address used for the purposes of such communications.*[7]

113.   A member present, either in person or by proxy, at any meeting of the company or of holders of any class of shares in the company shall be deemed to have received notice of the meeting and, where requisite, of the purposes for which it was called.

114.   Every person who becomes entitled to a share shall be bound by any notice in respect of that share which, before his name is entered in the register of members, has been duly given to a person from whom he derives his title.

115.   Proof that an envelope containing a notice was properly addressed, prepaid and posted shall be conclusive evidence that the notice was given. *Proof that notice contained in an electronic communication was sent in accordance with guidance issued by the Institute of Chartered Secretaries and Administrators shall be conclusive evidence that the notice was given.* A notice shall be deemed to be given at the expiration of 48 hours after the envelope containing it was posted *or, in the case of a notice contained in an electronic communication, at the expiration of 48 hours after the time it was sent.*[8]

116.   A notice may be given by the company to the persons entitled to a share in consequence of death or bankruptcy of a member by sending or delivering it, in any manner authorised by the articles for the giving of notice to a member, addressed to them by name, or by the title of representatives of the deceased, or trustee of the bankrupt or by any description at the address, if any, within the United Kingdom supplied for that purpose by the persons claiming to be so entitled. Until such an address has been supplied, a notice may be given in any manner in which it might have been given if the death or bankruptcy had not occurred.

WINDING UP

117.   If the company is wound up, the liquidator may, with the sanction of an extraordinary resolution of the company and any other sanction required by the Act, divide among the members in

---

[7] The words in italics in reg. 112 were inserted by Schedule 1 of the Companies Act 1985 (Electronic Communications) Order 2000 on 22 December 2000.

[8] The words in italics in reg. 115 were inserted by Schedule 1 of the Companies Act 1985 (Electronic Communications) Order 2000 on 22 December 2000.

specie the whole or any part of the assets of the company and may, for that purpose, value any assets and determine how the division shall be carried out as between members or different classes of members. The liquidator may, with the like sanction, vest the whole or any part of the assets in trustees upon such trusts for the benefit of the members as he with the like sanction determines, but no member shall be compelled to accept any assets upon which there is a liability.

INDEMNITY

118. Subject to the provisions of the Act, but without prejudice to any indemnity to which a director may otherwise be entitled, every director or other officer or auditor of the company shall be indemnified out of the assets of the company against any liability incurred by him in defending any proceedings, whether civil or criminal, in which judgment is given in his favour or in which he is acquitted or in connection with any application in which relief is granted to him by the court from liability for negligence, default, breach of duty or breach of trust in relation to the affairs of the company.

Appendix C

Index to 1985 Table A

Appendix D

Matters requiring shareholder approval under the Companies Act 1985 and the Insolvency Act 1986

Nature of resolution	Type of resolution	Companies Act 1985
Change of situation of registered office to Wales in memorandum of association	Special	s. 2(2)
Alteration of objects in memorandum of association	Special	s. 4(1)
Alteration of articles of association	Special	s. 9(1)
Alteration of conditions in memorandum that could lawfully be contained in the articles	Special	s. 17(1)
Change of company name	Special	s. 28(1)
Ratification of (and relief for) action by directors that is outside the capacity of the company	Special	s. 35(3)
Re-registration of private company as public	Special	s. 43(1)
Re-registration of unlimited company as public	Special	s. 48(2)
Re-registration of unlimited company as limited	Special	s. 51
Re-registration of public company as private	Special	s. 53(1)
Authority to directors to allot shares	Ordinary	s 80
To extend the period for which the general meeting may authorise the directors to allot shares under s 80 of CA 1985	Elective	s. 80A
Disapplication of pre-emption rights	Special	s. 95
Transfer to public company of non-cash asset in initial period	Ordinary	s. 104
Resolution that uncalled share capital shall not be called up except in a winding up	Special	s. 120
Alteration of share capital	Ordinary	s. 121
Variation of class rights (not attached by memorandum) for which the articles make no alternative provision with respect to variation.	Extraordinary	s. 125(2)
Reduction of share capital	Special	s. 135
Financial assistance by private company for acquisition of own shares	Special	s. 155
Resolution authorising terms of off-market purchase of own shares	Special	s. 164
Purchase of own shares under contingent purchase contract	Special	s. 165(2)
Authority for market purchase of own shares	Ordinary	s. 166
Assignment or release of company's right to purchase own shares	Special	s. 167

Nature of resolution	Type of resolution	Companies Act 1985
Purchase of own shares (payment out of capital of private company)	Special	s. 173
Resolution of dormant company not to appoint auditors	Special	s. 250
To dispense with the laying of accounts and reports before general meetings	Elective	s. 252
Removal of a director	Ordinary	s. 303
Approval of payment for loss of office to director	Ordinary	s. 312 & 313
Resolution making liability of directors unlimited	Special	s. 307
Approval of assignment of office by a director	Special	s. 308
Director's contract of more than five years	Ordinary	s. 319
Approval of political donations	Ordinary	s. 347C(3)
To dispense with holding annual general meetings	Elective	s 366A
To reduce the majority required to authorise short notice of meetings	Elective	s. 369(4) & s. 378(3)
Resolution to revoke elective resolution	Ordinary	s. 379A
Appointment of auditors by company in general meeting	Ordinary	s. 385 & 385A
To dispense with the annual appointment of auditors	Elective	s. 386
Resolution to fix remuneration of auditors	Ordinary	s. 390A
Removal of auditors	Ordinary	s. 391
Making provision for employees on cessation or transfer of business	Ordinary	s. 719
		Insolvency Act 1986
Resolution to wind up voluntarily	Special	s. 84(1)
Voluntary winding up of a company that cannot continue its business by reason of its liabilities	Extraordinary	s. 84(1)
Authorise liquidator to transfer assets of company to new company in exchange for securities in the new company	Special	s. 110(3)
Members' voluntary winding up, to sanction liquidator's proposals for a compromise with the company's creditors	Extraordinary	s. 165(2)
Resolution to be wound up by court	Special	s. 122(1)
		1985 Table A
Directions to directors	Special	reg. 70
Distribution by a liquidator of surplus assets in kind instead of realising them in cash	Extraordinary	reg. 117

Appendix E

Entitlements under 1985 Table A to receive notice and accounts and to attend and vote

Member, representative or officer	Entitled to			
	receive notice	receive accounts	attend meetings	vote at meetings
Members				
Voting shares	Yes (reg. 38)	Yes (s. 238)	Yes	Yes (reg. 54)
Non-voting shares	Yes (reg. 38)	Yes (s. 238)	Note 1	Note 1
Preference shares	Yes (reg. 38)	Yes (s. 238)	Note 1	No
Joint holders				
1st named	Yes (reg. 38)	Yes (s. 238)	Yes	Yes (reg. 55)
2nd, 3rd or 4th	No (reg. 112)	No (s. 238(2)	Yes	See reg. 55
Members overseas (no UK address)	No (reg. 112)	Yes (s. 238)	Yes	Yes (reg. 54)
Personal representative of deceased member	Yes (reg. 38)	Yes (s. 238)	No (reg. 31)	No (reg. 31)
Personal representative of bankrupt member	Yes (reg. 38)	Yes (s. 238)	No (reg. 31)	No (reg. 31)
Receiver in mental disorder	Send to member	Send to member (s. 238)	Yes (reg. 56)	Yes (reg. 56)
Member with calls unpaid	Yes (reg. 38)	Yes (s.238)	Yes	No (reg. 57)
Debenture holder	Note 1	Yes (s. 238)	Note 1	No
Auditors	Yes (reg. 38)	Yes (s. 238 & 390)	Yes (s. 390)	No
Directors who are not members	Yes (reg. 38)	Yes (s. 238 & reg. 38)	Yes (reg. 44)	No

Note 1: Not covered in Table A. Will depend on articles or terms of issue.

Appendix F

The Combined Code on Corporate Governance

SECTION 1 – COMPANIES

A. DIRECTORS

A.1 The Board.

Principle Every listed company should be headed by an effective board which should lead and control the company.

Code Provisions

A.1.1 The board should meet regularly.

A.1.2 The board should have a formal schedule of matters specifically reserved to it for decision.

A.1.3 There should be a procedure agreed by the board for directors in the furtherance of their duties to take independent professional advice if necessary, at the company's expense.

A.1.4 All directors should have access to the advice and services of the company secretary, who is responsible to the board for ensuring that board procedures are followed and that applicable rules and regulations are complied with. Any question of the removal of the company secretary should be a matter for the board as a whole.

A.1.5 All directors should bring an independent judgement to bear on issues of strategy, performance, resources, including key appointments, and standards of conduct.

A.1.6 Every director should receive appropriate training on the first occasion that he or she is appointed to the board of a listed company, and subsequently as necessary.

A.2 Chairman and CEO.

Principle There are two key tasks at the top of every public company – the running of the board and the executive responsibility for the running of the company's business. There should be a clear division of responsibilities at the head of the company which will ensure a balance of power and authority, such that no one individual has unfettered powers of decision.

Code Provision

A.2.1 A decision to combine the posts of chairman and chief executive officer in one person should be publicly explained. Whether the posts are held by different people or by the same person, there should be a strong and independent non-executive element on the board, with a recognised senior member other than the chairman to whom concerns can be conveyed. The chairman, chief executive and senior independent director should be identified in the annual report.

A.3 Board Balance.

Principle **The board should include a balance of executive and non-executive directors (including independent non-executives) such that no individual or small group of individuals can dominate the board's decision taking.**

Code Provisions

A.3.1 The board should include non-executive directors of sufficient calibre and number for their views to carry significant weight in the board's decisions. Non-executive directors should comprise not less than one-third of the board.

A.3.2 The majority of non-executive directors should be independent of management and free from any business or other relationship which could materially interfere with the exercise of their independent judgement. Non-executive directors considered by the board to be independent in this sense should be identified in the annual report.

A.4 Supply of Information.

Principle **The board should be supplied in a timely manner with information in a form and of a quality appropriate to enable it to discharge its duties.**

Code Provision

A.4.1 Management has an obligation to provide the board with appropriate and timely information, but information volunteered by management is unlikely to be enough in all circumstances and directors should make further enquiries where necessary. The chairman should ensure that all directors are properly briefed on issues arising at board meetings.

A.5 Appointments to the Board.

Principle **There should be a formal and transparent procedure for the appointment of new directors to the board.**

Code Provision

A.5.1 Unless the board is small, a nomination committee should be established to make recommendations to the board on all new board appointments. A majority of the members of this committee should be non-executive directors, and the chairman should be either the chairman of the board or a non-executive director. The chairman and members of the nomination committee should be identified in the annual report.

A.6 Re-election.

Principle **All directors should be required to submit themselves for re-election at regular intervals and at least every three years.**

Code Provision

A.6.1 Non-executive directors should be appointed for specified terms subject to re-election and to Companies Act provisions relating to the removal of a director, and reappointment should not be automatic.

A.6.2 All directors should be subject to election by shareholders at the first opportunity after their appointment, and to re-election thereafter at intervals of no more than three years. The names of directors submitted for election or re-election should be accompanied by sufficient biographical details to enable shareholders to take an informed decision on their election.

B. DIRECTORS' REMUNERATION

B.1 The Level and Make-up of Remuneration.

Principle Levels of remuneration should be sufficient to attract and retain the directors needed to run the company successfully but companies should avoid paying more than is necessary for this purpose. A proportion of executive directors' remuneration should be structured so as to link rewards to corporate and individual performance.

Code Provisions

Remuneration policy

B.1.1 The remuneration committee should provide the packages needed to attract, retain and motivate executive directors of the quality required but should avoid paying more than is necessary for this purpose.

B.1.2 Remuneration committees should judge where to position their company relative to other companies. They should be aware what comparable companies are paying and should take account of relative performance. But they should use such comparisons with caution, in view of the risk that they can result in an upward ratchet of remuneration levels with no corresponding improvement in performance.

B.1.3 Remuneration committees should be sensitive to the wider scene, including pay and employment conditions elsewhere in the group, especially when determining annual salary increases.

B.1.4 The performance-related elements of remuneration should form a significant proportion of the total remuneration package of executive directors and should be designed to align their interests with those of shareholders and to give these directors keen incentives to perform at the highest levels.

B.1.5 Executive share options should not be offered at a discount save as permitted by paragraphs 13.30 and 13.31 of the Listing Rules.

B.1.6 In designing schemes of performance-related remuneration, remuneration committees should follow the provisions in Schedule A to this Code.

Service Contracts and Compensation

B.1.7 There is a strong case for setting notice or contract periods at, or reducing them to, one year or less. Boards should set this as an objective; but they should recognise that it may not be possible to achieve it immediately.

B.1.8 If it is necessary to offer longer notice or contract periods to new directors recruited from outside, such periods should reduce after the initial period.

B.1.9 Remuneration committees should consider what compensation commitments (including pension contributions) their directors' contracts of service, if any, would entail in the event of early termination. They should in particular consider the advantages of providing explicitly in the initial contract for such compensation commitments except in the case of removal for misconduct.

B.1.10 Where the initial contract does not explicitly provide for compensation commitments, remuneration committees should, within legal constraints, tailor their approach in individual early termination cases to the wide variety of circumstances. The broad aim should be to avoid rewarding poor performance while dealing fairly with cases where departure is not due to poor performance and to take a robust line on reducing compensation to reflect departing directors' obligations to mitigate loss.

B.2 Procedure.

Principle **Companies should establish a formal and transparent procedure for developing policy on executive remuneration and for fixing the remuneration packages of individual directors. No director should be involved in fixing his or her own remuneration.**

Code Provisions

B.2.1 To avoid potential conflicts of interest, boards of directors should set up remuneration committees of independent non-executive directors to make recommendations to the board, within agreed terms of reference, on the company's framework of executive remuneration and its cost; and to determine on their behalf specific remuneration packages for each of the executive directors, including pension rights and any compensation payments.

B.2.2 Remuneration committees should consist exclusively of non-executive directors who are independent of management and free from any business or other relationship which could materially interfere with the exercise of their independent judgement.

B.2.3 The members of the remuneration committee should be listed each year in the board's remuneration report to shareholders (B.3.1 below).

B.2.4 The board itself or, where required by the Articles of Association, the shareholders should determine the remuneration of the non-executive directors, including members of the remuneration committee, within the limits set in the

Articles of Association. Where permitted by the Articles, the board may, however, delegate this responsibility, case by case, to a small sub-committee, which might include the chief executive officer.

B.2.5 Remuneration committees should consult the chairman and/or chief executive officer about their proposals relating to the remuneration of other executive directors and have access to professional advice inside and outside the company.

B.2.6 The chairman of the board should ensure that the company maintains contact as required with its principal shareholders about remuneration in the same way as for other matters.

B.3 Disclosure.

Principle The company's annual report should contain a statement of remuneration policy and details of the remuneration of each director.

Code Provisions

B.3.1 The board should report to the shareholders each year on remuneration. The report should form part of, or be annexed to, the company's annual report and accounts. It should be the main vehicle through which the company reports to shareholders on directors' remuneration.

B.3.2 The report should set out the company's policy on executive directors' remuneration. It should draw attention to factors specific to the company.

B.3.3 In preparing the remuneration report, the board should follow the provisions in Schedule B to this code.

B.3.4 Shareholders should be invited specifically to approve all new long-term incentive schemes (as defined in the Listing Rules) save in the circumstances permitted by paragraph 13.13A of the Listing Rules.

B.3.5 The board's annual remuneration report to shareholders need not be a standard item of agenda for AGMs. But the board should consider each year whether the circumstances are such that the AGM should be invited to approve the policy set out in the report and should minute their conclusions.

C. RELATIONS WITH SHAREHOLDERS

C.1 Dialogue with Institutional Shareholders.

Principle Companies should be ready, where practicable, to enter into a dialogue with institutional shareholders based on the mutual understanding of objectives.

C.2 Constructive Use of the AGM.

Principle Companies should use the AGM to communicate with private investors and encourage their participation.

Code Provisions

C.2.1 Companies should count all proxy votes and, except where a poll is called, should indicate the level of proxies lodged on each resolution, and the balance for and against the resolution, after it has been dealt with on a show of hands.

C.2.2 Companies should propose a separate resolution at the AGM on each substantially separate issue, and should in particular propose a resolution at the AGM relating to the report and accounts.

C.2.3 The chairman of the board should arrange for the chairmen of the audit, remuneration and nomination committees to be available to answer questions at the AGM.

C.2.4 Companies should arrange for the Notice of the AGM and related papers to be sent to shareholders at least 20 working days before the meeting.

D. ACCOUNTABILITY AND AUDIT

D.1 Financial Reporting.

Principle The board should present a balanced and understandable assessment of the company's position and prospects.

Code Provision

D.1.1 The directors should explain their responsibility for preparing the accounts, and there should be a statement by the auditors about their reporting responsibilities.

D.1.2 The board's responsibility to present a balanced and understandable assessment extends to interim and other price-sensitive public reports and reports to regulators as well as information required to be presented by statutory requirements.

D.1.3 The directors should report that the business is a going concern, with supporting assumptions or qualifications as necessary.

D.2 Internal Control.

Principle The board should maintain a sound system of internal control to safeguard shareholders' investment and the company's assets.

Code Provisions

D.2.1 The directors should, at least annually, conduct a review of the effectiveness of the group's system of internal control and should report to shareholders that they have done so. The review should cover all controls, including financial, operational and compliance controls and risk management.

D.2.1 Companies which do not have an internal audit function should from time to time review the need for one.

D.3 Audit Committee and Auditors.

Principle The board should establish formal and transparent arrangements for considering how they should apply the financial reporting and internal control principles and for maintaining an appropriate relationship with the company's auditors.

Code Provisions

D.3.1 The board should establish an audit committee of at least three directors, all non-executive, with written terms of reference which deal clearly with its authority and duties. The members of the committee, a majority of whom should be independent non-executive directors, should be named in the report and accounts.

D.3.2 The duties of the audit committee should include keeping under review the scope and results of the audit and its cost effectiveness and the independence and objectivity of the auditors. Where the auditors also supply a substantial volume of non-audit services to the company, the committee should keep the nature and extent of such services under review, seeking to balance the maintenance of objectivity and value for money.

SECTION 2 – INSTITUTIONAL SHAREHOLDERS
E. INSTITUTIONAL INVESTORS
E.1 Shareholder Voting.

Principle Institutional shareholders have a responsibility to make considered use of their votes.

Code Provisions

E.1.1 Institutional shareholders should endeavour to eliminate unnecessary variations in the criteria which each applies to the corporate governance arrangements and performance of the companies in which they invest.

E.1.2 Institutional shareholders should, on request, make available to their clients information on the proportion of resolutions on which votes were cast and non-discretionary proxies lodged.

E.1.3 Institutional shareholders should take steps to ensure that their voting intentions are being translated into practice.

E.2 Dialogue with Companies.

Principle Institutional shareholders should be ready, where practicable, to enter into a dialogue with companies based on the mutual understanding of objectives.

E.3 Evaluation of Governance Disclosures.

Principle When evaluating companies' governance arrangements, particularly those relating to board structure and composition, institutional investors should give due weight to all relevant factors drawn to their attention.

SCHEDULE A
Provisions on the Design of Performance-Related Remuneration

1. Remuneration committees should consider whether the directors should be eligible for annual bonuses. If so, performance conditions should be relevant, stretching and designed to enhance the business. Upper limits should always be considered. There

may be a case for part payment in shares to be held for a significant period.

2. Remuneration committees should consider whether the directors should be eligible for benefits under long-term incentive schemes. Traditional share option schemes should be weighed against other kinds of long-term incentive scheme. In normal circumstances, shares granted or other forms of deferred remuneration should not vest, and options should not be exercisable, in under three years. Directors should be encouraged to hold their shares for a further period after vesting or exercise subject to the need to finance any costs of acquisition and associated tax liability.

3. Any new long-term incentive schemes which are proposed should be approved by shareholders and should preferably replace existing schemes or at least form part of a well considered overall plan, incorporating existing schemes. The total rewards potentially available should not be excessive.

4. Payouts or grants under all incentive schemes, including new grants under existing share option schemes, should be subject to challenging performance criteria reflecting the company's objectives. Consideration should be given to criteria which reflect the company's performance relative to a group of comparator companies in some key variables such as total shareholder return.

5. Grants under executive share option and other long-term incentive schemes should normally be phased rather than awarded in one large block.

6. Remuneration committees should consider the pension consequences and associated costs to the company of basic salary increases and other changes in remuneration, especially for directors close to retirement.

7. In general, neither annual bonuses nor benefits in kind should be pensionable.

SCHEDULE B
Provisions on what should be included in the Remuneration Report

1. The report should include full details of all elements in the remuneration package of each individual director by name, such as basic salary, benefits in kind, annual bonuses and long-term incentive schemes including share options.

2. Information on share options, including SAYE options, should be given for each director in accordance with the recommendations of the Accounting Standards Board's Urgent Issues Task Force Abstract 10 and its successors.

3. If grants under executive share option or other long-term incentive schemes are awarded in one large block rather than phased, the report should explain and justify.

4. Also included in the report should be pension entitlements earned by each individual director during the year, disclosed on

one of the alternative bases recommended by the Faculty of Actuaries and the Institute of Actuaries and included in the Stock Exchange Listing Rules. Companies may wish to make clear that transfer value represents a liability of the company, not a sum paid or due to the individual.

5. If annual bonuses or benefits in kind are pensionable the report should explain and justify.

6. The amounts received by, and commitments made to, each director under 1, 2 and 4 above should be subject to audit.

7. Any service contracts which provide for, or imply, notice periods in excess of one year (or any provisions for predetermined compensation on termination which exceed one year's salary and benefits) should be disclosed and the reasons for the longer notice periods explained.

[Published June 1998]

Appendix G

ICSA's Guidance on Electronic Communications with Shareholders

The following summary sets out by chapter headings used in the guide:

- the points of recommended best practice (indicated in italics);
- the points which were not considered appropriate to be included as recommended best practice but which ICSA recommends that companies should consider (indicated in plain text).

Several chapters of the guide do not contain any specific recommendations.

Ch. 2: Authority
- *A company should take steps to amend its Articles to specifically facilitate the use of electronic communications as soon as is practical.*
- Take proper advice before amending Articles to avoid unforeseen effects on the meaning and application of other clauses.

Ch. 3: Types of e-communication
- *The invitation to shareholders to use electronic communications should include full details of any particular software or equipment specifications which will be required to enable the shareholder to take advantage of the options being made available.*
- *Shareholders electing to use computer based electronic communications should be warned that any electronic communication, including the filing of an electronic proxy form, found to contain a computer virus, will not be accepted by the company.*
- Consider carefully the practicalities of each method of electronic communication before offering them to shareholders noting for example the 'Proof of sending' requirements.
- Consider carefully which combination of alternatives to offer.
- Consider the Format and 'language' in which material will be placed on a web-site. Will the company need to provide free copies of software such as Adobe Acrobat?
- What steps may need to be taken to prevent the transmission or receipt of viruses?

Ch 4: Offering the facility
- *The offer and provision of a facility to communicate with shareholders electronically should not discriminate between shareholders of the same*

class and should include a statement reassuring shareholders of that fact. The invitation to participate and provision of the facility should be made available to all shareholders on equal terms and in such a manner as to make it as simple as possible for shareholders to participate.

- *The initial invitation to use electronic means of communications should be sent by post to each member of the company. The invitation should detail which documents will be available by which means and explain the procedures that will be adopted in each case.*
- *The list of alternative delivery mechanisms offered by the company should specifically include an option to continue to receive all material, in hard copy, by post.*
- *The company should, at least once each year, repeat the invitation to use electronic communications to those shareholders who continue to receive hard copy material. Such offer should be included, at the latest, with the Notice of the Annual General Meeting unless the company has elected not to hold an AGM.*
- Keep in mind any implications of other legislation such as the Disability Discrimination Act and the Data Protection Act.
- Consider how often the invitation should be repeated and the most cost effective way of doing so.

Ch 5: Registering a choice
- *The invitation to opt to use electronic communications should include clear advice on how to register an election. This should include any dedicated telephone number, fax number or e-mail address provided for the purpose and/or the address of an Internet website page where the election form may be completed on-line.*
- *Where a company is offering shareholders the opportunity to use electronic communications, all newly registered shareholders should, within 3 months of registration, be provided with a statement as to the company's policy on electronic shareholder communications together with a copy of the facility letter providing the shareholder with the opportunity to register his choice.*
- Consider how the company would prefer shareholders to register their choice and how they might be encouraged to use the company's preferred option.

Ch 6: Changing an election
- *The company's website should include fax and telephone numbers and an 'on-line' facility to enable shareholders to notify the company of any change in their choice of communication medium or contact details.*
- Consider ways to regularly remind shareholders to check the contact details being used by the company and to update them as necessary.

Ch 7: Notice of availability
- *Where the information being made available on a website includes a Notice of a General Meeting, the 'notification of availability' should draw specific attention to that fact; indicate the date, time and place of*

the meeting; highlight any applicable deadlines e.g. for the appointment of proxies

- *An e-mail notifying a shareholder that information is being made available on a website should contain a hyperlink direct to the appropriate pages of the website to enable the information to be accessed as simply as possible.*

Ch 8: Failed delivery or non receipt of information

- *When notices are delivered by telephone, the company should compile and retain a suitable evidential record, of all those contacted with the date and time of the call.*
- *When information or notifications of availability are sent by fax, a comprehensive transaction report or log generated by the fax machine should be suitably certified and retained by, or on behalf of, the company as 'proof of sending'.*
- *When information or notifications of availability are sent by e-mail, the company should ensure that it uses a system which produces either confirmation of the total number of recipients sent to or, preferably, a record of each recipient to whom the message has been sent. A copy of such record and any notices of any failed transmissions and subsequent re-sending, suitably certified, should be retained by or on behalf of the company as 'proof of sending'.*
- *The company should alert those shareholders electing to receive communications electronically that the company's obligation is satisfied when it transmits an electronic message and that it cannot be held responsible for a failure in transmission beyond its control.*
- *The company should, where it is aware of the failure in delivery of an electronic communication (and subsequent attempts do not remedy the situation) revert to sending a hard copy of the communication by mail to the recipient's last known postal address. This should be done within 48 hours of the original attempt. The company should include a standard notice advising the shareholder why he is being sent a copy by post and should take the opportunity of asking him to confirm his contact details.*
- Consider specifying in the company's Articles when notices (sent electronically) are deemed to be delivered.
- Consider specifying in the Articles the minimum number and frequency of attempts the company should be required to make to send to an electronic address before it resorts to sending hard copy by post.
- Consider sending a regular or periodic e-mail probe to check e-mail addresses held.

Ch 10: Electronic delivery of proxy forms

- *Electronic proxy forms should contain clear instructions as to the address to which the proxy form should be returned; a warning that an appointment of a proxy lodged electronically will only be valid if lodged at the 'address' supplied by the company.*
- *Each shareholder should be allocated a discrete identifier which should be required to be entered on the proxy form, used when logging on to the*

company's website to complete a proxy form 'on-line' or as part of the verification procedure in the case of proxy appointments lodged by telephone.

- Consider specifying in the Articles how the company will treat/ deal with proxy appointments submitted in an incorrect format or delivered to an address other than that specified by the company for the purpose.
- If proxy appointments are to be accepted by telephone consider what verification procedure will need to be adopted.
- Consider including provision in the Articles on the subject of the validity of proxy appointments.

Ch. 11: Proof of Delivery of Proxy Appointments
- Consider installing systems that will automatically acknowledge receipt of electronically delivered proxy forms.

Ch. 12: Record Date
- If the company decides to introduce a 'Record Date' for the purposes of freezing the register of Members at a point of time in advance of a general Meeting this should be addressed in the Articles.

Ch. 13: Security, use of a unique identifier, encryption
- Consider specifying in the Articles what constitutes an acceptable 'signature' on electronic communications such as electronically lodged proxy appointments.

Ch. 14: Retention of records
- *Where no poll is demanded, electronically lodged proxy appointments should be retained until one month after the meeting. Where a poll is held, records should be retained for a period of one year after the meeting.*
- *Any e-mail or other electronic address provided by the shareholder for the purposes of electronic communication should not be recorded as part of the publicly available part of the company's register of members.*
- Consider what records need to be retained, in what format and for what period.

Ch. 15: Identification of statutory and audited information
- *The company should liaise closely with, and obtain clearance from its auditors prior to the display of audited information and the Audit Report on a company web-site.*
- *The company should clearly identify 'statutory' information on its website and to so indicate when the information being viewed forms part of the audited accounts.*
- *The company should establish a routine system of checking that statutory or audited information made available via a website has not been tampered with and that the home page of the statutory section of the website contains a message indicating the time and date when the contents of that section of the site were last verified.*

- Heed the requirements of s. 240 Companies Act 1985 regarding the publication of financial information.
- Consider extending any website verification system to include non-statutory information.

Ch. 16: Overseas restrictions
Consider carefully the possibility that financial information placed on a website might be interpreted as an investment advertisement.

Ch. 19: Central depository/back-up
- *Companies should give serious thought to arranging a form of back up facility for their own web-site.*

The ICSA Guide, *Electronic Communications with Shareholders,* can be obtained from the Policy Unit, ICSA, 16 Park Crescent, London W1N 4AH (see *www.icsa.org.uk* or call 020 7580 4741 for details).

Appendix H

ICSA's aide-mémoire for preparing a schedule of matters to be reserved for the approval of the board

Companies Act requirements

1. Approval of interim and final financial statements. *
2. Approval of the interim dividend and recommendation of the final dividend. *
3. Approval of any significant change in accounting policies or practices. *
4. Appointment or removal of company secretary. *
5. Remuneration of auditors (where, as is usual, shareholders have delegated this power to the board) and recommendations for appointment or removal of auditors.*

Stock Exchange

6. Approval of all circulars and listing particulars (approval of routine documents such as periodic circulars re scrip dividend procedures or exercise of conversion rights might perhaps be delegated to a committee). *
7. Approval of press releases concerning matters decided by the board. *

Management

8. Approval of the group's commercial strategy and the annual operating budget.
9. Changes relating to the group's capital structure or its status as plc.
10. Appointments to boards of subsidiaries.
11. Terms and conditions of directors [and senior executives]. *
12. Changes to the group's management & control structure.

Board membership and board committees

13. Board appointments and removals. *
14. Terms of reference of chairman, vice chairman, chief executive and other executive directors. *
15. Terms of reference and membership of board committees. *

Cadbury recommendations

16. Major capital projects.
17. Material contracts of the company [or any subsidiary] in the ordinary course of business e.g. bank borrowing (above £xxx) and acquisition or disposal of fixed assets (above £xxx).
18. Contracts of the company [or any subsidiary] not in the ordinary course of business e.g. loans & repayments (above £xxx); foreign

currency transactions (above £xxx); major acquisitions or disposals (above £xxx).

19.   Major investments [including the acquisition or disposal of interests of more than [5] per cent in the voting shares of any company or the making of any take-over bid].
20.   Risk management strategy.
21.   Treasury policies (including foreign exchange exposures).

Miscellaneous
22.   Major changes in the rules of the company pension scheme, or changes of trustees or (when this is subject to the approval of the company) changes in the fund management arrangements.
23.   Major changes in employee share schemes and the allocation of executive share options.
24.   Formulation of policy regarding charitable donations.
25.   Political donations.
26.   Prosecution, defence or settlement of litigation (involving above ,xxx or being otherwise material to the interests of the company).
27.   Internal control arrangements.
28.   Health & safety policy.
29.   Environmental policy.
30.   Directors' & officers' liability insurance.

Note: Items marked * are not considered suitable, in any event, for delegation to a committee of the board e.g. because of Companies Act requirements or because, under the recommendations of the Cadbury Report, they are the responsibility of e.g. an audit, nomination or remuneration committee with the final decision on the matter required to be taken by the whole board.

Appendix I

ICSA's Code on Good Boardroom Practice

The Institute of Chartered Secretaries and Administrators (ICSA) believes that reliance on unwritten boardroom procedures and practices is no longer acceptable in the modern business environment. Whilst it is acknowledged that company law should not attempt to prescribe any particular style of boardroom management, ICSA believes that certain basic principles of good boardroom practice can be considered to be universally applicable.

Accordingly, ICSA has formulated this Code for directors and company secretaries as a guide to matters which it believes should be addressed and, wherever applicable, accepted formally by boards of directors in recognition of a commitment to adhere to an overall concept of best practice.

ICSA also recommends that boardroom procedures should be periodically reviewed to ensure both the satisfactory operation of the Code and the identification of matters which individual companies could advantageously bring within its scope.

Good Boardroom Practice: A Code for Directors and Company Secretaries

1. The board should establish written procedures for the conduct of its business which should include matters covered by this Code. A copy of these written procedures should be given to each director. Compliance should be monitored, preferably by an audit committee, and breaches of the procedures should be reported to the board.
2. The board should ensure that each director is given on appointment sufficient information to enable him to perform his duties. In particular, guidance for non-executive directors should cover procedures:
   (i) for obtaining information concerning the company; and
   (ii) for requisitioning a meeting of the board.
3. In the conduct of board business, two fundamental concepts should be observed:
   (i) each director should receive the same information at the same time; and
   (ii) each director should be given sufficient time in which to consider any such information.
4. The board should identify matters which require the prior approval of the board and lay down procedures (note 1) to be followed when, exceptionally, a decision is required before its next meeting on any matter not required by law to be considered at board level.
5. As a basic principle, all material contracts, and especially those

not in the ordinary course of business, should be referred to the board prior to commitment by the company.

6. The board should approve definitions of the terms 'material' (note 2) and 'not in the ordinary course of business' and these definitions should be brought to the attention of all relevant persons.

7. Where there is any uncertainty regarding the materiality or nature of a contract, it should normally be assumed that the contract should be brought before the board.

8. Decisions regarding the content of the agenda for individual meetings of the board and concerning the presentation of agenda items should be taken by the chairman in consultation with the company secretary.

9. The company secretary should be responsible to the chairman for the proper administration of the meetings of the company, the board and any committees thereof. To carry out this responsibility the company secretary should be entitled to be present at (or represented at) and prepare (or arrange for the preparation of) minutes of the proceedings of all such meetings.

10. The minutes of meetings should record the decisions taken and provide sufficient background to those decisions. All papers presented at the meeting should be clearly identified in the minutes and retained for reference. Procedures for the approval and circulation of minutes should be established.

11. Where the articles of association allow the board to delegate any of its powers to a committee, the board should give its prior approval to:
    (i) the membership and quorum of any such committee;
    (ii) its terms of reference; and
    (iii) the extent of any powers delegated to it.

12. The minutes of all meetings of committees of the board (or a written summary thereof) should be circulated to the board prior to its next meeting and the opportunity should be given at that meeting for any member of the board to ask questions thereon.

13. Notwithstanding the absence of a formal agenda item, the chairman should permit any director or the company secretary to raise at any board meeting any matter concerning the company's compliance with this Code of Practice, with the company's memorandum and articles of association and with any other legal or regulatory requirement.

Notes

1. If it is practicable, the approval of all the directors should be obtained by means of a written resolution. In all cases, however, the procedures should balance the need for urgency with the overriding principle that each director should be given as much information as possible and have an opportunity to requisition an emergency meeting of the board to discuss the matter prior to the commitment of the company.

2. Different definitions of the term 'material' should be established for 'contracts not in the ordinary course of business' and 'contracts in the ordinary course of business'. Financial limits should be set where appropriate.

Appendix J

Specimen briefing document for AGM

1. **Location**

   The company's AGM will take place at [Venue], [Address]

   The areas being used are as follows:

Registration	Foyer, ground floor
Cloakroom	Foyer, ground floor
Shareholders' catering	[Room 1], third floor
Customer Enquiries	[Room 1], third floor
Shareholder Enquiries	[Room 1], third floor
Exhibition	[Room 2], third floor
Board members' lounge	[Room 3], third floor
Registrars' room	[Room 4], third floor
Organisers' office	[Room 5], third floor
Press office	[Room 6], third floor
Investor relations office	[Room 7], third floor
Researchers' room	[Room 8], third floor
AGM	[Room 9 and Room 2], third floor
Lunch	[Room 10], second floor

2. **Car Parking**

   Chauffeurs bringing directors and their guests to the AGM may drive onto the forecourt of the [Venue]. If chauffeurs remain with their vehicles, they may wait on the forecourt but otherwise they must leave the area for the duration of the AGM.

   There are no car parking facilities for [Company] staff or shareholders on site, but there are car parks within walking distance at [Locations].

3. **Timetable**

   Thursday 2 August 2001

   Delivery and installation of stage set, display stands, question and answer system and exhibition panels throughout the morning.

1400	[Company] staff arrive for familiarisation tours and briefing
1430	Registrars' equipment delivery and installation
1600	Lighting check
1630	[Company] researchers arrive for briefing with Q & A personnel in the [Room 8]
1700	[Company] directors arrive for rehearsals

Friday 3 August 2001

0800	Chairman's rehearsal
0830	[Company] staff arrive
0845	Security briefing
0930	All staff at their posts
0945	All public areas to be ready
1000	Doors open
1030	All public areas to be ready
1055	Board escorted onto stage
1100	AGM commences
1300–1330	AGM ends
1330	Lunch commences
1400	Displays dismantled and removed according to agreed delivery schedule
1800	All [Company] equipment to be removed from the building

4. Security Procedures

In the event of an emergency, the security personnel at [Venue] will take all necessary action. If a suspicious object is discovered or if there is any other security or safety problem, please contact the organisers' office in [Room 5] immediately. The organisers can then take steps to contact all the relevant authorities.

5. First Aid Procedures

First aid staff from St John's Ambulance Brigade will be in attendance at the Meeting and there is a fully equipped first aid room on site. In the event of an emergency, please contact the St John's Ambulance Brigade representative in [Room 2] direct or contact the organisers' office in [Room 5].

6. Guidelines for [Company] Registration Personnel

Registration is the point at which it is established whether people have the right to attend the meeting and also the means whereby shareholder attendance numbers are obtained. [Company] personnel are to follow the procedures set out below:

(a) Shareholders should bring with them their admission card sent to them with the Company's annual report. (Samples will be provided to [Company] personnel involved).

(b) Shareholders producing such cards should be asked to hand you the card in return for which you should give them a yellow shareholder (voting) card and a folder containing the Chairman's welcome letter and notice for the meeting. Shareholders are also to be provided with a self-adhesive badge. It is imperative that you obtain their admission card *before* handing them a shareholder badge card and folder. Thereafter shareholders are free to make their way to the lifts for the exhibition and catering area and meeting room which are all on the third floor.

(c) Shareholders who wish to bring a guest into the meeting with them can do so but the guest is to be given a shareholder guest badge together with a pink guest card (which is non-voting), and a folder.

(d) Where two people are joint shareholders and both wish to attend, only the first named may have a yellow voting card, the second must be given a pink guest card and folder. Although the second shareholder is not technically a guest, this is the only practical way of preventing a double vote against a single holding.

(e) Staff shareholders who only hold free and matching shares are not entitled to attend the meeting and any staff producing any blue card should be referred to [Registrars] personnel.

(f) Institutional shareholders or corporate bodies are entitled to appoint a corporate representative to attend the meeting and vote on their behalf. Such corporate representatives should produce a letter of authorisation on their company letter heading to this effect. Such letters should be signed by their company secretary or director and strictly speaking should also bear their company's seal, but the latter is not always applied. If you consider this letter to be authentic, hand the representative a shareholder badge, a yellow shareholder voting card and folder. If you are in any doubt refer the individual to [Registrars] personnel.

(g) Shareholders without admission cards or anyone who says they are a proxy, should be referred to the desks staff by [Registrars] personnel.

(h) Likewise, there are separate registration procedures for the press and guests of the company who should be referred to the appropriate desk.

(i) Under no circumstances should anyone who does not have any means of identification be admitted. If in any doubt, refer to [Name] of [Registrars] who will contact security if necessary.

(j) Please retain all admission cards as these will be `wand' read by [Registrars] personnel during the meeting to enable an accurate count of shareholders attending.

7. **Guidelines for [Registrars] Verification Personnel**

Verification is the area which handles shareholders who cannot be admitted to the meeting directly through registration. Most of these will be shareholders who have forgotten their admission cards but there may also be proxies.

The clerical procedures are as follows:

(a) A person claiming to be a shareholder who has forgotten his voting card should be asked his name, address and number of shares. These details should be compared to the details on the computer and if the details agree the shareholder should be asked to sign the attendance record and is given a yellow shareholder voting card.

(b) A person claiming to be a proxy should be asked his name and that of the shareholder he represents. These details should be compared to the list of proxies provided and if the details agree the proxy should be asked to sign the attendance record and given a blue proxy card. Any proxy who is not on the list may not be admitted, except as a guest under certain circumstances.

(c) There will be separate registration procedures for people who are guests of the company or members of the press, and these people should be referred to the appropriate staffed desk by [Company] personnel.

(d) Employees who hold free and matching shares or share options are not shareholders and may only be admitted to the meeting if they have stock as well. If such staff are insisting on admission it is suggested that you contact [Name] and [Company]'s security adviser, who collectively will determine the appropriate course of action.

(e) At the end of the meeting the admission cards and signatures can be counted to establish how many people attended the meeting.

8. **Guidelines for Press Registration**

The [Company]'s press officer will brief the [Company] staff on the press desk as to the procedures to be adopted.

9. **Guidelines for Visitors' Registration**

[Company] staff on this desk will be provided with guest lists before the meeting. These lists will provide the names of the guests and their status, that is shareholder or guest, so that these staff may issue the appropriate cards, that is yellow or pink and folders.

10. **Displays**

There will be a series of small displays at the back of the main auditorium for shareholders' general interest before and after the AGM. The displays cover the main businesses such as [. . .].

[Company] personnel acting as stewards are to encourage shareholders to visit the display stands and models in the main auditorium. The doors to the main auditorium will be open at 1000 and a PA announcement will inform shareholders that the exhibition area is open.

11. **Customer and Shareholder Enquiries**

There will be a customer enquiry desk situated in [Room 1] staffed by [Company] personnel who will be pleased to answer queries on [. . .].

Shareholders with enquiries relating to their shareholding should be directed to the shareholder enquiry desk situated [. . .]. This desk will be staffed by [Registrars] personnel and [Company] personnel. The company's statutory registers will be available for inspection by shareholders at this desk.

12. **Question Points**

There will be four question points, two in [Room 1] and two in the auditorium, for any shareholder wishing to raise a question. All question should be registered in advance of the meeting as far as possible – details of this will be given to shareholders on their arrival. Included in the shareholders' folders will be a shareholder question card. The question card is for those shareholders who would prefer to receive a written answer – or if there is insufficient time for their question to be asked at the Meeting.

A number of questions that shareholders may have can be answered either at the customer enquiry desk or the shareholder enquiry desk and personnel at the question points should direct them as necessary.

13. **Question and Answer Management System**

The system consists of purpose-designed software running on a network of IBM compatible PCs. The configuration of the system consists of four question registration points, each with a computer and printer, two PCs and printers processing the answers to the questions and two further PCs outputting the next question (preview) or the 'on air' question (current). The system is split into four parts:

- front-of-house question registration points, two in [Room 1] and two in the auditorium;
- the research area behind the scenes;
- outputting information to the platform; and
- on-stage equipment.

At each registration point there is a computer and printer. There will be two personnel, a professional computer operator and a member of [Company] staff. The company employee is the first to meet the questioner. They make sure that he/she is entitled to ask a question (i.e. is a shareholder holding a yellow voting card). Proxies and visitors (i.e. those with blue and pink cards are not permitted to ask questions). They should have sufficient procedural knowledge to be able to allocate the question to the correct resolution by reference to the Notice of Meeting.

Shareholders may need assistance to compose their questions and therefore [Company] staff may wish to encourage questioners to draft questions on the pads provided at each point.

The question is then dictated to the computer operator. It is allocated a unique number which relates to the resolution to which it applies. Once the question has been entered, a print-out of the question is provided for the questioner to keep. A badge is also generated with all the essential information on it (i.e. question number, resolution number and the question point in the auditorium from which it is to be asked).

The badge is marked with a colour sticker and worn by the questioner to aid his or her identification of the questioner by

[Company] personnel and [Event Organisers] staff marshalling questioners within the auditorium.

As the question is printed out for the questioner it is simultaneously networked to the research area, stored on the file server, and printed out on two-part paper. In the research area there would be a number of senior company representatives with their own co-ordinator. One copy of the question goes to the co-ordinator who will then decide which researcher will answer it and pass it on. The other copy is filed as a control by the question controller backstage in [Room 8].

Once the question has been answered, hopefully with bullet points provided by the researchers, it is collected by either of two computer operators who add the answers to the questions. Once the answer has been added the page is re-stored on the fileserver and printed out again, locally, on two- part paper. One copy is given to the question controller and the other held as a paper back-up.

The PCs and operators output to the stage. They will output the questions in the order called by the question controller. One PC is dedicated to previewing the next question, the other outputs the current question. At any time additional information can be added to the displayed page to cope with supplementary or non pre-registered questions. Any alterations made on the screen will be reflected instantly on the on-stage monitors.

On the platform the Chairman will have one monitor dedicated to the current question and one dedicated to the next question, or preview. Executive directors will have one monitor each with a switch to select 'next' or 'on-air' and non-executive directors will have one switchable monitor between two.

14. **Entrance to the Auditorium**

[Company] personnel acting as stewards will monitor the admission of people entering the auditorium. Shareholders and their guests should have lapel stickers and have yellow or pink cards. Proxies should have a badge and blue card. Other personnel entering the auditorium should be wearing badges: either [Company] personnel, or [Registrars] personnel or representatives from the press or organisers.

15. **Seating Arrangements**

Seating for guests will be in the front row of the two seating blocks. Seating for questioners is in the back row of the two seating blocks, adjacent to the question points. Shareholders with pre-registered questions will be identified with badges and staff marshalling this area should seat questioners next to question point A or B in the auditorium as per the instruction on the badge. The question points are identified by overhead signs.

An area of the right side of the auditorium has been reserved for shareholders with wheelchairs and a signed area has been fitted with an induction loop system for the hard of hearing. This section will be clearly signed. Chairs will also be allocated for those accompanying the disabled.

Other shareholders may sit where they choose but if possible should be encouraged to sit near the front so that late arrivals sit towards the back. No special arrangements have been made for the press.

16.   Annual General Meeting

The meeting will commence at 1100. Prior to this background music will be played in the auditorium from 1000. A short opening sequence of slides will be shown during this period. Once the meeting has commenced, [Company] personnel may take their seats in the reserved area at the rear of the auditorium.

The finishing time of the meeting cannot be ascertained, but the anticipated time is between 1300 and 1330. At this time, **all** exhibition, registration and customer/shareholder enquiry personnel should resume their positions until the last shareholder leaves the building.

17.   Counting of Votes by a Show of Hands

[Registrars] personnel will be responsible for recording and counting the show of hands (that is, by shareholders raising their yellow cards) if it is not clear whether the resolution has been carried or not. [Name] of [Registrars] will be positioned near one of the Question Points in the auditorium so as to communicate with the Chairman.

18.   Poll

[Registrars] personnel are responsible for conducting a poll should the event occur. Again, [Name] of [Registrars] will be strategically placed near one of the question points so as to be able to communicate with the Chairman as to the validity of the poll request. The detailed procedure on the conduct of a poll will be dealt with by the Company Secretary at the Meeting. Ballot boxes and poll cards will be stored under lock and key in the registrars' office and only brought out by [Registrars] personnel in the event of a poll.

19.   Organisers' Staff

The [Company] AGM is organised by the [Venue] and [Event Organisers]. As well as technical crew, stewards, caterers and security staff, the following people will be on duty throughout the day.

[Name]	event director	[Event Organisers]
[Name]	question controller	[Event Organisers]
[Name]	senior producer	[Venue]
[Name]	producer	[Venue]
[Name]	centre co-ordinator	[Venue]
[Name]	head of security	[Venue]

In the event of any queries or problems, please go to the

organisers' office in room 3/10 on the third floor. They are both linked to the other members of the crew by walkie-talkie and can issue instructions as required.

20. **Communications**
The general telephone number for the [Venue] is [Tel. No.]. To contact representatives of the [Venue] or [Event Organisers], the direct lines to the [Company] AGM organisers' office are as follows:

[Tel. No.] telephone   [Tel. No.] facsimile
To contact [Company] staff, the direct lines to the investor relations office are as follows:
[Tel. No.] telephone   [Tel. No.] facsimile

21. **Catering**
Shareholders will be served tea, coffee, orange juice or mineral water in [Room 1] before and after the AGM. The catering service will operate from 1000 to 1100 and 1300 to 1400.

Light refreshments will be served for the board in [Room 3] before and after the AGM.

Lunch will be served to invited guests in [Room 10] from 1330 as a seated buffet.

Appendices
[Location Map of [Venue]]
[Plan of Registration Area (Room 1) and the Auditorium (Room 2 and Room 10)]

Appendix K

Uncertificated Securities Regulations 1995, reg. 34

Notices of meetings

34 – (1) For the purposes of determining which persons are entitled to attend or vote at a meeting, and how many votes such persons may cast, the participating issuer may specify in the notice of the meeting a time, not more than 48 hours before the time fixed for the meeting, by which a person must be entered on the relevant register of securities in order to have the right to attend or vote at the meeting.

(2) Changes to entries on the relevant register of securities after the time specified by virtue of paragraph (1) shall be disregarded in determining the rights of any person to attend or vote at the meeting, notwithstanding any provisions in any enactment, articles of association or other instrument to the contrary.

(3) For the purposes of serving notices of meetings, whether under section 370(2) of the 1985 Act, any other enactment, a provision in the articles of association or any other instrument, a participating issuer may determine that persons entitled to receive such notices are those persons entered on the relevant register of securities at the close of business on a day determined by him.

(4) The day determined by a participating issuer under paragraph (3) may not be more than 21 days before the day that the notices of the meeting are sent.

Appendix L

Chairman's scripts

This appendix includes specimen scripts for use by the chairman at general meetings. The examples given include scripts for:

- an annual general meeting (this is merely provided as an example and will need to be modified to reflect the resolutions to be proposed) (see para. 1.1);
- delaying the meeting to allow members to register (see para. 1.2);
- dealing with overcrowding in the meeting room (see para. 1.3);
- a poll called by the chairman or one demanded by a member (see para. 1.4)
- a resolution to adjourn (see para. 1.5);
- dealing with amendments (see para. 1.6);
- dealing with disruption (see para. 1.7);
- proposing a formal closure motion to put the question to the vote (see para. 1.8).

1.1 CHAIRMAN'S SCRIPT FOR ANNUAL GENERAL MEETING

Chairman: Ladies and gentlemen, I am pleased to welcome you to the annual general meeting of XYZ plc and declare the meeting open. With your permission, I will take the notice of the meeting as read.

SHORT PAUSE TO SEE WHETHER ANYONE OBJECTS

Chairman: Thank you. I now call upon [name of auditor] to read the report of the auditors to the members.

AUDITOR TO READ REPORT

Resolution 1 – Report and accounts
Chairman: Thank you. I propose:
THAT the report of the directors and the audited accounts for the year ended [date], now laid before the meeting, be received.

A copy of the report and accounts was sent to members with the notice of this meeting. But before putting the resolution to the vote, I would like to draw your attention to certain matters in the report and accounts and update you on the company's performance since the end of the financial year. I will then invite questions from the floor.

CHAIRMAN TO MAKE STATEMENT

Chairman: I now invite questions from the floor on the report and accounts. I will also take questions on my statement. If you have a question or a point to make, I would be grateful if you [could make yourself known to the staff at the question point nearest to you][raise your hand and wait until a member of staff has supplied you with a microphone]. Before asking your question, you should state your name and whether you are a shareholder or a corporate representative. [I would remind you that under art. [No.] of the company's articles of association proxies are not entitled to speak at this meeting.] [Unless the meeting objects, I propose for the time being to allow proxies to speak on any resolution before the meeting but reserve the right to change my ruling in this regard should it appear necessary in order to complete the business on the agenda.]

INVITE QUESTIONS FROM THE FLOOR

Chairman: If nobody has any further questions or points to make on the report and accounts (pause), I would now ask you to vote on the resolution before the meeting, namely:
THAT the report of the directors and the audited accounts for the year ended [date], now laid before the meeting, be received.
Those in favour [pause to count votes] – those against [pause to count votes] – I declare the resolution carried.

Resolution 2: Dividends

Chairman: I now propose THAT the final dividend of [5.8p] per share recommended by the directors of XYZ plc be declared payable on [date] to the holders of ordinary shares registered at the close of business on [date].

Does anyone have any questions or points to make on this resolution?

AFTER DEALING WITH QUESTIONS, IF ANY

Chairman: I now put the resolution THAT the final dividend of [5.8p] per share recommended by the directors of XYZ plc be declared payable on [date] to the holders of ordinary shares registered at the close of business on [date].

Those in favour [pause to count votes] – those against [pause to count votes] – I declare the resolution carried.

Resolutions 3 & 4: Re-election of directors

Chairman: I now turn to the re-election of directors retiring by
rotation. As you may be aware, under the company's
articles of association one third of your directors
(including the executive directors) must retire each
year and offer themselves for re-election. This year
the directors to retire are [name] and me. As I am one
of the directors seeking reappointment, it would not
be right for me to propose that resolution. I will
therefore ask my colleague [name] to do so when we
come to that item. However, before doing so I have
pleasure in proposing:

THAT [name], a director retiring by rotation, be re-elected a
director of the company.

INVITE QUESTIONS

Chairman: I now put the resolution to the meeting. Those in
favour [pause to count votes] – those against [pause to
count votes] – I declare the resolution carried.

I now call upon [name] to propose the next resolution.

[Name] Thank you, I propose:
THAT [name of chairman], a director retiring by rotation,
be re-elected a director of the company.

If there are no questions, I now put the resolution to the meeting.
Those in favour [pause to count votes] – those against [pause to
count votes] – I declare the resolution carried.

Resolution 5: Reappointment of auditors

Chairman: Thank you. The next resolution (resolution 5 in the
notice) is:

THAT [name of auditors] be reappointed auditors of the company
to hold office to the conclusion of the next general meeting at
which accounts are laid and that their remuneration be fixed by
the directors and I ask [name of shareholder], a shareholder, to
propose this resolution.

[Shareholder] I propose the resolution.

Chairman: Thank you. I now put the resolution to the meeting.
Those in favour [pause to count votes] – those against
[pause to count votes] – I declare the resolution carried.

Resolution 6: Amendment of articles

Chairman: I now turn to the last item of business on the agenda for today's meeting, namely resolution 6. I therefore propose as a special resolution:

THAT the regulations in the document produced at the meeting, and signed by the chairman so as to identify it, be adopted as the company's articles of association in substitution for and to the exclusion of all existing articles of association of the Company.

The reasons for recommending these alterations and their effect is explained on page [No.] of the notice of this meeting. In view of the number of changes it was decided that it would be easier to adopt new articles incorporating all of the changes to the existing articles. As the adoption of new articles is proposed, a separate resolution to renew the directors' authority to allot unissued shares in the capital of the Company will not be put to the annual general meeting. Instead, new section 80 and section 89 amounts have been inserted in the new articles of association and will become effective if the resolution to adopt the new articles is passed. The relevant amounts are set out on page [No.] of the notice.

I am happy to take questions on this item of business but will ask [name] from the company's solicitors to deal with any technical or legal points which arise.

INVITE QUESTIONS

If there are no further questions, I now put the resolution to the meeting. Those in favour [pause to count votes] – those against [pause to count votes] – I declare the resolution carried as a special resolution.

Close the meeting

Chairman: That concludes the business of the meeting and I thank you for your patience. Refreshments will now be served in [place]. All the directors will be available to answer any additional questions that you may have. We will be wearing red badges so that you can identify us. Thank you.

1.2 REGISTRATION INCOMPLETE

Chairman: Despite our best efforts to speed up registration there are still people who are waiting to register. I am told that registration is likely to be completed in about [15 minutes] and I therefore propose, with your consent, to delay the start of the meeting until [time].

IF ANYONE OBJECTS

Chairman: There is room to accommodate everyone now waiting

outside and I believe it would be courteous to them to wait [15] minutes so that they can be admitted.

Note: If necessary, temporary registration cards should be used so that those affected can be admitted. If a vote is required the votes of those with temporary cards could be taken by requiring them to register.

1.3 ROOM TOO SMALL

Chairman: Despite booking a room that we expected to be easily big enough, it is clear that not everyone can be accommodated in this room.

There are approximately [   ] people waiting to get in. People other than members present in person, by corporate representative or by proxy are reminded that they have no absolute right to be present at the meeting. In order to enable members who are outside to be accommodated in this hall, which is where the meeting is being held, it would be most helpful if about [   ] persons present who are not members or proxy holders or corporate representatives of members could volunteer to go to [another specified room]. [There is a one-way audio link so that those in the [specified room] will be able to hear the debate.]

IF ANNOUNCEMENT IS MADE AFTER TIME SET FOR THE MEETING

Chairman: I propose, with your consent, to delay the start of the meeting until [   ] to enable everyone to get settled.

IF ANYONE OBJECTS

Chairman: There is room to accommodate all members in this room and all non-members who cannot get into this room in the [   ] room. It would be courteous to those outside to wait [half an hour] to enable everyone to be accommodated.

Note: If after [fifteen minutes] non-members have left but registration is still not complete, temporary registration cards should be used so that those affected can be admitted. If a vote is required the votes of those with temporary cards should be taken by requiring them to register.

IF PEOPLE REFUSE TO MOVE OR THE ARRANGEMENTS FOR USING THE ROOM DO NOT WORK FOR ANY REASON

Chairman: It is clear that not everyone can be accommodated in this room. Unfortunately, if this meeting is to proceed to business it will be necessary for at least [   ] non-members to leave the meeting to enable members and proxy holders outside this room to get in. Will these people please leave [and go to the [   ] room].

IF INSUFFICIENT NON-MEMBERS LEAVE

Chairman: As non-members are unwilling to leave I propose to adjourn this meeting for [15] minutes while the stewards assist in accommodating them in the [   ] room. If insufficient non-members leave then this meeting cannot continue. If we have to reconvene this meeting further delay and additional expense will be incurred. This can be avoided if non-members (and that includes members of the press who are not themselves members) who have no entitlement to attend this meeting, now leave [and go to the [   ] room].

IF RESISTANCE IS ENCOUNTERED

Chairman: In the circumstances I have no alternative other than to propose the adjournment of this meeting to an alternative venue [which we have arranged at [   ] on [   ] at [   ]]. In order to ensure a valid vote on the question of adjournment I ask again if non-members will please leave now. They should not miss anything as they will have the opportunity to attend the adjourned meeting if the vote to adjourn the meeting is passed.

IF NON-MEMBERS DO THEN LEAVE AND MEMBERS GET IN – PUT MOTION TO ADJOURN TO A VOTE. IF NECESSARY CALL A POLL

IF EVERYBODY IS STILL NOT ACCOMMODATED

Chairman: There are still some members outside but I am going to put to the vote my proposal to adjourn to [   ] on [   ] at [   ] anyway. The stewards will attempt to count the votes of those outside.

IF THE VOTE IS LOST ON A SHOW OF HANDS, AN ATTEMPT SHOULD BE MADE TO PUT IT TO A POLL

Chairman: I also adjourn the meeting on my own authority pursuant to the inherent power vested in me as Chairman of this meeting. A further registration form will be posted to you to enable you to attend the adjourned meeting. [If you are uncertain whether you will be able to attend this meeting, proxy cards can be collected on the way out.] Proxies should be returned by [not less than 48 hours before the time of the adjourned meeting].

1.4 POLL PROCEDURES

Subject to the articles, the chairman has power to adjourn for the taking of a poll on a resolution. If the demand for a poll is valid, the poll is normally taken at the end of the meeting after any other business has been concluded unless the nature of the business requires it to be taken immediately (e.g. a poll on resolution to adjourn) or before the vote on the substantive resolution (e.g. a poll on an amendment to a resolution). See further Chapter 15 on voting, Chapter 21 on adjournments and Chapter 22 on amendments.

1.4A Called by chairman

Chairman: In the circumstances, I exercise my right as Chairman to call for a poll. The poll will be conducted at the end of the meeting and in the meantime I will proceed with the remaining business of the meeting.

WHEN REMAINING BUSINESS IS COMPLETE, GO TO 1.4C

1.4B Demand by a member

Member [Demands a poll.]

Chairman: I should point out that I hold over [No. of proxy votes] proxies in favour of the resolution and a further [No. of proxy votes] proxies which I may vote at my discretion. There are [No. of proxy votes] votes against the resolution. In view of this [considerable] support it seems likely that the resolution will be carried. As the conduct of a poll is a lengthy process, do those calling for a poll still feel that this is a worthwhile exercise?

IF MEMBER STANDS DOWN

Chairman Thank you. I will proceed with the business of the meeting.

IF MEMBER PERSISTS

Chairman: What is your full name and in what name is the holding registered?

ALLOW REGISTRAR TO TAKE DOWN FULL DETAILS

Chairman: Under the Company's Articles of Association, a poll can only be demanded by the Chairman or by [state relevant conditions].

Do you satisfy any of these conditions?

IF NO, RULE OUT OF ORDER.

IF YES:

Chairman: So that we can verify that the request is properly made, will you please make yourselves known to the Company's Registrar.

IF VALID DEMAND FOR POLL ON RESOLUTION TO ADJOURN, GO TO 1.4C

OTHERWISE

Chairman: If the poll has been validly demanded, it will be conducted at the end of the meeting and I will explain the procedures when the time comes. In the meantime, I propose to proceed with the other business of the meeting.

RETURN TO MAIN SCRIPT

WHEN REMAINING BUSINESS COMPLETE, GO TO 1.4C

1.4C Conduct of poll

Chairman: A poll on resolution [No.] [text of resolution] will now be conducted by our Registrars and I would ask the Secretary to describe the procedure for taking the poll.

Secretary: Please remain in your seats while the poll is being conducted. Polling cards will now be distributed.
On a poll each member present in person, by corporate representative or proxy has one vote for every share held. If you have already lodged a form of proxy you do not have to vote again now unless you wish to change the way you originally voted. If you do not wish to change your mind it will speed up the poll procedure if you do not vote again now.
A separate poll card should be used for each separate holding. If you are representing more than one holding, please ask for additional cards as necessary. You should indicate the number of shares to be voted in the appropriate box on the poll card. If you do not, all the shares registered in you name or in the name of the person you are representing will be included in the count. If two or more persons are jointly registered as shareholders, any one of them may vote either in person or by proxy. If more than one of the joint holders votes then only the vote of the joint holder whose name appears first on the register

of members will be counted.

Corporate representatives should complete the poll card with the full details of the name of the company they represent and provide the registrars with some form of identification and their written authority to exercise the votes.

Note. Articles rarely require presentation of authority and it should only be insisted upon if a reasonable suspicion exists of wrongdoing.

Completed cards should be placed in one of the boxes at the exits from the hall. if you are unsure as to what to do our staff will be pleased to answer your queries.

IN ADDITION TO CASTING HIS OWN VOTE, CHAIRMAN SHOULD COMPLETE VOTING CARDS FOR AND AGAINST THE RESOLUTION IN ACCORDANCE WITH THE PROXIES HELD BY HIM

AFTER A SUITABLE INTERVAL THE CHAIRMAN SHOULD GIVE NOTICE OF HIS INTENTION TO CLOSE THE POLL

Chairman: I intend to declare the poll closed in two minutes. Please ensure that your completed card has been given in.

WHEN THE CARDS HAVE ALL BEEN HANDED IN

EITHER:

Chairman: Thank you ladies and gentlemen, the poll is now closed. The poll cards will be processed by the scrutineers who will complete the poll as soon as possible. The results of the voting will be announced in this room but this will probably take about [   ] hours. I therefore adjourn the meeting pending the declaration of the result of the poll.

OR:

Chairman: Thank you ladies and gentlemen. The poll is now closed. As the results of the poll will need to be checked, it will not be possible to know the result for some time. The result of the poll(s) will therefore [be published in a Stock Exchange announcement on [   ] and will appear in [   ] on the same day]. This concludes the business of the meeting and I now declare the meeting closed. Thank you for attending.

1.5 ADJOURNMENT

1.5A Proposal by chairman

The motion for adjournment should include the day, time and place of the adjourned meeting or authorise the Board to determine such matters. The Chairman should give his views on or reasons for the proposal and invite debate from the floor.

The Chairman has an inherent power, in limited circumstances, to adjourn the meeting if it is necessary to enable members to debate and vote on the business of the meeting (e.g. if the room is too small to accommodate those entitled to attend or to deal with a disturbance).

If the meeting is adjourned, further proxies may become valid as the articles may allow proxies to be lodged up to 48/24 hours before the time of the adjourned meeting.

Chairman: In accordance with Article [   ] of the Company's Articles of Association I propose that this meeting be adjourned until [date, time and place, etc].

AFTER DEBATE ENDS

I now propose to put the proposal to adjourn to the vote. Ladies and gentlemen the proposal is that the meeting be adjourned to [date, time and place, etc]. Will those in favour of the proposal to adjourn please raise their hands / [colour] voting cards.

Thank you.

Those against. Thank you.

IF VOTE CARRIED EITHER:

Chairman: The proposal to adjourn the meeting has been carried.

This meeting stands adjourned to [place] on [date] at [time].

OR:

This meeting is now adjourned. Notice of the adjourned meeting will be posted to shareholders as soon as possible.

IF VOTE NOT CARRIED:

Chairman: I declare the resolution not passed on a show of hands and in accordance with article [No.] of the Company's Articles of Association I therefore exercise my right to demand a poll on the proposal to adjourn the meeting.

Note: The Chairman should state how he intends to vote the proxies that he holds. When deciding how to cast the votes of proxies the Chairman should consider the intentions of the shareholders who have appointed him as their proxy and act accordingly. Therefore how the Chairman votes will depend on the circumstances. If in doubt the Chairman should seek advice on the matter.

THE POLL MAY NEED TO BE TAKEN IMMEDIATELY

GO TO 1.4C

1.5B Proposal for adjournment from the floor

Member: I demand that the meeting be adjourned.

Chairman: Are you a member or a representative of a corporate member?

IF NO:

Chairman: Rule out of order.

IF YES:

Chairman: I will ask the Registrars to verify your status. Will shareholders please bear with me while this exercise is completed.

Note: This must be done immediately – no other business can be carried out if a valid proposal to adjourn is outstanding.

IF STATUS IS NOT CORRECT:

Chairman: The Registrars advise me that you do not have the required status to call for an adjournment. I therefore rule the proposed adjournment out of order. (Return to main script).

IF STATUS IS CORRECT:

Chairman: What exactly is your proposal? How long is the adjournment to be for?

Member: [At least [No. of days] – give reasons].

Chairman: Would your proposal then be to adjourn for a minimum of [No. of days] to a place, date and time to be fixed by the Board?

Note: The Chairman may have to assist the shareholders in formulating a suitable proposal.

Member: [Yes]

Note: The Chairman should allow the Member to explain his point of view and allow debate on the motion generally.

Chairman: I now propose to put the proposal to adjourn to the vote. Ladies and gentlemen, the proposal is that the meeting be adjourned to [day, time and place]. Will those in favour of the proposal place please raise their hands/[colour] voting cards.

Thank you.

PAUSE TO ESTIMATE VOTES

Those against. Thank you.

IF PROPOSAL IS CARRIED, CHAIRMAN SHOULD CALL FOR A POLL:

Note: When deciding how to cast the votes of proxies, the Chairman must consider the intentions of the shareholders who have appointed him as their proxy and act accordingly. Therefore how the Chairman votes will depend on the circumstances. For instance, if the intention of the adjournment is to defeat the resolution, the Chairman should cast the votes of those proxies who voted against the resolution in favour of the proposal to adjourn. If in doubt the Chairman should seek advice on the matter.

Chairman: In accordance with Article [No.] of the Company's Articles of Association, I call for a poll on the proposal to adjourn the meeting. On this poll on the proposal to adjourn I am assuming that those members who have appointed me with a direction that I vote in favour of [resolution [   ]] [the resolutions proposed in the notice of meeting] approve of the conduct of the business before the meeting at this time.

Accordingly, I intend to cast those votes against the proposal to adjourn. I also propose to cast against the proposal those votes where I have been given a discretion how to vote. These amount in total to [   ] votes. [I intend to abstain] in relation to those members who have appointed me with a direction that I vote against [resolution [   ]] [the resolutions proposed in the notice of meeting].

GO TO 1.4C.

IF PROPOSAL NOT CARRIED, PROCEED WITH BUSINESS OF MEETING

IF PROPOSAL IS NOT CARRIED BUT THERE IS A CALL FOR A POLL FROM THE FLOOR:

Chairman: A proposal to adjourn the meeting has been called for. Before I explain the procedure I think the meeting should be aware that on the poll I am assuming that those members who have appointed me with a direction that I vote in favour of [resolution [ ]] [the resolutions proposed in the notice of meeting] approve of the conduct of the business before the meeting at this time. Accordingly, I intend to cast those votes against the proposal to adjourn. I also propose to cast against the proposal those votes where I have been given a discretion how to vote. These amount in total to [ ] votes. I intend to abstain in relation to those members who have appointed me with a discretion that I vote against [resolution [ ]] [the resolutions proposed in the notice of meeting]. In view of the substantial majority of votes against the proposal to adjourn and as the conducting of a poll is a lengthy process, do those calling for a poll feel that this is a worthwhile exercise?

IF PROPOSAL IS WITHDRAWN PROCEED WITH BUSINESS OF MEETING

IF MEMBER PERSISTS, GO TO PARA. 1.4B

1.6 DEMAND FOR AN AMENDMENT TO A RESOLUTION

An amendment to an ordinary resolution must be relevant to the resolution and with the scope of the notice convening the meeting. Otherwise, it should be ruled out of order. In addition, the amendment must not be so fundamental as to destroy the intent of the original resolution. If it does, it should be ruled out of order. A special resolution may only be passed in the form set out in the notice, so any amendment (other than typographical or grammatical corrections) should be ruled out of order.

Chairman: Can you tell me whether you are a member or a corporate representative of a member.

IF NOT, PROPOSED AMENDMENT SHOULD BE RULED OUT OF ORDER

Chairman: What is your full name and in what name is the shareholding registered? I will ask the Registrars to verify your status. Will shareholders please bear with me while this exercise is completed.

IF STATUS IS NOT CORRECT:

Chairman: The Registrar advises me that you do not have the

required status to call for an amendment so I must rule the proposed amendment out of order.

RETURN TO THE MAIN SCRIPT

IF STATUS IS CORRECT:

Chairman: The Registrar advises me that your status has been verified. Would you now please state precisely what your proposed amendment is.

Member: [. . . . .]

Chairman: The proposal is that we amend Resolution [   ] to read as follows
[. . . .]

Note: Chairman gives his views on the amendment (taking advice as necessary) and invites debate from the floor, taking comments/questions in turn. After debate ends, the Chairman assesses the mood of the meeting and (if appropriate) asks whether in the light of the debate the person wishes to withdraw the proposed amendment. If the member does withdraw, return to the main script. If person does not withdraw, or there appears to be support for the amendment, the Chairman should propose a vote.

Chairman: I propose to put the proposal to amend the Resolution to the vote. [Repeat proposed amendment].

Those in favour of the proposal to amend please raise your voting cards.

Thank you.

Those against?

IF AMENDMENT IS CARRIED, CHAIRMAN MAY DEMAND A POLL

Chairman: In accordance with article [No.] of the Company's Articles of Association I exercise my right to demand a poll on the proposal to amend resolution [   ].

On this poll on the proposal to amend resolution [   ], I am assuming that those members who have appointed me with a direction that I vote in favour of the resolution which it is proposed to amend approve of the resolution in its existing form. Accordingly, I intend to cast those votes against the proposal to amend the resolution. I also propose to cast against the proposal those votes where I have been given a discretion how to vote. These amount in total to [   ] votes. I intend to abstain in relation to those members who have appointed me with a discretion that I vote against the resolution which it is proposed to amend.

GO TO 1.4C

IF AMENDMENT NOT CARRIED, PROCEED TO A VOTE ON THE SUBSTANTIVE RESOLUTION UNLESS A POLL IS DEMANDED FROM THE FLOOR, IN WHICH CASE, PROCEED AS FOLLOWS

Chairman: A poll on the proposed amendment to resolution [No.] has been called for. Before I explain the procedure I think that the meeting should be aware that on the poll I am assuming that those members who have appointed me with a direction that I vote in favour of the resolution which it is proposed to amend approve of the resolution in its existing form. Accordingly, I intend to cast those votes against the proposal to amend the resolution. I also propose to cast against the proposal those votes where I have been given a discretion how to vote. These amount in total to [   ] votes. I intend to abstain in relation to those members who have appointed me with a direction that I vote against the resolution which it is proposed to amend. In view of the substantial majority of votes against the proposal to amend the resolution, and as the conducting of a poll is a lengthy process, do those calling for a poll feel that this is a worthwhile exercise?

Note: As regards proxy votes against the resolution, it is difficult to decide whether the Chairman should vote them for or against the amendment. Accordingly, the safest course is to abstain. The proxy form should be drafted so as to give the Chairman the discretion to vote as he thinks fit on other business at the meeting (including adjournments and amendments validly coming before the meeting). The Chairman may wish to adopt the proposed amendment.

IF MEMBER WITHDRAWS:

Chairman: As you have now decided not to call for a poll, I will proceed with the business of the meeting. I therefore intend to propose the resolution in its original format. Are there any more questions on the resolution?

RETURN TO MAIN SCRIPT

IF MEMBER PERSISTS, GO TO 1.4B

1.7 DISRUPTION

Chairman: Would you please be quiet so that other members can ask questions and the meeting can carry on.

Member: No [or equivalent]

Chairman: If you do not stop I will have to ask you to leave the meeting.

Member: No [or equivalent]

Chairman: This behaviour is intolerable. With the consent of the meeting I propose to expel you from this meeting [pause to gauge dissension]. [Mr X] would you please arrange for the stewards to escort this gentleman/lady from the meeting.

IF DISRUPTION IS SUCH AS TO REQUIRE A BRIEF ADJOURNMENT

Chairman: It is quite impossible for this meeting to continue while this disruption is going on. In order to allow tempers to cool and to enable order to be restored I adjourn this meeting for 15 minutes.

Note: In the event that disruption comes from an external source – e.g. a fire alarm is set off – consult advisers. It may be possible to have a short interruption and avoid a full adjournment.

1.8 VOTE ON CLOSURE OF THE DEBATE

Chairman: We have now debated this proposal for [time] and I believe that despite the opposition of a small minority, most members would like now to vote on the resolution.

IF NO OPPOSITION, ANNOUNCE A VOTE ON THE RESOLUTION

IF THERE IS STILL OPPOSITION TO THIS

Chairman: In the circumstances I propose to put forward a separate motion first:

'THAT the debate be closed and a vote taken on the special/ordinary resolution'.

PROCEED TO VOTE ON A SHOW OF HANDS

Chairman: I declare the motion carried; we will now vote on the original resolution before the meeting.

IF CLOSURE MOTION IS NOT CARRIED, DISCUSSION ON THE RESOLUTION SHOULD BE ALLOWED TO CONTINUE

Appendix M

ICSA's Guide to Best Practice for Annual General Meetings: Summary of Recommendations

The guide contains the following 24 elements of best practice which listed companies in particular are encouraged to adopt.

Shareholder communications

1. All companies should engage in an active policy of communication with all shareholders (not just institutional shareholders).
2. Companies should arrange for all correspondence from shareholders to receive a full reply from the company secretary, the chairman, another director, or another designated senior executive. If the enquiry concerns a particular product or plant, it may be appropriate for the response to come from the head of the business division or a particular factory.
3. Communications with members should be handled appropriately but sensitively in accordance with the company's shareholder communications policy.

AGM notice and venue

4. The AGM notice and accompanying documents should be circulated at least 20 working days (excluding weekends and Bank Holidays) in advance of the meeting.
5. The venue for the AGM should be accessible by attendees who have disabilities, and have facilities for those with poor hearing.
6. Companies should ensure that each item of special business included in the notice is accompanied by a full and detailed explanation.

Directors

7. Directors standing for re-election to the board should be named in the notice and form of proxy.
8. A brief description should be given of the directors standing for election or re-election, including their ages; their relevant experience (not merely a list of other directorships they hold); the dates that they were first appointed to the board; and details of any board committees to which they belong.
9. The articles of association of public companies should require all the directors to be subject to retirement by rotation.
10. Wherever possible, all directors should attend the AGM, and be seated with the chairman, facing the shareholders.
11. The chairman should not propose his own election or re-election or propose any resolution in which he has an interest.

AGM procedure

12. The resolution to receive or adopt the accounts should be separate from any resolution to approve the payment of the final dividend recommended by the directors. It is also best practice generally to deal with different items of business by way of separate resolutions.

13. Boards should provide adequate time for shareholder questions at AGMs.

14. When moving the adoption or receipt of the accounts, the chairman should allow shareholders to raise questions on any item concerning the company's past performance, its results and its intended future performance. However, the directors need not answer questions which are irrelevant to the company or its business or which could result in the release of commercially sensitive information. Nor should they disclose price-sensitive information unless it can be done in compliance with the . . . Listing Rules and guidance regarding the release of price-sensitive information.

15. Before each resolution is put to the vote, the chairman should explain again its effect and purpose. If necessary, he should elaborate on the information previously provided in the explanatory circular which accompanied the notice of the meeting. He should also invite shareholders to speak.

16. Where concerns are raised by a shareholder at the AGM and the chairman undertakes to consider them, the shareholder should subsequently be sent a full report of the action taken.

Shareholder resolutions

17. Unless the company agrees at the outset to absorb all the costs of circulation, shareholder resolutions requisitioned under section 376 of the CA 1985 should automatically be accompanied (in any notice) by another resolution giving shareholders the opportunity to decide whether the company or the requisitionists should bear the relevant costs. If the directors feel that any particular case does not justify the adoption of such a resolution, they should, however, be free to recommend a vote against it.

Polls and proxies

18. When announcing the decision on a poll, the total number of votes cast in favour of, and against, the resolution should be disclosed.

19. If the chairman informs shareholders of the number of proxy votes he holds for and against a resolution, he should clarify that those numbers refer to the proxies lodged with the company (or its registrars) before the meeting and that some of those who lodged proxies may be present and, having heard the debate, could decide to vote differently.

20. All proxy forms should be worded to allow the proxy to vote or abstain on business which may come before the meeting which was not included in the notice, e.g. amendments and formal motions.

Enhancing the AGM

21. All companies should provide an updated trading statement at their AGM unless they have recently published a scheduled financial statement.
22. At least one of the executive directors of the company should make an oral report at the AGM, on those areas of the company's operations for which he or she has responsibility.

Disorder

23. All companies should establish procedures for dealing with disturbances at their AGMs.

Proxies' right to speak

24. All chairmen should seek the consent of the meeting to proxies speaking and participating in the debate.

Other recommendations

These 24 best practice points are supplemented by several other suggestions and recommendations intended to stimulate discussion and further development by companies. For example, the *Guide* suggests that:

- Companies could announce the date of their next AGM much earlier (possibly at the preceding AGM or with the interim report).
- Companies should avoid holding their AGM on the same day as others in the same sector in order to facilitate the attendance of shareholders with holdings across a particular sector.
- When a particular issue has been raised by a shareholder, the chairman can assist the flow of the meeting by inviting other shareholders who wish to speak on the same subject to do so at that time.
- Companies should invite shareholders to submit questions in advance, but should not use this practice as a method of manipulating the AGM by requiring written notice of questions or to replace spontaneity at the AGM.
- If a valid demand for a poll is made, shareholders should be issued with poll cards immediately and asked to deposit them as they leave the meeting. This allows the meeting to continue with the minimum of disruption and enables shareholders who have to leave the meeting early to vote on the poll.
- Although shareholders should be able to rely on the integrity of the company's registrars or auditors (properly supervised by and answerable to the company secretary, acting in that regard on behalf of the shareholders generally and not the directors) to act as scrutineers, one of the proposers of the poll could be invited to act as a joint scrutineer.

A Guide to Best Practice for Annual General Meetings can be obtained from ICSA, 16 Park Crescent, London W1B 1AH (see www.icsa.org.uk or call 020 7580 4741 for details).

Index